STUDIES IN CONTEMPORARY JEWRY

The publication of
Studies in Contemporary Jewry
has been made possible through the generous assistance
of the Samuel and Althea Stroum Philanthropic Fund,
Seattle, Washington

THE AVRAHAM HARMAN INSTITUTE
OF CONTEMPORARY JEWRY
THE HEBREW UNIVERSITY
OF JERUSALEM

THE PROTESTANT-JEWISH CONUNDRUM

STUDIES IN
CONTEMPORARY
JEWRY
AN ANNUAL
XXIV

2010

Edited by Jonathan Frankel
and Ezra Mendelsohn

Published for the Institute by

UNIVERSITY PRESS

OXFORD
UNIVERSITY PRESS

Oxford University Press, Inc., publishes works that further
Oxford University's objective of excellence
in research, scholarship, and education.

Oxford   New York
Auckland   Cape Town   Dar es Salaam   Hong Kong   Karachi
Kuala Lumpur   Madrid   Melbourne   Mexico City   Nairobi
New Delhi   Shanghai   Taipei   Toronto

With offices in
Argentina   Austria   Brazil   Chile   Czech Republic   France   Greece
Guatemala   Hungary   Italy   Japan   Poland   Portugal   Singapore
South Korea   Switzerland   Thailand   Turkey   Ukraine   Vietnam

Copyright © 2010 by Oxford University Press, Inc.

Published by Oxford University Press, Inc.
198 Madison Avenue, New York, New York 10016

www.oup.com

Oxford is a registered trademark of Oxford University Press

All rights reserved. No part of this publication may be reproduced,
stored in a retrieval system, or transmitted, in any form or by any means,
electronic, mechanical, photocopying, recording, or otherwise,
without the prior permission of Oxford University Press.

Library of Congress Cataloging-in-Publication Data
The Protestant-Jewish conundrum / edited by Jonathan Frankel and Ezra Mendelsohn.
p. cm. — (Studies in Contemporary Jewry, ISSN 0740-8625 ; 24)
Includes bibliographical references.
ISBN 978-0-19-974264-6
1. Protestant churches—Relations—Judaism—History. 2. Judaism—Relations—Protestant churches—History.
3. Evangelicalism—Relations—Judaism—History. 4. Judaism—Relations—Evangelicalism—History.
I. Frankel, Jonathan. II. Mendelsohn, Ezra.
BM535.P77 2010
296.3'96—dc22   2009053886

2 4 6 8 9 7 5 3 1

Printed in the United States of America
on acid-free paper

STUDIES IN CONTEMPORARY JEWRY

Editors

Jonathan Frankel (1935–2008)
Anat Helman
Eli Lederhendler
Peter Y. Medding
Ezra Mendelsohn
Uzi Rebhun

Institute Editorial Board

Michel Abitbol, Mordechai Altshuler, Haim Avni, Avraham Bargil, Yehuda Bauer, Daniel Blatman, Jonathan Dekel-Chen, Sergio DellaPergola, Sidra DeKoven Ezrahi, Allon Gal, Nitza Genuth, Moshe Goodman, Yisrael Gutman, Hagit Lavsky, Pnina Morag-Talmon, Dalia Ofer, Gideon Shimoni, Yfaat Weiss

Managing Editors

Laurie E. Fialkoff
Hannah Levinsky-Koevary

International Advisory and Review Board

Abraham Ascher (City University of New York); Arnold Band (University of California, Los Angeles); Doris Bensimon (Université de la Sorbonne Nouvelle); Bernard Blumenkrantz (Centre National de la Recherche scientifique); Solomon Encel (University of New South Wales); Henry Feingold (City University of New York); Martin Gilbert (Honorary Fellow, Merton College, Oxford University); Zvi Gitelman (University of Michigan); S. Julius Gould (University of Nottingham); Paula Hyman (Yale University); David Landes (Harvard University); Heinz-Dietrich Löwe (University of Heidelberg); Michael Meyer (Hebrew Union College–Jewish Institute of Religion, Cincinnati); Alan Mintz (Brandeis University); Gerard Nahon (Centre Universitaire d'Études Juives); F. Raphael (Universite, des Science Himanies de Strasbourg); Jehuda Reinharz (Brandeis University); Monika Richarz (Germania Judaica, Kölner Bibliothek zur Geschichte des deutschen Judentums); Ismar Schorsch (Jewish Theological Seminary of America); Michael Walzer (Institute for Advanced Study); Bernard Wasserstein (University of Chicago); Ruth Wisse (Harvard University)

Contents

Symposium
The Protestant-Jewish Conundrum

Ezra Mendelsohn, *Introduction: Volume 24, Jonathan Frankel, and the Future of* Studies in Contemporary Jewry,	3
Yaakov Ariel, *The One and the Many: Unity and Diversity in Protestant Attitudes toward the Jews,*	15
Susannah Heschel, *Confronting the Past: Post-1945 German Protestant Theology and the Fate of the Jews,*	46
Peter A. Pettit, The Passion of the Christ *and Its Ramifications with Reference to the Protestant Churches and Christian-Jewish Relations,*	71
Haim Genizi, *The Attitude of the World Council of Churches (WCC) toward the Israeli-Palestinian Conflict,*	91
Christopher M. Leighton, *The Presbyterian-Jewish Impasse,*	106
Mark Silk, *The Protestant Problem(s) of American Jewry,*	126
Timothy P. Weber, *American Evangelicals and Israel: A Complicated Alliance,*	141
Motti Inbari, *"Universal Temple"? Jewish-Christian Collaboration in Plans to Reestablish the Holy Temple in Jerusalem,*	158

Essay

Daniel Mahla, *Between Socialism and Jewish Tradition: Bundist Holiday Culture in Interwar Poland,*	177

Review Essays

Roger Kohn, *The Second Edition of the* Encyclopaedia Judaica: *"Snapshot" or "Lasting Monument"?*	193
Dan Avnon, *Is There a "Jewish" Morality? Amalek as a Touchstone,*	206

Book Reviews

(arranged by subject)

Antisemitism, Holocaust, and Genocide

Steven Beller, *Antisemitism: A Very Short Introduction*, MILTON SHAIN,	219
Judith M. Gerson and Diane L. Wolf (eds.), *Sociology Confronts the Holocaust: Memories and Identities in Jewish Diasporas*, WILLIAM HELMREICH,	222
Diane L. Wolf, *Beyond Anne Frank: Hidden Children and Postwar Families in Holland*, MANFRED GERSTENFELD,	225

Cultural Studies and Religion

Simeon D. Baumel, *Sacred Speakers: Language and Culture among the Haredim in Israel*, KALMAN WEISER,	228
Haim Chertok, *He Also Spoke as a Jew: The Life of the Reverend James Parkes*, LLOYD P. GARTNER,	231
Murray Friedman, *The Neoconservative Revolution: Jewish Intellectuals and the Shaping of Public Policy*, NANCY SINKOFF,	233
Leonard Glick, *Marked in Your Flesh: Circumcision from Ancient Judea to Modern America*, DIANE L. WOLF,	236
David Weiss Halivni, *Breaking the Tablets: Jewish Theology after the Shoah* (ed. Peter Ochs), SHUBERT SPERO,	239
Anita Norich, *Discovering Exile: Yiddish and Jewish American Culture during the Holocaust*, KENNETH B. MOSS,	242
Eugene R. Sheppard, *Leo Strauss and the Politics of Exile: The Making of a Political Philosopher*, MALACHI HACOHEN,	245
Fred Skolnik (ed. in chief), *Encyclopaedia Judaica*, 2nd. ed., ROGER KOHN,	193
Alan M. Wald, *Trinity of Passion: The Literary Left & the Antifascist Crusade*, EMILY BUDICK,	250
Michael Walzer (ed.), *Law, Politics, and Morality in Judaism*, DAN AVNON,	206

History and the Social Sciences

Steven E. Aschheim, *Beyond the Border: The German-Jewish Legacy Abroad*, MICHAEL A. MEYER,	253
Jocelyn Cohen and Daniel Soyer (eds.), *My Future Is in America: Autobiographies of Eastern European Jews*, TONY MICHELS,	256

Henry L. Feingold, *"Silent No More": Saving the Jews of Russia, the American Jewish Effort, 1967–1989*, EDITH ROGOVIN FRANKEL, 259

Marcie Cohen Ferris and Mark I. Greenberg (eds.), *Jewish Roots in Southern Soil: A New History*, JEFFREY S. GUROCK, 262

Robin Judd, *Contested Rituals: Circumcision, Kosher Butchering, and Jewish Political Life in Germany, 1843–1933*, MIRJAM ZADOFF, 264

Victor Karady, *The Jews of Europe in the Modern Era: A Socio-Historical Outline*, ROBERT NEMES, 267

Richard Mendelsohn and Milton Shain, *The Jews in South Africa: An Illustrated History*, GIDEON SHIMONI, 269

Emanuela Trevisan Semi, *Jacques Faitlovitch and the Jews of Ethiopia*, SHALVA WEIL, 272

Oren Soffer, *Ein lefalpel! 'Iton "Hazefirah" vehamodernizaziyah shel hasiah hahevrati hapoliti* (There is no place for pilpul! "Hazefirah" and the modernization of sociopolitical discourse), NATHAN COHEN, 275

Zionism, Israel, and the Middle East

Eliezer Ben-Rafael and Yochanan Peres, *Is Israel One? Religion, Nationalism, and Multiculturalism Confounded*, RUSSELL A. STONE, 278

Meron Benvenisti, *Son of the Cypresses: Memories, Reflections and Regrets from a Political Life*, trans. Maxine Kaufman-Lacusta in consultation with Michael Kaufman-Lacusta, MENACHEM KLEIN, 281

Yael Chaver, *What Must Be Forgotten: The Survival of Yiddish in Zionist Palestine*, LIORA R. HALPERIN, 283

Raymond Cohen, *Saving the Holy Sepulchre: How Rival Christians Came Together to Rescue Their Holiest Shrine*, YAAKOV ARIEL, 286

Zvi Ganin, *An Uneasy Relationship: American Jewish Leadership and Israel, 1948–1957*, SHLOMO SLONIM, 289

Benjamin Pinkus, *Meambivalentiyut levrit bilti ketuvah: yisrael, zarfat veyehudei zarfat 1947–1957* (From ambivalence to tacit alliance: Israel, France and French Jewry, 1947–1957), SIMON SCHWARZFUCHS, 293

Studies in Contemporary Jewry XXV, 297

Note on Editorial Policy, 299

Symposium
The Protestant-Jewish Conundrum

Introduction: Volume 24, Jonathan Frankel, and the Future of *Studies in Contemporary Jewry*

Ezra Mendelsohn
(THE HEBREW UNIVERSITY)

Jonathan Frankel, who passed away in May of 2008, conceived of the symposium subject of this volume of *Studies in Contemporary Jewry*, and worked energetically on it until a very short time before his death. He and his fellow editors thought of it as a companion volume to a recent issue of *Studies*, edited by Eli Lederhendler, which dealt with relations between Jews and Catholics. I took it upon myself to bring Jonathan's work to fruition, but the volume as it stands is basically his.

A book concentrating on the question of modern relations between Jews and Protestants faces a challenge more complex and multifaceted than one dealing with Jews and Catholics. True, Catholicism is no monolith, divided as it is today among a myriad of regional churches and clashing ideologies (the left-wing liberation theology of South America, "traditional Catholicism" that will not accept the reforms of the Vatican, various "Uniate" churches in such disparate places as Lebanon and Ukraine). But at least there is a commonly accepted hierarchy, presided over by a leader to whom all Catholics are expected to pay allegiance, and an official doctrine emanating from the corridors of the Vatican in Rome and enunciated, from time to time, by the Pope in his encyclicals and other official utterances and publications. Protestantism, on the other hand, boasts of no such centralized structure, and some Protestant denominations have virtually no structure at all (for example, the Religious Society of Friends, better known as the Quakers). There are Protestant sects and churches without end, and a bewildering range of views on theology, social problems, and politics. When I taught at Grinnell College, back in the mid-1960s, there were numerous churches in that small Iowan town, one or two Catholic, the rest Protestant of one denomination or another. The Protestant world is, to a large degree, a world of chaos rather than of order, which manages to encompass the most passionate evangelicals of the American Bible Belt and some African and South American countries and the stately, wealthy, Wasp Episcopalians and Anglicans of old New York and Boston and the British establishment.

This infinite variety is naturally reflected in attitudes toward Jews, Judaism, and Israel. So far as Israel is concerned, we have the passionate support given to the Jewish state by many evangelicals and Mormons, on the one hand, and the fierce criticisms voiced by some of the "mainstream" churches in America, for example, on the other. As in the case of Catholicism, theology, history (in particular the years 1933–1945 in Europe), and an ever-changing political and social landscape have their roles to play in the articulation of these attitudes.

Protestantism today, like all organized religions, is being sorely tested by such issues as the role of women in the church, homosexuality, abortion, evolution, and the like. Attitudes toward the Jews is another thorny issue, not so divisive, perhaps, but always present, and sometimes exploding into the public view. The importance of Jewish-Protestant relations for both sides is evident, as are the paradoxes of this relationship. Protestantism began its history as a revolt against the theological hegemony of Rome, and looked back to the so-called "Old Testament" and to ancient Jewish history for inspiration. Jews have traditionally flourished in countries where Protestants constituted the majority of the population, the most obvious examples being Holland, Britain, and North America, and surely Protestant traditions of toleration and pluralism have something to do with that; but they have also suffered terrible persecution in Protestant lands, such as Germany. As we are reminded in this volume, Martin Luther, who did so much to rediscover for Christianity its Jewish roots, did not like Jews of his time, and at any rate hoped for their conversion, as have Protestants ever since. Jews who believe in a future of prosperity and peace in the diaspora must hope for Protestant understanding and tolerance, while Protestants must grapple with the contradictory ways in which Jews and Judaism impinge upon and even challenge their theology and their understanding of history. Israeli foreign policy is based, in part, on efforts to win the active support of certain elements within the Protestant community, but evangelical Christians, while they support Israel, make no secret of their wish for the eventual conversion of the Jews to their faith, whereas the American Protestant establishment certainly harbored (and may still harbor) anti-Jewish sentiments. William Blake, a dissident Protestant and a great poet and artist, wrote of the pressing need to establish, in England's green and pleasant land, a new Jerusalem, but the new Jerusalem would presumably be a Christian city, not a Jewish one.

Our volume cannot pretend to cover in its entirety this vast and contentious territory. Indeed, I must admit that for some reason, perhaps connected to the fact that, for the first time in the history of our journal, the editor who began to work on a volume was unable to bring it to completion, we have had more than the usual number of mishaps—scholars pulling out at the last minute (an unpleasant fact of academic life), commissioned articles that could not be accepted because they did not meet our standards, and so forth. The result is a symposium rather smaller than those edited by Jonathan in the past (his were almost always our largest volumes, in accordance with his belief that almost every article, no matter how awful, has something of interest to say), and it may be that there are more gaps than is usually the case.

Nonetheless, we think that we have raised and analyzed the essential questions with which any serious consideration of relations between Protestants and Jews must contend. These include a survey of the historical framework in which were forged Protestant ideas regarding Jews and Judaism (Ariel); the depressing but highly revealing behavior of the German Protestant establishment during the Nazi years—surely the blackest era in the history of relations between Protestants and Jews—and its aftermath (Heschel); attitudes toward Israel and the Israeli-Arab conflict on the part of mainstream Protestantism (Genizi and Leighton) and elements within the vast evangelical community (Inbari and Weber); and Protestant reactions to Mel Gibson's famous (or notorious) film, "The Passion of the Christ" (Pettit). Another essay (Silk) tackles the question of Jewish attitudes toward Protestants.

In 1858, the American poet and scholar Henry Longfellow published a beautiful poem about the old Jewish cemetery in Newport. Longfellow describes his musings during his walk among the tombstones, and in the end he suggests that the Jewish people, though once a formidable presence, has come to an end, the cemetery being a metaphor for its present-day condition:

> But ah! What once has been shall be no more!
> The groaning earth in travail and in pain
> Brings forth its races, but does not restore,
> And the dead nations never rise again.[1]

Some time later, during the years 1890–1919, the distinguished American artist John Singer Sargent created a series of murals for the Boston Public Library, the subject of which was the history of religions. This splendid example of Christian triumphalism, titled "Triumph of Religion," includes in one panel a depiction of the synagogue as a reclining, defeated, blindfolded woman, in keeping with a long Christian iconographical tradition. The local Jewish community complained bitterly about this image, installed in 1919, but it was defended by the artist as justified in terms of the history of Christian art.[2] When I taught at Boston University I wanted to take my students to see it (none had ever heard of it), but the murals were then being restored and were not accessible.

These two outstanding representatives of American culture, both of Protestant background, turned out to be mistaken—Judaism and Jewry have not been defeated, and have not disappeared. Against all expectations, a Jewish state has been created in the cradle of Judaism, an event which neither Longfellow nor Sargent could have possibly imagined. The problem of Christianity, and of Christians, is how to deal with this new situation. Is it possible to revise the old, entrenched notions of Christianity as having "superseded" Judaism, which usually went hand in hand with strong antisemitic attitudes? How to deal with a long and powerful tradition of regarding the world of Christendom as the New Israel, and the conviction that with the coming of Christ the historic role of Judaism was over and done for? How to resolve Christian beliefs in the superiority of their religious tradition with the need for tolerance in a new, post-Holocaust world? How to (re)read the "New Testament" in light of the new and not so new scholarship that shows not only that Jesus was a loyal Jew, but that this was true even of Paul, the real founder of the new Christian church? These are the central issues with which this volume grapples.

As always, volume 24 of *Studies* includes a section devoted to essays not related to the symposium topic (only one this time, unfortunately), and a large number of book reviews. It could never have seen the light of day without the outstanding work of our two managing editors, Hannah Levinsky-Koevary and Laurie Fialkoff. In truth, given the special circumstances under which this volume was produced, their work was more important than ever. At a time when *Studies* is undergoing rapid change (on this, see below), they represent continuity, as well as an uncompromising dedication to the highest academic standards. My thanks to them, and to my fellow editors at *Studies*, for helping to produce this volume, the last that will appear under my name. I wish also to thank the Samuel and Althea Stroum Foundation, the Lucius N. Littauer Foundation, and the Nachum Ben-Eli-Honig Fund for providing us with the financial resources to publish our yearbook.

I first met Jonathan Frankel in the early 1960s (1962, I think), at Columbia University. He had come to Columbia from Cambridge University, where he had just completed his dissertation on Jewish socialism in Russia, and I, five years younger than he, had just finished my M.A. thesis on the Jews in the Second Socialist International.

In the 1960s a small group of young Jewish scholars, mostly American, began working on the subject of Jewish socialism in Eastern Europe (let us keep in mind that this was before "Jewish history" had become an accepted academic subject in the United States—the only secular institution in the entire country that employed a professor of Jewish history was my university, Columbia, where the great Salo Baron taught). Why this happened is an interesting question—perhaps they were looking for a "usable Jewish past," secular but national, or quasi-national, heroic, idealistic but pragmatic, responsible among other things for the creation of the state of Israel and its most renowned institution, the kibbutz. Among these people were Jonathan himself, Harold Shukman, Henry Tobias, Zvi Gitelman, and the writer of these lines. I should also mention Abraham Ascher, who wrote a pioneering biography of the Russian Jewish socialist Pavel Axelrod, and Israel Getzler, the biographer of the Menshevik leader Yulii Martov, who was the grandson of a leader of the Jewish enlightenment movement in Russia. In Israel, too, where Jewish history was an integral part of the university curriculum, there was considerable interest in this subject, and it attracted such notable scholars as Moshe Mishkinsky, Matityahu Minc, and Mordechai Altshuler. I remember, clearly, that Jonathan told me that he was drawn to this theme because he wanted to understand how the state of Israel had come into being, "how we got to where we are today" (in the 1960s, Zionist socialism ruled the roost in Israel, and no one imagined that Menachem Begin or anyone not associated with the Mapai political tradition would ever be prime minister).

I make no claim to special powers of prescience, or prophecy, but I remember being certain, even at that time, and especially after I had read the dissertation, that Jonathan was destined to become a great historian of the Jewish people. And so it proved to be. During his long and distinguished career at the Hebrew University, Jonathan published two major, prize-winning books, wrote a large number of brilliant articles,[3] and edited many volumes of collected works (including the volumes he edited in our series). This is not the place for a detailed analysis of Jonathan as a historian—fortunately, his great book *Prophecy and Politics* has been splendidly analyzed in print by his younger colleague, Benjamin Nathans—but I do want to say a few words about his work.[4] What made it so distinctive, so remarkable, so different from the kind of research undertaken by most of his colleagues in the now crowded field of modern Jewish history?

One obvious factor was its remarkably wide range. Jonathan saw modern Jewish history as transnational history, and made this insight a hallmark of his research. Thus his study of the roots of Jewish socialism in Russia demonstrated as never before how Jewish radicalism, rooted in the unique context of the 19th-century Russian empire, cannot be understood without taking into account its activities not only in the Pale of Settlement but also in the centers of the East European Jewish diaspora—America and Palestine, and to a lesser extent Galicia and other regions settled by *Ostjuden*. Jonathan demonstrated, thanks to his unprecedented command of the vast historical record, how Jewish radicals in New York, Odessa, Vilna, London, and Tel Aviv created a unique "Jewish radical world" characterized by fervent secularism (embraced by young men and women, many of whom had grown up in the old religious world of East European Judaism); Jewish nationalism of one sort or another; modern Yiddish (and to a much lesser extent Hebrew) culture; rejection of the old, "fossilized" Jewish world; and utopian, even messianic hopes, whether inspired by Marxism, some other radical doctrine, or the prophets of the Bible, for the creation of a new world in which Jews would take their rightful place as members of a just, socialist world order. His book on the Damascus affair also highlighted the international aspects of this dramatic event, dealing as it did with the situation of the Jews in the East (the Ottoman empire), and the reaction to their troubles on the part of western Jewry—so different from the Jews of the Orient, yet convinced of the need to defend and protect these Jews who were, when all was said and done, their brethren, their co-religionists, with whom they shared a common fate. In general, though Jonathan was at his core a historian of Russia, and of Russian Jewry, he was attracted to movements and ideas in the Jewish world that affected Jewish communities everywhere, to one degree or another—socialism, messianism, acculturation, religious reform, nationalism, and of course the impact upon diverse Jewish centers of the curse of antisemitism.

Jonathan was an archival historian—I well remember the many days we spent together working in the archives of the Jewish Labor Bund in New York back in the 1960s—and for him detail was the essence of historical writing. A classic example of this is his enthralling account of the American Jewish Congress movement during the First World War.[5] But he never lost track of the big picture, and he concentrated upon the big issues: what was the essence of the "Jewish question" in the 19th century, and how did Jews react to it? How strong were the forces tearing the Jewish community apart, and how strong were those acting to maintain some sort of unity among highly disparate elements? How much were Jews influenced by their surroundings, and to what extent were their activities and ideologies the result of internal Jewish currents and traditions? What was the significance of regional difference for Jewish behavior—for example, why did the Jewish labor movement develop so differently in Galicia than in the Russian empire? Why did the Jews provoke so much interest among non-Jews, whether positive (in the form of philosemitism, for example "gentile Zionism") or negative (the rise of modern antisemitism)? How could admiration for the Jews and hostility toward them coexist? How can we explain the forces that made possible the virtually unthinkable—the creation, in 1948, of the state of Israel? Why did radicalism attract the young Jews of Europe and America to such a degree, and what was the price paid by Jewry for this (fatal, perhaps) attraction? How did the clash between pragmatism and utopianism (or, as he put it, "politics and prophecy") play out on the "Jewish street"? How did Jews react to one of the central dilemmas of modern Jewish history—the clash between universalism and particularism, between the heritage of Isaiah and that of Joshua? These are truly the "big questions" every serious historian of modern Jewry must ask, and in Jonathan's works one can discover not only the formulation of these questions, but efforts to answer them—the answers being always complex, never simple.

Jonathan was, in many ways, a conservative historian, and in his writing there is almost no trace of the post-modernist jargon that has invaded the profession. But he was iconoclastic in many ways, and never afraid to tackle new subjects (for example, he edited the volume of *Studies* devoted to the issue of gender in Jewish life). He is responsible for a major "turn" in the historiography of the Bund, as he famously demonstrated that this pioneer Jewish Marxist, internationalist socialist party adopted a national program not because of pressure from below, from the Yiddish-speaking workers, as was accepted in the literature, but owing to influences emanating from the world of the radical Jewish intelligentsia of East European origin. He is also responsible for leading the struggle against the use of the word "assimilation" to describe the acculturating Jews of Europe and America, who combined a strong desire to integrate into general society with a no less strong feeling of Jewishness and of obligation to the Jewish people. Jonathan was one of the first to pay serious attention to the issue of historical memory among Jews, a subject that later became a growth industry in Jewish scholarship.[6] I would also contend that Jonathan is the father of the study of modern Jewish politics, of which he was a master like no other. He gave new meaning to the very term "Jewish politics," and suggested an approach to this subject, based on an original typology, that has been extremely influential.[7] His ideas on this problem were developed in an intellectually exciting seminar which he taught (together with Peter Medding and me) on Jewish politics at the Institute of Contemporary Jewry.

In general, Jonathan was a slayer of myths in Jewish historical writing, an enemy of easy answers, a fearless proponent of seeing and understanding all sides in the internal Jewish debate on the future of the Jewish people, from communists to haredim. He was influenced by the Jerusalem school of Jewish historical writing, but never wrote history according to the "Zionist narrative," which was too simple-minded for his taste. He was at home with the cunning of Jewish history, and enjoyed its manifold paradoxes, its surprises, its twists and turns. He believed that one could learn from the past, but that one could never predict the future, and I am certain that he would have enjoyed hearing the head of the Likud party, in his speech of June 14, 2009, come out in favor of the establishment of a Palestinian state.

One of the factors contributing to Jonathan's strength as a Jewish historian derived from the fact that he grew up in an educational system that made no distinction between "general history" and "Jewish history." He therefore always saw Jewish history as part and parcel of the history of the lands in which the Jews resided. He did not deny its uniqueness, but he never believed that Jews act and create outside history, in a realm of their own. As I have said, his primary area of expertise, before he turned exclusively to Jewish history, was Russian history, and in particular the history of Russian socialism. He edited a pioneering book on the work of a long-forgotten but important dissenting voice in Russian Marxism, Vladimir Akimov.[8] His intimate acquaintance with the ideas of Georgii Plekhanov and other Russian Marxist pioneers, including Lenin, enabled him to understand Ber Borochov and Jewish Marxism in general. Like all great Jewish historians, he demonstrated that separating Jewish from general history, as is done, unfortunately, in all Israeli universities, is an absurdity and—worse—often an obstacle to good historical thinking and writing.

Jonathan was an intellectual—Cambridge educated, living in the bubble of academia—but he had a surprising grasp of the realities of power and of the importance of personality in the making of history. He understood how politics works in the real world, and his books take full account of the influence of personal quirks and of the material situation, and age, of the protagonists in his historical drama. This helped him to master the intricacies of radical politics in Russia, in which ideology, personality, and the thirst for power all played their parts, and he grasped better than anyone else I have ever met the impossible complexities of Israeli politics, which in fact emerged from an East European context and from the history of the Yishuv, especially in the interwar years. He himself readily admitted that the events he had lived through influenced his perception of history (as can be said of just about every historian I can think of). Jonathan was well known for insisting that the wave of pogroms that struck southern Russia in 1881 (known in Hebrew as "hasufot banegev," the storms in the south) signified a decisive turning point in Russian Jewish history, and indeed in modern Jewish history in general. He presented the evidence for this, of course, but once told me that one factor that led him to this conclusion was that he had lived through the Second World War (as a young child) and, perhaps more importantly, lived in Israel in 1967. After the Six-Day War, he told me, "everything had changed." He felt that the same could be said about Russian Jewry and even world Jewry after 1881.

Jonathan was not only an extraordinary scholar, he was also, in his own way, a wonderful teacher and mentor. He was no stirring lecturer, in the Talmonian mold, but came into his own in small classes and in particular in seminars, where his pedagogical gifts were best displayed. I had the pleasure of co-teaching with Jonathan many times, and I saw how he taught his students to think historically, to place historical events in their context, to grapple with the problem of how Jewish history and general history interacted, to read difficult texts and tease out their meanings. It was an unforgettable experience, in which I, though also a professor, often felt more like a student than a co-teacher. It was also, sometimes, rather depressing to be confronted, again and again, with a master historian who knew much more than I and who thought more clearly than I could ever hope to do. He set high, really unattainable standards for himself, but was always prepared to deal kindly with students who were sometimes more ignorant and opinionated than they should have been. One could only remain silent, and fight off bouts of envy.

Jonathan was devoted to his students, and spent endless hours with them—reading their work, advising them, helping to find them jobs (if jobs were available), writing endless recommendations, even editing their dissertations. He had far more doctoral students than was allowed (but no one seemed to object), and while his colleagues often fled from the duties of mentoring he behaved in the opposite way. I think that his willingness to spend so much time with students—and with colleagues who asked for his assistance in reading their work—derived from his basic view of the seminal importance of the historical profession. Jonathan was a man with a typically English sense of humor, but he never spoke lightly or ironically of his profession, or his calling, which is a better word for it. He believed that good history writing was an essential aspect of high culture (and he was a highly cultured man), and that writing objectively and accurately about Jewish history, in all its complexity, had a great role to play in the formation of a modern, tolerant, self-confident but never arrogant Jewish nation. Thus his willingness to guide almost any student who wanted to work with him. A brilliant man himself, and highly critical of his own work, he actually suffered fools gladly, and thought that almost no one should be turned away if he or she wished to work seriously on some aspect of the Jewish past.

Jonathan did not seek fame as a writer of popular history, though he admired those good historians, like A.J.P. Taylor, Simon Schama, and Tony Judt, who were able to write blockbusters for the "educated masses." He was, in other words, a "historian's historian," who wrote for the ages. In this, as in many other ways, he was a bit of a throwback to the old days when universities prized great scholars, and did not necessarily seek out famous ones. Like many other great historians of the past, he also placed considerable emphasis upon style—he was a brilliant writer, whose mastery of English prose derived, no doubt, from a lifetime of reading the classics of English literature. He was also a great editor, able to turn, almost magically, dross into gold, as I observed many times while working with him on the volumes of *Studies*.

To my mind, Jonathan was a true heir to the great tradition of Israeli Jewish historians established by such men as Shmuel Ettinger (whom he very much admired), Jacob Talmon, and Jacob Katz. And yet he never became a well-known Israeli public intellectual (as were Talmon and another important figure, the historian of the United States Yehoshua Arieli). He was, however, an important figure at the Hebrew University, where he built up the Russian and East European program until it became one of the best in the world (this was before cuts in salaried positions and the retirement of faculty who were not replaced did their nefarious work).

Jonathan was certainly politically engagé, and very active in the Shalom Achshav (Peace Now) movement that emerged in the 1970s. A convinced Zionist, whose belief in the absolute necessity for the creation of the state of Israel never wavered, he was no less convinced that holding on to the newly acquired territories (conquered or liberated, according to one's point of view) was morally indefensible, pervasively corrupting, and in the end a serious threat to the preservation of Israel as a "Jewish state." Jonathan was an old-fashioned liberal, who found intolerance, racism, or chauvinism of any kind repugnant (while in New York in the 1960s, he even participated in the civil rights movement—together we attended meetings of CORE, the Congress on Racial Equality, led by James Farmer, and participated in the March on Washington of 1963). He was much admired by his colleagues and students, but never attained any sort of public fame in Israel. As I have noted, he did not write academic bestsellers. He never ran for office (as did some academics), and never wrote very much in the daily press on contemporary politics (as did Talmon and many others). He was almost never on television, even at a time when his colleagues were to be seen sounding off virtually every day on one program or another. Perhaps the reason for this was that he remained a bit of an outsider in Israeli life, despite his mastery of Hebrew (which he spoke very well, but with a pronounced accent that immediately gave him away as an "immigrant," even though he lived here for almost fifty years). He almost always wrote his books and articles in English (although some were later translated into Hebrew), and in his way of life, even in his understanding of Judaism, he stood outside the mainstream. He kept kosher and observed the Sabbath, but in all other ways behaved like a secular Israeli Jew, a combination virtually unknown in a country where one is either secular or observant (meaning Orthodox). He gladly and proudly served in the army reserves although, as an older immigrant, he was exempt from *sherut sadir,* the regular three-year stint that most Israeli-born men must endure. It is one of the facts of Israeli intellectual life that it is almost always the native-born, or those who are Central or East European-born but Israeli-raised and educated, who have the chance to attain some measure of fame. Rare it is for an "Anglo-Saxon" intellectual to enjoy much visibility in our cultural life. At any rate, Jonathan certainly did not seek a public role, and if I recall correctly, the few articles he did write on contemporary politics were published in the *Jerusalem Post* (before this once left-of-center newspaper lurched to the right). His festschrift was published not by Merkaz Shazar in Hebrew, but by a leading American university press in English. For some mysterious reason, the most glittering prizes Israel has to offer its scholars eluded him. So far as I know, he was not troubled by this.

Jonathan was an exceptional historian, and an exceptional man. He was modest by nature, but there was nothing in him of false modesty, for he knew his worth, though he never boasted. He was reserved, as the English tend to be, even the English Jews, and his inner life was not revealed to me, but he was a great friend with a real gift for friendship. He envied no one in his profession, was delighted when his colleagues won honors (just as he was pleased when such honors came his way), and entirely lacked that small-mindedness and pettiness that, unfortunately, flourish in the groves of academe. He fought fiercely for his colleagues, and often clashed with administrators, deans, and even presidents of the Hebrew University, but rarely if ever did these clashes result in rancor or anger. The key to his personality, I think, resided in his intense feelings of loyalty—to his family, his profession, his cultural and religious heritage, his university, his friends, for whom he would do anything (within reason). For many of us, he served as a moral compass, a man to turn to when the going got tough, when answers were needed, when decisions had to be made. He died too young, but he had a wonderful, rich life, sharing it with a woman who was also a talented academic as well as a loving life partner. He lived where he had always wanted to live, in Jerusalem, and taught at the university that he loved and served with the utmost devotion. He was a proud citizen of Israel, despite his severe critique of its post-1967 policies, and a proud Jew, despite his abhorrence of its fanatical and intolerant spokespeople. He stood for "Torah and derekh eretz," for Jewish learning and for civility, for pluralism and internationalism. He achieved what he hoped to achieve, and if he did not write even more than he did, the reason lay in his own decision to lavish so much time on his students, on the establishment of his department, and on fighting the good fight for his colleagues to win promotion and to be treated with respect by a sometimes unfeeling administration.

When I think of Jonathan, I think of what Hamlet said of his father: "He was a man. Take him for all in all, we shall not look upon his like again." "Old men forget: yet all shall be forgot," but so long as serious history is read, his works will live, and he will live through them. This is our consolation. Of course I never realized how important Jonathan was to me until he departed. How I miss him now, when I leave my apartment, in a neighborhood we shared for the last several years, and make my way to Givat Ram, where we both began our teaching careers in this country. In his last years, when the disease that killed him was still under control, we would meet and share our thoughts before the commencement of the working day. No longer.

When Moshe Davis decided that the Institute of Contemporary Jewry should publish a yearly journal dedicated to modern Jewish studies, he asked Jonathan to edit it, and Jonathan in turn asked me and Peter Medding to join him. We were all young, native English speakers from different points on the map of the "Anglo-Saxon" Jewish diaspora—London, New York, and Melbourne—two of us historians, the other a political scientist. As joint editors we were equal partners, but the truth is that Jonathan, slightly senior in terms of age and the wisest and most learned of us, was the *primus inter pares*, the first among equals (I hope that Peter will agree with me on this). If I recall correctly, it was his idea that the journal should feature, in every issue, a special symposium topic for which articles would be commissioned, as well as a number of essays on disparate subjects and a large number of book reviews. It is this scheme that has clearly distinguished our journal from the many other publications devoted to modern Jewish studies, many of which have emerged since the mid-1980s as a sure marker of the explosion of Jewish studies in the academic world.

The first volume, which appeared in 1986, was devoted to the subject of *Ostjuden* (Russian and Galician Jews) in the West, a subject that was emblematic of Jonathan's interest in transnational history, in internal Jewish controversies that were bitterly contested but eventually bore surprising fruit, and his understanding of Jewish history developing as the result of both internal Jewish dynamics and external forces (such as, in this case, antisemitism and restrictions imposed by most western countries on unwanted immigration from Eastern Europe).

This first volume, edited by Jonathan, set a standard that we have endeavored to maintain in the quarter-century that has passed. We have made every effort to recruit the best scholars in the field of modern Jewish studies in order to present our readers with the last word in Jewish scholarship on a wide range of subjects. This range has inevitably broadened over the years. I don't think that we anticipated producing volumes, alongside such obvious subjects as the Holocaust, American Jewry, the state of Israel, and Sephardic Jews, on much more arcane topics such as Jews and violence, Jews and the visual arts and music, Jews and Communism, and the issue of gender. We even did a volume on Jews and sports (a subject, by the way, that interested Jonathan very much—he was an avid mountaineer, and played rugby in his youth). The future historian of Jewish studies could do worse than to consider our journal as a guide to the changing nature of Jewish research, both in terms of topics discussed and the materials used in researching these topics. We have striven to keep up to date, while at the same time to remain accessible and lucid.

It has been a rewarding quarter century for me, one reason being the rare opportunity I had to work closely with Jonathan (and Peter, and more recently Eli Lederhendler, who was Jonathan's student). It has not always been easy. The relationship among the editors has almost always been good, based as it has been on mutual respect and trust. All editors know the misery that accompanies the submission of bad articles by colleagues, even friends, and the unhappiness attending the commissioning of articles that are promised, but never written. We shall never forget the case of a colleague who promised an article and even assured us that "it was in the mail" (in those days there was still mail), but which never arrived. Inevitably, we have, over the years, made a few enemies, but I think that we have made many more friends, who respect our aims and appreciate our close attention to editing. We would like to have a larger readership, of course (details on this sensitive issue are a state secret), but we are grateful that we still possess the wherewithal to survive, thanks in large measure to an endowment brought to the Institute by Yehuda Bauer. Much of our success, if it may be termed success, I attribute to our indefatigable managing editors, Laurie Fialkoff and Hannah Levinksy-Koevary, whom I mentioned above in connection with the appearance of this volume.

What lies ahead for our journal? The words of the prophets are written on the subway walls, but there are no subways (yet) in Jerusalem, and prophecy, so say the Jewish sages, is now given only to fools. Peter Medding and I have retired, and Jonathan is gone. Two new editors have been chosen: Anat Helman, a cultural and urban historian of the Yishuv and the state of Israel, and Uzi Rebhun, a sociologist and demographer who has worked on Israel and the United States. Uzi's presence ensures that the journal will maintain its interdisciplinary approach, which has always been a hallmark of our academic home, the Institute of Contemporary Jewry.

These two young scholars are splendid representatives of a new generation of Israeli-born researchers. I assume, and hope, that they will bring with them new perspectives, new ideas, and new ways of thinking about modern Jewish studies. Unlike us (by whom I mean Peter, Jonathan, Eli, and myself) they did not grow up in the diaspora, speaking English; their life experiences are quite different than ours. This means that *Studies* will change, and that is all for the good. But it must find a way to ensure its continued existence in a new, rather unfriendly environment. The Institute of Contemporary Jewry, Moshe Davis' creation, emerged at a time when the Hebrew University was in a period of rapid growth, both in terms of students and faculty, and at a time when some of the best young Jewish scholars in the world, Jonathan Frankel among them, were attracted by the state of Israel and by the opportunity to play a role in its development, and came to teach here. That was a long time ago. Today the Institute itself is engaged in a struggle for survival in a world of very few academic appointments, and its future is unclear. Nor is Israel's position in the world of Jewish scholarship what it once was. Brilliant young Jewish scholars are now employed in the best American and European universities, and fewer such people, it seems to me, are coming here. The best journals in history and related fields are open as they were not before to articles on Jewish studies, which renders it more difficult to recruit new talent to write for *Studies*. Prices of academic books are up, and readership is down. Our journal will have to make its way in a setting that is very different from the one in which it was born, back in the mid-1980s.

I do not wish to end on a note of pessimism. Jonathan's dream was that the libraries of the future would display to their users several shelves on which our yearly volumes are lined up and waiting to be perused. This has come to pass in many libraries in Israel and in the western world. I wish our new editors luck—they will need it, but they have a solid foundation on which to build. As for me, I have had a great run, which now is over. My deepest thanks to those on the editorial board of *Studies*, to my colleagues at the Institute, and to everyone else who supported *Studies*, contributed to it, bought it, and read it. So far as *Studies* is concerned, for me the rest is silence.

Notes

1. Henry Wadsworth Longfellow, "The Jewish Cemetery at Newport," first published in 1858; reprinted in idem, *The Complete Poetical Works of Henry Wadsworth Longfellow* (London: 1895), 191–192.

2. Sally M. Promey, *Painting Religion in Public: John Singer Sargent's Triumph of Religion at the Boston Public Library* (Princeton: 1999), esp. 176–225.

3. Some of them have been republished in Jonathan Frankel, *Crisis, Revolution, and Russian Jews* (New York: 2009).

4. See Benjamin Nathans, "Introduction," in *The Revolution of 1905 and Russia's Jews*, ed. Stefani Hoffman and Ezra Mendelsohn (Philadelphia: 2008), 1–12. This book is based on the three-day conference held in Jonathan's honor at the Hebrew University in 2004.

5. Jonathan Frankel, "The Jewish Socialists and the American Congress Movement," in *Essays on the American Jewish Labor Movement* (Yivo Annual of Jewish Social Science, vol. 16), ed. Ezra Mendelsohn (New York: 1976), 202–341.

6. See his "The 'Yizkor' Book of 1911: A Note on National Myths in the Second Aliya," in Frankel, *Crisis, Revolution, and Russian Jews*, 183–215.

7. My book *On Modern Jewish Politics* (1992) was inspired by Jonathan's views on this subject.

8. Jonathan Frankel (ed.), *Vladimir Akimov on the Dilemmas of Russian Marxism, 1895–1903* (Cambridge: 1969).

The One and the Many: Unity and Diversity in Protestant Attitudes toward the Jews

Yaakov Ariel
(UNIVERSITY OF NORTH CAROLINA AT CHAPEL HILL)

From its inception in the 16th century, Protestantism has been marked by complex and diverse attitudes toward the Jews—an understandable situation, given the fact that the Protestant movement, comprising various denominations, has never developed a unified tradition. When it came to the Jews, Protestantism was strongly influenced by its initial cultural heritage, with its attitudes often reflecting traditional Christian teachings as well as popular Christian European images that had been prevalent in the early modern era. However, a number of Protestant thinkers developed new understandings of the Jews and their role in history. This complicated relationship between Protestants and Jews was not merely a matter of denominational differences. At times, individuals within the same Protestant churches voiced varying opinions on the Jews, and a number of leaders and theologians expressed mixed and complicated sentiments that ranged from anger to appreciation—arguing that the Jews, by their refusal to accept Jesus, had halted the redemption of humanity at large, yet at the same time expressing their support for a Jewish national revival. As could be expected, such conflicting views gave rise to diverse encounters between Protestants and Jews in a variety of western societies in the centuries since the Reformation.

Overall, one can point to a number of core elements of Protestant attitudes that have persisted over time. One is the aforementioned plurality of views. Another is the manifest importance of Judaism and Jews to Protestant thinkers, whose understanding of their own tradition depends on defining the role and place of the Jews in God's plans for humanity. Finally, the highly complex Protestant attitudes toward the Jews are not given to easy compartmentalization. The simple categories invented by late 19th-century thinkers—"antisemitic" or "philosemitic"—do not readily apply.

Diverse patterns in the Protestant attitudes toward the Jews can be traced back to the 16th-century Reformation. Comprising a number of rebellions against the previous Roman Catholic religious order, the Reformation took place under a series of rulers or city councils in several different regions, which resulted in the severing of ties with the Roman church and the establishment of independent organizational, liturgical, and theological structures. Theologically, the boldest Protestant move was to abandon the priesthood and the sacramental system as mediating elements between God and the faithful, replacing it with the idea that individual Christians could approach God directly and "obtain justification" through the grace of God, on the basis of their faith.[1] Protestantism also did away with the adoration of Mary and the saints as well as eliminating much of the traditional iconography and priestly vestments. It transformed the Roman Eucharist, in which the sacrifice of Jesus was reenacted, into the more symbolic Lord's Supper. In a break with Roman tradition that had developed during the Middle Ages, Protestants regarded Scriptures alone, rather than the medieval tradition of the church, as being authoritative. At the same time, mainline Protestantism retained much of the western Christian dogma, accepting the decisions of the early church councils on the Trinity and Christology and respecting much of the theological writings of the early church fathers.[2] With minor changes, Protestants also adopted the same Christian Bible as their sacred scriptures. However, they placed more emphasis on the Bible than did Catholics, their interest extending to the biblical narratives about the Israelites' trials and tribulations. Many, if not most, Protestants agreed with Roman Catholics that Christianity had replaced Israel in its covenant with God. Yet some Protestants took a different approach, expressing an appreciation of the Jews both as continued heirs to the covenant between God and Israel and as objects of biblical prophecies about a restored Davidic kingdom in the land of Israel. However, even these more appreciative views were not always devoid of elements of anger and bitterness.

In pointing to characteristics of the Protestant-Jewish encounter, it is worth noting that Jews did not remain indifferent to Protestant opinions. The theological elite of both traditions was well informed with regard to the opinions promoted by the other group. Jews reacted strongly to Christian criticism, and the lively exchange that has taken place for centuries between Protestant and Jewish intellectuals has helped both communities define their boundaries and construct their self-image. Moreover, the importance of the Protestant relationship with the Jews can hardly be exaggerated. As one of the largest and more powerful religious traditions in the modern era, Protestantism has exercised much influence in determining popular opinions toward the Jews on a global scope. Protestant theological opinions have affected the policies of Protestant countries toward their Jewish minorities. Ultimately, such views have determined the civil status of Jews and their ability both to integrate into host societies and to live safety within them.

This essay, organized in a mostly chronological format, first explores the early relationship between Protestant Christianity and the Jews at the time of the 16th-century Reformation, which set the stage for generations to come. From there, I examine the paths taken by different Protestant reformers with respect to the Jews and the manner in which these reformers influenced European and colonial societies. A number of trends that emerged within Protestantism in the 17th, 18th, and 19th centuries, notably pietism and evangelicalism, are examined, as is the effect of the Enlightenment on Protestant thought and behavior. I note as well some of the major issues distinguishing between liberal and fundamentalist Protestant groups, offer a schematic overview of several dissenting groups, such as Jehovah's Witnesses, and examine the influence of racist theories on Protestants in the 19th and 20th centuries.

Finally, the rise of the movement of interfaith dialogue and reconciliation—which, especially after the Second World War, brought about unprecedented changes in the relationship between Protestants and Jews—is recounted. Overall, this essay emphasizes not only the diversity of Protestant (and Jewish) opinions, but also the dynamic nature of Protestant-Jewish relations over the centuries.

The Early Reformers and the Jews

In surveying Protestant attitudes toward the Jews, it is natural to begin with Martin Luther (1483–1546), who led much of the early and dramatic protest against the Roman Catholic church and whose own attitude toward the Jews was complex and even contradictory. During the early stages of his career as a reformer, Luther took an interest in the Jews and in the prospect of their conversion to Christianity; later on, he expressed virulently defamatory opinions with regard to them. Luther was initially inspired by Paul's *Letter to the Romans,* in which the apostle predicted the eventual redemption of the Jews. Luther thus justified the Jewish refusal throughout the centuries to convert to what he regarded as a corrupted form of the Christian religion. His tract of 1523, *That Jesus Christ Was Born a Jew*, demonstrated goodwill toward the Jews. Later, however, Luther became embittered when he realized that no major movement of Jewish converts to Protestant Christianity was underway. In 1543, he published an elaborate new tract, *On the Jews and Their Lies*, in which the reformer launched a sharp attack on Judaism—among other things, he believed the rumors that Jews were engaged in proselytizing and wished "to warn Christians to be on their guard against them."[3] Luther's views at this stage followed the traditional Christian understanding of Judaism, according to which the Jewish faith was based on an erroneous reading of the Scriptures. He also complained bitterly about what he considered to be a dismissive Jewish attitude toward Christianity.[4] In the latter part of his life, Luther recommended that if the Jews persisted in keeping their faith, Christian rulers should take harsh measures against them, including their banishment from Christian lands.[5]

Ironically, at least some Jews at this time were to some extent sympathetic to Protestantism. In the Ottoman empire, for instance, Sephardic Jewish thinkers generally viewed Protestantism as a faith closer to Judaism, liberated from what they considered to be pagan elements in other forms of Christianity such as the Orthodox and Middle Eastern Christian churches.[6] In other areas, such as Poland and Hungary, some Jews sympathized with Protestants as a fellow minority group. There were even Jews who looked upon Luther's early message, and the new wind blowing in the reformers' quarters, as a possible harbinger of the messianic age.[7] With rare exceptions, however, Jews did not convert to Protestantism.

Luther's shifting attitude toward the Jews can be viewed as a retreat into older and more prevalent Christian paradigms. Luther had inherited a painful legacy, including perceptions that had been formed both by early Christian writings and by images that had developed in the later centuries of the Middle Ages (among them, Jews poisoning wells and murdering Christian children for ritual purposes).[8] In his early career as a reformer, Luther stepped away from this medieval perception of the

Jews, promoting a fresh and more appreciative outlook, but he reverted to the older paradigm in his later, more embittered years. For centuries to come, Protestant attitudes would be influenced by this legacy of negative and suspicious attitudes toward the Jews as well as by more benevolent and appreciative views.

In the wake of the Second World War, a number of historians characterized Luther's opinions of the Jews as being a forerunner of policies of the Third Reich, pointing to the central historical role the Nazis ascribed to Luther as a presumed father of German nationalism and as having had "the right idea" about the Jews.[9] By extension, Lutheranism, if not all of Christianity, was blamed.[10] However, such an interpretation overlooks the complex and ambivalent attitude of Luther, and others like him, to the Jews. To be sure, Luther did have a role in influencing Protestant German opinions with regard to the Jews. Yet Luther alone did not define Protestant attitudes. A number of early Protestant leaders, including Heinrich Bullinger, Ulrich Zwingli's heir in Zurich, criticized Luther's anti-Jewish stand, as did Philipp Melanchthon (1497–1560), Luther's friend and fellow Lutheran theologian. Andreas Osiander (1498–1552), who played a role in the conversion to Lutheranism of Albert of Prussia and the adoption of the Reformation in Nuremberg in 1525, was another of those who were more sympathetic to the Jews, writing a tract that denounced the blood libel charges that had arisen in Western and Central European nations in the Middle Ages.[11] Osiander's own city of Nuremberg prohibited Jews from settling in its territory until the 19th century. Nonetheless, the relatively tolerant views voiced by Osiander and others counterbalanced more hostile opinions and may have had a role in preventing certain state or church actions against the Jews.

However, the Lutheran Reformation did not bring about a favorable transformation in popular attitudes. During the 16th-18th centuries, a number of Lutheran kingdoms and principalities in Scandinavia and Germany forbade Jews to settle in their midst. Moreover, well into the late 20th century, most Lutheran churches held to "replacement theology," the theological understanding that Christianity had superseded the Jews as heir to the covenant between God and Israel, the Jews having been cast out because of their refusal to accept Jesus as their redeemer. According to this traditional Christian view, Jewish law had come to an end with the sacrifice of Jesus on the cross and his atonement for human sins. Only through faith in Jesus Christ could an individual attain salvation; only if Jews joined the Christian church would they be morally and spiritually redeemed.

Protestant attitudes toward the Jews were also influenced by the fact that some Protestant reformers and scholars followed the Hebraist tradition, at least in a moderate measure. Influenced by the classicism of the Renaissance, they studied the Hebrew language, the Hebrew Bible and, in some instances, post-biblical Jewish writings. To be sure, Protestants had to contend with Catholic accusations that the fledgling Protestant tradition was a "Judaized" form of Christianity and, as such, a dangerous heresy. To counter such accusations, Philipp Melanchthon made sure in the Augsburg Confession of 1530 to respond to the Catholic claim of "Judaizing." However, while the Augsburg Confession condemns Anabaptists several times and argues tirelessly against the Roman tradition, it mentions the Jews only once, and this in an almost neutral manner.[12]

A more radical form of Protestant rebellion against the Roman tradition, which developed simultaneously but separately from the Lutheran tradition, became known as the Protestant Reform tradition. On the whole, Reformed Protestants had a more appreciative attitude toward the Jews. Leaders of the Protestant Reform tradition, such as Martin Bucer (1491–1551), Jean Calvin (1509–1564), and Theodore Beza (1519–1605), further distanced their communities both theologically and liturgically from Rome, removing all traces of the Catholic sacramental system and iconography. Leaders of the Reform tradition also put a greater emphasis on the Hebrew Bible, viewing it as equal in its importance to the New Testament. Calvin, the best-known Reformed theologian, wrote commentaries on a number of books in the Hebrew Bible and was highly impressed by the codexes of law in the biblical text.[13] Like Luther, Calvin had mixed feelings about the Jews, variously rejecting them and appreciating them. He mentioned them often in his theological writings, and when it suited his arguments he related to Jewish traditions as being both useful and commendable, as in his discussions of the Jewish Sabbath and the prohibition against graven images.[14] Although he was displeased with the Jewish refusal to accept the Christian tenets of faith, Calvin argued that when the Bible spoke about the sinfulness of the Jews, it referred to that nation as symbolizing all people: not only Jews but *all* of humanity stood guilty before the Lord. What happened to the Jews, he warned his readers, could also happen to Christians.[15] Most importantly, unlike Luther, who held that the role of the Jewish people, as an entity separate from Christianity, had come to an end, Calvin believed that while God was angry at the Jews, they could still be redeemed.[16] Theodore Beza, Calvin's successor, was even more sympathetic to the Jews. Like Luther in his early days as a reformer, Beza blamed the Christians for the Jewish historical refusal to accept the Christian faith. Although he, too, held the view that the Jews were being rightfully punished, he prayed daily for their redemption.

A number of Reformed theologians developed the understanding that the Jews had not been cast out by God for eternity. Rather, they continued to be the true Israel and as such were destined to play an important role in the unfolding of the divine plan of salvation. At the same time, Reformed thinkers, like other Protestants, were deeply influenced by the historical dispute between Christianity and Judaism. Calvin, for one, wrote a dialogue in which he argued with (perhaps an imaginary) Jewish polemicist; it is noteworthy that his presentation of the arguments in this dialogue was quite balanced.

The Early Modern Age

The mixed and ambivalent Reformed Protestant attitudes toward the Jews were relatively positive in comparison with more hostile Christian images of the Jews in Western and Central Europe at the time. To be sure, followers of the Reform tradition were influenced by the prevailing cultural stereotypes of Jews, as is seen, for instance, in Shakespeare's *The Merchant of Venice*, which portrays Jews as possessing troubled and greedy souls and as willing slaughterers of innocent Christians. For the most part, however, it was Reformed rather than Lutheran thinkers who would express interest in the Jews' prospect of national restoration and conversion to Christianity,[17] and in those countries where Reform Protestantism was influential—among them, England, France, and the Netherlands—Protestants displayed an increased measure of tolerance toward Jews.

Apart from accommodating a number of nonconformist Protestant groups, including the Anabaptists, who were not generally tolerated in Western Europe, the Netherlands was one of the first places where critical thinkers such as Benedictus Spinoza (who critiqued both Judaism and Christianity) could carry on their work and somehow voice their opinions.[18] During the 17th century there was no official edict of toleration directed at Jews or a declaration inviting Jews to settle in the Netherlands—some areas officially restricted their settlement. However, the relatively open atmosphere in the Netherlands made the country a magnet for thousands of Jewish emigrants, many of them originally from the Iberian peninsula, where open Jewish life had come to an end in the late 15th century. Joined by thousands of their brethren from Central and Eastern Europe, Jews in the Netherlands built a thriving and creative community.[19]

Dutch Reformed interest in the Jews went beyond benign toleration. A number of Protestant Dutch thinkers took special interest in the Jews, viewing them as the chosen people and closely following developments among that people, such as the rise of a large Jewish messianic movement in the mid-17th century that was sparked by Shabbetai Zevi's claim to be the Messiah. Various Dutch scholars, among them Gerhard Johann Vossius, a follower of Jacob Arminius (a late 16th-century Dutch Reformed theologian who promoted the idea of free will), wrote favorably on the Jewish rabbinical tradition.[20] A warm attitude toward Jews in general and rabbis in particular may also be evident in the art of Rembrandt. A friend of Rabbi Menasseh ben Israel, Rembrandt created four illustrations for the rabbi's book on the imminent messianic age; his biblical figures are modeled both on Menasseh ben Israel and on other Jews he encountered in the Sephardic Jewish neighborhood of Amsterdam.[21]

At about the same time, other Protestant thinkers in non-Reformed settings were producing virulently anti-Jewish tracts. One of the most notorious was *Entdecktes Judenthum* (Judaism unmasked) (1711), written by Johann Andreas Eisenmenger, a Lutheran scholar of Semitic languages. Although billed as an academic study, *Entdecktes Judenthum* was initially banned by the emperor, who recognized its potential for popular, anti-Jewish agitation. The initial censorship not withstanding, Eisenmenger's treatise became an enduring staple of anti-Jewish literature, propagating late medieval and early modern negative stereotypes of the Jews well into the 18th, 19th, and 20th centuries.

In England, the 16th-century Reformation gave rise to groups and ideas that promoted a new outlook on the Jews. England had been the site of the first anti-Jewish blood libel in the mid-12th century, and in 1290, the entire Jewish community had been expelled. Nonetheless, Jews continued to exert a hold on the popular imagination. As England became more Protestant, its images of the Jews became more nuanced. One important factor in this development was the King James translation of the Bible, which made the Christian scriptures far more accessible to English readers.[22] This, in turn, stimulated interest in eschatology, especially among Puritans, who were influenced by the Protestant Reform tradition. While some Puritan thinkers identified the English with ancient Israel and believed that a new Jerusalem could be built in England, others considered the prospect of a return of the Jews to Palestine and their conversion to Christianity.[23] This trend began in the late 16th century and became more predominant in the century that followed. One such visionary of Jewish restoration and conversion, Thomas Brightman, the rector of Hawnes, predicted that earthly Jerusalem would become the center of the universe as well as the center of a world-dominant Christianity.[24]

Premillennialist messianic convictions, based on a prophetic belief in Christ's return to establish the kingdom of God on earth, were also popular among the first generations of English settlers in what was to become the United States of America.[25] The New England Puritans were committed to building a perfect Christian polity in the new land, "a city built upon a hill," and they saw themselves as having entered into a covenant with God based on their perfect Christian faith and saintly membership.[26] They often referred to their experience in their new environment in biblical terms that were similar to those used to describe the Israelites entering Canaan.[27] While their eyes were directed toward the building of the kingdom of God in America, their messianic hopes also included the conversion of the Jews to Christianity and their restoration to Palestine.[28] Moreover, some Puritan thinkers, among them Increase Mather, attempted to convert American Indians, holding to the belief that the Indians were the Ten Lost Tribes of Israel.[29] Arguing that the evangelization of Israelites-Indians had to precede the return of Jesus, they urged the allocation of resources toward missionary efforts. A prominent Congregational minister and missionary to the Indians, John Elliot, spoke as well about the glorious future of the nation of Israel, in which he included the Ten Lost Tribes, the Indians.[30]

The civil war that began in England in 1642 gave further impetus to Puritan eschatological expectations, to the extent that Puritan leaders called for the cancellation of the Expulsion Act of 1290 and for the readmission of Jews to England. Basing themselves on Deut. 28:64 ("The Lord shall scatter thee among one end of the earth even unto the other"), some of them argued that in order for the Messiah to come, the Jews had first to be scattered to all corners of the earth, including England. Others noted that the readmission of Jews to England would make them more accessible to evangelization and would therefore hasten their conversion to Christianity.[31] Although the Whitehall Conference, convened in December 1655 by Oliver Cromwell, did not officially pass the resolution the Lord Protector had been hoping for, the bars against Jewish settlement in England were in effect removed. Consequently, a semi-clandestine community of Jewish Marranos who were living in London as Spanish and Portuguese merchants were allowed to express their Jewishness openly and build a synagogue. Other Jews, mostly from Central and Eastern Europe, followed, entering the country in small numbers throughout the 18th century.

Jewish patterns of immigration are significant, since they allow us to discern where Jews felt it would be advantageous for them to settle. During the 17th century, patterns of Jewish migration were reversed. Whereas Jews had previously emigrated eastward from Western and Central Europe, they now moved toward the west, from Catholic and Orthodox Christian lands to Protestant realms, including areas such as Sweden or Saxony in which they were officially prohibited from settling. Marranos wishing to return to Judaism discovered that Protestants did not care much about their previous Catholic identities, and at any rate there were no Protestant inquisitions. Similarly, Ashkenazic Jews increasingly sought to settle in Western or Central European Protestant states or in their overseas colonies.[32] This pattern of immigration persisted until the 1930s, when the rise of the Nazi regime brought the trend to a temporary halt. During the 19th and 20th centuries, English-speaking nations became particularly attractive to Jewish migrants. This, of course, did not mean that all Protestants welcomed Jews wholeheartedly. Long-rooted negative images persisted, and the Jews were often deemed both morally and spiritually deprived.

Pietism, Evangelicalism and the Jews

At the turn of the 18th century, a breakthrough in the relationship of Continental Protestants and Jews took place with the rise of the pietist movement. Unlike the Anabaptists and spiritualists of the 16th century, pietists did not challenge major Christian tenets of faith; generally speaking, they remained within the Protestant mainstream and demonstrated political conformity. Their basic quarrel was with the formal, hierarchical structure of Lutheran state churches. Unlike the Lutherans, the pietists stressed the individual's need to undergo personal spiritual religious experiences and to live committed Christian lives on both the personal and communal levels. Although pietist groups traced their roots to early Protestant apostolic movements in Bohemia and Moravia, the pietist wing that most influenced Protestant attitudes toward the Jews crystallized in 17th-century Germany.

Departing from mainstream Lutheran teachings, a number of pietist thinkers considered conversion of the Jews to be an essential step toward the advancement of messianic times.[33] Accordingly, a number of them pioneered Protestant missions to the Jews. These were not the first Protestants attempting to bring the Gospel to the Jews; such efforts had begun with Martin Luther and his contemporaries. However, the pietist mission differed sharply in its approach. Previous Christian scholars had generally looked upon the Jews as a people frozen in time, practicing a static and uniform tradition; few had taken notice of Jewish inner divisions or paid attention to the actual daily life of the Jews. In contrast, the Institutum Judaicum et Mahammedicum, founded in 1721 by a group of pietist leaders headed by Johann Callenberg (1694–1760), offered its missionaries a broad curriculum of Jewish culture, including Jewish languages. Apart from assembling an impressive library on Jewish themes, the mission (located in Halle, the center of German pietist activity) published a series of books relating to Jewish culture as well as lexicons and manuals, among them a manual for the study of Yiddish—one of the first of its kind.[34] Considering the Jews to be, in essence, God's chosen people who had been cast temporarily aside, they related to them more appreciatively than did most Lutherans.[35] The Instititium Judaicum set a model for a series of missions that were established in Protestant countries in the 18th and 19th centuries. Influenced by pietist theology and eschatology, such missions often promoted a messianic interpretation of the role of the Jews in history and became defenders of Jewish rights.[36]

Pietism strongly affected the evangelical movement that came about in English-speaking countries in the second part of the 18th century.[37] Like the pietists, the evangelicals did not consider formal baptism and church affiliation to be sufficient in defining an individual as a Christian; the only true Christians were those who had undergone religious experiences and had made personal commitments to live true Christian lives. Although evangelical Protestants did not hold to one school of thought, they all looked to the Bible as their source of inspiration and were deeply committed to spreading the Christian gospel. Even during the 20th century, when interfaith dialogue had become popular among a number of Protestant groups, evangelicals continued to regard non-Christian religions as faiths that could not offer salvation to their adherents (and thus refused to engage in such dialogue). In common with the pietists, they advocated a more literal interpretation of the Bible, opposing exegetical options that questioned the authenticity and accuracy of the biblical texts. To this day, biblical prophecies concerning the restoration of Israel to its ancestral land under the leadership of a Messiah descending from the House of David are accepted literally by many evangelical leaders and laypeople.[38]

In Britain, evangelicalism reached a zenith in the first half of the 19th century. The French Revolution, followed by the Napoleonic wars and the Industrial Revolution, were regarded by many as indications that an era was ending and that the apocalypse was about to begin.[39] Accordingly, a number of British religious and lay leaders tried to promote the conversion of the Jews to Christianity and their return to their ancestral homeland. In 1809, the London Society for Promoting Christianity amongst the Jews was established, which eventually became the largest 19th-century mission to the Jews, overseeing some 200 missionaries in more than 50 missionary posts around the globe.[40] Other missionary societies sponsored by Protestant churches and inspired by the pietists and evangelicals soon followed in places as varied as Norway, Scotland, Poland, and South Africa. In addition, there were a number of interdenominational missionary enterprises and many individual initiatives. By the turn of the 20th century, more than 700 full-time, paid Protestant missionaries, representing dozens of missionary societies, labored around the globe in large or medium-sized Jewish communities. Wives of missionaries and volunteers contributed their efforts as well. Missionaries published tracts and journals along with translations of sacred scriptures or other Christian literature. Wishing to demonstrate positive Christian values and attract potential converts, they also engaged in welfare activities among the Jews, including the offering of medical aid and educational opportunities. For their founders and sponsors, such missions were important far beyond the recorded few thousand Jews who were converted through missionary efforts. The missions' large and variegated literature was intended first and foremost to reeducate both Protestants and Jews as to the role of the Jews in history. Missionaries wanted the Protestant communities to adopt their premillennial theology in addition to disseminating the Christian message, in its pietist-evangelical form, to as many Jews as possible.

Many evangelical leaders also promoted the idea of the Jewish return to Palestine. Anthony Ashley-Cooper, the seventh earl of Shaftesbury, the leader of the evangelical movement in Britain and the president of the London Society for Promoting Christianity amongst the Jews, ardently believed in the imminent second coming of Jesus. In 1840, he suggested to the English foreign secretary, Lord Palmerston, that Britain should initiate the return of Palestine to the Jews, offering the rationale that a

Jewish Palestine would serve as a buffer against Egyptian encroachment in the Ottoman empire.[41]

It was in this atmosphere of intensified eschatological expectations in Britain and of a growing interest in the Jewish people and the prospect of their return to Palestine that dispensationalism, a new school of belief in the second coming of Jesus, was born. Dispensationalism promoted the view that history was divided into distinct eras, each of them featuring a different divine plan for humanity. This new system of explaining biblical prophecies was to have a more influential role in the 20th century among American Protestants than among the British. In Britain, the historical (non-dispensational premillennialist) school prevailed.[42] In America, with the rise of fundamentalism in the decades following the Civil War, the conservative evangelical elite became dispensational premillennialist and the conversion of the Jews was given greater priority than before. Indeed, at the turn of the 20th century, American Protestants created one of the largest of the missionary networks aimed at evangelizing among the Jews.[43] Noted evangelical leaders wrote of their expectations for the imminent second coming of Christ, which would usher in the kingdom of God on earth, and of their belief that, after recognizing Jesus as their true Messiah, the Jewish people would resume their place as the first nation of the Lord in the millennial kingdom.[44]

In the early 20th century, evangelical Protestantism was strongly shaped by the "modernism versus fundamentalism" controversy that split the ranks of Protestantism at that time.[45] Many evangelicals sided with the conservative point of view, insisting on the need to preserve "the fundamentals of faith," among which was the pietist-evangelical understanding that "no one can enter the kingdom of God unless Born Again."[46] For a number of decades, the conservative evangelical camp had a fundamentalist stamp. However, following the Scopes trial in 1925, when it became evident that American public opinion in general did not accept the more conservative outlook, fundamentalists disappeared to a great extent from the American public arena—even though, far from the public eye, they continued to evangelize and enlarge their ranks.[47] During the 1930s–1940s, a number of evangelical leaders decided to reform fundamentalism by accommodating it to the wider culture. In this way, they hoped, fundamentalism would be a means of shaping the values and agendas of a larger number of people. Between the 1940s and the 1960s, neo-evangelicalism—a more moderate and accommodating form of conservative Protestantism—emerged from the fundamentalist camp. Beginning in the 1970s, evangelicals such as Pat Robertson, Chuck Smith, John Walvoord, and Tim LaHaye entered the U.S. political and cultural scene, becoming known as ardent supporters of Jewish and Israeli causes.

The Enlightenment, Protestants, and Jews

Protestant attitudes toward the Jews in the 18th-20th centuries were strongly influenced by ideas apart from those of the pietists and evangelicals. In particular, the Enlightenment and its long-range effects transformed Protestantism. While it had different emphases in different realms, the Enlightenment generally challenged many long-held assumptions regarding faith and religious authority.[48] However, the effects of these intellectual transformations on Protestant-Jewish relations were mixed; like so many trends in the attitudes of Protestants toward Jews, the Enlightenment created both new opportunities and new challenges.

In undermining the theological basis for the political role of churches, the Enlightenment provided both for the separation of church and state and for the granting of civil rights to members of all religious and ethnic groups. These new outlooks served as a backdrop to the widespread discourse within European societies with regard to the emancipation of the Jews in the late 18th century and throughout much of the 19th century. During this interval, Jews gradually attainted equal citizenship—at least on the formal level—in most European countries. Among the long-term effects of the Enlightenment, especially in the English-speaking world, were interfaith dialogue and the beginning of a rapprochement between Judaism and Christianity. At the same time, the Enlightenment brought about a transformation of overtly Christian animosity against Judaism and Jews: such animosity was now more likely to be expressed in secular and pseudo-scientific jargon. Thus, the relationship between Protestant Christians and Jews entered a new phase in which Protestants did not fully abandon older religious sentiments, but rather made use of new concepts and arguments. Old cultural prejudices and accusations against the Jews were clothed in new and seemingly secularized garments. All of this occurred at a time when Jews and Protestants began more frequently to encounter one another, often in "neutral" social circles and meeting grounds.

To sum up, Protestantism did not necessarily become more accepting to Jews, at least not immediately. For one thing, Enlightenment thinkers who challenged Christian truths found it easier to lash out at Jewish pillars of faith rather than those of Christianity.[49] English deists such as John Toland denied the validity of the Hebrew biblical narrative, revelation, and prophecy, even though Toland himself (along with most other deists) had no objection to Jewish integration into European or American societies.[50] Others, however, blamed the Jewish tradition for corrupting western civilization.

Following the French Revolution, French Protestants took part in the public discussions that accompanied the rise of the new French republic. One of their major goals was ending the exclusive status of the Catholic church and creating a more neutral, religiously tolerant, civic society. A number of Protestant thinkers wrote in favor of offering the Jews civil liberties, often drawing a connection between their own status and that of the Jews as restricted minorities in a predominantly Catholic society. Similarly, a lively public debate broke out in Germany in the later decades of the 18th century on the issue of the Jews' place within the larger civic Christian society. Not all Protestant thinkers were sympathetic. Karl Grattenauer, a prominent Prussian jurist, compared the condition of Jews with that of the Huguenots—French Protestants who settled in Germany in the 17th and 18th centuries, especially in Prussia, and who were granted a civic status equal to that of Lutherans. According to Grattenauer, the Jews, unlike the Huguenots, were not willing to accommodate themselves to the larger society and were therefore inherently incapable of becoming citizens of a Christian nation. In contrast, Christian Wilhelm von Dohm, a senior Prussian administrator and intellectual, published a two-volume tract propagating the idea of

Jewish emancipation and integration into German society.[51] Dohm (who entered into debate with Moses Mendelssohn on the issue) believed that the pre-Enlightenment autonomous structure of the Jewish *kehilah* might be maintained, but he also argued that the Jews had to join the mainstream, to "Protestantize" themselves, as it were, even as they continued to maintain their ancestral faith. Put somewhat differently, he was willing to see the Jews become integrated citizens within European society on condition that they adopt the values and manners of European burghers and, not incidentally, change their occupations. Over time, the Jews began to contribute more directly and openly to the larger culture, including in areas—such as music, theater, art, and architecture—in which, for various reasons (among them, legal or social barriers) they had previously been underrepresented.

By the 19th century, Protestant European discourse regarding the Jews had become somewhat secularized, the focus shifting from the alleged failures of Judaism to the usefulness and decency (or lack thereof) of Jews as people and citizens. Max Weber, for instance, regarded the Jews, on the whole, as a positive element in modern society. Although it was Protestants who had developed and promoted the "spirit of capitalism," which Weber saw as the driving force in the building of successful premodern and modern societies, Jews, too, had made their contribution. Thus, while Weber was not entirely free of negative stereotypes of Jews, he more often than not went out of his way to defend the Jewish religion.[52] In contrast, Werner Sombart (1863–1940), an economist and political thinker who was an ardent socialist in his youth, blamed the Jews rather than the Protestants for the rise of capitalism.[53] In the view of Sombart and others, the Protestant Christian tradition promoted less greedy and more humane values.

Resentment of the processes of modernization, urbanization, and the rise of a capitalist technological society often translated into anti-Jewish sentiments. Many European Protestants deplored the shift taking place in the social standing of Christians and Jews: the outsiders became insiders, often besting their Protestant counterparts at their own economic, professional, and cultural games. It was within this context that Wilhelm Marr (1819–1904), a Protestant German intellectual, coined the term "antisemitische" (antisemitic), to designate his own (and others') inherent distrust of Jews. In contrast to the classic Christian resentment of the Jews as members of a religious minority who challenged the truths of Christianity, the new term gave expression to modern forms of political, ethnic, economic, and cultural hatred.[54] In this way, they went well beyond the historical Christian critique of Judaism as an obstinate sister faith that had refused to disappear.

As Jews became further integrated into European or American culture, they found themselves contending with Protestant ideas and modes of thinking. The Reform Jewish movement founded in the 19th century was influenced by Protestant liturgy and its more formal style of worship. In American and European universities, meanwhile, liberal Jewish scholars and leaders were exposed to the "scientific" scholarship of the Scriptures promoted by scholars such as Ferdinand Christian Bauer and Julius Wellhausen; they noticed, too, that these Protestant scholars, especially in Europe, reacted much more critically to the Jewish sacred texts and sacred narrative than to their own.[55] Jewish scholars, in particular those connected with the Wissenschaft des Judentums in Germany and their counterparts elsewhere, struggled to affirm the legitimacy and authenticity of Judaism against attacks by Protestant scholars.

Historians have paid little attention to the more favorable German Protestant attitudes toward Jews.[56] While these did exist, it is also the case that movements that promoted biblical-millennial faiths and related to the Jews as heirs and continuers of historical Israel were more marginal in German Protestantism than in the English, Dutch, or French-speaking counterparts. "Philosemitism," the expression of goodwill toward the Jews motivated by a Christian biblical faith, was a more subdued phenomenon in Germany and the European continent in general. Christian Zionism, a movement of support for Jewish restoration in Palestine motivated by a Christian messianic faith, had fewer adherents and more limited standing in German Protestant society than in English-speaking countries and was less successful in advancing the Jews' favorable reception in society.[57]

One of the long-lasting effects of the Enlightenment on modern Protestantism was the rise of a liberal wing that was to transform Christian attitudes toward Judaism and Jews. Liberal trends in Protestantism, which took shape during the 19th century, accepted many of the premises of the Enlightenment, including its insistence that a critical reading of the Bible must be based on scientific methods. Similarly, the liberals came to regard religious affiliation as a private, non-obligatory matter. One of the early pillars of liberal thinking, Friedrich Schleiermacher, grew up in the pietist community of Herrenhut and later became one of the more popular preachers and thinkers within the official Prussian church. Proponents of liberal Protestantism wished to adapt Christianity to the political, social, intellectual, and cultural developments of the times. Schleiermacher emphasized the personal and spiritual elements of religion, which he defined as "a sense and taste for the infinite."[58] Like many Protestants influenced by the Enlightenment, Schleiermacher's attitude toward Judaism was not entirely positive even though, on a personal level, he was friendly with a number of Jews. In a manner reminiscent of traditional Christian perceptions, he viewed Judaism as having come to an end, its "last effort" having been the bringing about of the messianic ideal—though he refused to credit Judaism with the emergence of Christianity.

The liberal camp did not develop as a monolith. Most mainline Protestant churches today contain strong liberal components as well as conservative wings. Despite this plurality of views, mainline churches have established interdenominational organizations that foster Protestant cooperation, as well as mutual theological seminaries, joint publications, and missionary and welfare groups. Likewise, Protestants have often looked to their intellectual and spiritual leaders as representing more than merely denominational opinions. Notwithstanding certain liturgical and organizational differences, mainline denominations have much in common in the realm of theology and ideology.

In the late 19th century, liberal Protestants embraced a progressive messianic outlook. As opposed to the conservatives, who believed that the world as we know it would come to an end in a catastrophic manner and that the messianic age would begin with the arrival of Jesus, liberal Protestants believed that humanity—aided by technology, improved forms of government, widespread education, and successful evangelism—could eventually build the kingdom of God on earth on its own.

(Until the First World War, this belief was also widely held by liberal Jews, although in their version, Judaism, not Christianity, best exemplified the purified ethical monotheism that humanity would eventually adopt.) Liberal Protestants also remained committed to an acceptance of scientific findings produced by the various academic disciplines, which were to be incorporated into their tenets of faith.[59] Accordingly, they promoted the "higher criticism" of the Bible, which gained a firm foothold in Protestant theological faculties and seminaries in the 19th century.[60] At the turn of the 20th century, liberal religious thinkers also became advocates of social justice. Theologians such as Walter Rauschenbusch emphasized responsibility toward the economically deprived, viewing it as a fulfillment of the basic tenets of Christianity.[61]

An especially important trend in modern Protestantism was the movement promoting international Christian unity and interfaith dialogue, which began to evolve just before the turn of the 20th century. Inspired by liberal Protestants, one of its first major gatherings was the World Parliament of Religions (WPR), which, convening in Chicago in 1893, brought together Protestants, Catholics, and Jews as well as Buddhists, Hindus, members of the Baha'i faith, Muslims, Greek Orthodox, members of Eastern Christian churches, and others. In 1906, liberal American Protestants established the Federal Council of Churches of Christ in America. During the 1920s, liberal Protestants, Catholics, and Jews established national councils of Christians and Jews in England (1924) and the United States (1928).[62] The immediate impetus for the establishment of the councils was the perceived need for a united campaign against the racist principles propagated by Christian reactionary groups, whose influence was increasing.[63] In 1948, John Mott, the director of the international department of the YMCA, was awarded the Nobel Peace Prize for his half-century of unflagging efforts to achieve unity among Christians throughout the world. Mott's lifetime dream partially materialized that same year, when the World Council of Churches (WCC) convened in Amsterdam. At its inception, the WCC included mainly Protestant denominations of more liberal leanings, but over the years it has been joined by Orthodox, Middle Eastern, and Third World churches, and its relation to the Jews and to Israel has undergone many changes.

During the 1930s and 1940s, the first calls for recognizing Judaism as a separate, legitimate religion were sounded among liberal Protestants in Great Britain and North America. These pioneers of Protestant-Jewish reconciliation also expressed support for the Zionist movement and the establishment of a Jewish home in Palestine. An early protagonist of this attitude was Reinhold Niebuhr, an American Protestant theologian who promoted "Christian realism"—a school of thought that cast doubt on the idea of progress while at the same time maintaining a liberal and socially conscious agenda. Niebuhr's initial exposure to Judaism took place in Detroit of the 1920s, where he encountered Jewish leaders and congregations and concluded that they were morally and spiritually worthy, even without benefit of the Christian gospel.[64] In England at about the same time, the Anglican Canon James Parkes reached similar conclusions and became another spokesman for this trend of thought.[65] In 1932, American liberal Protestants founded the Pro-Palestine Federation with the aim of promoting the Zionist agenda of building a Jewish commonwealth in Palestine. Ten years later, Protestants, most of them liberals, established the Christian Council on Palestine, which represented thousands of Protestant clergymen and leaders.

These organizations spoke out in the public debates that preceded the establishment of the state of Israel. This almost unprecedented liberal Protestant support of Jewish causes, which was by no means universal among members of the various liberal denominations, was not prompted by messianic premillennialist expectations; its proponents did not necessarily believe that the Jews were destined to play a major role in the unfolding of biblical prophecy.[66] Rather, their stand was the outcome of moral, political, and emotional considerations, not least of which was sympathy for a people that was being subjected not only to persecution but to mass extermination.[67] At the same time, however, other elements within mainline Protestant churches continued their missionary activity among the Jews, a fact that led to much resentment among Jewish leaders.[68]

Dissenting Protestant Denominations

Before turning to the Second World War and postwar eras, some mention should be made of the dissenting denominations within Protestantism—among them, Jehovah's Witnesses, the Seventh-day Adventists, and the Christian Scientists—all of which evolved in the course of the 19th century. These groups hold to the centrality of the sacred scriptures both in the building of a true Christian society and as a guide to daily life and belief. During the 20th century, dissenting Protestant groups became increasingly global, drawing the majority of their converts from outside the United States. With regard to the Jews, they have generally adhered to the traditional concept that Christianity inherited God's promises to the people of Israel, and that the role of Jews in history has come to an end.

The roots of the Seventh-day Adventists go back to the 1830s and 1840s, when a large movement of believers expectantly awaited the second coming of Jesus. Stirred by predictions made by a preacher named William Miller, the movement grew in membership until 1844, when the last of the dates set for Jesus' return came and went. However, the movement that Miller inspired did not fully disintegrate.[69] Some of Miller's followers became convinced that the messianic age had begun—not on earth, but in heaven. During the 1860s and 1870s, they established themselves as a non-mainstream Protestant denomination. Influenced by the Seventh-day Baptists, the Adventists chose to celebrate Saturday rather than Sunday as their Sabbath, in addition to promoting a healthy life based on exercise and vegetarianism. In spite of their biblical-messianic faith, their high regard for the Hebrew Bible, and their adoption of a code of dietary rules similar to that of the Jews, the attitude of the Seventh-day Adventists toward Judaism and Jews has for the most part been equivocal. Miller had no special place in his eschatology for the Jewish people, maintaining the traditional Christian belief that the Jewish role in history had terminated with Jesus' death on the cross. Likewise, he did not consider Palestine to have any significance for the coming messianic age. These attitudes continued to hold sway in the movement after it was reorganized under the leadership of Ellen White. Most Seventh-day Adventists, seeing no reason for the existence of a separate Jewish religious community, have considered the Jews to be a legitimate object of missionary activity.[70]

An exception was Clorinda S. Minor, one of Miller's lieutenants, who believed that the Jewish people would return to Palestine before Jesus' actual return to earth, and that her mission was to help restore the land and its Jewish inhabitants.[71] In the mid-19th century she settled in Palestine and aided in establishing agricultural colonies—first Artas, near Bethlehem, and later Mount Hope, near Jaffa.[72] Over the years, small groups of Adventists with similar convictions organized independently of the Seventh-day Adventists, evincing interest in the Jews, their return to Palestine, and the prospect of their conversion to Christianity (like Minor, some of them also went to Palestine).[73] By the turn of the 21st century, the Adventists had become influenced, to some extent, by the more liberal atmosphere that had developed among western Christians, and a number of Adventist thinkers joined the movement of Jewish-Christian reconciliation. Jacques B. Doukhan, a professor of Hebrew and Jewish studies at the Adventist-affiliated Andrews University in Michigan, established an institute for Jewish-Christian relations and reconciliation as well as a journal, *Shabbat Shalom*, dedicated to Christian-Jewish rapprochement. Doukhan's book, *Israel and the Church: Two Voices for the Same God,* reads much like other books of Protestant theologians who have come to accept the validity of Jewish existence outside of the church.[74]

Jehovah's Witnesses is the current name of a group founded in the 1870s by Charles Taze Russell (1852–1916), a conservative Protestant who was influenced both by the Adventists' "historical" vision of the "End Times" and by the "futurist" dispensationalist messianic faith. Russell believed in the central role assigned to the Jews in the heavenly plan of redemption and often preached on Jewish restoration to Zion.[75] However, his successor, Joseph Franklin Rutherford (1869–1942), instigated a theological turnabout.[76] The change in name, in 1931, from "Bible Students" to "Jehovah's Witnesses," expressed the group's new outlook of exclusivity. Jehovah's Witnesses have come to believe that they alone are fulfilling God's will, rejecting all other religious expressions. Likewise they maintain that all nation states are kingdoms of Satan, or at any rate carry out policies that have nothing to do with fulfilling God's will. Anticipating the kingdom of God as the only legitimate political entity, they take no part in politics, do not vote in elections, and refrain from serving in armed forces; they also refuse to take part in civil religious rites such as Thanksgiving and Christmas.[77] They have no use for the state of Israel and have no special attachment to Palestine. Not seeing special merit in either the land or the people, they, like the Seventh-day Adventists, consider the Jews to be a legitimate object of missionary activity.

The Church of Jesus Christ Scientist, popularly known as Christian Science, was established in the 1880s by Mary Baker Eddy. This offshoot of Protestantism developed new understandings of the deity, sickness, health, and death. Although it parted ways with traditional Christian dogma, Eddy's writings reflect traditional Christian perceptions of Judaism's alleged faults and failures. This, however, did not deter thousands of Jews from joining the new group, which drew much of its membership from the educated white middle class in the United States (many members were also women). Eddy's followers found her teachings empowering, since these emphasized the triumph of spirit over matter and the ability of people's minds to control their bodies, overcoming sickness and even death. Middle-class Jewish women and men, many of them the grandchildren of mid-19th-century German immigrants, joined the new group in relatively large numbers during the 1900s-1920s. A number of Jewish leaders, alarmed by the new development, constructed "Jewish Science," which came to offer similar teachings to those of Christian Science, while remaining within the realm of Judaism and the synagogue.[78]

Racist Protestantism and the Jews

Racist ideas affected Protestant thinking long before the Nazi rise to power in 1933. In far more benign form, as has been noted, such theories began to penetrate polite Protestant society in the late 19th century, finding expression in the social sciences and the humanities as well as in the life sciences. Ideas concerning the origins of peoples, cultures, languages, and religions influenced a new field of academic inquiry known as the history of religion or comparative religion.[79] The Protestant scholars who founded this discipline placed Christianity at the top of the religious evolutionary ladder, ranking Protestantism above other "less advanced" forms of Christianity and placing Judaism, considered by them to be a limited, less developed religion, as a stepping stone on the road to Christianity. Such discourse dominated theories of religions well into the mid-20th century.[80] The turn of the 20th century saw attempts to import theories from the realm of biology to the relations between ethnic groups and "races," which meant, among other things, reconstructing the dynamics of Protestant-Jewish relations in racial terms.

In Europe, and to some extent in America, Protestant thinkers helped develop a pseudoscience of racial differentiation. According to these views, the "Aryan race," comprising Northern Europeans, was superior to all others, including, of course, the "semitic" race to which Jews allegedly belonged. Protestants in the German- and Scandinavian-speaking regions of Europe were especially influenced by these ideas, but so, too, were those in the English-speaking world, particularly in the years between the two world wars.[81] Racial theories provided pseudoscientific justification to claims harking back to the discussions over Jewish emancipation at the turn of the 19th century—namely, that the Jews were unfit to become members of Christian societies. They also provided an explanation for the discomfort many Protestants felt toward Jewish converts to Christianity; according to the new racist understanding, Jewishness could not be erased by the baptismal waters. Racial theories thus represented a move away from traditional anti-Jewish views that were based on antagonism to the Jewish religion and its scriptural exegetical tradition: even in his later years, Martin Luther would have welcomed Jewish converts.

The relationship between German Protestantism and the Jews, complicated and ambivalent as it already was, took a sharp turn for the worse with the Nazi rise to power at the beginning of 1933. Within a relatively short period of time, the new regime's ideology had a pernicious effect on almost all of the German Protestant denominations. Leaders of the official state churches affiliated with the Union of Protestant Churches of Germany, and especially "German Christians," a newly created Nazi-oriented group, often became outright Nazi supporters, whereas nonofficial churches such as the Baptists or Methodists adopted an accommodationist pro-Nazi policy. The nonconformist Jehovah's Witnesses was the only group that firmly refused to adjust its ideas or norms to suit the Nazi demands.[82] Changes in Protestant theological perceptions were profound. Theologians and biblical scholars in German universities went so far as to recast Jesus as an "Aryan" instead of a Jew, dispensing with much of the Jewish biblical narrative as well as amending the New Testament.[83] In compliance with the racial theories promoted by the Nazis, Protestant churches also expelled Jewish converts to Christianity from their ranks. Likewise, the authorities forbade further Jewish conversions to Christianity and in 1941 put an end to Protestant missions to the Jews.[84]

Very few Protestant German leaders protested the anti-Jewish measures, although ample protests did occur in other Protestant quarters—even during the German occupation of France, for instance, there were Protestant French leaders who continued to speak out.[85] Before the outbreak of the war, a number of Protestant German thinkers went into exile. Among the most prominent was Paul Tillich, a theologian at Frankfurt University and a leader of the Christian-Socialist movement, who fled to the United States. There he continued his progressive Protestant theological work, first at Union Theological Seminary and later at Harvard and the University of Chicago; during the 1940s he was one of the Protestant American ministers who called for the establishment of a Jewish state in Palestine.

To the extent that German Protestant ministers protested the regime, they tended to limit their objections to the Nazi regime's termination of the theological autonomy of the churches and to its interference with Christian sacred texts. As a rule, however, this group of pastors, members of the Bekennende Kirche, "the Confessing Church," was not overly troubled by the Nazi treatment of the Jews.[86] While they did not, for the most part, endorse the measures the Nazis were taking against the Jews, they did not protest them, in contrast to their criticism of other Nazi policies. Thinkers associated with the Confessing Church, such as Martin Niemöller (1892–1984), did not consider Judaism to be a religious community on a par with Christianity, and they regarded the attempts at the complete integration of the Jews into European society to have been a mistake.[87]

Following the German defeat and the denazification of Germany, Nazi-oriented theology became discredited and non-Nazi church leaders replaced those who had supported the previous regime. Yet even after the war, German Protestant theologians would not be as inclined as their counterparts in English-speaking countries to concentrate their efforts on changing the Christian perception of Judaism—as will be seen, it took several decades for the legacy of the Holocaust to be applied to German Protestant theology. Overall, however, although racist Protestant groups have not completely disappeared, they have become marginalized—unaffiliated with mainstream churches and avoided even by most nonconformist churches.[88]

The Postwar Era

The relationship between mainstream Protestant groups, both liberal and conservative, and the Jewish people underwent momentous change in the era following the Second World War. During the past few decades, Protestant denominations and ecumenical groups have developed new understandings of the Jews' role in history and of Judaism's right to be regarded as a religion independent of Christianity. In 1946, for instance, Christian and Jewish activists established the World Council of Christians and Jews, which holds yearly international conferences on interfaith dialogue. A historical breakthrough in the attitude of Protestant churches toward Judaism occurred in the 1960s, both contemporaneously with and in the wake of Vatican II, the major Catholic council that transformed Christian life in the second half of the 20th century. Toward its conclusion in 1965, the council addressed Christian-Jewish relations, and the issue remained high on the Catholic church's agenda in the years that followed.[89] Changes in the Catholic attitude toward Jews were also positively received by mainstream and liberal Protestant bodies, which in turn issued a series of statements regarding the Jews that were similar in vein to those of Vatican II. In fact, some of these declarations went much further than the Catholic ecumenical council in their willingness for reconciliation with the Jewish people.

On the theological plane, liberal Protestants relinquished their claims to be both the only true interpreters of God's commandments to the human race and the only ones eligible to achieve salvation. The truly revolutionary step of recognizing Judaism's legitimacy as a religion that was able to grant its adherents spiritual succor and salvation was motivated in part by a sense of guilt with regard to the Holocaust—in particular, the realization that Nazi hatred of Jews had been nourished by ages of hostile Christian incitement.[90] This granting of recognition and legitimacy to Judaism, which had appeared in the works of Christian thinkers such as Reinhold Niebuhr and James Parkes before the Second World War, was pursued in the 1970s and 1980s by a number of other Protestant theologians, among them Paul Ricoeur of France and the American theologians Franklin Littell and A. Roy Eckardt.[91]

In the period during and after Vatican II, liberal Protestants proclaimed, sometimes even more emphatically than did Catholics, that the Jews were not guilty of deicide.[92] The National Council of Churches in the United States, an ecumenical and largely liberal Protestant organization, issued the following statement: "Especially reprehensible are the notions that the Jews, rather than all mankind, are responsible for the death of Jesus Christ and God has for this reason rejected his covenant people."[93] Having acquitted the Jews of responsibility with regard to the killing of Jesus, liberal Protestants now went one step further in order to clear the atmosphere of the hatred inspired by this and similar charges. In the late 1960s, Protestants revised textbooks then in use in Sunday school classes and elsewhere, removing passages with anti-Jewish overtones or stereotypes. A survey undertaken in 1972 found that the charge of deicide had almost vanished from Protestant textbooks.[94] Although this does not mean that all negative stereotypes of Jews have disappeared from Protestant popular culture, they are now, for the most part, "politically incorrect."[95] During the last several decades, various liberal Protestant scholars also undertook to examine the corpus of Christian theological writings with the aim of neutralizing ideas and claims that promoted negative images of the Jews.[96] Among the subjects they researched was that of attitudes adopted by the church fathers and leading theologians in the Middle Ages and the Reformation toward the Jews. Such studies often defended the New Testament against the charge of anti-Jewish bias, the claim being that anti-Jewish attitudes did not appear in the Holy Scriptures but rather in later Christian writings.[97]

Today, liberal Protestant theologians who characterize Judaism as a religious community in covenant with God can be assigned to one of two categories: those who believe that Judaism and Christianity are two legitimate interpretations of the same covenant, and those who point to two separate covenants with God.[98] Members of both categories share an outlook that places Judaism on an equal spiritual and moral footing with Christianity. This posture has been more readily adopted by English-speaking Protestants, especially in the United States. Within German and Scandinavian Protestantism, as well as Protestantism in the Third World, the more liberal interpretation of covenant theology has developed in a slower and more limited fashion, if at all.[99] However, some German Protestants have moved in this direction. One example is the German theologian Wolfhart Pannenberg, the author of *Jesus, Christ and Man*, who originally claimed that the foundations of Judaism had collapsed with the appearance of Jesus and that it was Jesus' rejection of Jewish religious law that led him to clash with the Jewish establishment of his day.[100] In a later book published after a visit to the United States, Pannenberg offered a modified view, namely, that the historical "God of Israel" stood above that corpus of religious law from which Jesus had dissented; consequently, the two religions had much in common and a dialogue between them was possible.[101] A similar transformation can be discerned in the views of Jürgen Moltmann, another major Protestant German theologian of the late 20th century. In his work of 1974, *The Crucified God*, Moltmann described the execution of Jesus as a direct result of his campaign against Jewish religious law. Although Moltmann rejected the traditional argument that Christianity had replaced Judaism, maintaining instead that the Jews were in fact the true Israel, he nonetheless insisted that only Christ could bring salvation to mankind. Yet three years later, in *The Church in the Power of the Spirit*, the German theologian called for an end to Christianity's "triumphalism" toward Judaism. "The more the Church frees itself from this abuse," he noted, "the more clearly it will recognize Israel as its enduring origin, its partner in history, and its brother in hope."[102] Claiming that the Jewish people would retain its unique mission side-by-side with the Christian church until the end of days and asserting that, upon his second coming, Jesus would be revealed as the Messiah of Christians and Jews alike, Moltmann entered into amicable dialogues with Jewish thinkers.[103]

The Nazi destruction of European Jewry had a notable effect upon liberal Protestant thinking, albeit not in the immediate postwar years. By the 1980s, Protestant theologians had begun to confront the significance of the Holocaust for Christianity and Christian consciousness.[104] While displaying sensitivity to the Jews' unique suffering, they also attempted to ascribe a universal Christian significance to the catastrophe over and above that of nationality.[105] Partly as a result of the Holocaust, mainstream and liberal Protestants also put a halt to their missionary endeavors among Jews; these are now the sole province of conservative-evangelical Protestants or of dissenting Protestant denominations.[106]

Perhaps the most impressive recent development in the attitude of liberal Protestants to Jews and Judaism has taken place in the field of academic studies. Protestant scholars (and students) have expressed growing interest in the study of

Jewish history and thought from the biblical period to the present, and Jewish studies have increasingly become part of the curriculum at Protestant theological seminaries and Protestant-affiliated universities. This development has aided in the uprooting of misinformed stereotypes and images. For instance, as influenced by works of Christian scholars (including E.P. Sanders and John Gager) and their Jewish counterparts (among them, Jacob Neusner, Geza Vermes, David Flusser, Paula Friedriksen, and Amy-Jill Levine), there is growing awareness concerning the historical role of Second Temple Judaism and its influence on early Christianity.[107]

Although many mainline and liberal Protestants have come to recognize the legitimacy of a separate Jewish existence alongside Christianity and have taken steps to uproot traditional hostile images of Jews and Judaism, it would be a mistake to assume that liberal Protestant attitudes toward Israel show the same measure of sympathy. In a process first set in motion by Israel's victory in the Six-Day War of 1967, which resulted in its occupation and partial settlement of the West Bank and Gaza, liberal Protestant circles became increasingly critical of Israel and its political and moral standing. Many liberal Protestants now express sympathy for the Palestinians while questioning the legitimacy of the Zionist endeavor.[108] Among the factors accounting for this shift is the fact that most Middle Eastern Protestants are Arabs (who are often identified as the remnants of authentic early Christianity). Additionally, in the past few decades, Protestant churches in developing countries have gained greater influence in international church councils. Whereas European and American churches generally try to maintain a modicum of evenhandedness, many Third World churches openly support the Arab cause.[109] Thus, the Middle East Council of Churches has given voice to anti-Israel sentiments, granting full credence to the Palestinian historical and political narrative. To be sure, Christian Arabs have not been altogether happy with the growth of radical Muslim movements in the Middle East, including in the West Bank and Gaza; many of them have decided to leave their ancestral homelands and immigrate to western Christian countries. Nonetheless, Palestinian Christian leaders regularly maintain an anti-Israeli stand.[110] Beginning in the 1980s, Palestinian Protestant thinkers such as Naim Ateek and Mitri Raheb promoted "Palestinian liberation theology," a Middle East application of "liberation theology," which, based on its reading of the Gospels, called for a struggle against political, social, and economic oppression. This theology had become popular among Third World Catholics and liberal Protestants during the 1970s and 1980s.[111] In an attempt to bolster his claim for political justice and to arouse international Protestant sympathy, Ateek titled his pioneering book *Justice and Only Justice*. Over the past two decades, he and other Palestinian Christian spokesmen have been welcome guests at liberal Protestant gatherings in Europe and America.

Of late, one of the best-known Protestant critics of Israel has been Jimmy Carter, who, as U.S. president, brokered the 1978 Camp David accords between Israeli prime minister Menachem Begin and Egyptian president Anwar Sadat. Carter subscribes to a progressive evangelical outlook and as such represents a minority stance within the evangelical movement. Progressive evangelicals (who belong to various denominations) share many tenets of faith with their conservative brethren, including the insistence that all individuals need to accept Jesus as their savior in order to be saved, but differ in their views on various social and political issues. As the title of Carter's recent book, *Peace Not Apartheid* (2006), suggests, his analysis of the Israeli-Palestinian conflict utilizes postcolonial terminology that equates Israel with repressive white European regimes. Carter's views have stirred resentment among Jews, some of whom were shocked by the extent of his criticism. In response, Carter has vehemently denied being anti-Israeli or anti-Jewish; liberal Protestants who hold views similar to those of Carter point to a number of post-Zionist historians, among them Ilan Pappé and Ian Lustick, in support of their views.[112]

In 2004, the U.S. Presbyterian church, the largest of the Presbyterian churches and one of the more liberal churches in the United States, passed a resolution to "initiate a process of phased selective divestment in multinational corporations operating in Israel,"[113] the argument being that such trade strengthened Israel in carrying out its misguided policies. Significantly, the Presbyterian church has not taken similar action with regard to any other country, including several whose regimes are blatantly dictatorial or even genocidal in nature, such as Sudan. Might it be that such liberal Protestant attitudes stem from a more demanding position vis-à-vis a Jewish nation and a Jewish state?[114] As first noted by Nathan and Ruth Perlmutter, the anti-Israel stand of liberal Protestants can be understood, in some cases, as part of a process by which traditional Christian antagonism has been transformed into anti-Israel sentiments.[115] In a more recent analysis of the writings of the Anglican clergyman Stephen Sizer, who has become one of the major Protestant spokespeople on Palestinian-Israeli issues, Margaret Brearley, an Anglican academician involved in Jewish-Christian dialogue, noted:

> Sizer utterly opposes Christian support for "Rabbinic Judaism" and for Israel. He tends to cite the most radical or populist strands of Christian Zionism, ignoring moderate or liberal writers and distinguished post-Holocaust theologians who championed Christian support for Jewish restoration to Israel, such as David Torrance, Franklin Littell, Roy Eckhardt, and Paul van Buren. Nor does he cite distinguished Anglican leaders such as the former Archbishops of Canterbury, Lord Coggan and Lord Runcie, and the newly retired Bishop of Oxford, Richard Harries, all of whom, while not Zionist, did have high regard for Judaism. Like other anti-Zionists, he ignores the devastating consequences of both Christian and Arab anti-Semitism and decontextualizes Israel politically.[116]

Some liberal Protestants also view the Arab-Israeli conflict through a wider prism—to a certain extent, their stance on Israel reflects internal conflicts between liberal and conservative Protestants. Sizer's anti-Israel writings, for instance, are mainly directed against Christian supporters of Israel—that is, conservative, premillennialist Christians who support Israel as a matter of religious ideology.[117]

As noted, evangelical Protestantism has become a growing and dynamic political force, particularly in the United States, but also elsewhere. Presenting their movement as an alternative to the open, permissive culture of liberal society, evangelicals have become increasingly aggressive in their efforts to shape society in conformity with their own beliefs. At the same time, they have replaced the term "fundamentalists," which was often associated with narrow-mindedness and reactionary ideas, with the more neutral term "conservative evangelicals" or often simply "evangelicals." These new terms have come to represent more moderate and accommodating versions of Christian fundamentalism.[118] Evangelicalism, especially in its charismatic form, has become ever more popular among college graduates and members of the middle classes.[119] Many people who came of age during the protest movements of the 1960s found themselves "born again" in the context of evangelical congregations, where they discovered a sense of existential and emotional security, along with clear answers to their dilemmas and doubts.[120] As noted, a majority of evangelical Christians subscribe to dispensationalist messianic beliefs, which offer an explanation of the course of human history as well as assuring believers of the divine promise of salvation for individuals and humanity at large.

As has been seen, dispensationalists have generally been supporters of the state of Israel. Thus, as their ranks have grown, conservative evangelicals have become an increasingly important source of pro-Israel lobbying, promoting Israeli interests and counterbalancing negative attitudes toward the Jewish state.[121] According to many American evangelicals, the United States is divinely destined to play the role of a modern Cyrus—that is, aiding in the restoration of the Jews to their land.[122] Beginning in the 1970s, dozens of pro-Israel conservative evangelical organizations formed around the globe. One of the more well known was the International Christian Embassy in Jerusalem, which was established by European evangelical and pietist supporters of Israel. This organization maintains branches throughout the world, distributing pro-Israel information and collecting donations for welfare aid in Israel. Other organizations, such as the Holy Land Fellowship of Christians and Jews, similarly engage in welfare projects.[123]

With all their goodwill, evangelical attitudes toward the Jews have remained complicated and somewhat ambivalent. Old European cultural images of the Jews have persisted among evangelicals, although they have weakened considerably in recent years. While believing that the Jews are destined to play a central role in the divine plan of salvation, evangelicals also maintain that until the Jews accept Jesus as their personal and communal Messiah, they will continue to be in a state of spiritual and moral deprivation, very much in need of the ameliorating Gospel. Evangelical Protestants do not think that Judaism (or, for that matter, any other religion except for evangelical Christianity) can grant salvation to its believers. A number of evangelical authors, including leading Christian Zionists such as William Blackstone and Arno Gaebelein, expressed disappointment with regard to the Jews' "blindness" concerning the truth of Jesus' messiahship: had they accepted Jesus at his first appearance, the kingdom of God would have come into being during Jesus' times.[124] Some conservative Protestant writers also portrayed Jews stereotypically as the avant-garde of secular ideological and political movements such as communism, socialism, and secular humanism—all of which were regarded as antithetical to Christian civilization.[125]

With all their enthusiasm about the Jewish state, evangelical Christians have looked upon the state of Israel with a mixture of admiration and suspicion. They have regretted its secular character (though they have also been apprehensive of the growing influence of the Orthodox Jewish community) and have bemoaned the fact that Israelis are unaware of their historical, messianic role. The present state, according to many conservative Protestant thinkers, is but a station, a stepping stone, on the way to the kingdom of God on earth, which will only be established with the second coming of the Messiah. In the apocalyptic events that will precede it, Israel will become the kingdom of the Antichrist, a (Jewish) impersonator of the Messiah.[126]

Despite this, a certain warming of hearts on the part of evangelical Christians toward Jews and Israelis has become more noticeable in recent years. Back in the mid-1980s, a study commissioned by the Anti-Defamation League showed a drastic decline in the extent of negative stereotypes among conservative evangelical Christians.[127] This change may be attributed in part to the increased interest in Jewish and Israeli affairs on the part of evangelical Christians in the aftermath of the Six-Day War, and to the growing encounters of evangelicals with actual Jews. What started as a "marriage of convenience" on the part of both evangelical and Jewish leaders seems to have turned into a truer friendship. This development is illustrated in the recent evangelical bestselling novel series, *Left Behind*, in which the Jews are portrayed as misguided yet decent and well-meaning people. Influenced by their encounter with Jews, a number of evangelical authors, including Tim LaHaye and Jerry Jenkins, have given up on the notion of the Jewish Antichrist, replacing him in the *Left Behind* series with a non-Jewish villain.[128]

Jews have been split in their reaction to evangelical supporters of Israel. With the Likud rise to power in the late 1970s, the Israeli government became more aware of evangelical support and the potential influence of evangelicals on U.S. (and other nations') policies. Likewise, a number of Jewish leaders came to the conclusion that promoting good relations with evangelical groups would be beneficial for Israel and for Jews in general. Whereas some Jews endorse the evangelical conservative political agenda, others have been uncomfortable with the growing alliance between conservative Christians and Jews, arguing that Jews should align themselves with progressive political groups.[129] Some Jewish leaders have also pointed to the aggressive evangelical missionary activity as hostile to Jewish interests.

Evangelical Christians have in fact persisted in their extensive missionary activity among Jews. The positive evangelical attitude toward the historical role of the Jews and the improved attitude toward the Jews after the Six-Day War have increased the missionary zeal to share the Gospel with God's chosen people. Missions have changed their strategies, if not their character, becoming champions of the Israeli cause and incorporating Israeli lore and culture. For instance, Jews for Jesus, which withdrew from the American Board of Missions to the Jews in 1974 in part because of criticism regarding its new, outgoing style of evangelism, named its musical band "The Liberated Wailing Wall." Missions have also organized yearly tours to the Holy Land for their Christian supporters.

Counted among the evangelicals are "messianic Jews" who have adopted the Christian faith while retaining their Jewish identity in the form of various symbols and the observance of Jewish holidays and the Sabbath.[130] Messianic Jewish communities (which also include Christian-born members) have become energetic promoters of the Jewish cause, as they see it, within the evangelical Christian community. Over the past few decades, they have helped reinforce evangelicals' favorable attitudes toward Israel. Other Jewish believers in Jesus belong to regular evangelical and charismatic churches and often serve as "the Jews" of their congregations—among other things, they conduct Passover services, which have also become popular among mainline Protestant congregations.

Although conservative Protestants, as noted, have generally opposed interfaith dialogue, there has been a series of evangelical-Jewish conferences and conversations. An actual dialogue in this case is, of course, problematic, since evangelical Christians are committed to propagating their faith while Jews are determined to safeguard their continued existence as a unique entity.[131] Ironically, however, a number of Orthodox Jewish leaders, including Yehiel Eckstein, Yehiel Poupko, and Daniel Lapin, have come to advocate evangelical Jewish cooperation, whereas Reform Jewish leaders, such as Eric Yoffie, have denounced it.[132]

Conclusion

Since the Reformation of the 16th century, Protestants have held strong opinions on the Jews and their historical role. By the very nature of Protestantism, attitudes toward the Jews have been diverse and variegated, and they have also changed and developed throughout the centuries. On the one hand, most Protestants initially adopted the traditional Christian attitudes toward Judaism and Jews. On the other hand, there were always Protestant groups and thinkers who moved away from the older paradigms, taking up innovative and more generous attitudes, often in response to new readings of the sacred Christian texts. There was also a minority among Protestants that considered the Jews to have an essential role in the advancement of history (and, in particular, the fulfillment of biblical prophecies concerning the end of days). This messianic outlook became especially significant in the 19th and 20th centuries.

Notwithstanding their diversity, Protestant views with regard to Jews and Judaism have also had much in common. Most Protestant groups, including mainstream, liberal, and conservative as well as dissenting Protestants, considered post-biblical Judaism to be a religious tradition that had no intrinsic merit of its own and could not offer true moral and spiritual guidelines to its adherents. Until fairly recently, almost all Protestants agreed that Jews had no chance of attaining personal salvation or communal redemption without accepting Jesus as their lord and savior. Differences of opinion among the various Protestant groups generally focused on the issue of whether the Jews could ever regain their ancient status as God's people.

Overall developments in Protestant theological attitudes vis-à-vis the Jews in the past few decades have been encouraging, leading to optimism as to the future of Protestant-Jewish relations. The attitude of both liberal and conservative Protestants toward Judaism and Jews improved in the second half of the 20th century in a manner that would have been impossible to predict only a few decades earlier. The official stance of liberal churches became one of recognition, dialogue, and willingness for exchange. Evangelical-conservative Protestants, for their part, modified their often stereotypical images of the Jews and further developed their understanding of the Jews as people who were destined to help fulfill the vision of the biblical prophets, becoming, as a result, enthusiastic supporters of the state of Israel.

Yet the canvas of contemporary Protestant-Jewish relations is not painted solely in bright colors. For one thing, the positive (and revolutionary) changes in attitudes vis-à-vis the Jews have not penetrated all Protestant denominations to the same degree, nor have they been fully recognized in various parts of the world. Not all liberal Protestants have unqualifiedly accepted the concepts that have granted legitimacy to the separate existence of the Jews as a religious entity outside of the church. Evangelical Protestants, for their part, have not unanimously accepted the idea of the central role of the Jews in relation to the arrival of the Messiah. And then there are those Protestant churches that are neither evangelical nor liberal; in many cases, their ambivalent attitudes toward Judaism and Jews have remained largely unchanged. Protestant churches in many developing nations, for instance, have not been impressed by the breakthrough in interfaith relations and have often retained "replacement theology" in their understanding of Judaism versus Christianity. Moreover, there is no telling if the unprecedented breakthrough in the attitudes of both evangelical and liberal Protestants toward the Jews is a long-lasting change or merely a temporary trend. There are certainly those among the liberals and the evangelicals who have voiced their discomfort with the new, more reconciliatory attitudes toward the Jews.

In light of all this, one might best regard the future of Protestant-Jewish relations with cautious optimism. Perhaps the only certain prediction is that Judaism and Jews will always be important to Protestant thinkers—not least, as a means by which to define their own tradition's theological purpose and historical role.

Notes

1. See Ronald H. Bainton's classic study, *Here I Stand!: A Life of Martin Luther* (New York: 1950).

2. On the Reformation of the 16th century in Europe and its ideals, see A.G. Dickens, *The Reformation, Historical Thoughts* (Cambridge: 1975); Evan Cameron, *The European Reformation* (Oxford: 1991); Lindburg Carter, *The European Reformation* (Oxford: 1996).

3. Martin Luther, *Luther's Works*, vol. 47, *Von den Juden und ihren Lügen, 1543*, trans. Martin H. Bertram (Philadelphia: 1971), 137–306.

4. Martin Luther, *On the Jews and Their Lies*, trans. Martin Bertram, online at http://www.humanitas-international.org/showcase/chronography/documents/luther-jews.htm (accessed 9 July 2009).

5. Haiko A. Oberman, *The Roots of Antisemitism in the Age of Renaissance and Reformation* (Philadelphia: 1984), 113–117.

6. Yaron Ben-Naeh, *Yehudim bemamlekhet hasultanim: haḥevrah hayehudit baimperiyah ha'otmanit bameah hashev'a 'esrei* (Jerusalem: 2007), 99–105.

7. Haim H. Ben-Sasson, *The Reformation in Contemporary Jewish Eyes*: Proceedings of the Israel Academy of Sciences and Humanities (Jerusalem: 1970).

8. Cf. Mark U. Edwards, Jr., *Luther's Last Battles: Politics and Polemics, 1531-46* (Ithaca: 1983), 115–121.

9. Lucy Dawidowicz, *The War Against the Jews, 1933–1945* (New York: 1986), 23; Robert Michael, "Luther, Luther Scholars and the Jews," *Encounter* 46, no. 4, (Fall 1985), 339–356; Johannes Wallmann, "The Reception of Luther's Writings on the Jews from the Reformation to the End of the 19th Century," *Lutheran Quarterly* (Spring 1987), 72–97.

10. See, for example, Rivka Schachter, *Hashorashim hateologiyim shel haraikh hashelishi* (Tel Aviv: 1950); Daniel J. Goldhagen, *Hitler's Willing Executioners: Ordinary Germans and the Holocaust* (New York: 1996), 111.

11. Joy Kammerling, "Andreas Osiander, the Jews, and Judaism" in *Jews, Judaism, and the Reformation in Sixteenth-Century Germany,* ed. Dean Philip Bell and Stephen G. Burnett (Leiden: 2006), 219–248.

12. The Augsburg Confession, article 24, clause 32; online at http://www.bookofconcord.org/augsburgconfession.php. On Melanchthon's attitudes toward Jews, see Timothy J. Wengert, "Philip Melanchthon and the Jews: A Reappraisal," in Bell and Burnett (eds.), *Jews, Judaism and the Reformation in Sixteenth-Century Germany*, 105–136.

13. See John Calvin's major theological tract, *Institutes of the Christian Religion*, ed. J. McNeil, 2 vols. (Louisville: 1961); François Wendel, *Calvin: Sources et évolution de sa pensée religeuse* (Paris: 1950); William Sourmee, *John Calvin: A Sixteenth Century Portrait* (New York: 1988).

14. Calvin, *Institutes of the Christian Religion*, vol. 2, ch. 30.

15. Salo Wittmayer Baron, "John Calvin and the Jews," in *Harry Wolfson Jubilee Volume*, ed. Saul Lieberman (Jerusalem: 1964), 2:141–163.

16. See Calvin's commentary on Matthew 27:25, online at http://www.ccel.org/ccel/calvin/calcom33.ii.xxxix.html?scrBook=Matt&scrCh=27-27&scrV=25-25#ii.xxxix-p11.1 (accessed 2 Sept. 2009).

17. Myriam Yardeni, *Huguenots and Jews* (Jerusalem: 1998), 83–112.

18. Yirmiyahu Yovel, *Spinoza and Other Heretics* (Princeton: 1991), introduction.

19. Yosef Kaplan, *From Christianity to Judaism* (London: 2000).

20. Frank E. Manuel, *The Broken Staff: Judaism through Christian Eyes* (Cambridge: 1992), 92–98.

21. On Rembrandt and the Jews, see, for example, Steven Nadler, *Rembrandt's Jews* (Chicago: 2003). Rembrandt's attitude toward Jews and Judaism remains controversial.

22. Christopher Hill, *The English Bible and the Seventeenth Century Revolution* (Harmondsworth: 1994).

23. Barbara W. Tuchman, *Bible and Sword: England and Palestine from the Bronze Age to Balfour* (London: 1983), 80–101; David S. Katz, *Philo-Semitism and the Readmission of the Jews to England, 1603–1655* (Oxford: 1982); Christopher Hill, *The English Bible and the Seventeenth Century Revolution* (Harmondsworth: 1994); Eitan Bar-Yosef, *The Holy Land in English Culture 1799–1917* (Oxford: 2005); Christopher Hill, "Till the Conversion of the Jews," in idem, *The Collected Essays of Christopher Hill*, vol 2: *Religion and Politics in 17th Century England* (Brighton: 1986); Robert M. Healers, "The Jews in Seventeenth Century Protestant Thought," *Church History* 46, no. 1 (1979), 63–79; Avihu Zakai, "The Poetics of History and the Destiny of Israel: The Role of the Jews in English Apocalyptic Thought during the Sixteenth and Seventeenth Centuries," *Journal of Jewish Thought and Philosophy* 5 (1996), 313–350; Mel Scult, *Millennial Expectations and Jewish Liberties: A Study of the Efforts to Convert the Jews in Britain up to the Mid-Nineteenth Century* (Leiden: 1978); Mayir Verete, *From Palmerston to Balfour* (London: 1992).

24. On visionaries of Jewish restoration in Elizabethan and Stuart England, see Franz Kobler, *The Vision Was There* (London: 1956); Peter Toon, "The Latter Day Glory," in *Puritans, the Millennium and the Future of Israel: Puritan Eschatology 1600 to 1660*, ed. Peter Toon (London: 1970), 23–41; Carl F. Ehle, "Prolegomena to Christian Zionism in America: The Views of Increase Mather and William E. Blackstone Concerning the Doctrine of the Restoration of Israel" (Ph.D. diss., New York University, 1977), 47–61; Katz, *Philo-Semitism and the Readmission of the Jews to England*. On Brightman's ideas concerning the future of the Jews, see, for example, Toon, "The Latter Day Glory," 26–32.

25. Iain H. Murray, *The Puritan Hope* (London: 1971); Avihu Zakai, *Exile and Kingdom: History and Apocalypse in the Puritan Migration to America* (Cambridge: 1992).

26. John Winthrop, "A Model of Christian Charity," quoted in Perry Miller and Thomas H. Johnson, *The Puritans* (New York: 1938), 198–199; Perry Miller, *Errand into the Wilderness* (Cambridge, Mass.: 1956); H. Richard Niebuhr, *The Kingdom of God in America* (New York: 1937); Robert T. Handy, *A Christian America: Protestant Hopes and Historical Realities* (New York: 1981); Ernest L. Tuveson, *Redeemer Nation: The Idea of America's Millennial Role* (Chicago: 1968).

27. For instance, William Bradford, the leader of the Pilgrims who settled in Plymouth, wrote: "May not and ought not the children of these fathers rightly say: Our fathers were Englishmen who came over this great ocean, and were ready to perish in this wilderness; but

they cried unto the Lord and He heard their voice, and looked on their adversity." William Bradford, *History of Plymouth Plantation, 1620–1647*, 2 vols. (Boston: 1912), 1:156–158. Bradford's words echo those of Deut. 26:5, 7.

28. On manifestations of this creed in 17th-century New England, see Ehle, "Prolegomena to Christian Zionism in America," 61–192; cf. E. Froom, *The Prophetic Faith of Our Fathers*, 4 vols. (Washington, D.C.: 1946-1954), 3:19–143.

29. Froom, *The Prophetic Faith of Our Fathers*, 74.

30. Sidney H. Rooy, *The Theology of Missions in the Puritan Tradition* (Delft: 1965), 230–242.

31. On the background to the readmission of the Jews to England, see Peter Toon, "The Question of Jewish Immigration," in Toon (ed.), *Puritans, the Millennium and the Future of Israel*, 115–125; Scult, *Millennial Expectations and Jewish Liberties*, 17–34; Tuchman, *Bible and Sword*, 121–146; Katz, *Philo-Semitism and the Readmission of the Jews to England*.

32. On patterns of Jewish migration, see Shmuel Ettinger, "Migration and Economic Activity in the Seventeenth and Eighteenth Centuries," in *A History of the Jewish People*, ed. H.H. Ben-Sasson (Cambridge, Mass: 1976), 733–740.

33. Christoph Rymatzki, *Hallischer Pietismus und Judenmission: Johann Heinrich Callenbergs Institutum Judaicum und dessen Freundeskreis, 1728–1736* (Halle: 2004); David Dowty, *Jewish-Christian Relations in Eighteenth-Century Germany: Textual Studies on German Archival Holdings, 1729–1742* (New York: 2006).

34. See *Catalogus* (Halle: 1739).

35. Peter Vogt (ed.), *Zwischen Bekehrungseifer und Philosemitismus: Texte zur Stellung der Pietismus zum Judentum* (Leipzig: 2007).

36. Christopher M. Clark, *The Politics of Conversion* (Oxford: 1995), passim.

37. George Marsden, *Understanding Fundamentalism and Evangelicalism* (Grand Rapids: 1991).

38. Timothy P. Weber, *Living in the Shadow of the Second Coming* (Chicago: 1988).

39. See, for example, Clarke Garret, *Respectable Folly* (Baltimore: 1975); W.H. Oliver, *Prophets and Millennialists* (Auckland: 1978).

40. On the premillennialist thinking promoted by leaders of the London Society for the Propagation of Christianity amongst the Jews, see From, *The Prophetic Faith of Our Fathers*, 3:415–433. On missions to the Jews, see Albert E. Thompson, *A Century of Jewish Missions* (Chicago: 1902), 93–106, 279–280. The London-based mission still exists, albeit with a more modest scope.

41. Tuchman, *Bible and Sword*, 175–207.

42. Premillenialists are so called because they believe that the Messiah will come before the millennium in order to establish the kingdom of God on earth.

43. On the history of Protestant missionary efforts in America, see David M. Eichhorn, *Evangelizing the American Jew* (Middle Village, N.Y.: 1978); Yaakov Ariel, *Evangelizing the Chosen People: Missions to the Jews in America* (Chapel Hill: 2000).

44. David Rausch, *Zionism within Early American Fundamentalism* (New York: 1978).

45. George M. Marsden, *Fundamentalism and American Culture: The Shaping of Twentieth-century Evangelicalism, 1870–1925* (New York: 1980).

46. *The Fundamentals of Faith as Expressed in the Articles of Belief of the Niagara Bible Conference* (Chicago, n.d.).

47. Joel Carpenter, *Revive Us Again: The Reawakening of American Fundamentalism* (New York: 1997).

48. James M. Byrne, *Religion and the Enlightenment: From Descartes to Kant* (Louisville: 1996).

49. See, for instance, Arthur Hertzberg, *The French Enlightenment and the Jews: The Origins of Modern Anti-Semitism* (New York: 1968).

50. John Toland, *Nazarenus or Jewish, Gentile and Mohametan Christianity* (London: 1716).

51. Christian Wilhelm von Dohm, *Über die Bürgerliche Verbesserung der Juden* (Berlin: 1781).

52. Max Weber, *The Protestant Ethic and the Spirit of Capitalism* (London: 1930), 71, 130, 244–245. Weber places Judaism in an inferior position to that of Puritans in relation to capitalism; see also idem, *Ancient Judaism* (Glencoe, Ill.: 1952).

53. Werner Sombart, *Die Juden und das Wirtschaftsleben* (Leipzig: 1911); for a good analysis of Sombart's understanding of Judaism and its alleged utilitarianism, see Sharon Gordon, *"Kol hamuẓak mutmar leavir, vekhol hakadosh—leḥulin": to'altanut veahavah basiaḥ 'al hamarat hadat shel yehudim begermaniyah bameah ha19* (Jerusalem: 2007).

54. Moshe Zimmermann, *Wilhelm marr: The Patriarch of Antisemitism* (New York: 1986).

55. Christian Wiese, *Challenging Colonial Discourse: Jewish Studies and Protestant Theology in Wilhelmine Germany* (Leiden: 2005).

56. Baruch Mevorach, "Be'ayat hamashiaḥ befulmus haemanẓipaẓiyah veharefcrmah 1781–1819" (Ph.D. diss., The Hebrew University, 1966).

57. Alan T. Levinson, *Between Philosemitism and Antisemitism: Defenses of Jews and Judaism in Germany, 1871–1932* (Lincoln: 2004).

58. Friedrich Schleiermacher, "Fifth Speech," in idem, *On Religion: Speeches to Its Cultured Despisers* (New York: 1958), 210–265.

59. For developments in Protestant thought during the final decades of the 19th and the early decades of the 20th centuries, see Claude Welch, *Protestant Thought in the Nineteenth Century*, vol. 2, *1870–1914* (New Haven: 1985).

60. In the post-Civil War period, this form of biblical criticism led to a rift between the progressives and the conservatives within American Protestantism.

61. See, for example, Walter Rauschenbusch, *A Theology for the Social Gospel* (New York: 1917; rpt. Nashville: 1977).

62. Yaakov Ariel, "American Judaism and Interfaith Dialogue," in *The Cambridge Companion to American Judaism* (New York: 2005), 327–344.

63. The establishment of these councils is described in William W. Simpson and Ruth Weyl, *The International Council of Christians and Jews* (Heppenheim: 1988), 11–19.

64. See, for example, Reinhold Neibuhr, "Jews after the War," *Nation* 21 (1942), 214–216.

65. On Parkes and his thought, see Robert A. Everett, *Christianity without Antisemitism: James Parkes and the Jewish-Christian Encounter* (Oxford: 1993); Haim Chertok, *He Also Spoke as a Jew: The Life of The Reverend James Parkes* (London: 2006).

66. Hertzel Fishman, *American Protestantism and a Jewish State* (Detroit: 1973).

67. See Ronald Stone, "The Zionism of Paul Tillich and Reinhold Niebuhr," *Christian-Jewish Relations* 15, no. 3 (1982), 31–43.

68. *The Theology of the Churches and the Jewish People: Statements by the World Council of Churches and Its Member Churches* (Geneva: 1988), 5–9.

69. On William Miller, the millenarian movement that he inspired, and its decline, see Leon Festinger, *When Prophecy Fails* (Minneapolis: 1956); Ronald L. Numbers and Jonathan M. Butler (eds.), *The Disappointed* (Bloomington: 1987).

70. Yona Malachy, *American Fundamentalism and Israel* (Jerusalem: 1978), 21–40.

71. Barbara Kreiger with Shalom Goldman, *Divine Expectations: An American Woman in 19th-Century Palestine* (Athens, Ohio: 1999).

72. See Clorinda Minor's account of the colony she established near Jaffa, found in her letter to Isaac Leeser in 1854, reprinted in Moshe Davis (ed.), *With Eyes Toward Zion* (New York: 1977), 183–186. The grandparents of American novelist John Steinbeck were members of Mount Hope; the community disbanded after his grandfather's murder by local Arabs.

73. For details on such groups, see Malachy, *American Fundamentalism and Israel*, 40–48.

74. Jacques B. Doukhan, *Israel and the Church: Two Voices for the Same God* (Peabody, Mass.: 2002).

75. On Russell and his attitude toward Zionism, see Malachy, *American Fundamentalism and Israel*, 59–68.

76. Ibid., 68–83.

77. David L. Weddle, "Jehovah's Witnesses," in *Introduction to New and Alternative Religions in America*, vol. 2, ed. Eugene V. Gallagher and W. Michael Ashcroft (Westport: 2005), 60–89.

78. Ellen Umansky, *From Christian Science to Jewish Science* (New York: 2005).
79. C. Samuel Preus, *Explaining Religion* (New Haven: 1987); 131–156; Eric J. Sharpe, *Comparative Religion: A History* (Chicago: 1986), 47-71.
80. It was not until Claude Levi Strauss published *The Savage Mind* in 1962 that attempts to rank cultures and communities of faith on an evolutionary scale came to an end.
81. See, for example, Glen Jeansonne, *Gerald L.K. Smith: Minister of Hate* (New Haven: 1988); Ralph L. Roy, *Apostles of Discord* (Boston: 1953).
82. *Stand Firm: Jehovah's Witnesses against Nazi Assault* (New York: 1996).
83. Susannah Heschel and Robert P. Ericksen (eds.), *Betrayal: The German Churches and the Holocaust* (Minneapolis: 1999); Susannah Heschel, *The Aryan Jesus: Christianity, Nazis and the Bible* (Princeton: 2007).
84. Christopher Clark, *The Politics of Conversion* (Oxford: 1995).
85. See, for example, the memoirs of the Protestant French pastor Mark Boegner, in Philipe Boegner (ed.), *Carnets du Pasteur Boegner* (Paris: 1992).
86. Wolfgang Gerlach, *And the Witnesses Were Silent: The Confessing Church and the Persecution of the Jews* (Lincoln: 2000).
87. Robert Michael, "Theological Myth, German Anti-Semitism, and the Holocaust: The Case of Martin Niemöller," *Holocaust and Genocide Studies* 2 (1987), 105–122.
88. *The Year in Hate: Intelligence Report*, Issue 125 (Spring 2007); "Aryan Nations/Church of Jesus Christ, Christian," online at www.adl.org/learn/ext_us/Aryan_nations.asp (accessed 9 July 2009).
89. Marcus Braybrooke, *Inter-Faith Organizations, 1893–1979* (New York: 1980); R.M. Brown, *The Ecumenical Revolution* (London: 1967); L.E. Dirk, *The Ecumenical Movement* (New York: 1969).
90. Franklin H. Littell, *The Crucifixion of the Jews: The Failure of Christians to Understand the Jewish Experience* (Macon: 1986).
91. For a recent work along those lines, see Eugene B. Korn and John T. Pawlikowski (eds.), *Two Faiths, One Covenant* (Lanham: 2005).
92. Helga Croner (ed.), *Stepping Stones to Further Jewish-Christian Relations* (New York: 1977), 87. For similar statements in the 1970s and 1980s, see idem (ed.), *More Stepping Stones to Jewish-Christian Relations* (New York: 1985).
93. Croner, *Stepping Stones to Further Jewish-Christian Relations*, 86.
94. Gerald Strober, *Portrait of the Elder Brother* (New York: 1972).
95. Nonetheless, the notion of Jews as the slayers of Jesus or as the moving cause behind his death still appears in popular literature as well as in musical and theatrical works, including contemporary passion plays such as *Jesus Christ, Superstar*.
96. Such efforts are still carried out today, albeit on a smaller scale.
97. See David Flusser, "Jewish-Christian Relations in the Past and Present," in idem, *Judaism and Early Christianity* (Tel Aviv: 1979), 454.
98. John T. Pawlikowski, *What Are They Saying About Christian-Jewish Relations?* (New York: 1980), 33–67.
99. Eva Fleischner, *Judaism in German Christian Theology since 1945* (Mutechen: 1975); Charlotte Klein, *Anti-Judaism in Christian Theology* (Philadelphia: 1978).
100. Wolfhart Pannenberg, *Jesus, Christ and Man* (Philadelphia: 1968).
101. Wolfhart Pannenberg, *The Apostles' Creed in Light of Today's Questions* (Philadelphia: 1972), foreword.
102. Jürgen Moltmann, *The Church in the Power of the Spirit* (New York: 1975), 136–137.
103. See Pinchas Lapide and Jürgen Moltmann, *Jewish Monotheism and Christian Trinitarian Doctrine* (Philadelphia: 1981), esp. 59-93.
104. For one of many examples, see Alice L. Eckhardt and A. Roy Eckhardt, *Long Night's Journey into Day* (Detroit: 1988); cf. Dan Diner, *Beyond the Conceivable: Studies on Germany, Nazism and the Holocaust* (Berkeley: 2000), 187, 189, 214, 227–228.
105. Eva Fleischner, *Auschwitz—Beginning of a New Era: Reflections on the Holocaust* (New York: 1977); Abraham J. Peck (ed.), *Jews and Christians after the Holocaust* (Philadelphia: 1982), 53–62; 87–108.

106. See John S. Conway, "Protestant Missions to the Jews 1810–1980: Ecclesiastical Imperialism or Theological Aberration?" *Holocaust and Genocide Studies* 1 (1986), 127–146.

107. E. P. Sanders, *Jesus and Judaism* (Philadelphia: 1985); John T. Pawlikowski, *Christ in Light of the Christian-Jewish Dialogue* (New York: 1982).

108. C.M. King, *The Palestinians and the Church*, vol. 1, *1948–1956* (Geneva: 1981); Larry Ekin, *Enduring Witness: The Churches and the Palestinians* (Geneva: 1985); Michel Prior (ed.), *They Came and They Saw: Western Christian Experiences of the Holy Land* (London: 2000); Nancy Gallagher, *Quakers in the Israeli-Palestinian Conflict* (New York: 2007).

109. R. J. Zwi Werblowsky, "Jewish-Christian Relations: New Territories, New Maps, New Realities," in *Judaism and Christianity under the Impact of National Socialism*, ed. Otto D. Kulka and Paul R. Mendes-Flohr (Jerusalem: 1987), 531–536; Paul C. Merkley, *Christian Attitudes toward the State of Israel* (Montreal: 2001), 183–186, 195–199.

110. Gershon Nerel, *Anti-Zionism in the Electronic Church of Palestinian Christianity* (Jerusalem: 2006).

111. Naim Ateek, *Justice and Only Justice: Palestinian Theology of Liberation* (Maryknoll, N.Y.: 1989).

112. See, for instance, Donald E. Wagner, *Anxious for Armageddon* (Scottsdale, Penn.: 1995), 240.

113. See "Resolution on Israel and Palestine: End the Occupation Now," online at www.pcusa.org/oga/publications/endoccupation03.pdf (accessed 9 July 2009).

114. Colin Chapman, *Whose Promised Land?* (Tring, U.K.: 1983).

115. Nathan Perlmutter and Ruth Ann Perlmutter, *The Real Antisemitism in America* (New York: 1982); Michael Lerner, *The Socialism of Fools: Anti-Semitism on the Left* (Oakland: 1992) esp. 71–129.

116. Margaret Brearley, *The Anglican Church, Jews and Multiculturalism* (Jerusalem: 2005), 13.

117. Stephen Sizer, *Christian Zionism: Road Map to Armageddon?* (Leicester: 2004).

118. George Marsden, *Reforming Fundamentalism* (Grand Rapids: 1987).

119. Vincent Synan, *The Holiness-Pentecostal Movement in the United States* (Grand Rapids: 1990).

120. George M. Marsden, "Unity and Diversity in the Evangelical Resurgence," in *Altered Landscapes: Christianity in America 1935–1985*, ed. David W. Lotz (Grand Rapids: 1989), 61–76.

121. Mark Silk, *Spiritual Politics* (New York: 1988), esp. 54–69.

122. See Yaakov Ariel, "Fundamentalistim amerikanim veyisrael," in idem, *Halakhah uma'aseh: zeramim fundamentalistim el nokhaḥ be'ayot ezorenu* (Jerusalem: 1989), 1–26.

123. See, for example, *The Jerusalem Connection, International*, online at www.tjci.org.

124. William E. Blackstone, *Jesus is Coming*, 3rd. ed. (Chicago 1908), 86.

125. Arno. C. Gaebelein, "Jewish Leadership in Russia," *"Our Hope* 27 (1921), 734–735.

126. Ariel, "Fundamentalistim amerikanim veyisrael," 6–8.

127. Lynne Lanniello, "Release for Press," *Anti-Defamation League*, New York (8 Jan. 1986).

128. Tim LaHaye and Jerry B. Jenkins, *Left Behind* (Wheaton: 1995).

129. See, for instance, the publication *Towards Tradition*; cf. www.jewsonfirst.com.

130. Arnold G. Fruchtenbaum, *Hebrew Christianity: Its Theology, History and Philosophy* (Grand Rapids: 1974); David A. Rausch, *Messianic Judaism: Its History, Theology and Polity* (New York: 1982).

131. A. James Rudin and Marvin R. Wilson (eds.), *A Time to Speak: The Evangelical Jewish Encounter* (Grand Rapids: 1987).

132. Shmuel Rosner, "Allying with Christian Zionists is Bad for Israel," *Haaretz* (3 April 2008), online at haaretz.com/hasen/spages/971196.html (accessed 6 Sept. 2009).

Confronting the Past: Post-1945 German Protestant Theology and the Fate of the Jews

Susannah Heschel
(DARTMOUTH COLLEGE)

As the audience at the Oberammergau Passion Play of 1934 watched Jesus being hoisted on the cross, many saw a parable of the Third Reich: "There he is. That is our Führer, our Hitler!"[1] The outcry was ambiguous: was Germany being crucified or was Hitler being identified as the savior? To complicate matters, agony and crucifixion were unheroic and thus unsuitable to the Nazi movement. Three years later, at the 1937 Nazi exhibit of Degenerate Art, depictions of Christ's anguish on the cross were displayed as examples of the unacceptable.[2] Christ was to be presented as an aggressive and manly warrior whose *life* was the focus of attention, not his death. Accordingly, artistic representations of Jesus increasingly aryanized his appearance and portrayed him in heroic poses, and archeological finds were interpreted as demonstrating his purported "Nordic" appearance.[3] At a minimum, his death had to be understood as the immediate prelude to a grand resurrection.[4]

At the conclusion of the Second World War, ambiguity continued to haunt Germany: had it capitulated to the Allies or had it been liberated from Hitler? For the postwar German Protestant church (Evangelische Kirche Deutschland [EKD]),[5] the dilemma was defined in theological terms: was the church guilty of a horrific collaboration with evil, a crucifixion of Christian morality alongside the murder of six million Jews, or it had now been liberated from a "pagan" Nazi regime that had sought the destruction of the church and Christianity? Following the widespread discourse of German victimhood that developed after 1945, elements within the church sought to present Christians and Christianity as victims of Nazism, just like the Jews, while using as its symbolic configuration the figure of Jesus—who had fallen victim to the Jews.[6]

The failure of the churches, both Protestant and Catholic, to address directly the moral and theological implications for Christianity of National Socialism and the Holocaust parallels the broader reluctance of German society, in the first decades after the war, to confront its past. Indeed, although reparations were paid to the new state of Israel and some trials of Nazis were held, broader questions of complicity were not raised for several decades. The most radical change, of course, was the immediate shift from a fascist to a democratic state (in the case of West Germany) and a greater involvement of laity in the governance of the Protestant church.

Just as it was only in the 1980s that German society began to engage in a widespread discussion of the Holocaust, so too it was in that decade that the churches began to address issues of Christian anti-Judaism and the need to develop a new kind of Christian theology in response to the Holocaust. At the same time, reactionary voices came to the fore, insisting that the violence of the Holocaust was not German in origin. Ernst Nolte, one of the leading figures in the notorious *Historikerstreit* of the late 1980s and 1990s, insisted that the crimes of Nazism were "Asiatic," whereas Christa Mulack, a Christian feminist theologian who became popular around the same time, argued that the Holocaust represented a "Jewish" morality of blind obedience to orders.[7]

For most German Protestant theologians during the first three decades after the war, the "sin" of Nazism was not primarily its persecution of the Jews or its suppression of democracy, but rather its overheated nationalism that had placed the authority of a secular ruler, Adolf Hitler, above Christ. The complex identification of Christians with Jews, facilitated by the ambiguity of Jesus' own identity as a Jew who was simultaneously the first Christian, was fostered by the equation of Nazism with paganism and paganism with secularism: Germany would need a rechristianization. According to the ethicist Helmut Thielicke, a member of the Confessing Church (the Protestant group that had arisen in 1934 in opposition to the German Christian movement), the Third Reich was the consequence of lapsed religiosity, Germans' abandonment of God: "National Socialism is the final and most terrible product of secularization."[8] This rationale overlooked the fact that Christian theological discourse had itself contributed to Germany's overheated nationalism, racism, and antisemitism both before and even after the Third Reich, providing symbols that shaped the wider cultural understanding of political developments.[9] During the last year of the First World War, for example, Matias Grünewald's famous Isenheim altar, depicting Jesus' agony on the cross, had been removed temporarily from a church in Colmar and put on display in Munich. The visitors who flocked to the museum interpreted this piece of art as an uncanny representation of contemporary war-era agony, meaningful only to Germans who could understand the Nordic message of the artist.[10] The connections between nation, race, and Christianity were configured to express a ressentiment: Germany was Christ on the cross, betrayed by Judas. After the war, such emotions were expressed in more secular terms when theories regarding how Germany had been "stabbed in the back" gained currency. Yet the identification of Germany with Christ persisted, as many pastors interpreted the Versailles Treaty as Germany's crucifixion at the hands of the victors, and later spoke of the promise of the Nazi party as Germany's resurrection. In 1931, for instance, a German Christian pastor, Julius Leutheuser (who was also a member of the Nazi party), wrote:

> In Adolf Hitler we see the powers again awakening which were once given to the Savior. For the National Socialists there is the experience of joy that finally one can sacrifice his life for something that will remain. . . . Our way is rough, but one thing we know, that we shall as a result maintain a pure soul. Golgotha is followed by the resurrection. We are still standing on the way to Golgotha. Some will remain on it, but the soul, it cannot be stolen. Into your hands we commend our spirit, for Adolf Hitler we will gladly die.[11]

Following the Second World War, formerly competing Protestant factions became united in their use of biblical imagery of the Israelites in exile in order to describe the "terrible plight" of Germans. Wolf Meyer-Erlach, a notorious Nazi propagandist and leader of the German Christian movement, wrote in 1947: "We are wandering through the wilderness like the Children of Israel. . . . We are like the generation of Israel that was in captivity in Babylon, who had to make bricks in Egypt and were in danger of perishing in the demoralizing service on the front."[12] It is noteworthy that, a few years earlier, Meyer-Erlach had expunged the Hebrew Bible (that is, what Protestants at the time called the "Old Testament") from the Christian Bible; now he was comparing postwar Germans to the children of Israel leaving Egypt. Meanwhile, a Confessing Church pastor, Werner Schmauch, termed the German civilian population "refugees" and compared them to Abram being told by God to leave his fatherland.[13] These former rivals within the church found common cause in identifying themselves as biblical Jews—that is, as politically innocent figures following a divine plan of salvation. Invocations of the Hebrew Bible by Christians remained in place for some decades after the Second World War in East and West Germany and were manipulated so as to exculpate Christians of responsibility for the fate of the Jews by transferring Jewish identity from Jews to Christian Germans.

The Protestant Church during the Third Reich

During the Nazi era, Germany's Protestants were divided between two main camps. The first, known as the German Christian movement, began to take shape in the late 1920s and became solidified as a movement within the Deutsche Evangelische Kirche (as the German Protestant church was then known) in 1932. This movement advocated the creation of a unified, national German church, to which Catholics, it was hoped, would convert, and which would also exemplify the nazified Christian spirit.[14] During the Third Reich, the movement claimed a membership of 600,000 pastors, bishops, professors of theology, religion teachers, and lay leaders, and it eventually attracted between a quarter and a third of Protestant church members. The movement was highly successful in gaining positions of influence at many of the university theological faculties and regional churches,[15] and its ideology was disseminated through lectures, conferences, and numerous publications that occasionally found common ground even among those in the main opposition, the Confessing Church, as well as those in the Catholic Church and in the much smaller "neo-pagan" groups that rejected Christianity in favor of a revival of Teutonic myths and rituals.[16]

Enthusiastically pro-Nazi, the German Christian movement sought to demonstrate its support for Hitler by incorporating Nazi images into Christianity: placing a swastika on church altars next to the cross, giving the Nazi salute at its rallies, and celebrating Hitler as a leader sent by God. It was ready to alter fundamental Christian doctrine in order to bring the church into compliance with the Reich, and it welcomed the April 1933 order that removed Jews from the civil service, demanding that the Protestant church do likewise by expelling baptized Jews from its ranks. That demand contravened the doctrine of baptism, according to which the sacrament transformed a Jew into a Christian, but German Christian leaders insisted that the Nazi racial laws took precedence and that baptism could not nullify race.

In May 1934, a group of disapproving Protestant theologians in Germany, including Karl Barth, one of the most distinguished theologians of his day, condemned the German Christian movement as heresy, issuing the now-famous Barmen Declaration. This document became the basis of a new movement within the German Protestant church that called itself the Confessing Church. Inspired by the neo-Orthodox theology of Barth, who left Germany for Switzerland in 1935, and who distinguished sharply between the word of God and humanly created religion, the Barmen Declaration insisted on Scripture as God's word and on Jesus Christ as the sole path to God.[17] While the document was a strong repudiation of the German Christian movement's efforts to synthesize Christianity with National Socialism, it included no mention of antisemitism, nor did it provide a theological basis to affirm the legitimacy of Judaism or any other non-Christian religion.

As a patriotic confederation of theologically conservative pastors, the Confessing Church eventually attracted the support of about 20 percent of Protestant pastors. Although some of its leaders, including Barth and the pastor and theologian Dietrich Bonhoeffer, became prominent opponents of Hitler, the Confessing Church did not officially oppose either Hitler or the Nazi regime or the persecution of the Jews.[18] Rather, its efforts were directed against the alterations in church doctrine, liturgy, and scripture that the German Christians had created in their synthesis of Christianity and National Socialism. In the early years of the Reich, enthusiasm for National Socialism and for Hitler prevailed among the public at large. Barth, whose theology inspired many in the Confessing Church, sharply reproached leaders of this church in 1936 for their silence regarding Nazi antisemitism: "This silence can be understood from the fact that in early 1933, when these evils were most flagrantly evident, the people who represent and sustain the cause of the Confessing Church today were deluded by the ideology of National Socialism. In 1933, whoever did not believe in Hitler's mission was ostracized, even in the ranks of the Confessing Church."[19] Indeed, when Bonhoeffer and a few others attempted to rally support for the Jews from members of the Confessing Church, they failed.[20] Formal support was forthcoming only for Jews who had been baptized, although some Confessing Church members did organize private assistance to Jews.

Tensions between the two factions within the church continued throughout the Third Reich, as the German Christians gained control of most of the regional Protestant churches in Germany, using the church's institutional structures and finances to promote their positions. On one issue, however, the two factions were not at swords' points: most members of the Confessing Church agreed with the German Christians that Germany needed to be rid of its Jews and that Judaism was a degenerate moral and spiritual influence on Christians.[21] However, in sharp contrast to the German Christian movement, the Confessing Church rejected the supremacy of the Nazi racial laws over the sacrament of baptism and spoke out firmly on behalf of Jews who had been baptized as Christians.

The extent of the German Christian movement's influence, which was initially downplayed by historians, was reevaluated in a major study by Manfred Gailus. Examining 147 Protestant church parishes in Berlin that were served by 565 pastors, he concluded that 40 percent of the pastors were oriented toward the German Christian movement at least at some point during the Third Reich, compared with slightly more than one-third who were sympathetic to the Confessing Church. One-quarter of the parishes were dominated by German Christian pastors, whereas half were split between the Confessing Church and German Christians. While no comparable detailed social historical studies of the churches in other regions have been carried out, Gailus' findings would undoubtedly find parallels elsewhere in Germany, and would perhaps reveal an even greater proportion of German Christian sympathizers. The movement infiltrated both university theological faculties and village parishes. Few Germans withdrew from the Protestant church on account of the new Nazi theology promoted by the German Christians, and German Christian rallies drew large crowds. Many pastors were sympathetic to the German Christian movement's theology, and their theological views were disseminated within the institutional structures of the Protestant church; there was no schismatic withdrawal and creation of alternative (that is, non-Protestant) churches, nor is there evidence of large-scale objections to pastors preaching a German Christian message.[22] Efforts made by the Nazi regime after 1937 to encourage Germans to withdraw from the church while still defining themselves as *Gottgläubige* (believers in God) met with only a minimal response. At the same time, the anti-Christian neo-pagan movements were unsuccessful in attracting large memberships.

In the spring of 1939, the bishops of Hannover, Württemberg, and Bavaria, all of whom maintained a non-aligned position vis-à-vis the Confessing Church and the German Christian movement, refused to sign the German Christians' Godesberg Declaration, which proclaimed that "Christianity is the unbridgeable religious opposition to Judaism."[23] Bishop Hans Meiser of Bavaria asked if "Jewish" referred to the "Jewish-talmudic religion" or to the apostle Paul's teachings (which were intended as a sharp refutation of the "Jewish-Pharisaic spirit"); "or was the declaration directed not against the genuine opposition between Jewish religion and Jewish spirit but rather against the divine revelation of the Old and New Testament?"[24] To clarify their position, the bishops formulated an alternative declaration that contained even stronger anti-Jewish language:

> The National Socialist worldview fights with all relentlessness against the political and spiritual influence of the Jewish race on our völkisch life. ... In the realm of faith there is a sharp opposition between the message of Jesus Christ and His apostles and [that] of the Jewish religion of legalism and political messianic hope, which is already being fought against in the Old Testament. In the realm of völkisch life an earnest and responsible racial politics is necessary for the preservation of the purity of our Volk.[25]

These two declarations formed the backdrop against which the formal opening in May 1939 of the Institute for the Study and Eradication of Jewish Influence on German Church Life was celebrated at the Wartburg Castle, a famous site of nationalist gatherings and the place where Martin Luther had translated the New Testament into German. The Institute published "dejudaized" versions of the New Testament that were purged of all positive references to the Hebrew Bible and Judaism, a hymnal purged of all Hebrew words, a revised catechism that proclaimed Jesus the savior of Aryans, and a vast array of scholarly and popular publications denouncing Judaism. With bishops, pastors, and numerous professors of theology as members, the Institute, financed by donations from regional Protestant churches and from church headquarters in Berlin, served as a vehicle for antisemitic propaganda.

The Initial Postwar Years

With the defeat of Nazi Germany, the theological "church struggle" between Protestant members of the German Christian movement and those of the Confessing Church was left unresolved. After 1945, the reins of many of the regional churches were transferred to former Confessing Church pastors and bishops as part of the denazification effort—but not all. For example, Christian Kinder, a prominent leader of the German Christian movement, became president of the church of Schleswig-Holstein in 1945, and the "neutral" bishops of the three "intact" churches, Theophil Wurm, Hans Meiser, and August Marahrens, retained their positions, although their stance vis-à-vis the regime and its antisemitism had been ambivalent, at best. Now it became the task of the new church leadership to supervise the denazification of German Christian pastors and to purge the church of their twelve-year reign. Yet "denazification" was largely a farce; hardly any pastors were removed from their positions, even those who had been most publicly and virulently pro-Nazi. One example is the Christian German leader and Nazi propagandist Wolf Meyer-Erlach, who was assisted by Martin Niemöller (a former Confessing Church pastor who was appointed president of the church of Hessen-Nassau in 1947). Presumably as a gesture of "reconciliation," Niemöller arranged for Meyer-Erlach to receive a pastorate in the Taunus mountains just north of Frankfurt. There he was able to launch a new and very public career as an anti-Soviet Christian propagandist, for which he was awarded, in 1962, the *Bundesverdienstkreuz* [Order of Merit] First Class by the Federal Republic of Germany, the highest civilian honor bestowed by the government.[26]

Even though most of the individual regional churches were now in the hands of former Confessing Church members, there was no unity among them, politically or theologically, regarding how to evaluate the immediate past or how to construct the future of the church. Barth, who had long criticized the Confessing Church, now insisted that Germans should not regard themselves as victims. In contrast, Bishop Wurm of Württemberg and church president Martin Niemöller of Hessen-Nassau called for forgiveness, accusing the Allies of vengeful behavior in their punishment of former Nazis. In fact, the ability of former Nazi supporters to retain their positions within the church was facilitated by the unwitting collaboration of Allied officials with church leaders who fabricated a myth of Christian resistance to National Socialism. According to that myth, the spiritual bulwark of faith had kept Christians from submitting to Nazism; at most, some theologians had compromised minor aspects of their religion in order to protect the church from destruction at the hands of the Nazi regime, which was always painted as anti-Christian. The portrayal of themselves as both victims and resisters fell on sympathetic ears; the Allies naively assumed that Germans who could demonstrate their involvement in the church could not have been Nazis. Letters attesting to regular church attendance from pastors—some of whom had themselves been Nazis—proved useful in efforts to achieve a denazified status. Such letters, often deliberate lies, were organized at the highest level of the EKD, as Robert Ericksen has shown.[27] Some bishops and pastors, notably Martin Niemöller, claimed that denazification investigations were demoralizing and were being undertaken in a spirit of revenge against Germans who had already repented. Niemöller thus urged Christians not to participate in the denazification tribunals and forbade clergy from involvement.[28] Then again, as Steven Remy has argued, the Spruchkammer [denazification courts] were nothing more than "a legal whitewash that facilitated the return of thousands of former Nazis to positions of influence in German public life."[29]

In the eyes of most Christians in the two postwar Germanies, the Holocaust was not the salient crime of Nazism, nor was the church implicated in any of the crimes committed against Jews, POWs, the handicapped, Sinti and Roma, members of resistance movements, and slave laborers. Instead, the church presented itself as the conscience of Germany that, together with the universities, could reestablish the moral integrity of the German people. This falsification of the church's role during the Third Reich was aided by the work of the church historian Wilhelm Niemöller (the brother of Martin), whose numerous publications about the Nazi era distorted the role of the Confessing Church by portraying it as having actively resisted the Third Reich.[30]

In addition to their claims regarding Christian resistance to Hitler, Protestant pastors and theologians fostered a myth regarding Nazi persecution of the churches.[31] Proving susceptible to this fiction, the Allies allowed the churches to conduct an independent self-examination rather than imposing on them a rigorous, external denazification procedure. As a result, even those with the most blatant Nazi involvement found that they could leave their past behind. An example is the case of Siegfried Leffler, one of the earliest and most prominent leaders of the German Christian movement, who had held a position in the Thuringian ministry of education during the Third Reich and was active as a Nazi propagandist. He was arrested and imprisoned in Ludwigsburg in July 1947, classified as guilty [*Belasteter*], level two, and given a punishment of one year in a work camp, a 2,000RM fine, and a five-year suspension from his profession. Immediately, he issued a public declaration of repentance and solicited support from a variety of prominent church figures. As the historian Doris Bergen notes, Leffler's "repentance" was joined to an insistence that he was not responsible for atrocities against the Jews, since he had always believed in "genuine tolerance and reconciliation."[32] Leffler's posturing as an atoning sinner innocent of any of the Reich's crimes was a perfect combination in the eyes of German Protestants, who presented his case sympathetically in church newspapers.[33] This stance, in fact, became a Christian staple in postwar Germany, as was reflected in the new image of Jesus that was promoted during that era: suffering and empathic, yet powerless against his enemies.[34] In less than a year, Leffler was released from the work camp, and by 1949 he had become a pastor for the church of Bavaria; he retired in 1970 and died in 1983.[35] The church's emphasis on forgiveness and reconciliation, more than repentance and reparation, promoted a morality that opposed punitive measures against former Nazis.

In the face of church claims regarding Christian resistance to the Nazi regime, it is worthy of note that some of those who had forfeited their lives because of their political resistance were denied church honors after the war. In the most notorious case, Bishop Hans Meiser of Bavaria refused to attend a 1953 memorial service for Bonhoeffer, who had been murdered by the Nazis in April 1945, on the grounds that he was a political martyr, not a Christian martyr.[36] Bonhoeffer and others, such as Hans and Sophie Scholl and their associates in the White Rose student resistance group, as well as resistance leaders (including Claus von Stauffenberg) who were responsible for the July 1944 assassination attempt against Hitler, were repudiated by the church for having attacked the state.[37] At the same time, Bonhoeffer served as an excuse for the church, a sign that it had offered resistance.[38]

Postwar Germany, a country that stood universally condemned, attempted to recover its national morality by bringing religious rhetoric into the public sphere. Clemens Vollnhals has demonstrated that the churches were perceived as one of the only German institutions to have survived the National Socialist era intact.[39] Till van Rahden has noted the increased popularity of Christianity in West Germany, among both Protestants and Catholics, after 1945. Pastors and bishops were influential within the government, particularly in establishing social policy; church publications were widely read; and the 1950s and 1960s saw the growth of lay religious organizations. Indeed, van Rahden writes, the "early Federal Republic experienced an epoch of 're-Christianization' among Protestants and especially Catholics."[40] Strict sexual morality became the template for rechristianizing Germany—premarital sex was forbidden and abortion and homosexuality were to remain outlawed.[41] A new focus on reconfiguring the role of the father and shaping a "democratic family," van Rahden has pointed out, became a hallmark of the West German quest for democracy.[42] Calls were made for an increased and independent voice for the laity within the church. Not only social conservatives, but democrats, too, proclaimed their allegiance to Christian moral teachings. Yet their moral concerns did not extend to public discussion of the Nazi crimes of eugenics, war, and murder, let alone church complicity in the National Socialist project. No objections were raised, on Christian grounds, to the establishment of the Federal Republic, but when Barth wrote in 1949 that the Jews, not the Germans, were the elect of God, and that the establishment of the state of Israel was a sign of the continued validity of God's covenant with the Jews, most Christians reacted with discomfort.[43] Classic elements of Christian anti-Judaism, which denied the continued Jewish covenant with God and the national identity of the Jewish people as part of that covenant, had not yet been confronted and overcome by the majority of German Christians.

Early Postwar Theological Declarations

In August 1945, following a national meeting of regional churches held in Treysa (Hessen) that established the new confederation of Lutheran, Reformed, and United churches known as the Evangelische Kirche Deutschland, a "Message to the Pastors" was issued. During the debate over this message, Barth insisted that Nazism had to be understood through Germany's particular history and demanded individual Christian repentance for it, whereas Martin Niemöller insisted that "the real guilt rests with the church."[44] In the end, the more conservative Lutheran viewpoint prevailed over Barth and the Reformed pastors: namely, that satanic forces had been at work in the Nazi movement and had eliminated reason and insight, and that the churches had attempted to take responsibility during the Third Reich, but had been kept in a "prison" by the Nazis.[45] At worst, German Christians had earned divine approbation—the statement concluded that "God's wrath has broken out over us"—yet that, too, had a silver lining: "according to the orthodox Lutheran understanding of the law and gospel, God's mercy always followed His wrath."[46]

The theology of the Confessing Church, with its emphasis on the need for greater Christian piety, lay behind the pastors' Stuttgart Declaration of October 1945, which was formulated for a non-German audience with the aim of gaining postwar acceptance for the German Protestant church. Like the Third Reich-era Barmen Declaration, which in part it echoed, this document made no mention of Nazi antisemitism, the Holocaust, or even the Jews.[47] Rather, the crime of Christians during the Third Reich was claimed to have been theological disloyalty to doctrinal discipline: a crime of the church against the church. The capitulation of the church to the German Christian movement during the Third Reich was explained as resulting from its failure to recognize the supreme authority of Christ due to its near-deification of the Volk and Hitler. As a result, denazification of those who had argued for an Aryan Jesus and who had called for a dejudaization of the church was made contingent upon their acknowledgment that the transcendent Christ held authority over any state leader.[48]

Consistent with his statements in Tresya, Martin Niemöller argued at Stuttgart that the guilt of the church was its turn away from Christian doctrine during the Third Reich, which opened the door to providing political support for many of Hitler's policies. A different view was taken by Hans Asmussen, who had been active in the Confessing Church: the church was guilty of complacency but not of complicity. The final document spoke of the German churches as having "struggled in the name of Jesus Christ against the spirit" of Nazism, so that the church now stood "in a great community of suffering with our people, but also in a solidarity of guilt. With great anguish, we say: Through us, infinite sorrow has been brought upon many peoples and countries." The use of the passive voice to speak of crimes committed "through us" was noteworthy: this became common parlance among postwar German theologians. In its concluding sentence, formulated by Asmussen, the declaration criticized Christians "for not witnessing more courageously, for not praying more faithfully, for not believing more joyously, and for not loving more ardently"—hardly a statement of moral or political responsibility. Yet even this pious language, as Matthew Hockenos has demonstrated, was viewed in some quarters as a capitulation by the German Protestant church to foreign interests.[49]

Religious subjectivity remained the dominant concern: confession of guilt, that is, disobedience of doctrine, a turning away from God. Following conservative Lutheran theological traditions, guilt remained a matter of inner religious sin, and religious sin was not linked to concrete political acts. Moreover, sin and guilt were essentially temporary; as Martin Niemöller stated at Stuttgart, God "can forgive all guilt that is confessed to Him."[50]

In the ongoing debates among theologians, pastors, bishops, and laity, there was little if any mention regarding the fate of the Jews. When the subject did come up, the tone toward Jews were generally disparaging. A fairly typical statement of the time was that of Bishop August Marahrens, who wrote in his weekly pastoral letter of August 1945: "However divided from the Jews we may be in our beliefs and although a number of them may have brought severe harm upon our people, they ought not to have been attacked in an inhuman fashion."[51] Although occasional comments took the church to task for failing to act on behalf of the Jews, none accused it of taking an active role in propagating and legitimating antisemitism, deportation, and murder. No recognition was given to the fact that, even if some pastors had supported the Nazi sterilization and euthanasia programs (others had protested against them), no theological justifications for those programs had ever been offered—in contrast to the theological justifications of antisemitism that had received ecclesial backing via the Institute for the Study and Eradication of Jewish Influence on German Church Life. Indeed, rather than identify and condemn the active theological support for antisemitism, the first explicit statement regarding the fate of the Jews issued by postwar German Protestants blamed the Jews for their own suffering: "By crucifying the Messiah, Israel rejected its election and intended purpose."

This "Message Concerning the Jewish Question" was formulated by a group of Protestants, most of them former members of the Confessing Church, that gathered in Darmstadt in April 1948. In the course of their deliberations, they received a letter from Bishop Theophil Wurm, which read in part:

> Can anyone in Germany speak on the Jewish question without mentioning how Jewish literature has sinned against the German Volk through its mockery of everything holy since the days of Heinrich Heine, and the ways farmers in many regions have suffered because of Jewish usurers? And if one wants today to take action about the rising antisemitism, can one remain silent about the misfortune of Jews holding in the palms of their hands the occupying powers, in order to express their understandable feelings of vengeance?[52]

As noted, the declaration ultimately placed the blame squarely on the victims: "Inasmuch as Israel crucified the messiah, it has lost its chosenness. . . . Christ was crucified and resurrected also for the people of Israel. This is the hope for Israel after Golgotha. That God's judgment follows Israel even into its rejection, is a sign of God's patience." Divine patience would be matched by Christian mission; Jews were welcome targets of conversion to the church.

A little-publicized "Address to the Churches" issued in 1947 in Seelisberg, Switzerland was unique in that it was formulated by a mixed group of Jewish and Christian theologians.[53] Unlike other early postwar declarations, the Seelisberg document also directly addressed the issue of antisemitism by specifying a number of Christian doctrines that lent support to anti-Jewish hostility, including Christian supersessionism, teachings about Jewish responsibility for the death of Jesus, and negative comments about Judaism. Despite its sophistication, the Seelisberg document remained little known and produced no immediate impact.

In 1950, as Jewish cemeteries in West Germany were being vandalized during a countrywide wave of antisemitism, representatives of the German Protestant church met in the Berlin suburb of Weissensee and formulated a statement declaring that the church "by omission and silence" was "implicated before God" in the "outrage which has been perpetrated against the Jews by people of our nation" (the terms Holocaust and genocide were not used). Although the statement asked Christians to "dissociate" from antisemitism and to protect Jewish cemeteries, it concluded with a hope for the eventual conversion of Jews to Christianity. The historian Matthew Hockenos notes the passive voice and the declaration's endorsement of continued proselytizing among Jews even as it recognized God's ongoing covenant with Jews: "If the Jews were still God's chosen people then why did the church need to pray that Jews would recognize Jesus as the Messiah?"[54] The declaration's affirmation of mission to the Jews hardly brought an end to Christian theological anti-Judaism. Notwithstanding, this statement was perceived as signaling a radical shift in German Protestant theology, and it stimulated further theological reflection in Germany on Christian-Jewish relations. Ultimately, such reflections led to the more important church statements of the 1980s and beyond.

In 1961, the German Protestant *Kirchentag*, a biannual convention of Protestant laity that had begun in 1949, included the topic of Judaism for the first time on its agenda. The meeting, at which several Jewish theologians were invited to speak, became a catalyst for renewed Christian consideration of Judaism's religious legitimacy. One topic of debate was whether God's covenant with the Jews remained in force or whether it had been broken as a consequence of the Jews' rejection of Jesus. Against those who argued for an ongoing covenant, some insisted that there could be no legitimate path to God or salvation without Jesus.[55] The supersessionism underlying that assumption became the key theological debate—several theologians could not accept the statement, based on Romans 11:2, that God had not rejected the Jewish people and that "Jews and Christians are linked in an unbreakable bond," since that would ignore the Jews' rejection of Jesus as the messiah. Nor could the Christian mission to the Jews be given up without abandoning the obligation to bear witness to Jesus. One theologian present at the *Kirchentag*, Günther Harder, argued in favor of continued Christian proselytizing among the Jews, although he added that such a mission should be undertaken with humility rather than arrogance.[56] More liberal theologians, among them Martin Stöhr and Gertrud Lückner, rejected the doctrine of a mission to the Jews quite forcefully. These two individuals later became active in lay organizations within the church that promoted Jewish-Christian dialogue groups (Christlich-Jüdische Gesellschaft)—or, more to the point, Christian groups discussing Judaism, since the few Jews remaining in West Germany had little interest in participating in interfaith dialogue.

The reaffirmation of Christian supersessionism in light of the Holocaust was made easier by identifying German Christians as "Old Testament" Jews and insisting on their victimhood. In 1961, the Jewish theologian Richard Rubenstein met with Heinrich Gruber, who, as a pastor in Berlin during the Third Reich, had provided assistance both to non-Aryan Christians and to Jews; in consequence, he spent three years in the Sachsenhausen and Dachau concentration camps. Gruber told Rubenstein that, in his understanding of Old Testament theology, Germany had simply served as the instrument of God's wrath toward the Jews; their murder, he told Rubenstein, was "part of God's plan."[57] Moreover, Germans had been punished "far worse than the people of the Lord" by Allied bombings and the division of Berlin into two sectors; according to Gruber, Germans were "now in the same situation as the Jews."[58] Rubenstein was horrified by Gruber's statements and concluded that a radical reconsideration of theology, within both Jewish and Christian contexts, would have to take place: "At the heart of the problem is the fact that it may be impossible for Christians to remain Christians without regarding Jews in mythic, magic, and theological categories."[59] Put somewhat differently, by identifying themselves as "theological" Jews, Christians in Germany were able to exonerate themselves from responsibility for the murder of very real European Jews.

Continuities in Academic Theology

In trying to decide what to do about postwar Germany's nazified universities and churches, the Allies were faced with a dilemma. Alongside the determination to eradicate Nazi influence was a desire to make use of Germany's spiritual and intellectual elites in the reconstruction of the country.[60] One of those urging for the latter was Karl Heinrich Bauer, the postwar rector at Heidelberg University, who argued that the universities and the churches should be placed at the Allies' disposal for the purpose of building a new spiritual leadership for West Germany.[61] This line of thinking, widely adopted in the early postwar years, worked against a thoroughgoing denazification of these institutions and also served as a screen to protect individuals, such as Bauer himself, from investigation of their Nazi involvements.[62]

Within the universities, those who had joined the Nazi party prior to 1933 were dismissed from their professorships by state authorities, but many others who had been active Nazi supporters retained their positions. According to the denazification rules established by the Allies, it was necessary to produce evidence that a particular faculty member had engaged in Nazi activities in order for that individual to be convicted and penalized. Membership in the Nazi party or affiliated organization was considered to be only limited proof; far more convincing were publications containing articles in which enthusiasm for Hitler was expressed. But the legitimacy of these publications was challenged in denazification hearings on the grounds that Nazi-era documents were tainted and non-objective.[63] Attorneys representing the accused argued that postwar reflections and letters of recommendation from friends and colleagues of the accused were far more reliable, since these were produced in a setting shorn of Nazi pressures and threats. In numerous cases, such reflections and recommendations—often self-exculpatory, disingenuous, and dishonest—won exoneration for former Nazis and Nazi sympathizers.

While several university faculties of Protestant theology were closed or consolidated during the Nazi era, those that remained open nazified their curriculum. Professors appointed after 1936 were virtually all members of the German Christian movement, and nearly all of them retained their professorships after the war or else were transferred to influential positions within the church. Scholarship was altered to include racial analyses of the ancient Israelite religion and post-biblical Judaism. Few theologians emerged from the Third Reich untainted by the antisemitism that had been integrated into academic theology. Indeed, the University of Jena's theological faculty had boasted of its effort to become a "bastion of National Socialism."[64] Such evidence refutes the argument made by the historian Trutz Rendtorff that the Protestant theological faculties were immune to National Socialism, thanks to the rigors of German theological scholarship.[65]

Moreover, Nazi-era theological traditions continued well after 1945. In the early postwar era, Walter Grundmann, the former academic director of the Institute for the Study and Eradication of Jewish Influence, published three major commentaries on the synoptic Gospels whose negative assessments of Judaism remained essentially unchanged from those of his earlier writings published during the Nazi era.[66] Nonetheless, these books were required reading for students preparing for ordination as pastors in East and West Germany until the early 1990s. Ethelbert Stauffer, professor of New Testament at the University of Bonn and an active member of the German Christian movement, enjoyed an influential postwar career in the field of New Testament. In his work of 1957, *Jesus: Gestalt und Geschichte*, Stauffer reiterated the German Christian view of Jesus as a lonely fighter against the tradition of Jewish legalistic pseudo-piety. The case of Hans F.K. Günther, a notorious racial theorist who had taught at the University of Jena and later the University of Berlin, was somewhat more nuanced. Following the war, he did not return to teach, but he continued writing academic works, some of them under a pseudonym. Writing as "Heinrich Ackerman," for example, he published two major scholarly studies on the representations of Jesus in modern theology, which essentially reiterated his prewar racial arguments.[67]

In these and other instances, postwar "Christian theology" was essentially an articulation of anti-Jewish ideas that were ascribed to allegedly objective theological scholarship on Judaism rather than to Nazi propaganda. In the case of theologians with academic training in Jewish texts, it was easy to obtain university appointments after the war: there were relatively few of them, for one thing, and for another, the naive assumption among Allied authorities was that those who had expertise in rabbinic texts must have been sympathetic to Judaism, or at least uninvolved in Nazi activities. In fact, the ranks of these scholars included several formerly active Nazis, such as Karl Georg Kuhn, Paul Fiebig, and Ethelbert Stauffer.

The perpetuation of negative images of Judaism as purveyed by German Protestants after the war was particularly striking in the third edition of a major, multivolume reference work titled *Religion in Geschichte und Gegenwart*, which was published between 1957 and 1965. In contrast to the second edition, published between 1927 and 1932, which had included Jewish scholars among its contributors, articles in the third edition were authored exclusively by Christians—many of them either former members or else students of former members of the German Christian movement. As a result, the third edition did not mention the Holocaust, nor did it examine the support of Christian theologians for the Third Reich. According to the historian Ulrich Oelschläger, the third edition also contained more anti-Jewish stereotypes than did the two preceding editions, a fact that indicated the extended influence of Nazi-era theology.[68]

Until the 1990s, there was very little examination of the German Christian movement on the part of church historians, with the exception of Kurt Meier's study of 1964 (which paid no significant attention to the movement's antisemitism).[69] Far more attention was given to the Confessing Church, which was presented as a heroic opponent of National Socialism. That myth, as we have seen, was carefully cultivated by Wilhelm Niemöller, among others.[70] For several decades, little was written about the antisemitism that had permeated both church factions. Wolfgang Tilgner, writing in the 1960s, articulated the classic Confessing Church position that the German Christians had ascribed near-divine qualities to the Volk because they had failed to maintain a strong incarnational theology—that is, a theology rooted in the belief that Jesus was God incarnate. For him, as for many others, the theological failures of the church during the Nazi era were due to inadequate doctrinal discipline.[71] Memoirs by Confessing Church theologians who had been active during the Third Reich usually did not mention Jews, antisemitism, or the Holocaust, whereas German Christian theologians avoided publishing their memoirs.[72] "Antisemitism" was not a category discussed in the massive historiography on the so-called *Kirchenkampf* (church struggle). Wolfgang Gerlach's important doctoral dissertation on Confessing Church attitudes toward Jews and responses to antisemitism was completed in 1970, but languished for years before being published in 1987.[73] To be sure, some church historians changed their positions over time. Leonore Siegele-Wenschkewitz, who in 1980 published the first critical examination of a major Nazi theologian, Gerhard Kittel, initially defined the central problem of the *Kirchenkampf* as a conflict over the nature of the church, but in later publications came to acknowledge that the Jewish question was in fact central.[74]

With the establishment of the German Democratic Republic (GDR) in 1949, two separate but intertwined German Protestant churches emerged, forming an important institutional link between the two Germanies.[75] The East German church was financially dependent on its West German counterpart, but it took an independent theological road, presenting itself as a "church within socialism." Within East Germany, as the historian Irena Ostmeyer has shown, the church was even more reluctant than was its West German counterpart to examine Christian responsibility for Nazi antisemitism and the Holocaust. This reluctance, she argues, served to reinforce the broader refusal of the GDR to discuss its own responsibility for Nazism and the Holocaust.[76] Theologians who were former Nazis were able to attain positions of power within the church of the GDR, in part because their earlier support of Hitler was known to the East German secret police, the Stasi, which then blackmailed them into serving as informants. Among them was Grundmann, who lost his professorship in New Testament at the University of Jena after the war, but who was then appointed rector of a seminary in Thuringia and remained an honored figure in the East German church until his death in 1974.

Within the GDR, attitudes toward Judaism and the Holocaust were ambivalent, at best. Whereas Jews living in East Germany could be included in the category of "victims of fascism" and be accorded the special privileges that accrued to those victims from the state, Jewish cultural distinctiveness and the practice of Judaism as a religion were discouraged on socialist grounds. Zionism and the state of Israel were particularly maligned, especially after the 1967 war. Yet the publication of books on Jewish history during the last years of the GDR aroused some public interest, particularly the 1988 study of antisemitism by Rudolf Hirsch and Rosemary Schuder, two well-known and very popular writers. Moreover, in contrast to most of the theological seminaries in West Germany, the Protestant theological faculty of Humboldt University in East Berlin included sympathetic instruction in Judaism and Jewish theology, as mandated by Heinrich Fink, professor of practical theology.[77]

Intimations of Change

Serious discussion of the Holocaust could not begin within Protestant theology until the continuities with the Third Reich, both institutional and ideational, were broken and the Holocaust itself was recognized and articulated as a historical and theological issue. That did not occur until the 1970s and 1980s, when German theologians began to speak not only of the genocide of the Jews but of Jewish texts and theological perspectives, including Jewish understandings of the Holocaust, as well as the imbrication of Christian anti-Judaism in the history of antisemitism and the challenge of the Holocaust to the continued theological legitimacy of Christianity.[78]

In 1975, the West German Protestant church's "Study Commission on Church and Judaism," comprising respected scholars with a strong interest in Judaism, published a theological document tracing some of the theological commonalities between Christianity and Judaism (one God, shared scriptures) as well as divergences in historical experience, Christian anti-Judaism and antisemitism, and the problematic nature of the Christian mission to the Jews.[79] Prepared for use by lay Christians, the study concluded that the Holocaust was a turning point for Judaism—but not for Christianity.

Recognition that Christianity stood under theological challenge was formulated by the Catholic theologian Johann Baptist Metz in an article published in 1979:

> The question as to whether there will be a Reformation, a return to the shared roots in the relationship between Christians and Jews, will always be decided ultimately, at least in this country, based on how we Christians stand on Auschwitz, how we Christians assess it for ourselves. Whether we allow it to be truly the end, the interruption that it was the catastrophe of our history from which one finds his way out only through a radical change, with new standards, or whether for us it is only a monstrous accident in our history that doesn't affect its course.[80]

Christian theology could not be pursued in the same way after Auschwitz, Metz argued, and his challenge was soon echoed by a group of sympathetic Protestant and Catholic exegetes and theologians who began dissecting the anti-Judaism within Christian theology, affirming the Jewish contexts of Jesus, Paul, and the Gospel authors, and asserting the continued centrality of the Torah for Judaism.

If, as Metz and others argued, Christians and Jews have shared roots, should Christians continue their centuries-long efforts to convert Jews? Missionary efforts had ceased early in the Third Reich with the rise of racial antisemitism. Complaints against converting Jews were filed with local churches throughout the 1930s, coming both from Nazi officials and lay people: "[J]ust as a pig remains a pig, even if you put it in a horse's stall, so a Jew still remains a Jew, even if he is baptized," declared a 1933 article in the journal *Arische Rundschau*.[81] Jewish requests for baptism continued, however, and when the Reich did not outlaw the practice,[82] those regional churches controlled by the German Christians ultimately took their own action by firing non-Aryan church employees, forbidding non-Aryan Christians from attending church services, and denying pastoral care to baptized Jews.

If the Christian mission to the Jews ceased because of antisemitism, its revival after the war was viewed, at least by some Christians, as philosemitic. The issue of mission to the Jews came to a head in the 1970s when the Rhineland synod prepared what came to be considered a ground-breaking statement on Christian-Jewish relations: published in 1980, this statement included a rejection of missionary efforts aimed at Jews.[83] This shift reflected the growing number of Protestant theological voices arguing that the Holocaust was the central theological issue arising out of the Third Reich, and that Christianity—which bore at least shared responsibility for Nazi antisemitism—would have to revise its attitude toward Judaism and the Jewish people. During the 1970s, the regional churches of the Rhineland, Baden, and Brandenburg began concerted efforts to analyze the anti-Judaism in Christian theological traditions and to forge a new affirmation of Judaism's continued vitality and legitimacy. It is worth noting that those efforts began among German synods influenced more by Calvinist than by Lutheran traditions. Back in 1960, individual pastors, such as Benjamin Locher of the Rhineland, played crucial roles in formulating a declaration by the EKD that in some ways anticipated the even more influential 1980 declaration by the Rhineland synod. Locher insisted that the Holocaust was not one of many Christian concerns, but rather the central problem of Christian theology: "Something is false in our faith. There must be something false at its heart that we as Christian teachers or practitioners are teaching or representing."[84] Other important voices in German discussions of the 1970s were those of the Reformed theologians Hans Joachim Iwand and Cornelius Miskotte, who sharply criticized the Lutherans' traditional distinction between the realms of church and state, arguing that it had resulted in the church's relinquishing its responsibility for promoting Christian values in the secular sphere.[85]

The Rhineland church's declaration of 1980 placed political concerns squarely at the heart of Christian theology. Mincing no words, the statement proclaimed the "recognition of Christian co-responsibility and guilt for the Holocaust." The continued existence of Jews was affirmed by the declaration as intrinsic to *Heilsgeschichte* (the biblically based belief that history was an unfolding of God's plan for the salvation of humanity), and Christian proselytizing among Jews was repudiated—a strong and sharp break with Christian tradition and scripture. Indeed, in the wake of the declaration, a lawsuit was filed against the synod by a number of member churches, claiming that renunciation of mission to the Jews was such a profound violation of Christian principles that, if permitted, the church's tax-exempt status would have to be withdrawn by the state.

Both the statement of the Rhineland synod and the growing popular discussion of the Holocaust in West Germany during the 1980s sparked a reassessment among a group of Protestant (and some Catholic) theologians in Germany with regard to the significance of Jews and Judaism within Christian theology. Renewed attention was paid to Paul's Epistle to the Romans, particularly chapters 9-11, which describe the relationship between Christianity and Judaism in terms of a tree and its roots: "it is not you that support the root, but the root that supports you" (Romans 11:18). A small but vocal number of professors of Protestant theology began writing on Christian-Jewish relations, dissecting and rejecting negative images of Judaism within Christianity. For instance, Friedrich Wilhelm Marquardt, professor of systematic theology at the Free University in Berlin, began to formulate a christology that would affirm Jesus as the embodiment of the Jewish faith, not as a teacher who sought Judaism's destruction. Marquardt's efforts begin with the question, "What meaning does it have for us [Christians] to speak of God after Auschwitz?"[86]

Examination of the theological significance of the Holocaust rested on the highly contested assumption that political events have theological meaning—and that scriptural texts have political consequences. Exegesis and the formulation of theological positions would have to be carried out with an eye to their past and future impact on society, as argued forcefully by Berthold Klappert: "The hermeneutical function of the Holocaust regarding new biblical insights signifies ... that only from the recognition of the history of interpretation and in giving up our anti-Jewish prejudgment will we be able to understand again the real intention of the biblical text itself."[87] Klappert's insistence that exegetes consider the political influence of scriptural verses and their hermeneutical traditions, especially as they have shaped anti-Jewish attitudes in Germany, has had a broad impact.

Critics such as Hannah Holtschneider have argued that placing the Holocaust at the center of a revised Christian theology implies a new version of Christian supersessionism.[88] By making Auschwitz the crucible, the place where Christianity itself lost legitimacy, that most Jewish event—the Holocaust—is transformed into a Christian experience. Klappert, among others, attempts to avoid supersessionism by emphasizing Christianity's dependence upon Judaism and Jewish history; Holtschneider responds that such dependence is itself a kind of exploitation. Drawing heavily from the work of Elie Wiesel, Klappert writes:

> For me, the fundamental dependence of the Christian church and theology upon the Jewish witnesses of the experience of God in Auschwitz is the distressing product of a theology after Auschwitz. Auschwitz is the most Job-like experience after the cross. The experience of the absence and presence of God there, the Jewish tale of the silence of God, from the terror of God up to the hanging and burning of God—which was only witnessed by Jews and can only be told by them, listened to in humiliation by us Christians—renders us dependent upon Judaism. Its storytellers and witnesses in Auschwitz reveal, as a fact, the eternal communion of the crucified with His suffering people.[89]

Like Marquardt, Klappert argues that, through Christian solidarity with Jews, the theology of the cross is radically altered, though not abandoned. Metz writes that because of Auschwitz, "Christians can protect their identity only in front of and together with the history of the beliefs of the Jews."[90]

Yet the awareness of the political implications of theology was accompanied by a theological reading of history; the line between human and divine responsibility was blurred. The Rhineland declaration, for example, while insisting on the responsibility of Christians and the church for the Holocaust, nonetheless asked why God permitted Jewish suffering: "[W]hy did God no longer guard his chosen people as the apple of his eye?" German responsibility for the Holocaust clashed with theological claims with regard to the divine authorship of history, and it was difficult to wean some theologians from older traditions of salvation history.

Among German liberation theologians, for whom political events are essential to understanding the Christian message, the Holocaust has not played a major role. Such theologians are more attentive to contemporary problems—which they define as American imperialism, nuclear weapons, poverty, environmental degradation, exploitation of women, and other manifestations of economic and social injustice—and have been relatively inattentive to anti-Jewish streams within Christian theology. At the same time, many of them have claimed that Germany's Nazi heritage of totalitarianism has made them particularly sensitive to issues of justice. A unique voice among German Protestants, Dorothee Soelle, opened her 1982 address to the World Council of Churches with a ringing declaration: "I speak to you as a woman from one of the wealthiest countries in the world; a country whose history is tainted with bloodshed and the stench of gas that some of us who are Germans have not been able to forget. ..."[91] Although the address continued without mentioning anything specific about the Holocaust, antisemitism, or the church's responsibility for Nazism, the opening sentences made her message clear; reflecting on those years in a later talk, she noted that "we drew the consequences of Auschwitz: we rethought our understanding of sin. We called that the 'politicization of conscience.' "[92] That she was roundly condemned in Germany for her declaration in 1982 reveals how uncomfortable many remained with the assumption of Christian responsibility for the Holocaust.

Other theologians are more subtle. Jürgen Moltmann, Germany's most famous contemporary Protestant theologian of liberation, has placed responsibility for political and economic justice at the center of his theology, yet does not speak of Christian responsibility for antisemitism. Instead, he places Christians together with Jews as joint victims of persecution, thus exonerating Christians from responsibility for that persecution:

> There is only one people of hope in the world, the one people of God. It is the one people of God, the people of the old and new covenant. Because Jews and Christians have a common hope for "the one who is to come," the Messiah, they are on the way together to God's kingdom and future. That is why they are persecuted together and suffer together. When Israel is led to the slaughter, the church goes with her—if things are as they should be.[93]

Elsewhere, Moltmann writes of "the cries for righteousness of those who are murdered or gassed," but then asks, "Or do the executioners ultimately triumph over their innocent victims? . . . does inhuman legalism triumph over the crucified Christ?"[94] Commenting on this passage, Nicholas de Lange calls it "a major stumbling block to dialogue between Christians and Jews" and asks whether "the only valid choice facing a Jew is to be reconciled to God by becoming a Christian?"[95] Moltmann, however, has dismissed the delineation of anti-Jewish motifs within Christian theology as "the signs of a neurotic German mentality."[96] For him, the Hebrew Bible consists of "texts of terror" that can only be read in light of the Gospels, and "in this redemptive light they seem shocking to me."[97]

The state of Israel posed a particular challenge to theologians of liberation, particularly after the 1967 war and the Israeli occupation of the West Bank and Gaza. Older Christian distinctions between a "carnal" Judaism concerned with regulating bodily needs and a "spiritual" Christianity concerned with the individual heart, soul, and conscience began to reappear in the form of questions pertaining to the theological meaning of a territorial dimension to Judaism. Perhaps because the theological meaning of Zionism and the state of Israel were so hotly disputed by some Christian theologians, students of theology were encouraged to study for a year or two at Israeli universities.

In response to the growing interest in analyzing the implicit anti-Judaism of particular biblical passages such as John 8 and Matthew 23, German theologians increasingly began developing new exegetical traditions to mitigate or alter traditional lines of interpretation. The rise of the feminist movement and its calls for altering or reinterpreting the sexism of scripture gave added weight to the quest for new hermeneutical methods that would make sexism and anti-Judaism both visible and theologically untenable. The recently published Bibel in Gerechter Sprache, a revised German translation of the Hebrew and Christian Testaments, attempts to eliminate the perceived misogyny and anti-Judaism of scripture. In one of the most promising revisions of Christian theology, the Old Testament theologian Frank Crüsemann has developed a new understanding of Torah as an expression of divine unity and as a "fundamental form of the gospel" and the very basis of Pauline theology.[98]

Conclusion

Within German Protestantism, there was no *Stunde Null* (zero hour) in 1945. Institutionally, the church continued to be governed by clergy who had, for the most part, supported the ideological underpinnings of the Third Reich. After the war, when overt support for race, nationalism, the cult of the Führer, and war could no longer be articulated, major theological trends were retained. The Hebrew Bible was reintegrated into the Christian Bible, but Judaism's role as the superseded religion of law remained entrenched. There was no recognition of the fact that Christian theology was deeply imbricated in National Socialism, nor was there any thoroughgoing examination of the church's history during the Third Reich. Thrilled by its new opportunity to play an influential role in German politics, the church entered the postwar era as a voice of moral authority for a newly established democracy grounded in Christianity. During this time, the German populace experienced a resurgence of interest in Christianity, with a significant number attending church regularly, reading church publications, and taking an active role in church lay organizations. All of this gave added support to a church eager to avoid examining its Nazi past.

With the fall of the Berlin wall and the reunification of the two Germanies in 1990, a new era emerged in the construction of postwar memory and politics. Ironically, the construction of the Jewish Museum and the Holocaust Memorial in Berlin as national monuments of memory has led to an intensified focus on the German experience. Helmut Schmitz has argued that German public discussion of the Holocaust has been followed by a growing discourse of German victimhood. Expulsion of Germans from areas of German settlement in the East in 1945, German suffering during the war, and the destruction and violence after the war have all have come to the fore in films and best-selling books. This, according to Schmitz, is in response to the institutionalization of Holocaust memory. By demanding empathy for all wartime victims and by decontextualizing the horrors of the war, Schmitz argues, this new attention to German suffering avoids dealing with the question of responsibility or the political implications of Nazism.[99] Similarly, within Christian theology, trauma and empathy have become increasingly important themes since the mid-1970s, with a growing literature emphasizing God as a suffering deity whose compassion is extended without distinction between sinner and victim, Christian or Jew. Moreover, during the past ten years, many of those who had been at the forefront of shaping a new and positive Christian appreciation of Judaism have either retired or died, among them Friedrich Wilhelm Marquardt and Bernard Schaller, and major new declarations regarding Christian-Jewish relations have not been issued by the Protestant church.

Since 1989, a growing number of voices have urged a turn away from Christian examination of its anti-Judaism and increasingly toward an affirmation of Christian identity; in more recent years, Judaism has taken a back seat to Islam and Christian-Muslim dialogue.[100] Moreover, the ambivalence within the Christian theological imagination regarding the Jewishness of Jesus continues, as do German Christian perceptions with regard to Jews, antisemitism, and the Holocaust. The question of the church's involvement in Nazism and responsibility for the Holocaust, with all its myriad theological consequences, remains a subject for new generations to debate.

Notes

1. Quoted in Dorothy Thompson, "Goodbye to Germany," *Harper's Bazaar* 170 (Dec. 1934), 46. On the Oberammergau play, see Saul S. Friedman, *The Oberammergau Passion Play: A Lance against Civilization* (Carbondale: 1984); James S. Shapiro, *Oberammergau: The Troubling Story of the World's Most Famous Passion Play* (New York: 2000). See also Günter Berghaus, "The Ritual Core of Fascist Theatre: An Anthropological Perspective," in *Fascism and Theatre: Comparative Studies on the Aesthetics and Politics of Performance in Europe, 1925–1945*, ed. Günter Berghaus (Providence: 1996), 63.

2. At the entry of the exhibit stood a wooden crucifix by Ludwig Gies, taken from the Lübeck cathedral; also on display was Emil Nolde's *Life of Christ*, which showed as well a Christ in physical agony.

3. Franz Wolter, *Wie sah Christus aus?* (Munich: 1930). See the discussion of the book by Hans F.K. Günther, "Wie sah Christus aus?" in *Volk und Rasse* 7 (1932), 118–119. The term "Nordic," which came into vogue in the 1920s and which was used interchangeably with "Aryan," was greatly popularized by Günther in his *Rassenkunde des Deutschen Volkes* (Munich: 1922). See Geoffrey G. Field, "Nordic Racism," *Journal of the History of Ideas* 38, no. 3 (1977), 523–540. On some examples of the biases inherent in scholarly interpretation, see Magen Broshi, "How to Recognize a Jew," *The Israel Museum Journal* 2 (1993), 81–83.

4. See, for example, Walter Grundmann, "Der Isenheimer Altar," in *Glaube und Freiheit: Ein Grüss an die Evangelischen Theologen an der Front*, ed. Emanuel Hirsch and Walter Grundmann (Leipzig: 1940), 129–135.

5. During the Third Reich, the church had been known as the Deutsche Evangelische Kirche (DEK).

6. Robert Moeller (ed.), *West Germany under Construction: Politics, Society, and Culture in the Adenauer Era* (Ann Arbor: 1997).

7. Susannah Heschel, "Configurations of Patriarchy, Judaism and Nazism in German Feminist Thought," in *Gender and Judaism*, ed. T.M. Rudavsky (New York: 1995), 135–156.

8. Helmut Thielicke, "Der Nationalsozialismus ist das letzte und furchtbarste Produkt der Saekularisation" (undated, 15-page typed manuscript), Repertorium des Archivs der Bekennenden Kirche Schleswig-Holstein (hereafter: BKSH), Nordelbisches Kirchenarchiv, Kiel (hereafter: NEK).

9. Susannah Heschel, *The Aryan Jesus: Christians and the Bible in Nazi Germany* (Princeton: 2008).

10. Ann Stieglitz, "The Reproduction of Agony: Toward a Reception-History of Grünewald's Isenheim Altar after the First World War," *Oxford Art Journal* 12, no. 2 (1989), 87–103.

11. Julius Leutheuser, *Peniger Tageblatt* (20 Jan. 1931); cited by Gerhard Besier, "The Stance of the German Protestant Churches during the Agony of Weimar, 1930–1933," *Kyrkohistorisk Årsskrift* (1983), 152.

12. Wolf Meyer-Erlach: "Wir wandern durch die Wüste wie das Volk Israel. ... Wir gleichen aber auch den Geschlechtern Israels, die in Babylon in der Gefangenschaft waren, die in Ägypten Ziegel streichen mussten und in der zermürbendem Frontdienst unterzugehen

drohten" (letter to Fritz Schmidt-Clausing, 26 May 1947, University of Lund archives, Odeberg materials).

13. Werner Schmauch, "Zur theologischen Frage des Flüchtlingsproblems" (undated, 15-page typed manuscript), BKSH, NEK.

14. While the Catholic Church was officially opposed to the German Christian movement and its theology, individual Catholic theologians and priests expressed similar ideas and some joined the Institute for the Study and Eradication of Jewish Influence; see Heschel, *The Aryan Jesus*, 133–136. For additional examples of Catholic engagement with German Christian theology, see Kevin Spicer, *Hitler's Priests: Catholic Clergy and National Socialism* (DeKalb: 2008).

15. The German Protestant church was divided into regional churches, each of which was headed by a bishop or a president (the positions are equivalent).

16. The neo-pagan movements viewed Christianity as a religion foreign to German sensibilities and rejected the possibility of dejudaizing or nazifying its teachings. Instead, they advocated a return to pagan rituals based on Teutonic myths, with gatherings centered on Wotan or Germanic heroes. (Interestingly, deceased members of the SS were accorded non-Christian, neo-pagan funerals, regard less of their church affiliation, though their families often held additional, private Christian ceremonies.) The neo-pagan groups remained small: the German Faith Movement had about 40,000 members, and others, such as the Ludendorff Tannenberg League, were even smaller. The Roman Catholic Church had about 20 million German members, compared with about 40 million members of the German Protestant church. Tensions between the neo-pagans and Christians have been exaggerated; see Heschel, *The Aryan Jesus*, 136–139.

17. Karl Barth was a theologian of the Reformed tradition, which emerged from Calvinism and constituted a small but important theological trajectory within the larger, Lutheran-dominated Protestant church of Germany.

18. Wolfgang Gerlach, *And the Witnesses Were Silent: The Confessing Church and the Persecution of the Jews*, trans. Victoria J. Barnett (Lincoln, Neb.: 2000).

19. Ibid., 231.

20. Ibid.

21. Catholics were in a position similar to the Confessing Church: too theologically conservative to alter either their doctrines or their liturgy to bring them in accord with Nazism, yet in basic agreement with their Protestant colleagues that Jews were a degenerate influence on German Christians. Munich's Cardinal Michael von Faulhaber, for example, delivered a series of Advent sermons in 1933 that attacked the German Christian movement—but his argument, almost identical to what the Confessing Church leaders came to claim, was that the Hebrew Bible need not be eliminated as a Jewish book, as some German Christians advocated. It was, rather, an anti-Jewish book, Faulhaber insisted, since the prophets were constantly condemning Israel for its sinful ways (see Michael von Faulhaber, Cardinal, *Judaism, Christianity and Germany*, trans. George D. Smith [New York: 1934]). Faulhaber's objection, then, was not to the German Christians' antisemitism, but rather their failure to realize that the Hebrew Bible itself was on their side.

22. Manfred Gailus, *Protestantismus und Nationalsozialistischen Durchdringung des Protestantischen Sozialmilieus in Berlin* (Cologne: 2001). This study was recently expanded; see Manfred Gailus and Wolfgang Krogel (eds.), *Von der Babylonischen Gefangenschaft der Kirche im Nationalen: Regionalstudien zu Protestantismus, Nationalsozialismus und Nachkriegsgeschichte 1930 bis 2000* (Berlin: 2006).

23. Zentral Archiv der Kirche (Central Archives of the Protestant Church), Berlin (hereafter: ZAK) 1/A4/170.

24. Letter from Bishop Hans Meiser to the Council of the Protestant Lutheran Church of Germany (Rat der Evangelischen Lutherischen Kirche Deutschlands), 5 May 1939, BKSH, NEK, Signatur 57, Neue Nummer 323.

25. "Grundsätze für eine den Erfordernissen der Gegenwart entsprechende Ordnung der Deutschen Evangelischen Kirche," ZAK 1/A4/168.

26. Heschel, *The Aryan Jesus*, 270.

27. Robert P. Ericksen, "Hiding the Nazi Past: Denazification and Christian Postwar Reckoning in Germany," in *A Lutheran Vocation: Philip A. Nordquist and the Study of History at Pacific Lutheran University*, ed. Robert P. Ericksen and Michael J. Halvorson (Tacoma: 2005), 137–156.

28. Frederick Spotts, *The Churches and Politics in Germany* (Middletown, Conn.: 1973), 105; Norbert Frei, *Adenauer's Germany and the Nazi Past: The Politics of Amnesty and Integration*, trans. Joel Golb (New York: 2002), 99.

29. Steven Remy, *The Heidelberg Myth: The Nazification and Denazification of a German University* (Cambridge, Mass.: 2002), 243–244.

30. Robert P. Ericksen, "Wilhelm Niemöller and the Historiography of the Kirchenkampf," in *Nationalprotestantische Mentalitäten in Deutschland—1870–1970*, ed. Manfred Gailus and Hartmut Lehmann (Göttingen: 2005), 433–452.

31. See, for example, Robert P. Ericksen and Susannah Heschel, "Historiography on the Churches and the Holocaust," in *Historiography of the Holocaust*, ed. Dan Stone (London: 2004), 296–318.

32. Doris L. Bergen, *Twisted Cross: The German Christian Movement in the Third Reich* (Chapel Hill: 1996), 223. See also Clemens Vollnhals, *Evangelische Kirche und Entnazifizierung, 1945-1949: Die Last der Nationalsozialistischen Vergangenheit* (Munich: 1989), 287.

33. This is documented by Bergen, *Twisted Cross*, 223.

34. For example, wives of imprisoned Nazis were urged to follow the example of a Jesus imagined in those terms; see Katharina von Kellenbach, "God's Love and Women's Love: Prison Chaplains Counsel the Wives of Nazi Perpetrators," *Journal of Feminist Studies in Religion* 20, no. 2 (2004), 7–24.

35. Leffler's postwar years are described in Anja Rinnen, *Kirchenmann und Nationalsozialist: Siegfried Leffers ideelle Verschmelzung von Kirche und Drittem Reich, Forum zur Pädagogik und Didaktik der Religion 9* (Weinheim: 1995). See also Vollnhals, *Evangelische Kirche und Entnazifizierung*.

36. Victoria Barnett, *For the Soul of the People: Protestant Protest against Hitler* (New York: 1992); 200; Renate Wind, *Dietrich Bonhoeffer: A Spoke in the Wheel* (Grand Rapids: 1992), 102.

37. Wind, *Dietrich Bonhoeffer*, 101.

38. See the autobiographical reflections by Jörg Zink in *How I Have Changed: Reflections on Thirty Years of Theology*, ed. Jürgen Moltmann (Harrisburg: 1997).

39. Vollnhals, *Evangelische Kirche und Entnazifizierung*.

40. Till van Rahden, "Paternity, Rechristianization, and the Quest for Democracy in Postwar West Germany," *Forschungsberichte des Duitsland Instituut Amsterdam* 4 (2008), 55–74; quote appears on p. 54.

41. Dagmar Herzog, *Sex after Fascism: Memory and Morality in Twentieth-Century Germany* (Princeton: 2005).

42. Van Rahden, "Paternity, Rechristianization, and the Quest for Democracy in Postwar West Germany."

43. Matthew D. Hockenos, *A Church Divided: German Protestants Confront the Nazi Past* (Bloomington: 2004), 163.

44. Gerlach, *And the Witnesses Were Silent*, 224.

45. Ibid., 225.

46. Matthew D. Hockenos, "Representations of the Nazi Past in the German Protestant Church in Early 1945," in *Christian Responses to the Holocaust: Moral and Ethical Issues*, ed. Donald J. Dietrich (Syracuse: 2003), 156.

47. See Gerhard Besier and Gerhard Sauter, *Wie Christen ihre Schuld bekennen: Die Stuttgarter Erklärung 1945* (Göttingen: 1985).

48. Minutes of the meetings held between Walter Grundmann and members of the church consistory, Landeskirchen Archiv (LKA) Eisenach (Archives of the church of Thuringia, in Eisenach), G 2402.

49. Hockenos, *A Church Divided*.

50. Gerlach, *And the Witnesses Were Silent*, 227.
51. Ibid., 223.
52. Letter from Bishop Theophil Wurm to the Bruderrat, 17 Jan. 1948, Landeskirchenarchiv Darmstadt 36/73; cited by Christoph M. Raisig, *Wege der Erneurung: Christen und Juden: Der Rheinische Synodalbeschluss von 2002* (Potsdam: 2002), 57 (n. 152).
53. Victoria Barnett, "Seelisberg: An Appreciation," *Studies in Christian-Jewish Relations* 2, no. 2 (2007), 54–57.
54. Hockenos, "Representations of the Nazi Past in the German Protestant Church in Early 1945," 151–167.
55. Eva Fleischner, *Judaism in German Christian Theology since 1945: Christianity and Israel Considered in Terms of Mission* (Metuchen: 1975), 72.
56. Ibid., 74–75. Harder was one of the founders of the Kirchentag's division on Christian-Jewish relations, Arbeitsgruppe für Juden und Christen, and he was also the founder and director of the Institute Kirche und Israel at the Kirchliche Hochschule in Berlin (now affiliated with Humboldt University in Berlin).
57. Richard L. Rubenstein, "The Dean and the Chosen People," in *After Auschwitz: Radical Theology and Contemporary Judaism*, ed. Richard L. Rubenstein (New York: 1966), 54.
58. Ibid., 55.
59. Ibid., 56.
60. Jürgen John, "Die Jenaer Universität im Jahre 1945," in *Die Wiedereröffnung der Friedrich-Schiller-Universität*, ed. Jürgen John and Volker Wahl (Weimar: 1998), 20. See also Mitchell G. Ash, "Verordnete Umbrüche – konstruierte Kontinuitäten: Zur Entnazifizierung von Wissenschaftlern und Wissenschaften nach 1945," *Zeitschrift für Geschichtswissenschaft* 43 (1995), 903–924 (esp. nn. 18, 20, 65).
61. On Heidelberg University after the war, see Remy, *The Heidelberg Myth*.
62. Reijo E. Heinonen, *Anpassung und Identität: Theologie und Kirchenpolitik der Bremer Deutschen Christen 1933–1945* (Göttingen: 1978), 181. On Bauer, a surgeon who published a book on racial hygiene in 1942, see Remy, *The Heidelberg Myth*, 88-90 and passim.
63. See Remy, *The Heidelberg Myth*.
64. Susannah Heschel, "For 'Volk, Blood, and God': The Theological Faculty at the University of Jena during the Third Reich," in *Nazi Germany and the Humanities*, ed. Wolfgang Bialas and Anson Rabinbach (Oxford: 2007), 365–398.
65. Trutz Rendtorff, "Das Wissenschaftsverständnis der Protestantischen Universitätstheologie im Dritten Reich," in *Theologische Fakultäten im Nationalsozialismus*, ed. Leonore Siegele-Wenschkewitz and Carsten Nicolaisen (Göttingen: 1993), 19–44.
66. Grundmann's commentaries on the Gospels were part of a huge oeuvre that comprised both scholarly and popular books. See Heschel, *The Aryan Jesus*.
67. Günther also published under the pseudonym Ludwig Winter; see Hans-Jürgen Lutzhöft, *Der Nordische Gedanke in Deutschland 1920–1940* (Kieler Historische Studien, vol. 14) (Stuttgart: 1971), 46.
68. Ulrich Oelschläger, *Judentum und Evangelische Theologie, 1909–1945: Das Bild des Judentums im Spiegel der ersten drei Auflagen des Handwörterbuchs* 'Die Religion in Geschichte und Gegenwart' (Stuttgart: 2005).
69. Kurt Meier, *Die deutschen Christen: Das Bild einer Bewegung im Kirchenkampf des Dritten Reiches* (Göttingen: 1964).
70. Ericksen, "Wilhelm Niemöller and the Historiography of the Kirchenkampf."
71. Wilfgang Tilgner, *Volksnomostheologie und Schöpfungsglaube: Ein Beitrag zur Geschichte des Kirchenkampfes* (Göttingen: 1966).
72. The absence of the Holocaust from the first generation of postwar memoirs by Christian theologians has been traced by Björn Krondorfer, *Mit Blick auf die Täter: Fragen an die deutsche Theologie nach 1945* (Gütersloh: 2006). Two such works are those of Klaus-Peter Hertzsch, *Sag meinen Kindern, dass sie weiterziehn: Erinnerungen* (Stuttgart: 2002)—Hertzsch grew up in Eisenach and taught practical theology at the University of Jena after the war; and Franz Tügel, *Mein Weg, 1888–1946: Erinnerungen eines Hamburger Bischofs*, ed. Carsten Nicolaisen (Hamburg: 1972). Tügel was bishop of Hamburg and active in the German

Christian movement; he was one of the initiators of the Godesberg Declaration. In contrast to these two memoirs, see a discussion of Tügel's Nazi-era activities: Manuel Ruoff, *Landesbischof Franz Tügel* (Hamburg: 2000); Kersten Krüger, *Beiträge zur deutschen und Europäischen Geschichte* (Hamburg: 2000).

73. Wolfgang Gerlach, *Als die zeugen Schwiegen: Bekennende Kirche und die Juden* (Studien zu Kirche und Israel, vol. 10) (Berlin: 1987).

74. See Leonore Siegele-Wenschkewitz, *Neutestamentliche Wissenschaft vor der Judenfrage: Gerhard Kittels theologische Arbeit im Wandel deutscher Geschichte* (Munich: 1980); cf. Leonore Siegele-Wenschkewitz (ed.), *Christlicher Antijudaismus und Antisemitismus: theologische und kirchliche Programme Deutscher Christen* (Frankfurt: 1994).

75. The two churches formally split in 1969, forming the Bund der Evangelischen Kirchen in der DDR (BEK; East Germany) and the Evangelische Kirche in Deutschland (EKD; West Germany).

76. Irena Ostmeyer, *Zwischen Schuld und Sühne: Evangelishe Kirche und Juden in SBZ und DDR 1945–1990*, (Studien zu Kirche und Israel, vol. 21) (Berlin: 2002).

77. See Rudolf and Rosemarie Schuder Hirsch, *Der gelbe Fleck: Wurzeln und Wirkungen des Judenhasses in der deutschen Geschichte* (Berlin: 1987).

78. Among the many important German Protestant theologians who have led the efforts for a positive Christian appreciation of Judaism are Berthold Klappert, Frank Crüsemann, Friedrich-Wilhelm Marquardt, Klaus Wengst, Peter von der Osten-Sacken, Ulrich Lutz, Johann-Michael Schmidt, Martin Leutch, Jürgen Ebach, and Leonore Siegele-Wenschkewitz. Among their prominent Catholic counterparts are Johann-Baptist Metz, Franz Mussner, Hans-Hermann Henrix, and Rainer Kampling.

79. *Christen und Juden: Eine Studie des Rates der Evangelischen Kirche in Deutschland* (commissioned by the Council of the Kirchenkanzlei der Evangelischen Kirche in Deutschland) (Gütersloh: 1975). See also Rolf Rentdorff (ed.), *Arbeitsbuch Christen und Juden: Zur Studie des Rates der Evangelischen Kirche in Deutschland, im Auftrag der Studienkommission Kirche und Judentum* (Gütersloh: 1979).

80. Johann B. Metz, "Ökumene nach Auschwitz," in *Gott nach Auschwitz: Dimensionen des Massenmords am jüdischen Volk* (Freiburg: 1979), ed. Johann Baptist and Eugen Kogon (Freiburg: 1979), 123.

81. "Schluss mit den Judentaufen," *Arische Rundschau* (1933); ZAK 1/C3/170, vol. 2, fol. 19; cited by Christopher M. Clark, *The Politics of Conversion: Missionary Protestantism and the Jews in Prussia, 1728–1941* (Oxford: 1995), 291.

82. By 1936, the only remaining official mission to the Jews was in Berlin; it was closed in 1941 by Gestapo action. See ibid., 301–302.

83. For an evaluation of the significance of the Rhineland synod declaration of 1980, see Siegfried Kreuzer and Frank Überschaer (eds.), *Gemeinsame Bibel, gemeinsame Sendung: 25 Jahre Rheinischer Synodalbeschluss zur Erneuerung des Vernhältnisses von Christen und Juden* (Neukirchen-Vluyn: 2006).

84. *Berlin 1960: Bericht über die vierte Tagung der zweiten Synode der Evangelischen Kirche in Deutschland vom 21. bis 26. Februar 1960* (commissioned by the Council of the Church Leadership of the EKD), 257; cited by Raisig, *Wege der Erneuerung*, 81.

85. On Iwand's role, see Hockenos, *A Church Divided*. On Miskotte, see Martin Kessler, *Kornelis Miskotte: A Biblical Theology* (Selinsgrove: 1997).

86. Friedrich Wilhelm Marquardt, *Von Elend und Heimsuchung der Theologie: Prolegomena zur Dogmatik* (Munich: 1988), 138.

87. Berthold Klappert, "Die Wurzel trägt dich: Einführung in den Synodalbeschluss der Rheinischen Landessynode," in *Umkehr und Erneuerung: Erläuterung zum Synodalbeschluss der Rheinischen Landessynode 1980*, ed. Berthold Klappert and Helmut Starck (Neukirchen-Vluyn: 1980), 45; cited by K. Hannah Holtschneider, *German Protestants Remember the Holocaust: Theology and the Construction of Collective Memory* (London: 2001), 46.

88. Holtschneider, *German Protestants Remember the Holocaust*.

89. Berthold Klappert, "Die Juden in einer christlichen Theologie nach Auschwitz," in *Auschwitz als Herausforderung für Juden und Christen*, ed. Günther B. Ginzel (Heidelberg: 1980), 504.

90. Johann Baptist Metz, "The Future in the Memory of Suffering," in *The Holocaust as Interruption*, ed. Elisabeth Schüssler-Fiorenza and David Tracy (Edinburgh: 1984), 28; cited by Holtschneider, *German Protestants Remember the Holocaust*, 43.
91. Dorothee Soelle, "Life in Its Fullness," *The Ecumenical Review* 35, no. 4 (1983), 377.
92. Dorothee Soelle, in Moltmann (ed.), *How I Have Changed*, 24.
93. Jürgen Moltmann, *Experiences of God*, trans. Margaret Kohl (Philadelphia: 1980), 22. For an excellent critique of Moltmann's anti-Judaism, see A. Roy Eckardt, *Long Night's Journey into Day: Life and Faith after the Holocaust* (Detroit: 1982), 87–110.
94. Jürgen Moltmann, *The Crucified God: The Cross of Christ as the Foundation and Criticism of Christian Theology*, trans. R.A. Wilson and John Bowden (New York: 1974), 175.
95. Nicholas de Lange, "Jesus Christ and Auschwitz," in *The Future of Jewish-Christian Dialogue*, ed. Dan Cohn-Sherbok (Lewiston, Canada: 1999), 12.
96. Jürgen Moltmann, *A Broad Place: An Autobiography* (Minneapolis: 2008), 280.
97. Edna Brocke, "Seit Auschwitz muss jeder wissen, das Schlimmeres als Krieg moeglich ist," in *Kirche und Israel* no. 1 (1991), 61–74; Jürgen Moltmann, "Das christliche jüdische Verhältnis und der Zweite Golfkrieg," *Kirche und Israel*, no. 6 (1991), 163–185. See also the correspondence between Brocke and Moltmann in *Kirche und Israel*, no. 2 (1991), 163–185; 179–180.
98. Frank Crüsemann, "The Torah and the Unity of God," *Word and World* 21, no. 3 (2001), 248.
99. Helmut Schmitz (ed.), *A Nation of Victims? Representations of German Wartime Suffering from 1945 to the Present* (Amsterdam: 2007).
100. For instance, in 2003, shortly before his election as head (Vorsitzender) of the EKD, Bishop Wolfgang Huber of Berlin-Brandenburg argued that the Muslim headscarf symbolizes a cultural divide, whereas the Christian cross has nothing to do with social tensions. See Mark Siemons, "Voilà Integration: Das Kopftuchverbot erzeugt die Bedrohung, der es wehren will," *Frankfurter Allgemeine Zeitung* (13 Nov. 2003), 37. See also Michael Gassmann, "Kreuz und Kopftuch nicht in einen Topf: Unverzichtbarer Distinktionsunterricht: Bischof Wolfgang Hubers politische Theologie," *Frankfurter Allgemeine Zeitung* (5 Feb. 2005), 41.

The Passion of the Christ and Its Ramifications with Reference to the Protestant Churches and Christian-Jewish Relations

Peter A. Pettit
(MUHLENBERG COLLEGE)

There have been no large-scale retributions against Jewish communities nor even any reported individual acts of anti-Jewish violence tied to Mel Gibson's The Passion of the Christ in the more than five years since the movie's Ash Wednesday release in 2004. Although it had the widest release ever for an independent film and grossed more than $600 million in worldwide box office sales, a recent survey indicates that it produced no noticeable spur in anti-Jewish feelings among audience members.[1] Neither has the film become a staple of Holy Week programming on North American television or cable channels. What, then, makes it anything more than a flash-in-the-pan point of controversy, albeit one that was fueled by arguably the savviest marketing campaign in entertainment history?[2]

For the Roman Catholic world, *The Passion of the Christ* stands as a test case of the long-term influence of the Second Vatican Council, which declared in *Nostra Aetate* that "what happened in [Christ's] passion cannot be blamed upon all the Jews then living, without distinction, nor upon the Jews of today."[3] That particular issue has been examined extensively—from the application of internal church guidelines for passion portrayals to the public response of the U.S. Conference of Catholic Bishops; from the supposed remark of a pope nearing his death to the influence of Mel Gibson's father and the circles of traditionalist Catholic activism.[4] Under Pope Benedict XVI, the Vatican has sent a number of ambiguous signals regarding the relationship of the church to the Jewish people. With the dramatic assertions of *Nostra Aetate* seemingly under reinterpretation, the appearance of Gibson's film just 14 months prior to Benedict's election as pope can be regarded as a tantalizing key to contemporary conundrums in Catholic-Jewish relations.[5]

What of the Protestant world? The more specific issues that drew attention in the Roman Catholic controversy were absent from Protestant discussions. Vatican II is not normative for Protestants, who have no corresponding guidelines for presenting passion portrayals; Gibson is not a Protestant himself; the disputes he and his father may have with the modern Catholic church are of little consequence to Protestants; and there is no Protestant hierarchy corresponding to the U.S. Catholic bishops' conference that might be a bellwether of Protestant response to the film. Among Protestants, we can only judge by observation and by a variety of more or less influential writings what the phenomenon of the film could mean.

In this regard, it is instructive to consider a sample of North American Protestant literature regarding *The Passion of the Christ* dating to the time of the film's release and the several years subsequent to that.[6] This sample includes more than two dozen articles in theological journals, denominational publications and the public media, as well as four edited volumes about the film (containing contributions by several Protestant writers)[7] and numerous stories appearing in major daily newspapers. (It is noteworthy that, among North American Protestant institutions, only the Evangelical Lutheran Church in America [ELCA] issued anything resembling a denominational statement regarding the film, namely, a set of "concerns and recommendations" formulated by the church's Consultative Panel on Lutheran-Jewish Relations, which was published prior to the film's release.)[8]

In analyzing this literature, denominational differences among Protestants proved to be of minimal consequence as a factor in determining attitudes and primary concerns. Even hermeneutical differences among various theologians—that is, their stated relationship to Scripture or their acceptance or rejection of historical-critical methodology in interpreting the Bible—were of secondary import. What instead proved to be decisive were the theological meta-narratives implicit in the various Protestant responses, which makes the phenomenon of the film and the controversy surrounding it particularly relevant in the context of contemporary Protestant-Jewish relations.

On a broad range of contemporary social issues ranging from reproductive rights to church-state issues and from responses to the Arab-Israeli conflict to creationism/evolution debates, the Protestant world can seem confusing and contrary. Representatives of the same denomination can hold widely divergent views and yet speak to them in the framework of their Christian faith. Knowledge of a Protestant's theological training or cultural context (urban/rural community, economic class, educational level, and the like) does not necessarily yield a basis for projecting the individual's views on any of these issues—something more than theology and biblical interpretation clearly is at work in shaping Protestant views. The case of the controversy surrounding Gibson's film can present us with some of the lines along which divisions are drawn, with potentially useful implications for future Protestant-Jewish dialogue.[9]

A Variety of Responses

Both the broadly positive and the broadly negative responses to the announcement of Gibson's film—and it only took the announcement to generate vehement responses—are by now well known. Congregations bought blocks of tickets and either resold them or gave them away to ensure that congregants would have the opportunity to see the film. Religious leaders who were invited to private screenings by Gibson and his production company, Icon Productions, wrote with great enthusiasm about the evangelistic potential of the film, its powerful impact on them personally, and the moving ways in which Gibson and the actor portraying Jesus, James Caviziel, spoke of the production experience. An array of affiliated marketing sites popped up on the internet, and promotional kits from Icon were distributed widely to Christian congregations. Indeed, one of the central avenues of marketing for the film was the evangelical Christian network.[10]

Meanwhile, a group of Roman Catholic and Jewish scholars who had reviewed a pre-release copy of the script, understanding that they had at least tacit approval from Gibson and Icon to make their comments on it, criticized it strongly in relation to the "Guidelines for Portrayals of the Passion" that had been published by the U.S. Conference of Catholic Bishops in 1988.[11] The Christian Scholars Group for Jewish-Christian Relations put out a viewer's guide titled *Facts, Faith, and Film-Making*.[12] As noted, the Consultative Panel on Lutheran-Jewish Relations also came out with a set of concerns and recommendations. Jewish organizations, with the Anti-Defamation League's president Abraham Foxman in the lead, expressed grave concern about the portrayal of Jews and the potential for fanning antisemitism. In addition, the major news magazines and several monthlies carried stories covering the controversy.

With the film's release, the focus of much commentary turned on four key points: the extreme, graphic violence; the accuracy of the narrative vis-à-vis the gospel accounts and other sources; anti-Jewish aspects of the film; and the powerful emotional and spiritual impact of the film on viewers. Among Protestant commentators, each of these themes was widely discussed and debated.

Some argued that the violence was a powerful presentation of the suffering that Jesus underwent for the sake of believers and that it therefore confronted the audience with a transcendent reality, no matter how difficult it was to watch.[13] Others analyzed the film as an example of the "snuff" genre in which the central action is the death of the main character.[14] Some represented the film as faithful to the gospel accounts while others contested even the possibility of such an accomplishment, given the differences among those accounts.[15] Some took the inclusion of elements from an early modern meditational text by a 19th-century stigmatic nun, Anne Catherine Emmerich, to be inspired, while others regarded it as pandering to emotions at the expense of historical veracity.[16]

The dress, posture, verbal and nonverbal interactions, prominence and positioning of Jewish characters throughout the film (including Jesus' opponents, disciples, and family as well as "the crowd") all underwent extensive scrutiny for evidence of anti-Jewish animus.[17] Gibson and others pointed to the explicit portrayal of Satan, the presence of Gibson's own hand nailing Jesus to the cross,[18] and the traditional Christian view that "the sins of all humanity crucified him," as evidence that any charges of anti-Jewishness were absurd and misguided. Most agreed that the film was powerful in its impact, though the effect of its impact—positive or negative—was widely debated, and some argued that the sheer duration of the brutality shown on the screen rendered *The Passion of the Christ* both boring and stultifying.[19]

Protestant respondents made use of analytical tools drawn from various disciplines including theology, psychology, sociology, and film studies. This may partly account for the lack of consensus regarding the source or significance of their divergent reactions to the film.[20] Yet the matter appears to go much deeper than a mere difference in analytical approach. Why did one viewer see a heinous execution portrayed on the screen while another perceived a sublime story of universal salvation? Why did one enjoy "the best portrait of Jesus that I've seen in film"[21] while another experienced "a reversal of the true meaning of the Passion of Jesus Christ"?[22]

A Limited Narrative Arc

The Passion of the Christ offers a very limited narrative arc across the eighteen hours of Jesus' life that it depicts. As Stuart Robinson notes, the film "is a visceral contemplation of the agony of Jesus' willing sacrifice."[23] Leaving aside the issue of the sacrifice (which Robertson himself might agree is a theological assessment more to be found in Gibson's commentary on the film than in the film itself), this leaves simply the agony, contemplated. And this, absent the audience's reflective engagement, leaves a narrative arc that can be summarized in four words: *They killed the guy.*

The film opens on the last night of Jesus' life, as he prays in Gethsemane just prior to his arrest. His impending death is quickly foreshadowed by a snake slithering menacingly toward him, which he crushes underfoot. Gibson thus evinces the divine curse of Gen. 3:15 that set Satan and humans in mutual enmity, "they [Eve's offspring] shall strike at your head, and you shall strike at their heel." From that image forward, through the arrest, abuse, condemnation, flogging, and crucifixion, there is but one story line, and it all leads to Jesus' death. Had Gibson succeeded in his original intention of releasing the film with its Latin and Aramaic dialogue, sans subtitles, the effect would have been even greater: with no understandable dialogue to guide the viewers' interpretation, only the unremitting march to Calvary would have registered with most audience members. Indeed, even with the subtitles, it is questionable how much dialogue most of the audience recalls. What none can forget is the brute fact of the slaughter.

Such a spare narrative leaves room for ample elaboration by those who view the film. Thus we come to the central dynamic that can account for the wide variation in interpretation, particularly in Protestant circles. As James F. Moore put it, "a focus on the story, that is, how the story is told, is precisely what is central to a Protestant Christian approach."[24]

The formal principle of the Protestant Reformation is *sola scriptura*, "by scripture alone."[25] In contrast to the Roman Catholic church, which enshrines periodic changes of interpretation in the magisterium (its official set of theological teachings),[26] Protestants continually return to the biblical story in an effort to make the word of God live anew in each age. The focus is not only on the details of the text but also on the reader's repeated encounters with it, in ever-changing circumstances of life and community. This continual engagement with the Bible is deemed to be of major importance in discerning God's truth, which in principle can never be fully or permanently captured in any dogmatic formulation. As Edmund Schlink, a Lutheran theologian notes: "All human thought, emotion, and activity is subjected to Scripture. . . . What Scripture as a whole teaches must be the teaching of the church. What Scripture does not teach must be rejected as doctrinal pronouncements of the church."[27]

Putting the "focus on the story," as Robertson has said, is not, however, a kind of pedantic textualism; rather, the encounter in which scriptural meaning is revealed becomes a focal point of its own. Thus Luther's account of his dramatic "Tower Experience" (in which he discerned, through diligent and extended meditation on a New Testament text, the principle of justification by grace through faith), is as well known to Lutherans as many Bible stories.[28] Similarly, John Wesley's "strange warming of the heart" in Aldersgate is as much a touchstone for the shared identity of his Methodist followers as any detail of his theological work.[29] A Protestant approach to theological understanding, then, characteristically turns to the particulars of the story being told and discerns meaning as a function of the living encounter with that story, taking full cognizance of the interpreter's circumstances as relevant factors in the experience.[30]

What, then, is one to do with *The Passion of the Christ*, whose story is told with so little elaboration? How is one to discern and enlarge upon its meaning when its narrative arc is so brief, no matter how long the suffering drags on?

Meta-narratives and Meaning

Among the Protestant commentaries and analyses reviewed for this essay, we discovered an unexpectedly large number of references to the personal lives and experiences of the authors. It has perhaps become a truism to say that every commentary is situated by the life-experience of the commentator; in many fields of linguistic and cultural analysis, scholarly work now regularly includes reference to the particulars of the author's worldview. As we will see, the personal character of the comments we reviewed were of a somewhat different nature, occasionally becoming the focus of the analysis and always figuring directly, where they were mentioned at all, in the substance of the analysis. The writers were suggesting, or sometimes saying outright, that a viewer of the film had to have had certain experiences or had to bring a certain background to *The Passion of the Christ* in order to see or understand something important about the film. We will refer to these necessary settings for understanding as meta-narratives,[31] and see how they function in generating widely divergent meanings from the film.

Some meta-narrative references are clearly autobiographical, as is the case with this commentary by Jeffrey Siker:

> I confess as I approached the release of Mel Gibson's *The Passion* and its possible consequences for relations between Christians and Jews, I had no small personal interests at stake. I grew up in a household with a Jewish father and Roman Catholic mother. I had an uncle who was a conservative rabbi and a great aunt who was a mother superior. Somehow, this turned me into a Presbyterian minister who works primarily as a professor teaching and writing about early Jewish-Christian relations at a Roman Catholic University. . . . [T]he release of the Gibson movie has provided a significant place for both personal and critical reflection.[32]

Siker does not elaborate on the personal dimension of his reflection in any detail, but his approach to the whole question of interpreting Jesus' passion, death, and resurrection points in the direction of sorting out his own complicated background of personal relationships and communal identities:

> The death of Jesus is located at the heart of Christian faith. . . . Christian reflection and theologizing on the meaning of the death of Jesus has always been an important barometer of both internal Christian identity and Christian relations to external groups, especially Jews and Judaism.[33]

In a similar vein, Stephen T. Davis, a Presbyterian minister in the philosophy department at Claremont-McKenna College in California, offers a preliminary note to his article on "Crucifying Jesus: Antisemitism and the Passion Story": "As a philosopher of religion, I do not often address in print the topic of relations between Jews and Christians ..., but I have thought a great deal about it."[34] The autobiographical tone is even more apparent in the first paragraph of the article, in which Davis notes that he grew up in the 1940s and 1950s in a family of mixed Presbyterian-Roman Catholic background. In that setting, he writes, he cannot remember when he "first heard the canard that all Jews were 'Christ killers,' but it must have been when I was old enough to recognize the absurdity of the charge because I have never believed it." Davis' choice to include so much autobiographical detail leads one to ask whether his conclusion—"That Jews as a people ought to be singled out for punishment is, in my opinion, contrary to Christian teaching"—derives more from his careful scholarly work or his own personal background.

Stephen R. Haynes, of Rhodes College, offers the most extensively autobiographical response to the film. His article, titled "A March of Passion; or, How I Came to Terms with a Film I Wasn't Supposed to Like,"[35] is a kind of journal covering a period of 15 days in late February and early March 2004, when he saw the Gibson film and then had a series of encounters in relation to it. Haynes lays out his struggle to resolve his conflicting responses to the film, which are variously mirrored and derided by family members, colleagues, and students. In the final installment, he writes:

> The time had come to examine my own psyche for the roots of my dilemma. . . . Gradually it became evident that it was not simply empathy for religious folk or respect for my parents that led me to a semidefense of *The Passion*. It was my own deep-seated affinity for images of a God who suffers. This affinity reveals itself in my cinematographic preferences as much as in my research interests. . . . Then there is my obsession with the martyr Dietrich Bonhoeffer. . . . Remembering these things forced me to acknowledge that something in my understanding of the Christian faith makes me want to view suffering redemptively.[36]

All of these authors note that there is a personal context within which their engagement with the film and its meaning took place. More or less explicitly, the context is shown to correlate with the meaning that the commentator ascribes to the film. This same dynamic is apparent in the counsel provided by the Lutheran consultative panel to those who may view the film (or any Passion portrayal). The panel noted that the Gibson film had the potential to "shape or reshape understandings of this central Christian story" and that "such influence should be exercised with due regard for the powerful heritage of the Passion as gospel truth for Christians and as human tragedy for many Jews."[37] The simple biographical detail of Christian or Jewish affiliation can provide a meta-narrative that will largely determine how accounts of the Passion are perceived.

For D. Andrew Kille, a Baptist minister serving an ecumenical Episcopal community, the very fact of such a broad range of responses is meaningful. "When something elicits such a spectrum of responses, especially such strong responses, the psychic dynamics of projection are at work. Viewers project their inward lives onto the external world, and thus any response to the film may prove to be more autobiographical than anything else."[38] Kille cites work by Norman Holland on readers' assimilation of new material to describe the role of an "identity theme" (or, in our terminology, a meta-narrative) in making sense of unfamiliar material: "The viewer links the film to what he or she finds meaningful, filling in the gaps without being aware of doing so."[39]

Mary Boys draws on a similar analytical tool from the work of John Hull in the field of education. Hull, she writes, developed "personal construct theory" to account for the ways in which "all of us order our worlds by construing experience a certain way."[40] This ordering, in Hull's words, "is intended to offer prediction about the way things will be."[41] Boys adds: "A person's construct system is the entirety of what she or he has learned thus far," with one result being that each term or image within the person's experience, such as the Passion or the figure of Jesus, "carries associations that are often individual and highly personal."[42] In relation to the Gibson film, Holland and Hull both support Kille's observation that "what you find in the movie seems to depend greatly upon what you brought into the theater by way of experience, belief, or expectation."[43]

Our research suggests that it is not only specifically autobiographical or intimate personal experience that shapes the meta-narrative brought by Protestants (and presumably others, as well) to the film. For many, what is most significant is the more broadly personal or even communal experience. For instance, Connie Corbin, the coordinator of a Protestant coffee-shop ministry in Buckhead, Georgia, responded to the film in this way: "Personally, I believe that in my Christian walk, it's very important that I literally go to the cross and see what happened."[44] Clearly this particular motivation for seeing the film will have a strong impact on the viewer's perception of the film's meaning. Corbin's perspective is echoed by many of those quoted in news reports about the film.

It was not only the average pew-sitter or local ministry coordinator who identified the film's meaning in terms drawn from their communal Christian experience. A noted Protestant author and speaker, Lee Strobel—formerly the pastor of Willow Creek Community Church, the original "mega-church"—wrote the following:

> For the first time in my life I felt as if I were really *experiencing* what Jesus had endured. Book research, library studies, and interviews with scholars had given me cognitive knowledge, but now my heart engaged with history as never before. . . . It wasn't until I endured the visual intensity of Gibson's film that I was able to absorb the emotional impact of the passion of Jesus.[45]

The emphasis of both Corbin and Strobel on the realism of the portrayal supports Leslie E. Smith's observation that "[evangelicals] gauged *The Passion*'s accuracy not by measures of specific historicity but rather by the emotions the film evoked in the viewer and the extent to which it could lead to a conversion experience."[46] According to the editor of *Christian Century*, a prominent North American Protestant journal, even the extreme violence of the film, which "most critics" agreed was a "major flaw," was deemed acceptable by evangelical Christians (who would normally be expected to oppose scenes of graphic violence) because it served their own metanarrative of evangelical truth.[47] Mark Juergensmeyer, a sociologist at the University of California at Santa Barbara, suggests that this violence is familiar to Christian viewers as "part of an age-old template of Christian experience." They are familiar with "cosmic war" narratives depicting all-encompassing struggles of good against evil, and they have seen the pain that such war can cause in current-day wars and terrorist attacks. Despite the severity of the suffering shown in *The Passion of the Christ,* "they know that in the end, good will prevail because, as Gibson's movie so amply demonstrates, God already has entered the struggle [and] ultimately he will win."[48]

Gibson himself would agree that enduring the visual spectacle of Jesus' suffering, and understanding its larger context, are both integral to his purpose in making the film. In an interview with ABC television news correspondent Diane Sawyer, he said:

> Jesus Christ was beaten for our iniquities. He was wounded for our transgressions and by his wounds we are healed. That's the point of the film. ... I wanted it to be shocking, and I also wanted it to be extreme. I wanted to push the viewer over the edge ... so that they see the enormity—the enormity of the sacrifice—to see that someone could endure that and still come back with love and forgiveness, even through extreme pain and suffering and ridicule.[49]

Jeffrey Siker reports that Gibson reiterated this view in a personal exchange following a film screening, and did so in especially autobiographical terms: "[H]e thought ... that the sacrificial death of Jesus was everything, as it helped to remind him of his own sin and his need for constant redemption."[50]

Recognizing this "age-old template" requires a certain personal experience, however. Many commentators pointed out that, for viewers lacking a Christian background, some of the film's most basic references and depicted actions could be difficult or even impossible to understand. Kille, for instance, noted that one of the scenes (a flashback that presumably provided some of the slight context from Jesus' life that could help the viewer understand the Passion) was "especially incomprehensible to the uninformed viewer." Commenting more generally on Gibson's intention to be "extreme" in the film, he concluded that "even for those who understand the core faith statement 'Jesus died for our sins,' Gibson's interpretational slant may not be clear."[51] In the words of another reviewer, writing in the *Houston Chronicle*: "All you will see is a man being hit over and over and over again, such extravagantly brutal torture that you cringe and pray for it to be done. If you know the Gospels, however, you might see something more than violence. You might see the embodiment of Christ's message."[52]

Knowing the Gospels is only a beginning, according to Daniel Harlow, who teaches in the Religion Department at Calvin College of the Reformed Church in America. Harlow documents extensively the Hebrew Bible, New Testament, and even traditional Jewish images that appear throughout the film, noting that "of course, it takes a biblically literate Christian to catch these resonances."[53] Methodist bishop Larry

M. Goodpaster recognizes, too, that "you really had to know the story to catch some of the symbolism"[54] but also goes beyond that observation. For him, the larger story of Jesus, that which makes sense of the "gut-wrenching" experience and which provided "a deeper, more vivid awareness of the agony that Jesus endured for me—and, indeed, for the whole world," is the story of the resurrection:

> Remember that the Passion and the crucifixion are not the end of the story. Without the resurrection, as Paul points out in Corinthians, our faith is in vain. I found myself profoundly thankful for the last 30 seconds of the movie and wished that part had been longer, but it was enough. God raised Jesus from the dead. After all the suffering, the pain and the cruelty of humanity, God redeems and transforms it all.[55]

According to Goodpaster, this form of "redemptive" meta-narrative may serve to counter any impulse toward anti-Jewish hostility: "Anyone who harbors anger, resentment, hostility or outrage toward Judaism has not heard the whole story of the love and mercy of Jesus himself."[56]

As one delves more deeply into the various Protestant responses to *The Passion of the Christ*, it becomes clear just how significant the meta-narrative is in drawing meaning from Gibson's "they-killed-the-guy" plot. This is because different meta-narratives emphasize different elements of the configuration—that is, some will focus on the "they" who killed Jesus, whereas others will concentrate on the killing itself or on Jesus as a victim. Several examples will illustrate each possible option.[57]

The focus on Jesus as the victim can emerge from a number of meta-narratives based on different experiences. Harlow, a mainline Reformed professor, reports that he undertook his graduate studies at the University of Notre Dame, a Roman Catholic school, where he was "struck by the ubiquity of crucifixes on the campus." Indeed, he writes:

> They adorned the wall of virtually every room of every building. Over time, I came to appreciate why Catholics have Jesus still hanging on their crosses. It is too easy for Protestants like me to forget that the cross was not a big piece of jewelry but the ancient equivalent of the electric chair or the hangman's noose. We have been bought with a price. Christ is risen indeed, but he remains Christ crucified.[58]

This is "one feature that distinguishes Catholic from Protestant piety," notes Harlow, and "it is one from which Protestants have something to learn." By viewing the film in the framework of a meta-narrative shaped by Roman Catholic mystical streams and "reverential devotion to Jesus' shed blood," Harlow sees "the five sorrowful mysteries of the rosary and the Stations of the Cross," with Christ as the innocent victim, the "contemplation of [whose] agony enables believers to participate in the redemption his death secured."[59]

Many evangelical Protestants subscribe to a different meta-narrative focusing on Jesus as the victim—one that reflects their own sense of being marginalized or even victimized in a North American culture that is increasingly characterized by religious pluralism and challenged by secularism. Mark Juergensmeyer argues that Gibson encourages the perception of victimization by his excessive focus on the violence done to Jesus, the movie being "an orgy of bloodshed that goes far beyond the Christian tradition's norm for portraying the agony and sacrifice of Jesus."[60] Moreover, since the transformative outcomes of the suffering—that is, redemption and purification—are not shown in the film, it is "not really about sacrifice at all but about victimization."[61] Leslie E. Smith, for her part, argues that Gibson's film "provides a rallying point for evangelicals who feel that American culture long has waged war on their values and deprived Christians of their share of positive cultural attention. ... Evangelicals see in the suffering Jesus a mirror of what they believe is their own persecution."[62] A somewhat different slant is that offered by James Dobson, the president of the evangelical organization Focus on the Family, who suggested that "the real problem the liberal establishment has with the movie is that it has the audacity to portray Christ as he really was ... as the Savior of mankind. This is an offense to the postmodern sensibilities of our morally relativistic culture."[63] A similar sentiment was expressed more succinctly in one of the messages posted on "a pro-*Passion* website": "Thanks for finally recognizing the Christians!"[64]

Marian Ronan, a Roman Catholic scholar teaching at the American Baptist Seminary of the West in Berkeley, does not restrict the meta-narrative of victimization to evangelicals. Rather, she argues, based on research done by Renana Brooks,

> we have come to see ourselves as a nation of victims, beginning with our identification with the victims of the World Trade Center bombing, continuing in our subsequent identification with the innocent victims of sex abuse by Roman Catholic priests, implicit representatives of a foreign power, and now in our identification with our wholesome servicemen and women under attack in Iraq. ... This identification between American victimization and Jesus is very satisfying, of course, because, as Mel Gibson makes abundantly clear, Jesus' death is not the last act. Those responsible for his victimization pay for it in a big way, with their temple destroyed and a warrior Jesus rising from the tomb on his way to kick some ass.[65]

Thus, whether rooted in the centuries-long pieties of Roman Catholic devotion, the intra-Christian and religious-secular dynamics of American society, or the most recent sense of siege that has been cultivated in American consciousness, the meta-narrative of victimization provides a powerful framework for many Protestants viewing *The Passion of the Christ*.

Whereas meta-narratives emphasizing Jesus as a victim are generally devoid of antisemitic overtones, those focusing on the "they" who killed Jesus must contend with the charged history of Jewish-Christian relations, and more specifically the centuries-long labeling of Jews as "Christ-killers." On this specific question, the debate surrounding *The Passion of the Christ* was marked by deep divisions and very strongly held opinions. What is irrefutable, however, is the observation that, for many viewers, Gibson's film not only evoked the doleful history of passion plays and other anti-Jewish expressions of Christian piety but was itself a new, wide-screen version of that tragic story.

In the words of John Buchanan in *Christian Century*, "you can't know much about the dreadful history of Christian antisemitism and feel very good about Mel Gibson's movie."[66] Even one who could feel reasonably good about the movie—for instance, Harlow, who wrote in praise of it—noted that "Jews bring to their experience of The Passion nearly two thousand years of Christian anti-Judaism and anti-Semitism, the theological roots of which are to be found in the pages of the New Testament itself. Christians should sympathize with the discomfort of Jews."[67] Tammi Reed Ledbetter, a Baptist, recognized the potentially pernicious effect of a personal background that was informed by anti-Jewish attitudes deriving from the church or elsewhere, arguing that the film could stir up hostility toward Jews among those with "a culturally ingrained anti-Jewish view." Implicitly acknowledging the dynamics that surrounded medieval passion plays, she also pointed out that an audience that had spent two hours watching excessive personal violence might well be inclined to find someone to blame, and the film offers Jews as the primary candidates.[68]

Laird Stuart, for his part, notes that his own personal background disposed him *not* to perceive any antisemitism in Gibson's film (characterized by him as "a modern presentation of a Passion play"), since, "for a very long time, probably since I was in seminary, I have not believed it was the Jews who killed Jesus." However, he continues, "someone who did not have that background would obviously come away thinking it was the Jews who killed Jesus."[69] Such differences in background and resulting meta-narrative were not confined to individuals. Christopher Hitchens, a *Vanity Fair* columnist writing on *Slate*, commented: "In America, I hope and believe, the sinister effect [of the film's antisemitism] will be blunted by generations of civilized co-existence. But think for a minute what will happen ... from screenings of the film in Egypt and Syria, or in Eastern Europe, where things are a bit more raw."[70] In a similar vein, Stuart Robertson indicated that "what might develop in parts of Europe or the Middle East where the movie might nourish existing anti-Jewish fermentation remains to be seen."[71]

Finally, while a number of observations regarding the violence of Gibson's film have already been noted, some commentators focus specifically on the film's emphasis on the act of killing, in an era when genocidal killing provides important context. Among those who have articulated this theme are James F. Moore from Valparaiso University (for Protestants) and John Pawlikowski (for Roman Catholics). Moore takes exception not only to the scapegoating of Jews (which could conceivably open the path back to Nazi-like genocide), but also to the continuation of a Christian theology of suffering that fails to take account of the reality of Auschwitz, or that imagines that God had gone missing during the Nazi era. "Suffering," he argues, "is not salvific, and we know this absolutely after Auschwitz." Precisely because Gibson's exclusive focus is on suffering, "Protestant theologians should have a problem with this telling of the story." In his view, "most of us who have thought about passion plays in a post-Shoah world would believe that telling the story of the passion must be done in a post-Shoah framework."[72]

What is pertinent in these observations for contemporary Jewish-Protestant relations is not the particulars of the various meta-narratives, nor the accuracy with which the commentators identify the dynamics behind Gibson's film. In that sense, the film has already gone on its way.[73] Rather, the point worth noting is the common dynamic of the responses, the way in which the film was integrated into the viewers' sundry meta-narratives, and thereby took its meaning from them.

For Protestant-Jewish interaction, this insight suggests that the story that Protestants tell about God and themselves and the world, all in relation to one another, is a key starting-point for any theological or interreligious engagement. Often that story will have a strong autobiographical component as it sets the terms for encountering the other and the environment. To be sure, in the course of that encounter, the language of theology, the analysis of scripture, the tools of historical and literary and cultural criticism, the insights of sociology and psychology, the perspectives of anthropology, and the rhetoric of philosophy may all find a place. They have all been brought into play in Protestant commentary on the Gibson film. However, what has repeatedly proven determinative of the way those tools are used and the conclusions to which they lead is the place that the film filled in the meta-narrative into which the commentator placed it.

One broadly recognized characteristic of the film is the very limited exposure it gives to Jesus' own life and teachings as a context for the Passion.[74] It is likely that a fuller portrayal of Jesus' interactions with Jewish opponents, with his disciples, with the wider public, and with Roman authorities, as well as his teaching and other actions, would have constrained the tendency to use story frameworks from outside the film to make sense of it. We have seen in the examples of Wesley and Luther, though, that a Protestant theological dynamic will in any case give significance to the wider personal and social stories that are the context of any interpretive encounter. The meta-narratives are rather those of the commentators and their communities, in which either the character of Jesus or the film as a whole played a vital role. Whenever an alternative understanding of the film found expression, the vehement debate that usually ensued demonstrated how hard it was to consider the film outside the larger narrative arc that each viewer brought to it. Gibson simply played into this dynamic by making the film's arc so nugatory and plastic that it could be fitted into many different frameworks rather easily.[75]

A Timely Parallel

In the summer of 2004, just months after the release of the Gibson film and while the discussion around it was still lively, a presumably unrelated event shook the world of Protestant-Jewish relations in North America. The Presbyterian Church (USA) voted in its general assembly to undertake a process of phased, selective divestment from Israel in protest against the policies of the Israeli government with regard to West Bank and Gaza Palestinians and to the Oslo peace process. A firestorm of controversy erupted; meetings and consultations were both called and cancelled in the wake of the divestment vote; Presbyterians and other mainline Protestant leaders met and spoke again and again with their Jewish counterparts. Clearly the Presbyterian action had caught the Jewish world off guard. Just as clearly, the vehement Jewish response shocked and surprised the Presbyterian leadership.[76]

Through the course of the ensuing debate and discussion, Ethan Felson of the Jewish Council for Public Affairs developed a cogent analysis of the communications patterns at work in many of the meetings. His analysis attempted to account for the miscommunications that often took place and the sense of frustration that quickly developed among many participants. The analysis was circulated informally as "Israel Advocacy with Mainline Protestant Influentials" and summarized in a number of places orally.

Felson's observation was that Jewish participants mounted arguments based on historical dynamics, legal principles, theories of justice, and standards of international diplomacy. Protestant participants, by contrast, relied heavily on narratives and anecdotes portraying Palestinian suffering and deprivation. While not unaware of the more abstract and scholarly evidence that their Jewish counterparts deployed, they circumscribed their understanding of that evidence with the emotional content of the stories that embodied for them the conflict's core issues. Ironically, their sympathies for the underdog and marginal figure were in fair measure cultivated in their appreciation of the paradigmatic redemption story of Israel's exodus from Egypt. However, the dominant narratives of Palestinian suffering with which they were familiar afforded little flexibility in understanding a complex historical and reciprocal experience of oppression and suffering. As in the case of the Gibson film, meta-narratives were at work: Israel's objectionable actions found their place in a larger story of Israeli expansionism or (more broadly) Western imperialism and colonialism.

The emergence of the divestment controversy so close to the release of *The Passion of the Christ* affords a serendipitous opportunity to see this central dynamic of Protestant theological engagement in quite different settings.[77] In both cases the Protestant community was grappling with ambiguity: in regard to Gibson's film, ambiguity derived from the paucity of narrative content, whereas in the divestment controversy it was the outcome of an excess of competing narrative options. In each instance, however, a key determinant in the Protestant response was the narrative framework, whether autobiographical or anecdotal, that the interpreter brought to the encounter.

Conclusion

Our review of Protestant responses to and commentary on Mel Gibson's 2004 film, *The Passion of the Christ,* shows a wide range of assessments fitting no clear denominational or theological pattern. A consistent element has been shown across much of the literature, however; it is the application of a meta-narrative drawn from outside the film to interpret the truncated narrative arc of the film itself. For those engaged in Protestant-Jewish encounter, the "meta-narrative phenomenon" offers the useful insight that prior theological (and often even very personal) narratives are apt to exercise a controlling influence on Protestants as they develop their theological understandings. Thus, the pertinent questions for interreligious dialogue may not be "what do you see there," or "how do you understand that," or "what does this mean to you," but rather "where does this fit in the story of your life and faith?" The visual, cognitive, and semiotic responses to a given issue are likely to be secondary formations, whereas narrative inquiries may be more likely to open up fruitful paths of exchange and understanding.

Notes

1. Statistics about the film's distribution and box office sales can be found online at www.the-numbers.com/movies/2004/PASON.php (accessed 18 April 2009). On anti-Jewish feelings among audiences, see Ann Rodgers, "Gibson's 'Passion' Remains a Concern over Portrayal of Jews," *Pittsburgh Post-Gazette* (21 March 2004), cited in William J. Brown, John D. Keeler and Terrence R. Lindvall, "Audience Responses to *The Passion of the*

Christ," Journal of Media and Religion 6, no. 2 (2007), 92. Cf. John Pawlikowski, who draws attention to "a 2004 Pew Research Center survey in which the number of people attributing responsibility for Jesus' death to the Jews has risen by some 9 percent" subsequent to the film's release ("Gibson's *Passion*: The Challenges for Catholics," in *Mel Gibson's* Passion*: The Film, the Controversy, and Its Implications*, ed. Zev Garber [West Lafayette: 2006], 130. This is likely the same Pew survey reported more generally by Gary Gilbert as showing that "just over one-quarter of Americans believe that the Jews were responsible for Jesus's death" and that "this belief is more prominent among those who have seen *The Passion* than among those who have not" ("Antisemitism without Erasure: Sacred Texts and Their Contemporary Interpretations," in *After* The Passion *Is Gone: American Religious Consequences*, ed. J. Shawn Landres and Michael Berenbaum [Walnut Creek: 2004], 125–136; quotation on p. 136, with bibliographic reference to the Pew survey in an endnote on p. 318.

2. Brown, Keeler, and Lindvall, "Audience Responses to *The Passion of the Christ*," 88, 90–91.

3. *Nostra Aetate* §4, in *The Documents of Vatican II*, ed. Walter M. Abbott, S.J. (n.p.: 1966), 666.

4. "Report of the Ad Hoc Scholars Group Reviewing the Script of *The Passion*" (2 May 2003) (hereafter: "Ad Hoc Scholars Report")—photocopy of a report produced without institutional sponsorship by nine scholars: Mary C. Boys, Michael J. Cook, Philip A. Cunningham, Eugene J. Fisher, Paula Fredriksen, Lawrence E. Frizzell, Eugene Korn, Amy-Jill Levine, and John T. Pawlikowski. For an overview of the controversy surrounding the report, see Mark Silk, "Almost a Culture War: The Making of *The Passion* Controversy," in Landres and Berenbaum (eds.), *After* The Passion *Is Gone*, 23–34; Peter Boyer, "The Jesus War," *The New Yorker* (15 Sept. 2003), 64–67.

The pope's reputed comment, "it is as it was," was first reported independently by *The Wall Street Journal* and the *National Catholic Reporter* (17 Dec. 2003); the latter may be found online at www.nationalcatholicreporter.org/update/bn121703.htm (accessed 28 June 2009). See also the subsequent report in the *National Catholic Reporter* regarding the "mess" of media coverage, online at www.nationalcatholicreporter.org/word/pfw012304.htm (accessed 27 July 2009).

Catholic traditionalists, with whom Gibson and his father are affiliated, reject the authority of the Second Vatican Council and the reforms it instituted in the Roman Catholic church, including the modernizing of the Mass, the ecumenical recognition of Protestants as faithful Christian brothers and sisters, the acknowledgment of God's truth in other religions, and the intimate continuing connection of the church to the Jewish people. For helpful discussions of this group in relation to the film, see Peter J. Boyer, "The Jesus War," and Julie Ingersoll, "Is It Finished? *The Passion of the Christ* and the Fault Lines in American Christianity," in Landres and Berenbaum (eds.), *After* The Passion *Is Gone*, 77–78.

5. Commenting on the papal visit to Israel in April 2009, Debbie Weissman, president of the International Council of Christians and Jews, noted that "the present pope has expressed somewhat ambivalent or, at least, ambiguous views on certain key topics of concern to Jews" and quoted John Pawlikowski as saying, "Perhaps the best we can hope for is no further backward steps" (*Jerusalem Report* [8 June 2009], 12).

At a meeting held in June 2009, the U.S. Conference of Catholic Bishops "clarified" a 2002 document, "Reflections on Covenant and Mission," by noting its inadequate theology of evangelization and affirming that Catholics cannot be prohibited from preaching the gospel to Jews. In a letter to *The Times* (London) on January 31, 2009, Edward Kessler, the director of the Centre for Jewish-Christian Relations in Cambridge, summarized a series of "key topics of concern to Jews" in this way: "The Vatican's decision to readmit ... the Holocaust denier Bishop Richard Williamson follows closely on from controversies over the proposed canonization of the wartime Pope Pius XII, and the revised Good Friday prayer, calling for conversion of Jews. ... [This] is another example of the marginalisation by the Vatican of relations ... with Jews..." (online at www.timesonline.co.uk/tol/comment/letters/article5621541.ece [accessed 28 June 2009]).

6. The preliminary survey of literature and development of an unpublished, annotated bibliography (covering 26 journal articles and pamphlets and seven public media reports), was

compiled by Ashley Eldredge-Martin under a collaborative research grant from the Provost's Office of Muhlenberg College, with the assistance of Kelly Cannon of the College's Trexler Library. I am grateful to both Ashley and Kelly for their substantial research support contributing to the project; responsibility for the judgments and opinions expressed here remains that of the author alone.

7. The four volumes are: Garber (ed.), *Mel Gibson's* Passion; Landres and Berenbaum (eds.), *After* The Passion *Is Gone*; Philip A. Cunningham (ed.), *Pondering the Passion: What's at Stake for Christians and Jews* (Lanham: 2004); and S. Brent Plate (ed.), *Re-Viewing the Passion: Mel Gibson's Film and Its Critics* (New York: 2004).

8. Consultative Panel on Lutheran-Jewish Relations, Department for Ecumenical Affairs, Evangelical Lutheran Church in America, "*The Passion of the Christ*: Concerns and Recommendations in Anticipation of the Forthcoming Film" (4 Jan. 2004), online at http://archive.elca.org/ecumenical/interreligious/thepassion/gibson_statement.html (accessed 28 July 2009). The present author was instrumental in the publication of this and the Christian Scholars Group study guide (see n. 12).

A later assessment by members of the panel was not distributed by the ELCA but rather emerged as a free-lance document garnering approximately 125 signatures from both Catholic and Protestant scholars and clerics. It may also be noted that the Lutheran World Federation issued a "theological reflection" on the film that characterized it as a "timely challenge facing churches of our Lutheran communion." The preface to this pamphlet made it clear that the comments within represented the author's view and were not to be regarded as an official expression on the part of the Lutheran World Federation. See Reinhard Böttcher, *The Passion of Jesus the Jew* (*Thinking It Over...*, issue no. 5) (Geneva: 2004); published simultaneously in German as *Die Passion des Juden Jesus* and in Portuguese as *A paixão do Jesu Judeu*.

9. See Julie Ingersoll, "Is It Finished? *The Passion of the Christ* and the Fault Lines in American Christianity," in Landres and Berenbaum (eds.), *After* The Passion *Is Gone*, pp. 75–87, for an excellent, related assessment of the lines drawn by responses to the film.

10. Leslie E. Smith, "Living *in* the World, but Not *of* the World: Understanding Evangelical Support for *The Passion of the Christ*," in Landres and Berenbaum (eds.), *After* The Passion *Is Gone*, 47, 53; Phil Kloer, "Touched by 'The Passion,'" "*Atlanta Journal-Constitution* (9 April 2004), 1H.

11. "Ad Hoc Scholars Report."

12. Christian Scholars Group, *Facts, Faith, and Film-Making: Jesus' Passion and Its Portrayal: A Study Guide for Viewers and Reviewers* (Chestnut Hill, Mass.: 2004), http://www.bc.edu/research/cjl/meta-elements/sites/partners/csg/passion_guide.htm (accessed 2 Aug. 2009).

13. "It is the most brutally violent and simultaneously holy thing I have seen" (Steve Beard, United Methodist News Service, [24 Feb. 2004]); "a visceral contemplation of the agony of Jesus' willing sacrifice" (Stuart D. Robertson, "A View from the Pew on Gibson's *Passion*," in Garber [ed.], *Gibson's* Passion, 158); "Book research, library studies, and interviews with scholars had given me cognitive knowledge, but now my heart engaged with history as never before. . . . It wasn't until I endured the visual intensity of Gibson's film that I was able to absorb the emotional impact of the passion of Jesus" (Lee Strobel, quoted in Smith, "Living *in* the World, but Not *of* the World," 51).

14. "A sacred snuff film" (Maureen Dowd in the *New York Times*, cited in "Gibson's Passion: Few Signs Of The Kingdom Of Grace," *Catholic New Times* [21 March 2004], online at http://findarticles.com/p/articles/mi_m0MKY/is_5_28/ai_n13470858 [accessed 18 July 2009]); see also Matthew Myer Boulton, who cites *The Los Angeles Times* ("almost sadistic"), *The Boston Globe* ("obscene"), and *The New Yorker* ("a sickening death trip") in his "The Problem with *The Passion*," *Christian Century* (23 March 2004), 18. According to James F. Moore, the film is "nearly pornographic in its violence" ("Mel Gibson's *The Passion of the Christ*: A Protestant Perspective," in Garber [ed.], *Gibson's* Passion, 141), see also Björn Krondorfer, "Mel Gibson's Alter Ego: A Male Passion for Violence," *Crosscurrents* (Spring 2004), 16–21; and James Brownson, who argues that "this film is most emphatically *not* 'just

another slasher film' " ("Mel Gibson's *The Passion of the Christ*: A Theological Critique," *Perspectives: A Journal of Reformed Theology* [April 2004], online at www.rca.org/Page.aspx?pid=3297 [accessed 2 Aug. 2009]).

15. See the following articles in Garber (ed.), *Gibson's* Passion: S. Scott Bartchy, "Where is the History in Mel Gibson's *The Passion of the Christ*?" 76–92; Gordon D. Young, "History, Archaeology, and Mel Gibson's *Passion*," 70–75; and Robertson, "A View from the Pew on Gibson's *Passion*," 144–153. See also George M. Smiga, "Separating the True from the Historical: A Catholic Approach to the Passion Narratives," in Cunningham (ed.), *Pondering the Passion*, 55-64.

16. Anne Catherine Emmerich, *The Dolorous Passion of Our Lord Jesus Christ* (Rockford: 1983). According to Penny Wheeler:

> This is an account of the visions of a nineteenth-century German mystic named Anna Katharina Emmerich, an Augustinian nun. Emmerich, however, did not write this volume. The actual author was Clemens Brentano, a contemporary who sat with Sister Anna Katharina and wrote down her visions as she described them to him. ... A stigmatist is one whose meditations upon the Passion and in particular the crucifixion of Jesus has resulted in physiological phenomena—usually bleeding lesions—situated in approximately the same areas as were the wounds received by Jesus during his actual crucifixion" ("Gibson at the Crossroads," in Garber [ed.], *Gibson's* Passion, 13–14).

Gibson made use of Emmerich's visions for many of the more vivid and graphic scenes in his film—for instance, the arrest, the flagellation, and Mary's mopping up of Jesus' blood after the flagellation—for which the gospel accounts are laconic at best. See also Robertson, "A View from the Pew on Gibson's *Passion*," 157 ("that Gibson borrowed so freely from Sr. Anna Katharina Emmerich's nineteenth-century meditations on Christ's Passion does not matter to Protestants"); and James White, who, writing on a conservative Protestant blog, aired "his concerns about the presence of 'unbiblical and extraneous Marian elements' " and concluded that the film "is not nearly as accurate as we were told; it is truly a prize for Rome" (*Apologetic Blog*, Alpha and Omega Ministries, online at www.aomin.org; cited in William J. Cork, "Passionate Blogging: Interfaith Controversy and the Internet," in Landres and Berenbaum [eds.], *After* The Passion *Is Gone*, 40).

17. Boulton, "The Problem with *The Passion*," 19; Judy Yates Siker, "Anti-Judaism in the Gospels According to Matthew, Mark, Luke, John, and Mel," *Pastoral Psychology* 53:4 (March 2005), 303-312; Gordon R. Mork, "Dramatizing the Passion: From Oberammergau to Gibson," in Garber (ed.), *Gibson's* Passion, 117–123.

18. Mork, "Dramatizing the Passion: From Oberammergau to Gibson," 121; Smith, "Living *in* the World, but Not *of* the World," 51; Steve Beard, " 'Passion' Drives Home Gritty Reality of Christ's Sacrifice," *United Methodist News Service*, online at http://archives.umc.org/interior.asp?ptid=1&mid=3380 (accessed 28 July 2009).

19. James F. Moore says he "was amazed to hear so many say that when they saw the film they realized 'what Jesus really went through' " ("Mel Gibson's *The Passion of the Christ*," 141). Adrienne Alexander of Duluth, Georgia, reports that her sons Charles and Christopher stood up to accept Jesus as their savior at the end of the film: "They've always understood that he died for our sins, but the severity of the scourging is glossed over so much. ... This movie gave them more of an understanding of what Jesus Christ went through to save them" (cited in Rick Bade, "Passions Run Deep," *Atlanta Journal-Constitution* [7 March 2004]). By contrast, Laurie Goodstein reported that "an interfaith panel of eight Christian and Jewish clergy ... were in full agreement [after screening the film]: they were disturbed by what they had seen. They said the movie ... fell flat emotionally and was numbingly violent" (" 'Passion' Disturbs a Panel of Religious Leaders," *New York Times* [25 Feb. 2004]). Björn Krondorfer noted that "when I left the theatre, I was speechless and stunned. None of my students, with whom I went to see the movie, was able to talk either. Public spectacles of violence immobilize. They shock, attract, stimulate, but ultimately paralyze" ("Mel Gibson's Alter Ego," 20). Stephen T. Davis reported: "Like many viewers, I found the unremitting violence of the movie numbing"

("Crucifying Jesus: Antisemitism and the Passion Story," in Landres and Berenbaum (eds.), *After* The Passion *Is Gone*, 219–228; quotation at 226).

20. This absence of consensus is evidenced by the tendency among publishers and editors to offer anthologies of articles from a variety of commentators, rather than definitive summations of the responses; see the four collections referred to in n. 7.

21. Jeff Wells, quoted in "Area Pastors Say 'Passion' Film Could Help Fill Pews on Easter," *Houston Chronicle* (4 April 2004) ("This Week," p. 7).

22. Boulton, "The Problem with *The Passion*," 20.

23. Robertson, "A View from the Pew on Gibson's *Passion*," 158; Robertson is a Presbyterian minister and an adjunct professor in the Jewish Studies Program at Purdue University.

24. James F. Moore, "Mel Gibson's *The Passion of the Christ*: A Protestant Perspective," in Garber (ed.), *Gibson's* Passion, 140; Moore is professor of theology at Valparaiso University, a Lutheran school.

25. Edmund Schlink, *Theology of the Lutheran Confessions* (Philadelphia: 1961), 1–11; John Dillenberger and Claude Welch, *Protestant Christianity* (New York: 1954), 52–53; Bernhard Anderson, "The Bible," in *A Handbook of Christian Theology* (New York: 1958), 35–40.

26. Richard P. McBrien, *Catholicism* (Minneapolis: 1981), 64–74.

27. Schlink, *Theology of the Lutheran Confessions* 3–4.

28. Luther recounts his experience in the tower of Wittenberg's Black Cloister in the Preface to the 1545 *Complete Edition of Luther's Latin Writings*, saying,

I was raging with wild and disturbed conscience. I constantly badgered St. Paul about that spot in Romans 1 and anxiously wanted to know what he meant. I meditated night and day on those words until at last, by the mercy of God, I ... began to understand that in this verse the justice of God is that by which the just person lives by a gift of God, that is by faith. . . . All at once I felt that I had been born again and entered into paradise itself through open gates. Immediately I saw the whole of Scripture in a different light (text of quote online at www.fordham.edu/halsall/mod/1519luther-tower.html [accessed 28 July 2009]).

29. Wesley reports that his "conversion" took place on May 24, 1738 at approximately 8:45 p.m., while he was listening to the preface to Luther's *Commentary on Romans*. The "strange warming" of his heart conveyed a feeling of trust in "Christ alone, for salvation." As the renowned historian Williston Walker remarks, "of the far-reaching significance of this experience there can be little question. It determined thenceforth Wesley's estimate of the normal mode of entrance on the Christian life" (*A History of the Christian Church*, 3rd. ed. [New York: 1970], 459, where the Wesley quotation is also cited).

30. In this description, one might perceive interesting parallels between Protestant and traditional Jewish interpretation, especially as seen in responsa and in the homiletical traditions. Although the language of revelation may differ somewhat, both Protestants and Jews shy away from fixing an interpretation "in stone" at any given point in the community's life and encourage a return to the normative revelation, whether written or oral Torah (in Jewish terms), to discern through a new encounter what the meaning for a new day might be. Roman Catholicism has its own means of maintaining openness to new circumstances and flexibility in moral discernment, but the magisterium has traditionally been characterized by a more fixed set of scriptural interpretations expressed in doctrinal and dogmatic propositions that constitute the received theology of the church.

31. Meta-narratives can and do function as much for any audience member as they do for the commentators and analysts reviewed here. Indeed, many of these writers suggest fairly explicitly that a worthwhile understanding of the film is dependent on a particular meta-narrative.

Meta-narratives can function in many different genres, referring in general to any broader, longer story with which an audience member is familiar and into which the particular experience of viewing a film is fitted. It may fit as an example, as a segment, as a continuation, or as a climax of the meta-narrative, and it may be either the plot of the film or the experience of viewing the film that is related to the meta-narrative. Imagine, for example, a young girl who dreams (in her own personal meta-narrative) of one day being swept away by a handsome young man who will love her, provide for her every need, and rescue her from a life of insignificance. She is likely to view *Cinderella* as a confirmation of her hope and as encouragement to await her "Prince Charming." By contrast, a social critic who is familiar with the disempowering role of fairy tales in women's experience will see *Cinderella* quite differently. For the critic, it will be one more installment in a long line of toxic influences from which young girls should be protected, lest their capacities for self-assertion and autonomous responsibility be undermined.

32. Jeffrey S. Siker, "Theologizing the Death of Jesus, Gibson's *The Passion*, and Christian Identity," in Landres and Berenbaum (eds.), *After* The Passion *Is Gone*, 137.

33. Ibid., 139.

34. Stephen T. Davis, "Crucifying Jesus: Antisemitism and the Passion Story," 219–228.

35. Stephen R. Haynes, "A March of Passion; or, How I Came to Terms with a Film I Wasn't Supposed to Like," in Landres and Berenbaum (eds.), *After* The Passion *Is Gone*, 193–204.

36. Ibid., 203–204.

37. Consultative Panel on Lutheran-Jewish Relations, *"The Passion of the Christ"* (see n. 10).

38. D. Andrew Kille, "More Reel than Real: Mel Gibson's *The Passion of the Christ*," *Pastoral Psychology* 53, no. 4 (March 2005), 341–350; quotation on 341–342.

39. Ibid., 343.

40. Mary C. Boys, "Educating for a Faith that Feels *and* Thinks," in Cunningham (ed.), *Pondering the Passion*, 186.

41. John Hull, quoted in ibid.

42. Ibid., 187.

43. Kille, "More Reel than Real," 341.

44. Quoted in article by Phil Kloer, "Touched by 'The Passion,'" *Atlanta Journal-Constitution* (9 April 2004), Features 1H.

45. Lee Strobel and Garry Poole, *Experiencing the Passion of Jesus* (Grand Rapids: 2004), 5–6, cited in Smith, "Living *in* the World, but Not *of* the World," 51.

46. Smith, "Living *in* the World, but Not *of* the World," 51.

47. James M. Wall, "Gibson's Gospel," *Christian Century* (6 April 2004), 69.

48. Mark Juergensmeyer, "Afterword: The Passion of War," in Landres and Berenbaum (eds.), *After* The Passion *Is Gone*, 279–287; quotations on 286; "cosmic war" description on 285–286.

49. Cited in Kille, "More Reel than Real," 343–344.

50. Siker, "Theologizing the Death of Jesus, Gibson's *The Passion*, and Christian Identity," 146.

51. Kille, "More Reel than Real," 343–344. This judgment, which is repeated by numerous other commentators, points to the "informed" community as the most likely to understand and respond to the film. Interestingly, when questioned about his intended audience, "'the church or the unchurched,' Gibson replied, 'Oh, that's easy, the unchurched'" (quoted in Smith, "Living *in* the World, but Not *of* the World," 47).

52. Leonard Pitts, Jr., "Violence Aside, 'Passion' Reveals Christ's Message," *The Houston Chronicle* (1 March 2004).

53. Daniel C. Harlow, "How Has Mel Offended? In Praise of *The Passion of the Christ*," *Perspectives: A Journal of Reformed Thought* (April 2004); online at www.rca.org/Page.aspx?pid=3296 (accessed 28 July 2009).

54. Larry M. Goodpaster, "Brutal 'Passion' Worth Seeing, Discussing," *United Methodist News Service*, online at http://archives.umc.org/interior.asp?ptid=1&mid=3556 (accessed 28 July 2009).

55. Ibid.

56. Ibid.

57. See David Morgan's essay, "Manly Pain and Motherly Love," in Landres and Berenbaum (eds.), *After* The Passion *Is Gone*, 149–157, where the wide-ranging social and historical analysis moves well outside the orbit of these three themes. However, Morgan, too, fits the film and its imagery into several meta-narratives from American religious history.

58. Harlow, "How Has Mel Offended?"

59. Ibid.

60. Juergensmeyer, "Afterword," 280.
61. Ibid.
62. Smith, "Living *in* the World, but Not *of* the World," 54–55.
63. Cited in ibid., 55. Focus on the Family was founded by Dobson in 1977. According to its website, its mission is to "cooperate with the Holy Spirit in sharing the gospel of Jesus Christ with as many people as possible by nurturing and defending the God-ordained institution of the family and promoting biblical truths worldwide" (www.focusonthefamily.com/about_us.aspx [accessed 25 May 2009]).
64. Cited in Smith, "Living *in* the World, but Not *of* the World," 55.
65. Marian Ronan, "Mel Gibson's *Passion* and the Many Uses of Christ's Suffering," *Pastoral Psychology* 53, no. 4 (March 2005), 379.
66. John M. Buchanan, "Another Take," *Christian Century* (23 March 2004), 3.
67. Harlow, "How Has Mel Offended?"
68. Tammi Reed Ledbetter, "Critics Seek Changes in 'Anti-Jewish' Mel Gibson Film," www.crosswalk.com/news/religiontoday/1216893.html (accessed 28 July 2009).
69. Laird J. Stuart, "Reflections on *The Passion of the Christ*," *Pastoral Psychology* 53, no. 4 (March 2005), 381–382. For a thorough analysis of the passion play heritage and its relevance for analyzing the Gibson film, see Karen Jo Torjesen, "The Journey of the Passion Play from Medieval Piety to Contemporary Spirituality," in Landres and Berenbaum (eds.), *After The Passion Is Gone*, 93–104.
70. Christopher Hitchens, "Schlock, Yes; Awe, No; Fascism, Probably," *Slate* (27 Feb. 2004), online at www.slate.com/id/2096323 (accessed 15 July 2009).
71. Robertson, "A View from the Pew on Gibson's *Passion*," 155. A measure of that "fermentation" was taken by David I. Kertzer, an anthropologist at Brown University, even before the Gibson film was announced ("The Modern Use of Ancient Lies," *New York Times* [9 May 2005]). Regarding the film itself, something of what "remained to be seen" became clear when "a top Shiite cleric ... urged Kuwait to let Mel Gibson's film *The Passion of the Christ* be shown in this conservative state because it 'reveals crimes committed by Jews against Christ'"(reported in the *Journal and Courier* [Lafayette, Ind.] [28 March 2004], 3; cited in Young, "History, Archaeology, and Mel Gibson's *Passion*," 73).
72. Moore, "Mel Gibson's *The Passion of the Christ*," 141–142. In Moore's telling of the story, it should be noted, the cross has a place only as "the political/moral image of resistance" rather than as the locus of salvific suffering; what is redemptive is the act of resisting evil and rescuing those who are suffering. From this it follows that there is no real point to the killing of Jesus, other than to illustrate the ultimate cost of the resistance to evil. Moore's argument stands in clear contrast to Gibson's theology, as reported by Jeffrey Siker, that "Jesus lived in order to die ... as an atoning sacrifice" ("Theologizing the Death of Jesus, Gibson's *The Passion*, and Christian Identity," 145). Moore rejects this meta-narrative because it affords no basis for giving meaning to the suffering of Jewish genocide victims (which, he believes, must be a constitutive element in any post-Holocaust reading of the Passion), and he considers Gibson's film "nearly pornographic in its violence" ("Mel Gibson's *Passion of the Christ*," 141).
73. None of the Protestant commentators or the communities they represent can be shown to have initiated significant changes in either practice or belief as a result of the film. Rather, the film more or less briefly played into various groups' meta-narratives and allowed them a vehicle to carry their message to a wider public.
74. "The portrayal of the person and mission of Jesus is partial and skewed" ("Ad Hoc Scholars Report," section II.B: 4); Stuart, "Reflections on *The Passion of the Christ*," 383; Harlow, "How Has Mel Offended?"; Laurie Goodstein, " 'Passion' Disturbs a Panel of Religious Leaders."
75. According to James Brownson: "My hunch is that it is precisely this film's ambiguity that makes it such a vehicle for controversy" ("Mel Gibson's *The Passion of the Christ*"). See also Bartchy, "Where is the History in Mel Gibson's *The Passion of the Christ*?" 80.
76. For a detailed account of the divestment initiative and its fallout, see the essay by Christopher M. Leighton in this volume, "The Presbyterian-Jewish Impasse," esp. 116–119.

77. Some of the meta-narratives that helped to shape the understanding of the Gibson film, particularly those that posited Christian victimization and the ultimate vindication of Christian experience, could also generate meaning from the juxtaposition of the film and the divestment controversy. That story might read something like this: an energized Christian community, experiencing the vicarious vindication that came from the Gibson film's remarkable commercial success, embarked on a much more aggressive course of action in relation to perceived injustices perpetrated by the Jewish state.

The Attitude of the World Council of Churches (WCC) toward the Israeli-Palestinian Conflict

Haim Genizi
(BAR-ILAN UNIVERSITY)

The World Council of Churches (WCC), an umbrella organization for the major Protestant and Orthodox Christian denominations in the world, was established in September 1948 both in order to promote understanding and cooperation among its member churches and to highlight the ethical demands of the gospel in a worldwide setting. Its main objects are unity and the renewal of the Christian spirit, and it provides a forum through which its members may work, talk, and pray together in a spirit of tolerance and understanding. Headquartered in Geneva, its most important body is the assembly, which appoints a Central Committee consisting of 120 members (an executive committee of 12 individuals conducts day-to-day operations). Although it comprises 349 member churches based in more than a hundred countries, it is not an all-encompassing organization—the Roman Catholic Church, the Southern Baptists in the United States, and some evangelical churches have chosen not to join.

Insisting on "peace, justice, and the integrity of creation," the WCC, since its establishment, has supported the Jewish people and their right to a state of their own. However, because of deep-seated theological ambivalence on the part of some member churches with regard to Judaism and the Jews, the WCC has demonstrated an equivocal attitude toward Israel. Equally significant is the fact that, as an international organization, the WCC is committed to political and social causes, including support for national liberation movements and the human rights of oppressed minorities. Consequently, it has been particularly subject to influences and pressures from religious and political forces in Asia and Africa, which are different from those in the West.

A combination of several powerful factors has led to the gradual formulation of a sympathetic (and arguably one-sided) approach toward the Arab cause in the Middle East. Among these factors are the aforementioned anti-Jewish theological traditions; the influence both of missionary groups operating in Arab countries and of Protestant churches in the Middle East that are dominated by Arab clergy; the plight of Palestinian refugees, deprived almost everywhere of their human rights; and finally, the decision by the Palestine Liberation Organization (PLO) to declare its aim for a just peace and self-determination, in the form of an independent state. At the same time, there are several important factors exerting countervailing pressure—among them, the sensitivity to Jewish opinion in the light of the Holocaust and the concomitant necessity to condemn antisemitism; the aspiration for interfaith dialogue with the Jews; and the active support for Israel by several evangelical churches. In response to these varied factors, the WCC has repeatedly called for a comprehensive peace that would assure the rights and security of both Israel and the Palestinian people.

The Arab-Israeli question came up at the first assembly of the WCC, held in Amsterdam in September 1948. A resolution from that assembly reads as follows:

> The establishment of the state "Israel" adds a political dimension to the Christian approach to the Jews and threatens to complicate anti-Semitism with political fears and animosities. On the political aspects of the Palestine problem and the complex of "rights" involved, we do not undertake to express a judgment.[1]

The WCC called upon nations to treat the "Palestine problem" not as a political issue, but rather "as a moral and spiritual question that touches a nerve center of the world's religions." This neutral position was the outcome of a compromise between the missionary groups, which were hostile to the Zionist idea, and the West European church representatives, who supported the necessity of a haven for Jewish survivors of the Holocaust. At the time, Arab influence in the WCC was marginal.[2] However, at its second assembly, held in Evanston, Illinois in 1954, a coalition of representatives from Arab and Asian countries, as well as from the United States, was able to prevent any reference to Israel as a political entity. The heated debate on Jewish nationalism demonstrated how difficult it was for the Protestant world to confront the theological implications inherent in the establishment of a modern Jewish state.[3]

In contrast, humanitarian issues—namely, those regarding Palestinian refugees—were easier to deal with. In May 1951, the WCC served as co-sponsor (together with the International Missionary Council) of a conference held in Beirut on the Arab refugee problem. The conference dealt mainly with the issue of relief work for the refugees. It was agreed that the Near East Christian Council (NECC) would be responsible for coordination of the aid; that the WCC would pay for administrative expenses; and that American churches would cover the operational costs.

The conference also confronted the problem of priorities: should the stress be put on welfare projects or on political action—that is, supporting repatriation efforts? Dr. Elfan Rees, a British clergyman and an expert on refugee problems who was serving as a consultant to the Commission of the Churches on International Affairs, reported his findings about a tour he had made in Arab refugee camps. His contention was that their miserable condition was caused by the refusal of the Arab host countries to help them. He called for international financial backing for the integration of refugees into neighboring Arab states, maintaining that the refugees would be absorbed in Muslim and Arabic-speaking societies more easily than in Israel. In the end, the following resolution was approved:

Palestinian refugees are the victims of a catastrophe for which they themselves are not responsible. A deep injustice has been inflicted upon them. ... We are convinced that there can be no permanent solution of the problem of the Palestinian refugees until there is a settlement of the outstanding political differences between the Arab states and Israel. Churches are not competent to lay down the lines of a political solution. ... A careful appraisal of the total situation has compelled us to conclude ... that many Palestinian refugees will have to settle in new homes.[4]

Eight years later, the gradual rise of Arab nationalism, the growing influence of the Arab-dominated Middle Eastern Protestant churches, and American missionary influence were evident when the WCC rejected Rees' proposed program for the integration of Palestinian refugees into Arab host countries. The WCC now preferred to emphasize the political aspect of the problem and to press Israel to agree to repatriation: in real terms, this meant relegating humanitarian solutions to second place.[5]

The Six-Day War of 1967 was a turning point that led to heightened animosity toward Israel in certain church circles. The Israeli occupation of East Jerusalem, the West Bank, and Gaza, along with the significant growth in the number of Palestinian refugees (which was increasingly becoming an international, rather than a local issue) turned many church members away from a sympathetic or even a neutral position vis-à-vis the Jewish state. Israel's speedy victory also went against a long-entrenched image of the Jews as underdogs: in the eyes of many, David had become a Goliath. As a result of all these factors, the WCC became increasingly critical of Israel.

In part, this response reflected the growth of national liberation movements during the 1960s. The WCC was determined, as a matter of ideology, to fight colonial oppression and white racist regimes; from a pragmatic point of view, such a stance also ensured support from the emerging Third World countries.[6] To be sure, the financial help given by the WCC to a number of liberation movements—among them the Rhodesian Patriotic Front, for the purpose of purchasing weapons—met with some criticism in church circles. This support was provided during the 1970s, and by the end of the decade there were a number of critics who argued that the Council was "controlled by radical, even revolutionary elements" in the Third World.[7]

The shifting policy of the WCC with regard to Israel is apparent in two statements on the Middle East that were adopted in the period following the Six-Day War. The first was issued in Heraklion (Crete) on August 23, 1967, in which the Central Committee of the WCC called for "a just and durable peace." Although the WCC refrained from entering into the details of a political settlement, it did outline some elements essential "to any peace founded upon justice and recognition of the equality of all peoples in the region." It deplored the occupation of the conquered territories, demanded the withdrawal of Israeli forces, and proposed effective international guarantees for "the political independence and territorial integrity" of all nations, including Israel and the Arab states. It also called for the repatriation of refugees who had fled during the recent war. Further, the committee demanded free access to all religious sites and advocated an end to the arms race. The great powers were held responsible for providing political and economic leadership for the welfare of the whole region.[8] Missing from the statement was any criticism of Egyptian president Gamal abd al-Nasser, whose actions (expelling U.N. forces from Sinai and blocking the

Straits of Tiran) had triggered the hostilities, or any mention of the Arab states' refusal to alleviate the situation of the refugees residing in their countries.

Two years later came a more revolutionary statement that became the basis for all subsequent WCC Middle East policies. Issued in Canterbury in August 1969, the statement declared that,

> in supporting the establishment of a Jewish State in Palestine, without recognizing the rights of the Palestinians to self-determination, the Great Powers have done an injustice to the Palestinian Arabs, and this injustice should be redressed.
>
> No lasting peace is possible without respecting the legitimate rights of the Palestinian and Jewish people presently living in the area and without effective international guarantee for the political independence and territorial integrity of all nations in the area, including Israel.[9]

Whereas the previous resolutions had characterized the Palestinians as "refugees" who should be helped and repatriated, the Canterbury statement emphasized the "legitimate rights" of the Palestinians for "self-determination" and "political independence." By adopting the Palestinian demand for an independent state, the WCC became a major sponsor of the Arab cause; the expectation was that Protestant churches worldwide would follow the same policy. The *Oikoumene*, the quarterly newsletter of the WCC, reported in December 1970 that the Canterbury declaration "aroused on the Jewish side, especially in Anglo-Saxon countries, a surprise not far removed from scandal."[10]

In September 1969, a "consultation on the refugee problem" took place in Nicosia. The prevailing atmosphere and resolutions adopted at this gathering were different from those of two previous conferences held in Beirut, where a majority of the delegates had hailed from western countries. In Nicosia, the majority of the delegates were Arabs (including Palestinians) who were members of the Middle Eastern churches. Accordingly, what had previously been an ambivalent approach gave way to clearly pro-Arab positions. A political approach was now emphasized rather than programs of relief and rehabilitation, which were not considered an appropriate response to the Palestinians' aspirations for self-determination and nationhood. As one of the resolutions declared: "We consider it our duty to call upon the churches of the world to use all their influence towards a just solution involving necessarily the recognition of the rights of the Palestinians." Among other things, this meant that churches should exert influence on their respective governments to intervene in the United Nations on behalf of the refugees; they were also asked to "promote an informed Christian discussion on the Palestine question."[11] The Nicosia decisions caused "very understandable annoyance to leaders of Jewish organizations." The WCC was caught in a dilemma, as was explained in the organization's newsletter:

> In spite of the WCC's desire for justice and their will to be impartial, these various declarations encouraged the belief that in considering the Palestinian conflict the WCC was unduly influenced by the Arab Churches and had taken up a unilateral position. It would even appear that Palestinian organizations took advantage of the presence of these churches at the Council to use it for purposes of propaganda.[12]

Clearly, the Council's efforts to play an impartial role were being subverted by the Arab-dominated Middle Eastern churches. This was apparent as well after the outbreak of the Yom Kippur War in October 1973, when the WCC's general secretary, Philip Potter, called for a stronger role for the U.N. in the Middle East, warning world powers against the dangers of military intervention.[13]

A rare exception to the WCC's generally hostile posture vis-à-vis Israel was its "unequivocal opposition" to the U.N. resolution equating Zionism with racism. In November 1975, Potter expressed his organization's "deep concern" about this resolution, stating that "Zionism has historically been a movement concerned with the liberation of the Jewish people from oppression, including racial oppression" and warning that the resolution had the "seriously damaging effect of exacerbating the already explosive situation in the Middle East." Potter, therefore, appealed to the General Assembly of the U.N. "to reconsider and rescind this resolution," though he also called upon the parties involved in the Middle East crisis to find ways "to enable the Palestinian people to achieve their legitimate rights to nationhood and statehood."[14]

In sharp contrast to its stance with regard to the Israeli-Palestinian conflict, the WCC developed a more positive approach to the Jewish people and to Judaism. At the time of its establishment in 1948, the organization went on record as condemning antisemitism, and over the years it has persistently called on its member churches to combat prejudice and anti-Jewish hostility. Beginning in 1962, the WCC received a number of requests from Jewish leaders to set up Jewish-Christian consultation groups. Informal meetings gradually assumed a more official character, culminating in 1970 in the establishment of a top-level group comprising representatives of the WCC and the International Jewish Committee on Interreligious Consultations (IJCIC). Consultations between Christian and Jewish leaders became an ongoing concern, and frequent meetings continue to take place, providing an opportunity to discuss non-theological subjects such as racism in Africa, human rights in the Soviet Union (a subject of particular interest during the 1970s and 1980s) and social justice.

For several years after its establishment, the WCC refrained from sponsoring discussions regarding the Middle East crisis or the theological meaning of the Jewish state, since these issues aroused considerable disagreement even among member churches. Between 1971 and 1974, however, the WCC took the bull by the horns, sponsoring study groups on "Biblical interpretation and its bearing on Christian attitudes regarding the Middle East." It was the first time the WCC had sought to bring a range of Christian denominations from different theological and geographical backgrounds into a serious evaluation of the Middle East crisis, and the results were summarized by Franz von Hammerstein of the WCC as "a promising if sometimes difficult exercise in inter-Christian communication.... Christians from different continents, such as Africa or Asia, as well as Christians from oriental or Orthodox churches, continue to disagree strongly with Christians from Europe and North America."[15] Among other things, he noted, church leaders in the Third World perceived Israel as a creation of 19th-century European imperialism, and thus regarded it as a colonialist nation.[16] Consequently, the WCC as an umbrella organization was compelled to take a middle line, attempting to bridge over the opposing positions of its member churches.

In its biennial consultation in June 1975, the WCC's Committee on the Church and the Jewish people criticized the Council's position with regard to the Middle East conflict. Members of the committee, all of them Christians, declared that statements on the Arab-Israeli crisis made by various church organizations "were not always balanced as between Jews and Arab Palestinians, and it was urged that much greater care should be taken in future to achieve a fair representation of the conflicting views."[17] In February 1976, representatives of the WCC and IJCIC decided to "engage in wider patterns of relationship in the future." A liaison committee was established in order to further mutual understanding, "help combat prejudice, prevent misconceptions and permit both faiths to improve conditions for living together."[18] The dialogue process helped to clarify some misunderstandings and created a more positive atmosphere. Or, as von Hammerstein put it in an optimistic report: "We want to go ahead informing each other on mutual developments, including difficulties, studying together important aspects of our faiths, working together where it is possible for the benefit of mankind."[19]

Despite appeals for a more balanced approach toward the Israel-Palestinian conflict, the course of the WCC did not appear to change. Its decisions on Jerusalem were a case in point. Israel's conquest of East Jerusalem in 1967 had roused strong resentment in a variety of Christian circles. What bothered them was not the fact that non-Christians ruled the Holy City; Jerusalem under Muslim control had proven to be acceptable to them. It was, rather, the incongruity of a Jewish military victory on such a large scale that caused disquiet, as this did not accord with deep-rooted Christian preconceptions of the Jews as underdogs.

On several occasions WCC bodies issued statements concerning Jerusalem.[20] Since Jerusalem was a holy city to the three religions, the organization declared that its importance to any religion should not be minimized. In 1980, for instance, the Central Committee criticized the Israeli government's unilateral proclamation declaring united Jerusalem to be the nation's capital. It urged a dialogue between the three religions, hoping that this might lead to a "mutually acceptable agreement for sharing the city."[21] Three years later, at the WCC's sixth assembly, held in Vancouver, the organization appealed to its member churches to maintain a Christian presence in Jerusalem and to increase ecumenical interest in the fate of the Muslim and Christian communities "suffering from the repressive actions of the occupying power." Although Israeli law guaranteed free access to holy sites, the war and political reality had created "serious difficulties and [Christians] are often prevented from visiting the Holy City." The Vancouver declaration insisted that the "status quo of the Holy Places must be safeguarded and confirmed"; at the same time, the demand for the internationalization of Jerusalem was dropped.[22]

Events in the Middle East between 1982 and 1992 exerted a clear impact on the WCC position toward the region. The beginning of the period saw the Israeli invasion of Lebanon and the continuing occupation of the southern part of that country; Arab terrorist activities and Israeli retaliations; and the emergence of the Palestine Liberation Organization (PLO) as the widely recognized representative of the Palestinians. In December 1987, the intifada, the civil uprising of the Palestinians, began, and Israeli measures to suppress it quickly followed. All these events sharpened the World Council's criticism of Israel's policies. Thus, the Vancouver assembly of the WCC, going beyond the specific issue of Jerusalem, adopted a statement that strongly attacked Israel. The Lebanon war and the continuing occupation of the West Bank and Gaza, it declared, created a dangerous situation that "threatens the peace of the whole world"; hence the churches had a responsibility to intervene. The statement also blamed Christians who "uncritically supported Israel" because of their guilt over the fate of the Jews at the hands of Christians through the centuries, thereby "ignoring the plight of the Palestinians." It accused Israel of "flagrantly" violating the basic rights of the Palestinians, expelling, relocating and imprisoning them, and it called upon the U.N. to revise Resolution 242 in light of changes that had occurred since 1967, upholding "the rights of the Palestinians to self determination including the right of establishing a sovereign Palestinian state." The statement also demanded the inclusion of the PLO in negotiations for a peaceful settlement. The WCC called upon its member churches to increase their awareness of the fate of the Palestinians, to encourage dialogue between Palestinians and Israelis, and to support peace movements in Israel.[23]

The Vancouver resolutions served as the basic document for the Christian-Arab dialogue initiated in Canada in 1983 between the Canadian Council of Churches, the Anglican Church of Canada, and the Canadian Arab Federation.[24] The continued war in Lebanon, which brought great suffering to the Lebanese people, caused "deep concern" to the WCC. From time to time the Central Committee issued statements in which it expressed sympathy for the Lebanese and demanded the immediate cessation of hostilities and the withdrawal of foreign forces. It also expressed appreciation for the work done by the Middle East Council of Churches, and called upon the churches to continue their financial support for the churches in Lebanon. Although Israel was not mentioned specifically in these communiqués, it was implicitly included in the phrase "the withdrawal of foreign forces." Furthermore, the connection between Lebanon and the Palestine issue was always made. The invasion of Lebanon surely taught Israel that no solution could be achieved by the use of force, maintained Ghassan Rubeiz, secretary of the WCC's Middle East Commission on Inter-Church Aid, Refugee and World Service.[25]

The intifada, which began in December 1987 in Gaza and later spread to the West Bank, increased world sympathy for the plight of the Palestinians. Children throwing stones at armed soldiers provided TV news with sensational footage. Summarizing world opinion, Rubeiz of the WCC wrote: "The psychology of today's events shows that the Palestinian question is more powerful when it portrays the Palestinians as militarily weak and morally strong. Rock throwing is very symbolic as a strategy of the victim facing colonials."[26] Indeed, for five long years Israel confronted the difficult—almost impossible—task of handling the civil uprising. Its efforts to suppress the unrest by military means were far from successful, attracting harsh criticism not only from abroad but from within Israel itself. The WCC recognized the intifada as "a genuine expression of the national aspiration of the Palestinian people," and it protested the violations of human rights and the closing of schools and colleges in the territories. Only a peaceful solution, it maintained, could stop bloodshed, and the WCC therefore strongly supported the idea of convening an international peace conference. The Central Committee expressed its solidarity with the Christian churches in the region that were suffering, particularly those in Jerusalem. It demanded that Israel dismantle Jewish settlements in the occupied territories and avoid establishing new ones.[27]

On November 15, 1988, the Palestine National Council, the umbrella organization of the various Palestinian groups, issued both a declaration of independence and a political statement that emphasized the urgent need for an effective international peace conference under U.N. auspices. Emilio Castro, general secretary of the WCC, welcomed the declaration and expressed "appreciation for the positive spirit" it demonstrated. He pointed out that the political statement of the Palestinians was "very much along the lines taken by the WCC" and regarded the occasion as "a decisive moment for the Middle East, offering a unique opportunity for peace-making."[28]

The presentation made by the WCC before the U.N. Commission on Human Rights in February 1989 may be considered a faithful summary of the Council's position on the Middle East crisis. Rubeiz opened his oral presentation by declaring that the WCC was "a friend of the peoples of Palestine and Israel," and that peace could be attained only by the recognition of their "legitimate aspirations." He reiterated the WCC's position that the Israeli occupation was "unlawful and must terminate to allow for the establishment of a Palestinian state neighboring to the state of Israel." The suppression of the civil uprising was "morally unacceptable and in contravention of the Geneva 1949 Conventions," whereas Yassir Arafat's implicit recognition of Israel as a neighboring state was "a new sign of the changing times." Rubeiz added:

> Solutions based on greed, on simplistic understanding of history and on exclusive theology, have proven to receive decreasing support from the international community. This year ought to be the year of a major breakthrough in peace making. The Palestinians have made significant initiatives, which deserve positive reciprocation from the side of Israel.

To Israel, he advised an "exchange of land for peace"; to the Arabs he recommended "creative thinking." Israel was considered strong enough to take some risk in making peace. The WCC, concluded Rubeiz, was calling for the convening of an international peace conference under U.N. auspices with PLO participation.[29]

From the mid-1990s, the WCC intensified its concern with regard to Jerusalem as a "key to peace in the wider region," appealing for its recognition as a "shared city" for Christians, Jews, and Muslims. The heads of the Jerusalem churches insisted on a plan to establish "a shared and open Jerusalem, which respects the rights and sovereignty of the three religions and two peoples." The WCC also deplored the deterioration of security in the Holy City and the "discriminatory practices against Palestinians," which, in its view, forced Christians to leave the country.[30] The appeal of the Jerusalem church leaders "to help bring an urgent conclusion to the conflict affecting the lives of thousands in this land" obviously affected the WCC's position. Church leaders complained about intensified violence in the city and "respectfully request[ed] protection for all our people" as well as asking churches abroad to help those in need in the region, since "many are desperate for food, clothing, shelter and the like."[31]

With the failure of the Camp David peace conference in 2000; with (what a WCC source called) the "provocative visit" of Ariel Sharon to the Temple Mount, and with the "resulting second Palestinian uprising," the Council increased its campaign for international protection of Christian churches in Jerusalem. In February 2001, the

Central Committee called on the WCC's general secretary, Conrad Reiser, to make greater efforts "towards a negotiated peace in the Middle East, based on international law, paying special attention to the future status of Jerusalem."[32] In addition to the Jerusalem church leaders, the Middle East Council of Churches (MECC)—representing the major Christian churches in the Middle East—exerted an important influence on the WCC's attitude toward the Israeli-Palestinian conflict. The General Secretariat of the MECC declared that it "sympathizes with the events in the Occupied Palestinian Territories ... and condemns Israeli practices ... rang[ing] from infractions of holy sites, [and] indiscriminate shootings of Palestinians, to threats of war and use of violence. The violation of human rights, the adoption of apartheid and the dissection of towns and villages from one another all contribute to a worsening of economic, health and educational conditions." What was needed to accomplish a just peace, in the view of the MECC, was unity among the Palestinians, coupled with the right of self-determination and the right of refugees to return to their former homes.[33]

The outbreak of the second intifada in 2000 led to intense activity in WCC circles. On October 10, 2000, Reiser sent a letter of support to U.N. General Secretary Kofi Annan in the wake of a U.N. Security Council session, convened by Annan, that had called for an immediate cessation of violence and the return to negotiations. Although Reiser acknowledged that "both sides have suffered from this renewed violent confrontation," he accepted the Security Council's statement that "this wave of violent confrontation was set off by a provocative act in Jerusalem."[34] (The charge that the violence was caused by Sharon's visit to the Temple Mount was denied by Israel, which put the blame on what it claimed was Arafat's decision to launch a renewed and armed uprising.)

On February 5, 2001, the WCC's Central Committee declared its "grave concern" over the renewed violence in Israel:

> We share the frustration and disappointments of our Palestinian sisters and brothers. We are deeply disturbed by and deplore a pattern of discrimination, routine humiliation, segregation and exclusion which restricts Palestinian freedom of movement, including access to the holy sites, and the disproportionate use of military force by Israel, the denial of access to timely medical assistance [and] the destruction of property.

The Council called on its member churches "to increase their efforts to condemn injustice and all forms of discrimination, to end Israeli occupation, [and] to pray for and promote a comprehensive and just peace in the Middle East."[35] A negotiated peace, declared the WCC, should be based on the right of return of the Palestinians; the dismantlement of Israeli settlements; the enforcement of all U.N. resolutions; and the withdrawal of Israeli forces from all occupied territories. The statement likewise insisted that peace-loving forces in Israel and among the Palestinians should be provided with broad international support.[36] Clearly, the position of the WCC at this stage perfectly matched that of the MECC, which was dominated by Arab clergy.

To prepare a detailed peace plan, an ecumenical delegation was sent to the region in 2001 with a mandate to report its findings, advise on strategies, and suggest a program of action to the upcoming international ecumenical consultation. The 12 high-ranking members of the delegation met with a group of individuals ranging from

Israeli government officials to Hezbollah activists and found themselves impressed by both the miserable conditions of the Palestinians and the complexity of the political problems. However, as the representative of the Methodist church in Ireland noted: "There were voices which the delegation had not heard and the delegation made no claim to understand fully the life of the region or offer solutions to its serious and urgent problems."[37] In accordance with recommendations of the delegation that were reviewed by the international consultation, including the member churches in Jerusalem, the WCC decided to focus on "coordinated action and advocacy: on an Ecumenical campaign to end the illegal occupation of Palestine; [on] support [for] a just peace in the Middle East and on an Ecumenical Accompaniment Programme in Palestine and Israel."[38] Member churches of the WCC followed up with a joint letter sent on April 10, 2002 to the president of the United Nations Security Council.

In this letter, the Security Council was urged to take action "to deploy observers to monitor compliance with human rights and international humanitarian law standards." The Israeli occupation, it noted, could be ended only by the withdrawal of the Israeli forces, as stated by Security Council Resolution 242. However, in the 35 years since this resolution, the Security Council had failed to take effective steps to carry out this resolution; during this time, the violations of human rights by the Israeli army had been growing in number. Quite exceptionally, the letter referred as well to Israeli victims of terrorism, though here, too, the language remained critical of Israel: "The occupation has also given rise to growing Palestinian violence, including suicide bombings against innocent Israeli citizens, resulting in many tragic deaths and injuries. Such violence directed against Israeli citizens, while abhorrent, does not justify the occupation which gives rise to such acts nor the misguided incursions and assaults now under way in response to them."[39] The WCC asked the Security Council "to promote a cease-fire and to explore immediate steps towards a resolution, based on two sovereign states, enjoying full recognition and peaceful relations with their neighbors."[40]

Another step taken by the WCC, in 2005, was to encourage its members to consider "economic measures that are equitable, transparent and non-violent as a new way to work for peace, by looking at ways to not participate economically in illegal activities related to the Israeli occupation."[41] It sought, in other words, a boycott on Israeli products originating in the occupied territories. In addition, seeking to enlist worldwide support for the Palestinian cause, the WCC invited international agencies to a special meeting in March 2006, urging them "to participate in the worldwide week of Christian advocacy for a just peace." Since the situation was worsening and there were no current openings for peace,

> it is crucial for Christians to make their voices heard vigorously in the public arena.... Lawmakers and politicians in your country need to know that the churches are well aware of the on-going suffering caused by the Occupation and the subsequent insecurity and are becoming even more actively involved in seeking a just peace.

Church leaders of Jerusalem appealed to member churches around the world to arouse the concern of lawmakers in their respective countries regarding the Palestinian issue. They complained that, despite the unilateral withdrawal of Israeli forces from the Gaza Strip in August 2005, the situation in the West Bank and Jerusalem had deteriorated. Therefore, members of the WCC were asked to hold services in solidarity with the Palestinian Christians on March 12, 2006 in order "to launch the International Church Action for Peace in Palestine and Israel and lift up the Christian voice for a just peace."[42]

Continuing this forceful line, the Executive Committee of the WCC issued a statement titled "The Time Is Ripe to Do What Is Right." In its meeting in Geneva in May 2006, it reached the conclusion that "Peace must come soon or it may not come to either people for a long time." After noting the suffering of the Palestinians and the unacceptable actions of the Israelis, including the isolation of the legitimately elected Hamas leaders, the Committee called on the churches to speak out from a moral and ethical point of view. The Israeli actions, it stated, "cannot be justified morally, legally or even politically." It urged the international community to establish contact with Hamas, and it called for the renewal of peace negotiations based on U.N. resolutions, along with the recognition of the pre-June 1967 borders. It also appealed to the Middle East "Quartet" (the United States, Russia, the European Union, and the U.N.) to let Hamas, as the newly elected Palestinian authority, assert its control. Furthermore, it appealed to the Quartet and the U.N. "to exercise even-handedness when dealing with the conflict," implying that this body could be expected to support the Israeli side.[43]

The outbreak of the Second Lebanon War in July 2006 aroused the WCC to intensive action. In addition to appealing to the U.N. Security Council and to the international community generally, it issued its own statements. For instance, the WCC's general secretary, Samuel Kobia, wrote to members of the Security Council on July 21, 2006, while the fighting was still on, that the war in Lebanon presented a "critical opportunity." Describing the suffering both of the people of Lebanon and of the "citizens of Israel [who] fear death from the sky," he argued that "it is time to demonstrate the unique potential of the Security Council to bring peace. Joint and conclusive action is necessary." Kobia linked the Palestinian problem to the Lebanese issue, stressing that parallel to the tragedy in Lebanon, the "residents of Gaza mourn new losses day after day," and he demanded that multinational forces be deployed not only in Lebanon but also in Gaza. He also appealed to members of the Security Council to implement all of the U.N. resolutions regarding peace, both in Lebanon and in the occupied territories, and he noted that the WCC was urging the release of all Palestinian prisoners held in Israel.[44]

In a different message, Kobia appealed to the international community, mainly the United States, Great Britain, and Israel, to stop the bombing, reach a ceasefire and negotiate a comprehensive peace. The letter concluded with a prayer for the Christians and Muslims in Lebanon, and for the people of Israel, "who have fallen victims to the missiles that continue to be fired indiscriminately into their towns and villages."[45] In his report to the WCC's Central Committee on August 30-September 6, 2006, Kobia suggested the establishment of a "Palestine-Israel Ecumenical Forum" with the aim of providing "a space for coordination of advocacy based on moral and theological principles and [for] translat[ing] recommendations into actions that influence the political process." He demanded "deeper engagement" in confronting such difficult issues as the right of return and the establishment of final borders between Israel and the Palestinian state. Kobia insisted that the proposed forum could mobilize "our collective energies and resources." One of the participants in the Central Committee meeting, Jean-Arnold de Clermont, president of the Conference of European Churches, pleaded: "Do not remain content with praying. Do something!" The proposed program of the Middle East forum indicated that the WCC put the Middle East very high on its list of priorities.[46] In its "Statement on the War in Lebanon and Northern Israel, and Ecumenical Action for Middle East Peace," the Central Committee publicized the decisions adopted at its meeting —namely, the call for an unconditional ceasefire; the demand that the U.N. establish an international inquiry to investigate the violations of international law; and the appeal for governments to suspend the transfer of arms to the combatants (in the context of this last item, the WCC made its first mention of Hezbollah).[47]

In conclusion, we can see the long way the WCC has traveled, from a neutral position in 1948 with regard to the aspirations of the Palestinians, to its supporting the demand for an independent Palestinian state in the 1980s. Sympathy for Third World liberation movements, combined with the constant pressure of Middle Eastern churches dominated by Arab church leaders, together influenced the WCC to take a sympathetic approach toward the Palestinians. In the last decade and a half, the WCC has not only issued statements of support for a "just peace" for the Palestinians but has sought to enter the field of political action. It has organized an annual week of "international church action for peace in Palestine and Israel," which promotes worldwide educational campaigns for the Palestinian cause, and has even suggested the boycott of Israeli products produced in the occupied territories. The proposed Palestine-Israel ecumenical forum was the cornerstone of the WCC's efforts to unite worldwide church initiatives for peace—which translated into Israeli withdrawal from all occupied territories; the implementation of all U.N. Security Council resolutions; the right of return for the Palestinians; and the establishment of a Palestinian independent state.[48]

Despite this trend, one should bear in mind that the WCC has always recognized the legitimacy of the state of Israel and its right to live within secure borders; condemned antisemitism and the equation of Zionism with racism; and initiated successful dialogues with Jewish leaders. As a result of its international stature and its well-informed organization, the policies of the World Council of Churches have frequently been echoed by national and local church bodies such as the Canadian Council of Churches and the National Council of Churches of Christ in the United States. It was easier for such churches to issue pro-Arab statements when they could rely on the Geneva-based senior institution—hence the important role that the WCC has played in Middle East international diplomacy.

Notes

1. WCC, *The First Assembly of the WCC: Official Report* (New York: 1949), 160–164.
2. Hertzel Fishman, *American Protestantism and a Jewish State* (Detroit: 1973), 155; WCC, *The First Assembly of the WCC*, 160–164.

3. Fishman, *American Protestantism and a Jewish State*, 158. It is worthy of note that a proposal calling for evangelization of the Jews was rejected at this assembly.

4. Resolution quoted in *Christianity and Crisis* (11 June 1951), 78–79.

5. Fishman, *American Protestantism and a Jewish State*, 133–135, 139.

6. Robert O. Matthews, "Lobbyist or Prophet: The Christian Churches and Canadian Foreign Policy in Human Rights," prepared for the Committee on Church and International Affairs (CCIA) Conference on Domestic Groups and Foreign Policy, Carleton University (June 1982), 4 (Archives of the Canadian Council of Churches, Toronto [henceforth: CCC]).

7. Clifford Longley, "Can WCC Grants to Guerilla Movements be Defended?" *Canadian Churchman* (Anglican), 104 (Nov. 1978), 8; "Political Involvement of World's Churches is Criticized," ibid. 105 (Jan. 1979), 12; Donald Smith, "The WCC and its Critics," *Presbyterian Record* (June 1980), 2–3; *Presbyterian Record* (July-Aug. 1980), 21–22 (quote on 22).

8. "WCC Central Committee Adopts Statement on Middle East," 25 Aug. 1967 (Archives of the Anglican Church in Canada, Toronto [henceforth: ACC], GSA, CSS, GS–75–106, b.11, CIA, minutes).

9. Canterbury statement cited in WCC, Middle East Task Force, John B. Taylor to "Dear Friends," 5 Sept. 1975 (Archives of the United Church of Canada, at Victoria University, Toronto, files of the Committee on Church and International Affairs [henceforth: UCA, CCIA], 82,250C, b.7, f.9).

10. *Oikoumene*, Newsletter of the World Council of Churches, Committee on the Church and the Jewish People, no. 4 (Dec. 1970) (Archives of the Roman Catholic Archdiocese of Toronto [henceforth: ARCAT], OCO4, WCO1).

11. Consultation on the Palestine Refugee Problem, 29 Sept.-4 Oct. 1969 (UCA, CCIA, 88,088C, b.2, f.1).

12. *Oikoumene*, no. 4.

13. Philip Potter, "Statement on the Middle East Conflict," 17 Oct. 1973 (Ontario Jewish Archives, Toronto [henceforth: OJA], MG/8S, b.54, f.41).

14. "WCC Appeals to the UN Assembly to Rescind Resolution on Zionism," 13 Nov. 1975 (UCA, A.C. Forrest papers [henceforth: ACF], 86,104C, b.21, f.10).

15. Franz von Hammerstein, "The Christian-Jewish Dialogue: An Account by the WCC," in *Jewish-Christian Dialogue: Six Years of Christian Consultations. The Quest for World Community: Jewish and Christian Perspectives* (published by the International Jewish Interreligious Consultations and the WCC's Sub-Unit on Dialogue with the People of Living Faiths and Ideologies [Geneva: 1975]), 14.

16. Ibid. On the Jewish approach to interfaith consultations, see a different article in ibid., "The Jewish-Christian Dialogue: An Evaluation by the International Jewish Committee on Inter-Religious Consultations," 16–23.

17. Peter F. Gilbert, "Exploring Christian-Jewish Relations," *Presbyterian Record* (Oct. 1975), 10.

18. WCC and IJCIC, Liaison Committee (Jerusalem), 29 Feb. 1976 (Canadian Jewish Congress National Archives [henceforth: CJCNA], Montreal, DA 15.1 4:13).

19. Von Hammerstein, "The Christian-Jewish Dialogue," 15.

20. Such statements included those of the WCC's fifth assembly, held in Nairobi in 1975; of the Central Committee, in August 1980; and of the sixth assembly, held in Vancouver in 1983.

21. "Statement Issued by the Sixth Assembly of the WCC in Vancouver" (14 July-10 Aug. 1983), 8 (CCC, Canadian International Development Agency, Middle East Task Group, Dialogue, 1983–1984); this statement cited the earlier declaration made by the Central Committee in 1980. Canadian Jewish leaders were among those who had angrily criticized the declaration on Jerusalem, arguing that it was "wholly political in character and is flagrantly partisan, it disregards established facts and distorts reality." They had also complained about the unbalanced information relied upon by the WCC—whereas Arab Christians, as members of the WCC Central Committee, were able to press their pro-Palestinian point of view, Jews had no direct voice in the WCC. In response, members of the WCC Christian-Jewish dialogue offered

"to seek further ways by which the voices of the Jewish community can be freely heard within the WCC." See "Middle East Information Distorted, Angry Jewish Groups Tell WCC," *Canadian Churchman* 106 (Nov. 1980), 10.

22. "Statement Issued by the Sixth Assembly of the WCC in Vancouver."

23. Ibid.

24. "Middle East Working Group to Members of the Christian Delegation, Re: the Talks with Canadian Arab Federation," n.d.; Brian Prideaux to Tad Mitsui, 1 June 1984 (CCC, CJP, MEWG, 1983–1984).

25. Ghassan Rubeiz, Lebanon/Palestine, 1988, Jan. 1988 (CCC, Commission on Justice and Peace, Middle East Working Group [henceforth: CJP, MEWG], 1988).

26. Ibid.

27. WCC, "Statement on the Occupied Territories," n.d.; WCC, Central Committee, "Message to the Heads of the Christian Communities in Jerusalem," n.d. (CCC, CJP, MEWG, 1988). On another occasion the Central Committee urged the churches to press their governments for an international peace conference, and to pressure Israel to halt new Jewish settlements and to consider dismantling the existing ones. See "Council Seeks Middle East Peace," *Anglican Journal* 115 (Oct. 1989), 5.

28. "WCC on Palestinian Declaration of Independence," *Ecumenical Press Service* (3 Jan. 1989).

29. "WCC Presentation on Palestine," 24 Feb. 1989 (CCC, MEWG, 1989, b.183).

30. WCC, International Affairs, Regional Concerns, "The Palestine-Israel Question" (21 Feb. 2005), 1–2 (hereafter: "The Palestine-Israel Question"). An almost identical text, titled "The WCC and the Palestinian-Israeli Conflict," may be found online on the updated WCC site at www.oikoumene.org/en/programmes/public-witness-addressing-power-affirming peace/palestine-and-israel-eappi/history.html (accessed 4 May 2009); "Church Leaders in Jerusalem Urge World Churches and all Christians to Advocate for Peace," 6 Feb. 2006, online at www.oikoumene.org/en/resources/documents/other-ecumenical-bodies/23-03-06-church-leaders-in-jerusalem-urge-world-churches-and-all-christians-to-advocate-for-peace (accessed 23 Feb. 2009). Jerusalem was mentioned in WCC statements in 1974, 1975, 1980, the "status of Jerusalem" in 1998, and "Jerusalem final status negotiations" in 2000.

31. "Appeal From the Churches of Jerusalem," 24 March 2001, online at www.wcc-coe.org/wcc/what/international/conflict10.html (accessed 23 Feb. 2009).

32. "The Palestine-Israel Question," 2. This survey article makes reference to the earlier declarations of the Central Committee.

33. Middle East Council of Churches, "Church Statements on the Palestinian-Israeli Conflict," Beirut, 10 Oct. 2000, online at www.wcc-coe.org/wcc/what/international/conflict3.html (accessed 23 Feb. 2009).

34. WCC, press update, "WCC Supports Kofi Annan's Intervention in the Israeli-Palestinian Conflict," 2 Oct. 2000, online at www.wcc-coe.org/wcc/news/press/00/33pu.html (accessed 25 Feb. 2009).

35. WCC, Central Committee, "Minute on the Situation in the Holy Land after the Outbreak of the Second Palestinian Uprising" (29 Jan.- 6 Feb. 2001), online at www.oikoumene.org/en/resources/documents/wcc-commissions/international-affairs/regional-concerns/middle-east/29-01-01-israeli-palestinian-conflict-minute-on-the-situation-in-the-holy-land-after-the-outbreak-of-the-second-palestinian-uprising.html.

36. "The Palestine-Israel Question," 2.

37. "Ecumenical Delegation Returns from the Middle East," 26 March 2001, online at www.wcc-coe.org/wcc/what/international/conflict15.html (accessed 23 Feb. 2009).

38. "The Palestine-Israel Question," 3.

39. "Misguided incursions and assaults" is apparently a reference to Operation Defensive Shield, a wide-scale military operation carried out in the West Bank in March-April 2002 in response to a series of suicide bombings and terrorist attacks that had resulted in more than a hundred Israeli deaths.

40. "Churches' Joint Letter to the UN Security Council," 10 April 2002, online at www.wcc-coe.org/wcc/what/international/april10churchesletter.html (accessed 23 Feb. 2009).

41. "The Palestine-Israel Question," 4; see also "The WCC and the Palestinian-Israeli Conflict" (n.d.), online at www.oikoumene.org/?id=6260 (accessed 1 March 2009).

42. "Church Leaders in Jerusalem Urge World Council and All Christians to Advocate for Peace," 6 Feb. 2006, online at www.oikoumene.org/?id=2143 (accessed 1 March 2009).

43. Executive Committee Statement on Israel/Palestine, "The Time is Ripe to Do What is Right," 19 May 2006, online at www.oikoumene.org/?id=4512 (accessed 1 March 2009).

44. "WCC Letter to Members of the U.N. Security Council," 21 July 2006, online at www.oikoumene.org/en/resources/documents/general-secretary/messages-and-letters/21-07-06-letter-to-members-of-un-security-council.html (accessed 25 Feb. 2009).

45. "An Appeal to the International Community," Geneva, 3 Aug. 2006, online at www.oikoumene.org/en/resources/documents/general-secretary/messages-and-letters/03-08-06-appeal-to-the-international-community.html (accessed 25 Feb. 2009).

46. Central Committee news release, "Kobia Calls for Comprehensive Response to the Middle East Crisis," 31 Aug. 2006, online at www.oikoumene.org/en/events-sections/cc2006/news-media/news/display-single-english-news/browse/2/article/1722/kobia-calls-for-comprehen.html (accessed 25 Feb. 2009).

47. "Statement on the War in Lebanon and Northern Israel, and Ecumenical Action for Middle East Peace," 30 Aug.-6 Sept. 2006, (final report of the WCC public issues committee), 14-15, online at www.oikoumene.org/en/resources/documents/central-committee/geneva-2006/reports-and-documents/final-report-of-the-public-issues-committee-adopted.html (accessed 25 Feb. 2009); see also "New Middle East Forum to Unite Church Efforts for Peace," 5 Sept. 2006, online at www.oikoumene.org/en/news/news-management/eng/a/browse/6/article/1722/new-middle-east-forum-to.html.

48. Eventually, the Palestine-Israel Ecumenical Forum was established in 2007 in Amman, Jordan. Its purpose was "to catalyze and co-ordinate" new and existing church advocacy for peace. See the founding document, online at www.oikoumene.org/en/resources/documents/wcc-programmes/public-witness-addressing-power-affirming-peace/middle-east-peace/20-06-07-the-amman-call.html.

The Presbyterian-Jewish Impasse

Christopher M. Leighton
(INSTITUTE FOR CHRISTIAN &
JEWISH STUDIES, BALTIMORE)

On the grand scale of global affairs, the interplay of Presbyterians and Jews may not register as an earthshaking concern. Yet Presbyterian responses to Judaism and the Jewish people are indicative of the complex, often conflicted attitudes that characterize many Christians within the United States. The confusion and the ambivalence are rooted within unsettled and unsettling theological dispositions, which in turn find expression within the denomination's debates and policies. Recent denominational actions have made an impact on other Protestant denominations as well as the Jewish community, and the reverberations will be felt far and wide for many years to come. More important, the manner in which the conflicts between Presbyterians and Jews are handled will have serious political implications, for the terms of the Presbyterian-Jewish engagement disclose some unfinished tasks of a nation that continues to struggle with the challenges of living in a religiously pluralist world.

In this essay, I will first examine two Presbyterian requests, known in Presbyterian parlance as "overtures," which were both directed to and approved by the denomination's 216th General Assembly, which was held in Richmond, Virginia in July 2004. I will then trace the debates that these resolutions generated and analyze the theological undercurrents within the denomination in the period leading up to the 217th General Assembly meeting in Birmingham, Alabama in June 2006. The two resolutions addressed "messianic Judaism" and the Israeli-Palestinian conflict, and the debates that followed exposed some of the deepest fissures within the church while also shedding light on a broader range of challenges facing mainline Protestants and Jews. My reading of these events is rooted in the strong conviction that Jews and Christians are still learning to break out of the reactive legacies of an anguished past. The imperative to develop a new set of intellectual reflexes stems from the belief that the destinies of both communities are more deeply interwoven than either is inclined to acknowledge. My partisan position is that neither Jews nor Christians will be able to move beyond the script of ancestors locked in adversarial battle until both communities discover, understand, and honor something of the beauty and wisdom that belongs to the other and that must not be claimed as one's own.

A few brief observations will be useful in orienting readers who are not at home in the sectarian currents of the Protestant world. The Presbyterian Church (U.S.A.) is the largest and most theologically progressive of the Christian denominations that adhere to a presbyterian form of church governance in North America. This movement grew out of the Protestant Reformation and took hold in parts of the Netherlands, Switzerland, France, and Scotland in the 16th century. Presbyterian immigrants to America, in particular those from the British Isles, brought with them a system of ecclesiastic organization that sought to steer a path between the authoritarian tendencies of an episcopacy (the rule of bishops within Roman Catholicism and Anglicanism) and the decentralized localism of Congregationalism. Presbyterians have championed the Protestant doctrine that insists upon the priesthood of all believers by balancing the authority of ministers with elected lay leadership. This distribution of responsibility extends from the local congregation to the presbytery (a geographically defined region composed of many local congregations) to the synod (comprising elected clergy and lay leaders from several presbyteries), to the general assembly (an ecclesiastical body with elected clergy and lay leaders who represent all of the nation's presbyteries and synods). The presbyterian form of governance seeks to achieve uniformity through democratic process.

Presbyterians within the United States are demographically in decline. With 2,314,000 members at the end of 2005 (down from 3,800,000 in 1990), the Presbyterian Church (U.S.A.) is struggling to develop a clear and compelling theological identity that will attract new congregants or at least stanch the current hemorrhage. Like other mainstream Protestant denominations in America, Presbyterians find themselves polarized by issues that defy ecclesiastical resolution. In addition to the interminable clash over the rights of gays, the Presbyterian Church has become embroiled in debates over American domestic and foreign policies in which ideological alignments, partisan polemics, and political maneuvering have consistently eclipsed reasoned engagement with biblical and theological traditions. In the battles to develop clear positions on all of these issues, Presbyterians have enlisted their sacred texts and their doctrinal norms and have used them as political weapons to defeat their opponents within the church. At every turn, combatants have entered the fray with the conviction that they were battling to preserve the very soul of the community. The General Assembly actions that have weighed so heavily on the Jewish community have provided yet another instance of this splintering of Presbyterians into warring factions.

Presbyterian Outreach and the Jews

On January 29, 2002 the Presbytery of Philadelphia endorsed a proposal for a Messianic New Church Development project. This resolution gave life to Avodat Yisrael, which the congregation translates as "the service of Israel." This fledgling congregation on the outskirts of Philadelphia was headed by the Reverend Andrew Sparks, an ordained Presbyterian minister with extensive experience in the Messiah Now Ministry, an evangelical initiative that is directed at Jews. He was the principal organizer and "spiritual guide" of this venture. The congregation presented itself as a spiritual home where differences between Jews and Christians were bridged, and its outreach was directed to secular Jews and families from mixed marriages. In the debates about the appropriateness of evangelical projects that specifically targeted the Jewish people, supporters of Avodat Yisrael noted that this venture directed its aim at nonobservant Jews for whom Judaism had become little more than an atavistic cultural attachment. The case was made that, just as Presbyterians accommodate the national and linguistic needs of Koreans, Indonesians, and varied African heritages, so too there was room (and the need) to frame the Christian story within a Jewish idiom. Advocates maintained that a congregation wherein Jews and Gentiles overcame ethnic divides and discovered an underlying unity would offer a theological model of universality utterly lacking in most Presbyterian churches.

Accepting these arguments, many evangelical and conservative members of the Presbyterian family enthusiastically supported the Avodat Yisrael outreach project. For some, this endeavor simply made good on the evangelical imperative to bring all peoples to Christ. For others, the congregation offered a path that promised to ameliorate the tragic legacy of antisemitism while simultaneously advancing the goal of a more inclusive and diverse denomination. Champions of this initiative observed that many interfaith couples drift into a limbo in which competing and exclusive religious claims divide families and leave many uprooted and dispossessed. The search for a spiritual home that harmonizes both traditions rarely comes to a satisfactory conclusion, and congregations such as Avodat Yisrael would seem to fill an urgent void.

Avodat Yisrael launched its first worship services on Rosh Hashanah in September 2003. Support for this initiative came from the local Philadelphia presbytery ($145,000), but the project subsequently garnered funding from the Synod of the Trinity, which includes the region of Pennsylvania and parts of West Virginia and Ohio ($75,000), and from the highest governing body, the General Assembly ($125,000). Despite this broad platform of sponsorship, the Avodat Yisrael project generated intense opposition from its inception. A significant group of Presbyterian clergy and lay leaders concluded that it contradicted the direction charted in the 1987 General Assembly paper titled "A Theological Understanding of the Relationship between Christians and Jews,"[1] and they called for a withdrawal of church support.[2] Efforts were made within the presbytery to rescind support for Avodat Yisrael, and on February 26, 2002, a majority of the presbytery leadership (63-44) cast its votes in opposition to the project—this vote, however, failed to overturn the earlier action because a two-thirds majority was required for motions not filed at least ten days prior to a presbytery meeting. Meanwhile, local and national representatives of the American Jewish community vehemently attacked the Avodat Yisrael initiative.[3]

Fierce debates continued to roil the Presbytery of Philadelphia and thrust the larger Presbyterian community into a political and theological quagmire. At the July 2004 meeting of the General Assembly, proposals from four presbyteries called for an examination of the appropriate forms of Christian witness (outreach) to Jews in general, and the Avodat Yisrael plan in particular. In response, the General Assembly issued a two-part plan of action.[4] On the one hand, it mandated a study "to examine and strengthen the relationship between Christians and Jews and the implications of this relationship for our evangelism and new church development"; on the other, by a vote of 260 to 233, it rejected the proposal to suspend national funding for Avodat Yisrael and similar new church developments.

The resolution of the General Assembly revealed a deeply divided church unable to develop a compromise that would satisfy both the progressive and the conservative factions. The liberal dream of reaffirming and strengthening the relationship between Presbyterians and Jews was trumped by the decision to sustain a policy of evangelism. Thus, the action of the General Assembly registered as a serious setback both to progressive Presbyterians who had committed themselves to interfaith partnerships and to their Jewish neighbors who felt betrayed by the Presbyterian alignment with messianic Judaism (sometimes referred to as Hebrew Christianity). Church officials did their best to control the damage by noting that the decision had been based primarily on ecclesiastical protocol: "The primary decisions regarding the funding of new church developments are made at the presbytery (regional) level of our denomination; in nearly all cases, national funding for such work is made only to complement funds already committed by presbyteries and synods with the understanding that presbyteries take the lead in determining the appropriate projects."[5] In other words, the vote had been linked to a commitment to honor the authority and autonomy of the presbytery. Such procedural considerations overrode the question of the appropriateness of messianic evangelism.

Needless to say, this explanation did little to mollify the critics of Avodat Yisrael, who charged that the General Assembly had proven itself unable or unwilling to confront the hard questions of missionary activities targeting the Jews. The conflict within the Presbytery of Philadelphia and the larger church continued to fester in the months to follow. An administrative commission was formed to oversee Avodat Yisrael, and a report of its findings was delivered before a meeting of the Philadelphia presbytery in November 2004.[6] This report included a theological statement by Dr. Mark Wallace that summarized the unresolved questions. To work systematically through the issues would have demanded an enormous expenditure of time and effort—the task would no doubt have exacerbated tensions within both the Philadelphia presbytery and the larger Presbyterian community. So there was a collective sigh of relief when the Presbytery of Philadelphia voted on March 29, 2005 to withdraw support from Avodat Yisrael. This decision, however, was not linked to theological considerations. Instead, presbytery leaders noted that Avodat Yisrael had not demonstrated sufficient progress as a congregation, having fallen short in terms of membership growth, worship attendance, and particularly congregational giving. Whereas the formal ties that bound Avodat Yisrael to the Presbyterian Church were severed, the presbytery continued to recognize the Reverend Andrew Spark's call as a validated ministry.

Had Avodat Yisrael succeeded as a congregation, the Presbyterian Church might have confronted a range of biblical, historical, political, and theological issues that have long haunted Presbyterian-Jewish relations. As matters stand, the stage is set for repeat performances of the same imbroglio. The conflicted positions about the theological status of the Jews will continue to reinforce the ambivalence that many Christians have about Judaism. The Avodat Yisrael debacle has disclosed three specific areas in which the interplay of American Jews and Protestants is strained:

- *Defining Judaism as an ethnicity*. The mission of Avodat Yisrael speaks of Judaism and the Jewish people in terms of ethnicity. Yet Avodat Yisrael and other messianic Jewish congregations incorporate traditional Jewish religious practices into their services, and in the process overlay rituals that are constitutive of Jewish identity with interpretations that misrepresent and offend core affirmations of the Jewish tradition. To encourage members of the messianic congregation to don prayer shawls, to follow the Jewish liturgical calendar, to invoke Hebrew prayers, to use a Torah scroll, and to order the sacred space with Jewish symbols—all of these gestures are regarded by traditional Jews as an offensive expropriation of religious content. When the advocates of this mission claim that these elements are simply ethnic embellishments that enable unaffiliated Jews to feel at home, the Jewish community has good reason to assess this kind of outreach as a deceitful ploy.

The nature of this offense is powerfully illustrated in the ways that these messianic Jews celebrate the Passover seder. Rituals, symbols, and narratives that lie at the very heart of Judaism are adapted to advance an altogether different religious agenda. Each element is given a Christological significance, and the subsequent decoding of the Passover seder indicates that traditional Jews miss the underlying truth of their own story. These messianic Jews march through the seder with the conviction that Jesus has unlocked its hidden spiritual depths. Whereas the messianic Jew maintains that this is simply a complementary reading of the Passover service, it has impressed the Jewish community at large not only as a gross misrepresentation but as an act of religiously sanctioned piracy.

- *Synthesizing Judaism and Christianity.* Messianic Jews maintain that they are recovering a neglected movement within the earliest church, an ancient tradition with a pedigree going back to the church's beginnings. They are quick to note that Jesus and his earliest disciples were all Jewish, and that there is evidence of Torah-observant followers of Jesus stretching into the 7th or 8th centuries of the Common Era. While the recognition of the Jewishness of Jesus, the apostles, and most especially Paul has emerged as an important corrective within a tradition that has all too often obscured or debased its Jewish origins, the notion of hurdling almost two thousand years of anguished history to retrieve a form of religiosity rejected by both the dominant Jewish and Christian traditions seems less than desirable.

Both rabbinic Judaism and Christianity unfolded in the wake of the destruction of the Second Temple, and scholars as diverse as E.P. Sanders, Shaye Cohen, James Dunn, Amy-Jill Levine, Alan Segal, Paula Fredriksen, and John Meier all agree that a complex of pressures led the vast majority of Jews and Christians to pursue paths that refused to accommodate the other. Within the Christian tradition, the Jewish insider was redefined as an outsider, and Jewish followers of Jesus increasingly found themselves at radical odds with both the early church and rabbinic Judaism. This beleaguered minority was compelled to make a choice between the church and the synagogue. To affirm the beliefs and practices that were and remain constitutive of the Christian family was judged as apostasy within Judaism. To live in the light of the Torah and to follow the covenantal practices that defined the Jewish community was condemned as heretical by orthodox Christians. To add Jewish observances to the

The Presbyterian-Jewish Impasse 111

gospel was not only seen as a superfluous exercise, but also called into question the sufficiency of faith in Jesus Christ as the basis of Christian identity.

Moreover, as orthodox Christianity developed, distinctions were made between the Jewish Sabbath and Sunday worship. The Jewish calendar no longer served as the touchstone in the calculation of Christian holy days. The confessions and creeds that defined the normative tradition did not accommodate or even make reference to Jewish practices. Both Christians and Jews came to understand that they belonged to two distinct religious traditions, and any efforts to tear down the walls of separation were recognized as an assault on the integrity of each.

Thus, the claims of messianic Jews ignore the boundaries bequeathed to both communities by their ancestors. There is no recognition that the Judaism of Jesus' time is profoundly different from the dynamic reality that became the rabbinic Judaism of subsequent centuries. This observation may appear as an empty abstraction to many Presbyterians—indeed, Christians are in large measure oblivious to the fact that Jews had no option, in centuries past, to embrace publicly both traditions and to join them into a harmonious union. Today, the notion of such a merger registers in the minds and hearts of most Jews as an invitation to defile the memory of the faithful, most especially those who chose martyrdom over apostasy.

While the history of Christianity is littered with syncretistic ventures—efforts, for example, to integrate goddess worship, Gnostic spirituality, Marxism, or any number of other religious/ideological practices and beliefs within the Presbyterian heritage—Presbyterians have insisted that they cannot be all things to all people. Not only do Presbyterians do violence to the integrity of others, but they also imperil the coherence of their own tradition when they relinquish their confessional and creedal boundaries. A new tradition may yet emerge that weaves together Jewish and Christian beliefs and practices, and this communal arrangement may meet the deepest yearnings of spiritual seekers from interfaith marriages. However, this new religious reality will have a very tenuous connection to the traditions for which previous generations of Jews and Christians lived and died.

- *Sanctioning evangelical subterfuge.* All Christians are obliged to provide a witness that demonstrates the transformative power of the gospel. That is, the words that Presbyterians proclaim and the deeds that they perform are all animated by the hope that all peoples will come to recognize the redemptive truth of Christ. Many understand this affirmation as the basis for evangelical outreach, and they actively seek the inclusion of all humanity within the Christian faith. With respect to the Jewish people, this understanding of mission is usually driven by the logic of supersessionism, a theological position maintaining that the old covenant with the Jewish people has become obsolete, having been replaced by the new covenant in Christ. According to this viewpoint, the church supersedes the synagogue as the locus of God's redemptive purpose for the world.

While this missionary approach has deep roots within the Christian tradition, evangelical efforts to bring Jews into the covenantal framework of the Christian church are increasingly regarded as a symptom of a theologically incoherent and ethically flawed position. The rationale given to justify God's dismissal of the covenant with the Jewish people Israel is chilling in its simplicity: in their rejection of Jesus, the

Jews also rejected God; since the Jews rejected Jesus, God rejected them. This calculus undercuts one of the most fundamental affirmations of the Protestant Reformation, namely, that people are embraced by God's love not because they are deserving or even loveable. Put somewhat differently, God does not give up on his covenantal partners. If God abandons the Jewish people, then Christians have no reason to trust that the covenant formed in and through Jesus Christ will long endure. Similarly, if Presbyterians maintain that God's gracious embrace is trustworthy when applied to them, why would the same fidelity not obtain in the case of the Jewish people?

The problem of missionary overtures to convert the Jewish people does not reside simply in the flawed and inconsistent reasoning of Christian theologians. From a Jewish perspective, a church that dreams of the conversion or the absorption of Jews into the Body of Christ ends up supporting an ideology of spiritual genocide. Presbyterians must ask themselves if they want to support practices that aim at the elimination of the traditions that have sustained the Jewish community over the centuries. In fact, in the wake of the Shoah, many Christians have begun to rethink the nature of the Christian witness to the Jewish people. They maintain that the evangelical imperative does not require Christians to convert the Jewish people, and that the truth of the gospel does not exhaust the covenantal possibilities open to God and the rest of the world. At a minimum, they argue that Christians cannot proclaim God's fidelity without acknowledging the irrevocable bond between God and the Jewish people (Romans 11:29). As Franz Rosenzweig once noted, it may be true that there is no way to come to the Father except through Jesus Christ. However, the Jews are already with the Father; they thus have no need to embark upon a different path to enter into a divine partnership. Their challenge is to remain true to the call that radiates from Sinai, and to make good on the commandment to be a blessing to the nations by continuing to witness and work for the ultimate redemption of humankind.

Issues regarding the legitimacy of the Christian mission to the Jews will remain a source of heated debate for years to come, not only among Presbyterians, but also among other Protestants and Roman Catholics.[7] These tensions will endure until the church comes to grips with the inescapable reality of religious pluralism. Despite these contentious divisions, Presbyterians of every persuasion have consistently agreed that missionary activity of any sort must respect the freedom and dignity of those to whom they witness. Coercion and manipulation denigrate the integrity of others and contradict the ethical imperative of the gospel. In this regard, whereas Avodat Yisrael and other messianic Jewish congregations are not coercive, they have systematically engaged in manipulation and deception.

When Andrew Starks, the ordained Presbyterian minister of Avodat Yisrael, presented himself as a rabbi, the stage was set for a breakdown in trust. When the signage in front of the congregation made no mention of its alignment with the Presbyterian Church, there was a failure to state the truth publicly. When the worship did not connect with the confessional claims of the Presbyterian tradition and followed the liturgical rhythms of Judaism, disaffected Jews and interfaith families may have felt more at ease. But the cost of this comfort was purchased at the expense of ethical integrity.

The fierce debates about the appropriateness of funding a messianic Jewish congregation may strike some readers as much ado about nothing. It may appear to be a procedural problem that spun out of control; some may feel that it would have been out of order for the larger church to interfere with the local affairs of the Philadelphia presbytery. Yet Presbyterians need to recognize that there is much more at stake than an evangelical anomaly that providentially fell flat. In fact, the mix of attitudes that surfaced in the debates about Avodat Yisrael form an important backdrop for the consideration of the second resolution from the 216th General Assembly. Taken together, these two actions dramatically changed the landscape of Jewish-Presbyterian relations.

Presbyterian Peacemaking and the Israeli-Palestinian Impasse

The second overture that was delivered to the 216th General Assembly called for a process of phased, selective divestment of companies doing business with Israel, specifically targeting corporations that were profiting from the alleged oppression of Palestinians. The Assembly's decision to endorse this proposal demonstrated a denominational commitment to translate words into action and to apply pressure on the prevailing policies of the Israeli government and its military. While this intervention was intended to exhort all parties involved in the Israeli-Palestinian conflict, including the United States, to overcome an intransigence that had repeatedly undermined any significant movement toward a peaceful resolution, the overture placed the greatest burden of responsibility on the state of Israel. In its tone and content, the resolution provoked rancorous debate within the Presbyterian community and deepened the rift in Presbyterian-Jewish relations.[8]

The implications of this denominational action are difficult to assess without a more comprehensive understanding of the historical linkages that bind Presbyterians to the Middle East. Furthermore, an inquiry into these entanglements reveals longstanding tensions that are built into the organizational structure of the Presbyterian Church. Contrasting, if not competing agendas have set two groups at odds: on the one hand, those who have missionary connections to the Middle East and who have pursued peacekeeping initiatives in cooperation with their Palestinian brethren; on the other, those Presbyterians who have committed themselves to interfaith relations, most especially within the context of the United States.

Since the founding of the state of Israel in 1948, the Presbyterian Church has juggled a set of incompatible obligations born of irreconcilable narratives. Palestinians recount a saga of eviction and land confiscation, brutal military domination, economic exploitation, political paralysis, chronic violations of human rights, and imperialist appropriation of natural resources on the part of Israelis. In this rendering, Israelis exercise almost total control over the destiny of Palestinians, who in turn have been reduced to desperate victims of injustice. Israelis, for their part, recall the Palestinian refusal to accept the United Nations proposal for a two-state solution and the subsequent attack by Syria, Egypt, Jordan, Lebanon, and Iraq on May 15, 1948. They highlight the rights of citizenship granted to Arabs who remained in Israel during and after the War of Independence, and they contrast this treatment with the surrounding Arab nations who refused to assimilate their Palestinian populations, using them as pawns in a cynical propaganda campaign against Israel. They remember that the Six-Day War in 1967 and the Yom Kippur War of 1973 were initiated by hostile Arab neighbors who went into battle with the dream of eliminating the Jewish state—a goal explicitly championed in the charter declaration of the PLO and still endorsed by the leadership of Hamas. The invasion of Lebanon in 1982 is construed by Israelis as defensive, and the recurrent intrusions into Gaza and the West Bank are presented as either preventive measures or as acts of retaliation designed to counter Palestinian extremists. According to this narrative, it is the Israelis who are the victims of Arab belligerency and Palestinian intransigence.

Given these conflicting accounts of the Israeli-Palestinian conflict, Presbyterians have found themselves pressed into acknowledging that both sides have legitimate claims and grievances. Thus, they have decried the legacy of antisemitism and have repeatedly insisted on the right of Israel to exist within secure and internationally recognized borders. In 1969, 1974, 1977, 1983, and 1989 the General Assembly approved resolutions that explicitly affirmed these commitments. At the same time, the denomination has cited a history of missionary involvement in the Middle East stretching back almost two hundred years. Presbyterians have noted the deteriorating circumstances of Christians in much of the Middle East and have directed particular attention to the beleaguered condition of the Palestinian population. The General Assembly has consistently spoken of the Palestinian right to self-determination. Beginning in the 1980s, Presbyterian resolutions (in 1984, 1986, 1987, and 1988) endorsed the international community's efforts to work for the creation of an independent Palestinian state in the West Bank and Gaza. In addition, Presbyterians have repeatedly condemned the building of Israeli settlements in the occupied territories (1988, 1990, 1992, 1997, and 1998) and have argued that the continuation of U.S. aid to Israel should be made contingent upon an end to additional settlements and the cessation of human rights violations (1990, 1995, and 1998).[9]

To most observers within the Jewish community, the Presbyterian Church has demonstrated a pro-Palestinian bias over the decades; this assessment is shared by many Presbyterians involved in the Jewish-Christian dialogue. Yet from the perspective of other Presbyterians, particularly those who have interpreted the Israeli-Palestinian conflict through the lens of liberation theology, the denomination has taken the path of least resistance. Many Presbyterians, it is claimed, are too easily intimidated by accusations of antisemitism or too easily seduced by the neo-conservative dreams of American power and influence in the region. The passionate volley of charges and countercharges has often deepened the divides between these two Presbyterian camps. Both sides, however, have acknowledged that Presbyterian efforts at peacemaking in the Middle East have yielded very meager results.

"End the Occupation Now"

During the past decade, the professional leadership of the Presbyterian Church has become more outspoken in its condemnations of Israel. This criticism hardened in the wake of the 214th General Assembly in June of 2002. The asymmetry in Israel's power was presented as the basis of greater accountability, and the emergent positions of the Presbyterians signaled an abandonment of policies that were aimed at evenhandedness and neutrality. The pro-Palestinian tilt was boosted by the election of the Reverend Fahed Abu-Akel, the Mission Pastor of the First Presbyterian Church in Atlanta, Georgia, as the new Moderator, the titular head of the church who is elected at the General Assembly to serve a two-year term as the denominational spokesperson. Abu-Akel was born in the Galilee region of Israel, and he carries the memories of fleeing from his home with his father and brothers in 1948. In his capacity as the official voice of the Presbyterian community, he repeatedly put the spotlight on the plight of the Palestinians and decried their oppression at the hands of the Israelis.

It was during Abu-Akel's tenure that the "Resolution on Israel and Palestine: End the Occupation Now" was developed and presented to the 215th meeting of the General Assembly in 2003. This document provides a historical synopsis of "Israel's unremitting repression of the Palestinian people," yet it is riddled with serious misrepresentations and marred by a lack of diplomatic balance. Take, for example, the following passage about the partition of Palestine:

> ...the General Assembly [of the United Nations] in 1947 decided to partition Palestine into two states, one Arab and one Jewish, with special international status for Jerusalem. Though the proposed Palestinian state did not materialize, the land was partitioned in 1949 when an armistice divided the new Jewish state from other parts of the Mandate of Palestine.[10]

There is no mention that the reason the Palestinian state did not "materialize" is because the Palestinians rejected the U.N. proposal and the surrounding Arab countries attacked Israel. Similarly, the document fails to acknowledge that Israel was later besieged in 1967 and in 1973. In similar fashion, the Israeli occupation of the West Bank and Gaza is presented as the source of the Palestinian predicament, but there is no mention of the fact that this situation was in large measure created by the military aggression of surrounding Arab neighbors who sought Israel's destruction. Also overlooked is the fact that the option of ending the occupation has never rested exclusively in the hands of Israel, but has rather depended upon a negotiated settlement between Israelis and Palestinians that would in turn be supported by the surrounding Arab nations and the international community. This larger web of relationships all too frequently fades from the Presbyterian picture.

With regard to the 1991 Gulf War, the document notes that the Palestinian leadership's opposition to the invasion of Iraq was "hurtful to the Palestinian cause." Left unmentioned is the fact that the Palestine Liberation Organization (PLO) was not merely against the western invasion; it sided with Saddam Hussein and expressed enthusiastic support when Iraqi Scud missiles were fired at Israel. The evidence of fiscal mismanagement and dishonesty within the Palestinian Authority under Yassir Arafat is overwhelming, yet the Presbyterian resolution makes do with a limp observation that "corruption is feared to be prevalent." Noting that there is "genuine anxiety" among Palestinians that Israel might adopt a policy "often referred to as 'transfer,' and compared sometimes to ethnic cleansing in the former Yugoslavia," the document fails to point out that only a small minority among the Israeli populace and in the Knesset supports such measures, whereas most major parties in Israel explicitly reject the "transfer" option. This pattern of underlining the worst elements within Israel while muting or explaining away the worst tendencies among Palestinians runs through the entire resolution, and the results make a mockery of Presbyterian claims about its role as "peacemakers."

The seriousness of this accusation requires elaboration on a particularly crucial issue. The General Assembly document makes several references to U.N. Security Council Resolution 242 as requiring Israeli withdrawal to "the pre-1967 boundaries" and the return of "all the territory" occupied in the course of the Six-Day War of June 1967. This is a disturbing misstatement of what Resolution 242 actually calls for, namely, an Israeli withdrawal from "territories occupied during the war." The omission of the word "the" or the phrase "all the" territories was intentional, as it was meant to allow for the possibility of territorial adjustments in the course of the peace agreement. Moreover, the simplistic call made in "End the Occupation Now" for "the right of return of Palestinian refugees" fails to consider the implications of this action: given the large number of refugees and the dramatically higher birthrate among Palestinians, Israel would soon be transformed into a state in which Jews were a minority of the population.

The 2004 Divestment Overture

The "Resolution on Israel and Palestine: Initiating Divestment and Ending Occupation" reiterated the commitment to initiatives that would advance peace in the Middle East and restated the demand that "the occupation must end; it has proven to be at the root of evil acts committed against innocent people on both sides of the conflict."[11] The General Assembly resolution concluded by calling upon "The Mission Responsibility through Investment Committee (MRTI) with instructions to initiate a process of phased selective divestment in multinational corporations operating in Israel, in accordance [with] General Assembly policy on social investing, and to make appropriate recommendations to the General Assembly Council for action." The divestment resolution was approved by a vote of 431 in favor, 62 opposed, and 7 abstentions in June 2004.

Although representatives from the Presbyterian Church have insisted that divestment was directed at all those who were deriving profits from the Israeli-Palestinian conflict, the tone and content of the resolution were utterly lacking in balance. For instance, it failed to address the fact that attacks by Palestinian radicals against Israel have been covertly funded and sustained through channels that are impervious to Presbyterian pressure. Nor have Presbyterians advanced any policies to provide Palestinians with positive economic or political incentives to enter into negotiations with Israel. The divestment overture singled out the Israeli military, and by extension, the Israeli government, as the sole target for substantive rebuke. Furthermore, the resolution was essentially redundant, since previous investment guidelines for the Presbyterian pension fund had already established ethical norms that prohibited financial holdings linked to the industrial military complex. In sum, Presbyterians appeared to be judging Israel with a set of standards that were not applied equally to other countries. Certainly Israel was not the only or the worst exemplar of human rights abuse, and yet no other nation was subjected to similar censure.

Presbyterian officials have insisted that divestment is selective, and that this policy does not amount to a boycott of Israel. Advocates of divestment believe that they are performing a surgical procedure that targets a specific disorder, namely the expansion of Israeli settlements and the excessive use of military force. Yet there is little or no evidence to support the claim that Israel has ever responded positively to clumsy demands mounted by a Christian denomination whose outlook was demonstrably partisan. Moreover, in the debates surrounding the 2004 overture, repeated comparisons were made to previous divestment initiatives, beginning in the mid-1970s, against the apartheid government in South Africa—which were essentially designed to topple the regime. Although the implied analogy between South Africa and Israel is widely recognized by most Presbyterians and Jews to be deeply flawed, the psychological payload of this comparison continues to deliver a jolt.[12] Presbyterians, to be sure, are in no position to inflict a decisive blow against the Jewish state, but a number of other mainline Protestant denominations have considered similar directives, and this causes an understandable anxiety that liberal Christians are actively undermining the American commitment to the Jewish state. There is little doubt in anyone's mind that the withdrawal of American support for Israel would seriously threaten its future, and Presbyterian assurances to the contrary have done nothing to alleviate a profound sense of betrayal.

Finally, Presbyterian criticism of Israel has cited the construction of the "separation barrier" as an egregious example of Israeli oppression.[13] There is no mention of the fact that the proposal to construct a barrier between Israel and the West Bank/Gaza was first adopted by Israeli Labor party doves in order to serve two purposes: to thwart terrorist infiltration, and as a means of preventing the annexation of additional territories from the West Bank. The initial proponents of the barrier actually intended to have the lines drawn more or less according to the 1949 armistice line. In any event, the actual positioning of the barrier has in some instances posed serious questions of territorial encroachment, which in turn have been brought before the Israeli supreme court (in several rulings, the court demanded that portions of the barrier be redrawn). At the same time, the number of terrorist incidents has declined markedly since construction of the barrier first began in 2002, and a significant majority of Israelis have concluded that the barrier is necessary so long as the climate of intense hostility persists.

While the placement of the security barrier requires careful scrutiny and critical review, the blanket condemnation of "the wall" invites further reflection. Christian peacemaking is animated by the conviction that the love of enemies breaks the cycle of violence and overcomes patterns of hostility. The practice of the Christian faith urges adherents to pull down walls of separation. The prophet Isaiah presents a vision of God's Kingdom in which all the nations come to Zion to worship: they will beat swords into ploughshares, and the reign of death will yield to a harmonious life in which all participate fully. This messianic dream orients Christians to work for a world that is not defined by borders. Yet an ominous shadow falls between this dream and the current reality of the Middle East.

How are Christians to respond when the antagonists in the Israeli-Palestinian conflict have developed such a deep hatred for one another? How are Presbyterians to conduct themselves when others refuse to play by Presbyterian rules of order and decency—indeed, when these other peoples align themselves with militant ideals of violent revolt and the bloody defeat of their enemies? What are Christians to make of their own affirmations if love does not conquer all?

Presbyterians have an understanding of sin that makes them highly suspicious of the deployment of force. Given the human aptitude for self-deception and the dangerous application of military might around the globe, there is a solid warrant for skepticism. Yet Presbyterian expectations of the Peaceable Kingdom all too often operate with romanticized notions of powerlessness that obscure the complex compromises demanded of people and nations. When fact and myth are inseparably bound together and used to sanction political intransigence among both Israelis and Palestinians, theological prescriptions need to be tempered with the realization that American Christians may have a more modest role to play in mediating this clash. A mix of arrogance, naiveté, and ignorance was stirred into the divestment recommendation, and noble intentions were unable to conceal the blunders in the proposal.

When the General Assembly was asked to consider the divestment overture, the Presbyterian commissioners listened to the impassioned entreaties of the Rev. Dr. Mitri Raheb, the Palestinian pastor of the Evangelical Lutheran Christmas Church in Bethlehem. Other Palestinian Christians with close ties to the Presbyterian Church were intimately involved in the development and dissemination of the overture. However, there was little or no opportunity for the commissioners to hear the views of American or Israeli Jews. This failure to engage the Jewish community undermined the ideals of collaborative peacemaking. The absence of Jewish participants also signaled the mistaken notion that there is a shortage of Jews with whom Presbyterians can work in order to advance greater justice for Palestinians. With the acceptance of the divestment resolution, Presbyterians were drawn into a zero-sum gamesmanship that divided the world in two: winners and losers, the mighty and the downtrodden, right and wrong, just and unjust. The approval of divestment generated a dangerously simplistic reading of the political and economic realities, but more significantly betrayed the deepest insights of the Presbyterian (often referred to as the Reformed) theological tradition—namely, the recognition that people are, in the words of John Calvin, "curved in on themselves." Self-interest and group loyalties tend to blind people to the legitimate needs of others, leading them to endow their finite attachments with transcendent significance. This sober assessment of the human condition applies to Palestinians no less than to Israelis, to Presbyterians no less than to Jews and Muslims.

In the aftermath of this General Assembly, a storm of protests erupted within both the Presbyterian and Jewish communities. The outrage and deep sense of betrayal expressed by many American Jews was far greater than most Presbyterians anticipated, and the best efforts of Presbyterian officials to soften the anti-Israel rhetoric did little to allay the anxieties. In cities across the United States, local rabbis and Presbyterian ministers entered into searching conversations with their congregations. While most Presbyterians continue to believe that their church must not ignore the violations of Palestinian rights and must take positive steps to promote a two-state solution, there is now a far greater acknowledgement that their own contributions depend upon collaborative engagement with the Muslim and Jewish communities. Furthermore, a greater number of Presbyterians began to arrive at a shared conclusion: strategies that threaten punishment, especially when the pressure cannot be evenly distributed, accelerate the polarization of the opposing factions and darken an atmosphere already thick with intimidation and resentment. Grassroots initiatives such as

"Presbyterians Concerned for Jewish and Christian Relations" not only advocated the rescinding of the divestment resolution, but also championed a more constructive approach that would embody the positive values behind the Presbyterian commitment to peacemaking.[14] To this end, presbyteries around the country began to abandon the highly charged language of divestment and instead adopted a constructive model of engagement by promoting economic and educational investments in the region.

A Change of Direction: The 217th Meeting of the General Assembly

By the time the General Assembly met in June of 2006 in Birmingham, Alabama, 26 presbyteries had submitted overtures concerning the Israeli-Palestinian conflict, the overwhelming majority of them critical of the divestment resolution. Church officials made efforts to table these overtures until a specially appointed commission had studied the issues and developed recommendations that could be presented to the next General Assembly. Some feared that the proposed commission would be stacked with members with an anti-Israel bias and would embark on a study process without putting a hold on the divestment policy. In the end, the proposal to table the various overtures was rejected by the Peacemaking and International Relations Committee. By a vote of 483 in favor, 28 opposed, and one abstention, a new resolution was approved that charted a revised course of action for the Presbyterian Church.

The content and tenor of this resolution stand in dramatic contrast to the previous General Assembly's statement. It begins:

> We acknowledge that the actions of the 216th General Assembly (2004) caused hurt and misunderstanding among many members of the Jewish community and within our Presbyterian communion. We are grieved by the pain that this has caused, accept responsibility for the flaws in our process, and ask for a new season of mutual understanding and dialogue.[15]

The resolution replaced the language of "divestment" with a policy advocating "investment in Israel, Gaza, East Jerusalem, and the West Bank." It encouraged dialogue and partnerships with American Jews and American Palestinians (Christian and Muslim) as well as Israelis and Palestinians. There is a call to pursue peaceful means of ending the occupation, but the resolution backs away from a blanket condemnation of "the security wall," noting instead that "the General Assembly supports fair criticism of the security wall insofar as it illegally encroaches into the Palestinian territory and fails to follow the legally recognized borders of Israel since 1967 demarcated by the Green Line."

Conclusions

During the past decade, Presbyterians have advanced positions that have placed an unprecedented strain on their relationships with Jews. At the most recent meeting of the General Assembly, the denomination took vital steps to reverse the downward spiral. To be sure, the road ahead will hold many twists and turns. As an example, the leadership of the Presbyterian Church has delivered an odd interpretation of the action adopted by the 2006 General Assembly—according to the Reverend Clifton Kirkpatrick, the Stated Clerk, who functions as the chief executive of the office of the General Assembly and its ecumenical representative, this resolution did not rescind the previous one: "Divestment is still an option, but not the goal. Instead, this assembly broadened the focus to corporate engagement to ensure that the church's financial investments do not support violence of any kind in the region."[16] Insofar as the Presbyterian leadership assumes a defensive posture with respect to divestment policies, the stage is set for more serious discord. The polemical outcries of networks such as the National Middle Eastern Presbyterian Caucus reveal Presbyterian constituencies caught within an enduring trauma. Their inability to see beyond their own pain, to fathom a more tangled web of accountability, or to envision any possibilities for creative engagement is etched into their protest of January 31, 2008, titled "A Call to End the Siege of Gaza."[17]

The degree to which the Mission Responsibility through Investment Committee can develop positive strategies to invest in the region while at the same time applying economic pressure with balanced and equitable policies remains to be seen. However, the conflicts that have erupted during the past few years are rooted in deeper communal habits and theological dispositions. The discord within the Presbyterian family, and between Presbyterians and the Jewish community, signals an impasse that will be broken only when the denomination confronts its internal theological contradictions and develops more creative responses to the competing, often conflicting claims of diverse religious traditions. Recent disputations have brought the following challenges into the open:

- *Mission and evangelism*. The Presbyterian Church affirmed the ongoing integrity of God's covenant with the Jewish people in a 1987 study paper titled "A Theological Understanding of the Relationship between Christians and Jews."[18] The second core affirmation declares, "Christians have not replaced Jews." However, the statement then offers an explication that concludes with an assertion undermining this positive recognition: "At the same time ... faithfulness to the covenant requires us to call *all* men and women to faith in Jesus Christ." Although the Presbyterian Church has taken steps to repudiate the ideological alignments of Christian supersessionism, the denomination remains caught on the horns of a dilemma. Presbyterians cannot forge relationships of trust with Jews if they hold fast to the assertion that there is no salvific integrity in the covenantal relations between God and the Jews. There can be no firm basis of peacemaking without the theological recognition of the ongoing legitimacy of the Jewish tradition. Yet such affirmation would preclude Jews as legitimate targets of proselytizing overtures, contradict evangelical commitments of the church's past, and call for the repudiation of interpretations of New Testament texts that have often been deployed to sanction a global spiritual conquest.

- *The battle for the Bible*. The competing conceptions of the evangelical mission of the Presbyterian Church grow out of tensions within the New Testament and subsequent traditions of interpretation. Many Christian groups, most notably the

Roman Catholic church, have moved away from missionary outreach to Jews on the basis of their reading of Paul's Letter to the Romans, most especially chapters 9–11.[19] The foundational text is the assertion that "the gifts and calling of God are irrevocable" (11:29). There are of course other New Testament texts that indicate that a "new covenant in Christ" has rendered the "old covenant" obsolete (Hebrews 8:13). In other words, the New Testament can be enlisted to support at least two conflicting visions about the character of God's covenant with the Jewish people. The status of the Jewish people in the eyes of many Protestants will depend upon the adjudication of these competing biblical notions.

At the same time, Presbyterian interpretations of the Bible continue to shape perceptions concerning the Jewish attachment to the land of Israel. Norman Habel, among others, has noted that there are several ideologies of the land that run through the Bible.[20] Most Reformed Christians espouse a view that insists that the land of Israel belongs first and foremost to God. This land was entrusted to the people Israel, but its possession was contingent on the people's ethical behavior, most particularly the just and compassionate treatment of the vulnerable. When the people Israel failed to abide by these moral standards, God rendered a judgment that resulted in the withdrawal of this sacred gift.

The primacy of this interpretative model sustains two critical attitudes common among Presbyterians. First, current policies within Israel that impinge on the rights and dignity of the Palestinian people are often read as a negation of Jewish claims to the Holy Land. Second, Presbyterians have adopted the criteria of modernity in their assessment of the Jewish attachment to this territory. In other words, the assertion that the land of Israel is imbued with a holiness that distinguishes it from any other land is regarded as an unintelligible, if not idolatrous assertion. From this perspective, the Jewish people are guilty of a serious theological blunder when they assign infinite value to a finite reality.

Clearly, the hermeneutical principles accepted by most Presbyterians put them at odds with many, if not most Jews. By and large, Presbyterians have not developed a theology of the Holy Land, and they tend to unleash negative judgments in response to the foundational covenantal claims of Judaism that link peoplehood, Torah, and the land of Israel into a seamless entity.[21] This critical predilection will remain an active factor until Christians recognize that they have a theological and ethical stake in the flourishing of Judaism. Does the commitment to reverse the adversarial habits of mind and heart within the Christian tradition also entail the recognition that the flourishing of Judaism is inseparable from the flourishing of the Jewish people in the land of Israel?

Israel is the only nation in the world where Jews constitute the majority of the population. Although in most ways a modern state that sees all of its citizens as legally equal, its democratic ideals are in tension with the commitment to Israel as a "Jewish homeland." When Christians and Muslims visit the Holy Land, they find themselves in existential terms as guests in someone else's home. This situation does not mesh easily with the historical memories or the prevailing definitions of theological identity within either Christian or Muslim communities. The question is whether Christians and Muslims have something of vital theological importance to discover from being a guest in a Jewish setting. Bishop Krister Stendahl maintains that the greatest challenge facing every religion is the discovery that, in God's eyes, we are all minorities. If so, Israel provides an opportunity for Christians and Muslims to learn what cannot be discovered anywhere else in the world, namely, what it means to affirm Jewish sovereignty on land deemed holy by all three traditions. This recognition does not negate the legitimate political aspirations of Palestinians, nor is it intended to enshrine a position of Christian and Muslim civic inferiority. Rather, the Christian and Muslim affirmation of a Jewish state points to a paradigm shift in which both honor the interwoven destinies of all three traditions. The centuries-old fusion of theological, political, and military power in the quest for global dominance has proven a dysfunctional fantasy. Israel provides a context in which our interdependencies might yet be discovered and our mutual aspirations advanced. Until both Christians and Muslims can live and learn within a sacred context in which they do not seek to displace the power of the majority, there is little likelihood that either community will recognize the legitimacy of the Jewish state and offer support for its continued existence and welfare. On the other side, the Jewish nation will need to recover and put into practice the biblical and rabbinic requirements of hospitality if these essential new insights are to take hold of the hearts and minds of Christians and Muslims.

- *Dreams and delusions*. Deep fractures within the Presbyterian community were exposed in the debates over the Presbyterian endorsement of Avodat Yisrael and in the church's pursuit of a divestment policy. The impasse has spilled into the public arena, generating the most serious rift between Presbyterian and Jewish communities in recent memory. Notably, the most successful efforts to prevent the collapse of the Presbyterian-Jewish relationship did not emanate from the leadership of the General Assembly nor emerge in response to the strident denunciations of Jewish defense agencies. Rather, the most potent corrective to disengagement from the Jewish community came from local Presbyterian churches and synagogues across the country where both Presbyterians and Jews had forged strong ties. The reversal in the actions of the 216th General Assembly depended upon a web of friendships that outflanked the lamentable habits of Christian supersessionism.

There are powerful indications that the conflicted attitudes about Judaism and Israel will remain within Presbyterian circles, because the church's leadership is understandably reluctant to confront theological complexities that will polarize the members of an already beleaguered denomination. Therefore, the future of Presbyterian-Jewish relations, and indeed that of mainline Protestant-Jewish relations, will depend upon a range of grassroots initiatives that can result in lasting partnerships. This approach is also well understood among champions of the Palestinian cause who have invested their time and resources in networks such as the Sabeel Ecumenical Liberation Theology Center and the Presbyterian Middle East Caucus.

During the course of the past few years, critics of Presbyterian policies have suggested that the denomination is incorrigibly antisemitic and hopelessly partisan in its pro-Palestinian alignments. However, these facile dismissals permit little understanding of a deeply conflicted community and end up concealing a far more serious challenge: how is it that good intentions and simplistic solutions continue to cloud the vision of significant segments of the Christian population in the United States? The angry backlash of Israel's supporters has often reinforced the nasty habit of substituting one set of caricatures for another, thereby adding new layers of antagonism.

When it comes to the Presbyterian-Jewish impasse, there is little possibility of making a positive contribution if participants in these debates fall into a scripted drama. The quest for a one-sided victory fans the flames of indissoluble antipathies, and the yield is carnage on every side of the border. When it comes to the dueling allegiances within the Presbyterian family or theological clashes with the Jewish community or the struggle between Israelis and Palestinians, the promise of authentic engagement and transformative encounter become ever more remote if people are captivated by dreams of quick fixes and happy endings.[22]

Michael Oren has examined the interplay of faith and fantasy in his historical portrayal of America's involvement in the Middle East. From the Puritans to Woodrow Wilson, the United States has consistently embraced a moralistic mission to serve as "a light to the nations."[23] The legacy of America as "chosen" both to spread democracy and to bring peace to a desperate world continues to animate Middle Eastern policies. Oren demonstrates that, in recent decades, the seductions of this national myth have proven to be irresistible, with presidents from Jimmy Carter to George W. Bush embracing the role of the United States as messianic mediator and liberator. However, efforts to establish the *pax Americana* have led to the exercise of economic, political, and military power that have greatly complicated the nation's entanglements in the region while at the same time engendering deep-seated resentments.

In similar fashion, Presbyterian initiatives to save the region too often reflect its exaggerated sense of its own importance. Before the Presbyterian Church can make a positive impact on the Middle East and reinvigorate constructive relations with its Jewish and Muslim neighbors, the General Assembly and its leadership will need to tone down their rhetorical excesses and abandon their delusions of grandeur. They are far more likely to succeed if they build their church's policies on a solid foundation of grassroots initiatives that demonstrate the possibilities of working collaboratively with peoples who see the world in radically different terms.

Notes

1. See "A Theological Understanding of the Relationship between Christians and Jews," online at www.pcusa.org/theologyandworship/issues/christiansjews.pdf (here and elsewhere, online citations were accessed on 13 July 2009).

2. "A Presbyterian Understanding of the Relationship between Christians and Jews: A Counter Witness to the Presbytery of Philadelphia's Messianic New Church Development," *Jewish Exponent* (2 Oct. 2003), 11. This statement is signed by approximately 140 members of the Presbytery of Philadelphia.

3. See, for instance, "Jewish Community Statement on New Messianic Congregation in Greater Philadelphia," written by Rabbi Carol Harris-Shapiro, signed by Rabbis David Gutterman and Burt Siegel, and distributed on June 18, 2003. The statement was prepared with the

collaboration of the Jewish Community Relations Council and the VAAD: Board of Rabbis of Greater Philadelphia.

4. See Emily Enders Odom's report "Christian-Jewish Relations to be Studied," online at www.pcusa.org/ga216/news/ga04080.htm.

5. Clifton Kirkpatrick, "Statement from the Stated Clerk of the General Assembly of the Presbyterian Church (USA) Concerning Actions of the 216th General Assembly (2004) Regarding Israel and Palestine and Outreach to Jewish People" (July 2004), online at www.pcusa.org/pcnews/2004/04329.htm.

6. "Report of the Administrative Commission Overseeing Congregation Avodat Yisrael to the Presbytery of Philadelphia, November 23, 2004," written by Mark Wallace and Bill Borrow for the Presbytery of Philadelphia. This document is filed within the Minutes of the Presbytery of Philadelphia, although public access has been restricted.

7. The controversy regarding the Good Friday prayer "For the Conversion of the Jews" within the Tridentine Mass highlights deep divides within the Roman Catholic community as well as with the Jewish community. See online reports at www.spiegel.de/international/world/0,1518,542872,00.html, www.the-tidings.com/2007/072707/popelatin.htm, and www.haaretz.com/hasen/pages/ShArt.jhtml?itemNo=952188&contrassID=1&subContrassID=1.

8. Divestment overtures are not a uniquely Presbyterian phenomenon. Lutherans (ELCA), the Disciples of Christ, the Episcopalians, and most recently the Methodists have all entered into passionate debates about the advisability of applying this kind of political pressure on the state of Israel. For the outcome of the Methodist petitions, see "United Methodists Explore Divestment Proposals" (29 Jan. 2008), online at www.umc.org.

9. See "A Brief Summary of Presbyterian General Assembly Statements," online at www.pcusa.org/worldwide/israelpalestine/resources/17gastatements.pdf.

10. "Resolution on Israel and Palestine: End the Occupation Now," online at www.pcusa.org/oga/publications/endoccupation03.pdf.

11. "General Assembly Action Resolution on Israel and Palestine: Initiating Divestment and Ending Occupation," online at www.pcusa.org/worldwide/israelpalestine/israelpalestineresolution.htm#1.

12. Former U.S. President Jimmy Carter's book, *Palestine: Peace Not Apartheid* (New York: 2006), provides a striking example of this misleading linkage. Clarence B. Jones, former counsel and draft speech writer for Martin Luther King, Jr., provided a trenchant critique of this comparison in a speech titled "Israel is Neither South Africa Nor Racist," delivered on May 18, 2006 at the conference "The Church, Israel, and the Middle East" (Central Presbyterian Church, New York City); summarized online at www.enddivestment.com/jones.html.

13. Known in Hebrew as *geder hahafradah* (the separation fence), the barrier is actually a fence in some areas and a wall in others.

14. This group has an online site at www.pcjcr.org.

15. See "Action of the 217th General Assembly (2006) regarding Israel/Palestine," online at www.pcusa.org/interfaith/pdf/ga217response.pdf.

16. Moderator Joan Gray and Clifton Kirkpatrick's "Pastoral Letter" of 25 June 2006, online at www.pcusa.org/pcnews/2006/06330.htm.

17. See www.pcusa.org/middleeastern/pdf/gazastatement.pdf.

18. See n. 1.

19. Prominent advocates of Roman Catholic-Jewish relations are struggling to determine if the Good Friday prayer in the Tridentine Mass amounts to a theological regression. Some apologists for the Vatican insist that the prayer frames an eschatological hope that does not authorize proselytizing among Jews in our day.

20. Norman C. Habel, *The Land Is Mine: Six Biblical Land Ideologies* (Minneapolis: 1995); also see Walter Brueggemann, *The Land* (Minneapolis: 1977); W.D. Davies, *The Territorial Dimension of Judaism* (Berkeley: 1982); Robert Wilken, *The Land Called Holy* (New Haven: 1992); W. Eugene March, *Israel and the Politics of Land* (Louisville: 1994).

21. See the condemnation of Christian Zionism, online at www.pcusa.org/worldwide/israelpalestine/resources/21christianzionism.pdf.

22. Instead of seeing the Israeli-Palestinian conflict through an economic and political lens that revolves around divestment strategies, the insights in Paul Collier's *The Bottom Billion* (New York: 2007) provide a fresh approach to the challenges. Collier puts forth a compelling argument for economic and political collaboration that defies conventional wisdom and that offers sound reasons for Israelis and Palestinians alike to sit at the same table.

23. Michael B. Oren, *Power, Faith, and Fantasy: America in the Middle East 1776 to the Present* (New York: 2007).

The Protestant Problem(s) of American Jewry

Mark Silk
(TRINITY COLLEGE)

In his 2007 book on the "Judeo-Evangelical alliance" in George W. Bush's America, the journalist and sometime Israeli political apparatchik Zev Chafets wrote that "[n]o Christian Zionist in the United States is more red hot" than Pastor John Hagee. Head of San Antonio's huge Cornerstone Church, Hagee is a longtime enthusiast of Israel who has for decades led his parishioners on trips to the Holy Land. A staunch premillennialist who preaches an "End Times" theology with its elements of "rapture," "tribulation," and Christ's second coming, he raised millions of dollars for the ingathering of Russian Jews in Israel; in 1999, he became the first non-Jew ever to be honored with the San Antonio B'nai B'rith Council's Humanitarian of the Year Award. In February 2006, Hagee assembled 300 prominent evangelicals from around the country to kick off Christians United for Israel—"a national organization through which every pro-Israel church, para-church organization, ministry or individual in America can speak and act with one voice in support of Israel in matters related to Biblical issues." In March 2007, he was invited to speak at the annual meeting of AIPAC, the powerful pro-Israel lobby, where he was received with "multiple standing ovations."[1]

Six months later, on December 23, Mike Huckabee, a former Baptist pastor and governor of Arkansas who was then seeking the Republican party nomination for president, made an appearance at Cornerstone Church. What followed was a flurry of protest from within the American Catholic community. "Hagee has a history of denigrating the Catholic religion," declared Bill Donohue, president of the Catholic League for Religious and Civil Rights, the premier national Catholic defense organization.[2] Nor was the famously combative Donohue alone. The Catholic News Agency featured a report headlined "Mike Huckabee to Speak at Strongly Anti-Catholic Preacher's Church," in response to which a prominent Catholic blogger (and self-described Huckabee supporter) described Hagee as "a raving anti-Catholic bishop."[3] What had Hagee done to acquire the reputation of being a zealous opponent of Catholicism? The evidence adduced by Donohue and company was principally a YouTube video showing Hagee outlining an End Times scenario in which the "Roman Church" was identified as the Whore of Babylon—a centuries-old tradition of Protestant anti-Catholic propaganda.[4]

Two months after the Huckabee visit, the controversy repeated itself when the then-presumptive victor in the Republican nomination contest, John McCain, also appeared at Hagee's church and, to considerable fanfare, received the pastor's endorsement. This time, Donohue issued a press release charging Hagee with having "for the past few decades ... waged an unrelenting war against the Catholic Church.[5] In the tempest that followed, McCain eventually rejected Hagee's anti-Catholicism while insisting that he was glad to have the pastor's endorsement. All the while, however, Hagee's much-courted Jewish friends said not a word.

Once upon a time, Jewish self-defense agencies saw it as their business to war against religious bigotry wherever it occurred. The legal scholar Samuel Rabinove has pointed out that, over the years, the American Jewish Committee, the American Jewish Congress, and the Anti-Defamation League (ADL) intervened in more cases involving non-Jews than those involving Jews.[6] In 1946, the ADL's Leo Shapiro spoke to the American Catholic Sociological Society on "Religious Tensions in the U.S.—A Social Problem." The social problem in question was the religious prejudice directed at Jews and Catholics by Protestants in American society; it followed that the two minority groups had an interest in standing up for each other. Shapiro's imagined examples were a Jewish physician and a Catholic lawyer who were both handicapped by their religious affiliations.[7] A half century later, such barriers to professional accomplishment were barely a memory in the United States. Even so, it was striking that in the midst of the Hagee-Catholic controversy, the ADL's president, Abraham Foxman, should have declared outright that this was "not a Jewish issue." Responding to the *Forward*, the weekly Jewish newspaper, Foxman asked, "Are we troubled by Hagee's support of McCain and McCain's acceptance? The answer is no, and that's where it ends for us."[8] His answer testified not only to a shift in the perceived interfaith responsibilities of American Jewry, but also to the radically enhanced place of evangelical Protestants such as Hagee in Jewish communal life. Their support of Israel in the post-9/11 world set the seal on their status as the principal Gentile ally of the American Jewish establishment, decisively supplanting what had come to be known as mainline Protestantism.

Toward a Judeo-Christian Nation

The mid-20th-century alliance between Jews and mainline Protestantism first took shape in the 1920s, with the rise of the "Goodwill movement" within the Protestant establishment.[9] At a time of significant interreligious strains in American society, this movement provided a countervailing trend. It was spearheaded by the Federal Council of Churches, an ecumenical organization whose members comprised the principal mainline Protestant denominational groups, including Presbyterians, Congregationalists, Methodists, and Episcopalians. The Federal Council's Committee on Goodwill between Jews and Christians was an expression of the Protestant establishment's concern that Jews (and Catholics) participate in a range of institutions designed to promote civil and political reform. Foremost among the interfaith institutions that sprang up at the time was the National Conference of Christians and Jews (now known as the National Conference for Community and Justice), whose leader,

Everett R. Clinchy, propounded a version of religious pluralism that would not come into its own until after the Second World War. To be sure, the movement was not without its opponents in the mainline Protestant world, which harbored a significant number of traditionalists who believed that the best thing one could do for those of other faiths was to lead them to Jesus. As Benny Kraut makes clear, the moderates in the Federal Council who favored harmonious relations among America's several faiths were often on the defensive.[10] Yet in a real sense the Goodwill movement was the leading edge of mainline Protestantism, carrying forward the modernist banner on the interfaith front at the same time as fundamentalists within the mainline denominations were going down to defeat.

The Jewish community was to some extent suspicious of Protestant goodwill. Mixed messages frequently emanated from the Federal Council, and it was easy enough to suspect that the Protestant hegemons were concealing a hard fist of unrepentant evangelism within the velvet glove of interreligious amity. Nonetheless, from civic efforts such as the Community Chest charity to campaigns against religious discrimination, Jews saw much to gain in the alliance. Indeed, the largest financial backer of the National Conference of Christians and Jews was B'nai B'rith. For its part, the American Jewish Committee (under the National Conference's auspices) silently funded a study conducted by Drew University, a Methodist institution, with regard to references to Jews in religious textbooks used to instruct Protestants in churches and seminaries. As a small minority faith community worried about fending for itself, American Jewry in this regard behaved differently than the far more sizeable body of American Catholics. The Vatican's condemnation of the "Americanist heresy" at the turn of the century had left the American Catholic church very wary of interfaith activities of all sorts, particularly those that threatened to put Protestant denominations on any kind of equal footing with the Catholic church. In 1928, Pope Pius XI issued an encyclical that effectively forbade ecumenism, and while liberal Catholics sought to interpret it in such a way as to permit cooperative efforts to advance human welfare, the Catholic participation in the goodwill movement never came close to that of Jewish organizations. Not coincidentally, Jews sided with Protestants on virtually every social and political issue on which Catholics and Protestants differed; such issues included Prohibition, keeping religion out of the public schools, easing divorce laws, and allowing access to birth control. Catholics noted with some resentment the ability of Jews to put antisemitism on the Protestant establishment's agenda, something they had not been able to manage for anti-Catholicism.

Of prime importance in the narrative of Jewish-Protestant relations in the mid-20th century is the emergence of the idea of a "Judeo-Christian tradition" to identify a common faith for America. I have recounted this story at length elsewhere, but it is useful to review a few of the highlights.[11] As a political shibboleth, the term "Judeo-Christian" can be traced to the need to find a substitute for "Christian" as a marker of religious commonality in the 1930s, inasmuch as "Christian" had been co-opted by fascist and antisemitic organizations such as the Christian American Crusade and publications such as the *Christian Defender*. Not surprisingly, liberal Protestants led the way in devising the new terminology. In a 1941 handbook, *Protestants Answer Anti-Semitism*, the left-liberal *Protestant Digest* identified itself (for the first time) as "a periodical serving the democratic ideal which is implicit in the Judeo-Christian tradition."¹² Initially, the term received mixed notices in the American Jewish community. On the one hand, Julian Morgenstern, president of Reform Judaism's Hebrew Union College, called during the war for a partnership between Judaism and Christianity, saying, "We speak now, with still inadequate but steadily expanding understanding, of the Judeo-Christian heritage." Each faith, Morgenstern said, had its own unique and necessary contribution to make "to what we may truthfully call Judaeo-Christianity, the religion of tomorrow's better world."[13] On the other hand, Trude Weiss-Rosmarin, a well-known publicist, considered the very idea to be dangerous nonsense. Judaism and Christianity, she wrote, were not one entity at all; it was "a totalitarian aberration" to tie Jewish-Christian goodwill to a shared religious identity.[14]

Like it or not, "Judeo-Christian" became a familiar part of American political rhetoric during the cold war—a new definitional component of the American way of life. No less importantly, from the Jewish community's point of view, it signified a joint Judeo-Protestant theological enterprise that obscured (even if it could not banish) the supersessionist theology that, from the earliest days of the church, lay at the heart of Jewish-Christian enmity. Since the late 1930s, some American Protestant theologians had begun to emphasize what Christianity had in common with Judaism. These were not the standard Social Gospel liberals of the earlier part of the century but rather followers of the continental theology of crisis—the neo-Orthodox, as they came to be called.[15] Scorning the optimistic image of man and his works that dominated 19th-century Protestantism, they emphasized humanity's sinful nature and its obligation to transform itself through faith in the absolute. Central to their religious vision was a downgrading of classic Christian theology based on ancient Greek philosophical categories in favor of a "biblical" theology better equipped to convey the personal relationship between God and the individual. Works by such prominent Protestant Bible scholars as G. Ernest Wright and Paul Minear, while hewing to orthodox Christian beliefs, abandoned the traditional apologetic goal of showing the New Testament as fulfilling and superseding the Hebrew Bible. Rather, their aim was to demonstrate the extent to which the New Testament belonged to the world of Hebrew Scriptures and to stress, against 19th-century theology, the centrality of the Hebrew religion for Christianity.

America's most prominent Protestant theologian, Reinhold Niebuhr, was also the leading Christian "Hebraist." It was the Hebrew prophets who inspired Niebuhr's great theme of the moral complexity of historical existence. As he wrote in 1944: "I have, as a Christian theologian, sought to strengthen the Hebraic-prophetic content of the Christian tradition." In fact, over the years, Niebuhr's conception of the Christian tradition grew increasingly Hebraic and less supersessionist. In his 1939 Gifford lectures, which were later published in revised and expanded form, he stated: "The Christian belief that the meaning of both life and history is disclosed and fulfilled in Christ and his Cross, is in a sense a combination of Hellenic and Hebraic interpretations of life." But in his last major theological work, *The Self and the Dramas of History* (1955), he contended that the "essence of Christian faith is drawn from the Hebraic, particularly the prophetic, interpretation of life and history, and is erroneously interpreted as the consequence of a confluence of Hebraic and Hellenic streams of thought."[16] For Niebuhr, Hebraism, with its personal God, its sense of covenant community, and its memory of historical revelations, was far better equipped than Hellenic high culture and abstract thought to penetrate the mysteries of human existence. Hebraism revealed humankind for the problematic and imperfect thing it was and at the same time exalted the prophets' refusal to abide the problems and the imperfections. This was, for Niebuhr, the essential contribution of "Hebraic-Christian culture" to the moral and political crises of the mid-20th century.[17]

Neo-Orthodoxy insisted on the limited and historically conditioned character of all earthly institutions, including religious ones. The great sin, endemic to humanity, lay in overrating their moral worth; this was idolatry. The great virtue, embodied in the prophetic tradition, was constantly to question society's false absolutes in the name of the only true absolute: the God who transcends history. Among the false absolutes were the church and its theology. For the neo-Orthodox, Christianity—as an institution embedded in history—needed to be modest about its exclusive claims to truth, especially vis-à-vis Judaism. Paul Tillich held that Christianity could be seen as a Jewish heresy and Judaism as a Christian one, and this position was adopted by Niebuhr as well: "At best, the two can regard themselves as two versions of one faith, each thinking of the other as an heretical version of the common faith."[18] In *Christianity and the Children of Israel* (1948), the Methodist clergyman and religious studies professor A. Roy Eckardt developed a neo-Orthodox "theology for the Jewish question" that specified a "peculiar function which Judaism performs in the divine economy, that of testifying on behalf of a universal God of justice." Such testimony was meant to ensure that Christianity did not place unwarranted limits on divine grace. "We are confronted with the paradoxical fact," Eckhardt noted, "that, while Christianity originally broke away from Judaism partly for the purpose of universalizing the Judaeo-Christian message, today Judaism has the function of protesting on behalf of universalism against the particularization of that message by Christianity."[19] Such contentions came very close to an acknowledgment that God's covenant with the Jews was still intact, thus abjuring the age-old Christian claim that Jesus was the exclusive path to salvation.

Not only secular Jewish intellectuals such as Waldo Frank and Alfred Kazin, but also the leading Jewish theologian of the day, Abraham Heschel, grasped the outstretched hand of neo-Orthodoxy.[20] The foremost Jewish exponent of the neo-Orthodox vision of the Judeo-Christian, however, was Will Herberg, a self-made sociologist and theologian whose 1955 study, *Protestant Catholic Jew*, did much to set the terms of religious pluralism in postwar America. After turning from Marxism to religion in the late 1930s, Herberg considered becoming a Christian but was dissuaded by Niebuhr, who told him that he could not become a good Christian until he was first a good Jew. (In a paper read before a joint meeting of the Jewish and Union Theological seminaries in 1958, Niebuhr claimed that Judaism and Christianity were "sufficiently alike for the Jew to find God more easily in terms of his own religious heritage than by subjecting himself to the hazards of guilt feeling involved in a conversion to a faith, which whatever its excellencies, must appear to him as a symbol of an oppressive majority culture."[21]) Herberg's theological opus was *Judaism and Modern Man* (1951), a confession of faith that went beyond Judaism per se to express a neo-Orthodox belief in "the fundamental religious affirmation and commitment held in common by Judaism and Christianity."[22]

From a theological standpoint, the Catholics were far less in accord than the other two members of the tripartite coalition. Prior to the Second Vatican Council of 1962–1965, Catholicism was wedded to a confident, "Hellenic" system of thought derived from the work of Thomas Aquinas that was as far from neo-Orthodox "Hebraism" as could be imagined. Under the circumstances, not even John Courtney Murray, American Catholicism's lonely pre-Vatican II champion of religious pluralism, could have any use for the Jewish-Christian faith of Niebuhr and company. Protestantism, Catholicism, and Judaism were, in Murray's view, "radically different" styles of religious belief, none of which was "reducible, or perhaps even comparable, to any of the others." The best that might be hoped for was "creeds at war intelligibly" under "the articles of peace which are the religion-clauses of the First Amendment."[23]

The Jewish-Protestant theological alliance was mirrored in the contemporary religious policy agenda, which saw Jews and Protestants allied in supporting greater church-state separation, as against the Catholic goals of gaining public funding for parochial schools and obtaining a U.S. ambassador to the Vatican. On all fronts, the most robust interfaith alliance of the postwar period was that between Jews and mainline Protestants. Persisting through the 1960s, this alliance was notable for its liberal domestic policy agenda centered on civil rights. Indeed, when trouble arose toward the end of the decade, it was not because of a domestic issue. Rather, it was the Six-Day War of 1967 that proved to be a watershed in Jewish relations with mainline Protestantism.

A Fading Alliance

In the anxious weeks preceding the Six-Day War, American Jewish support for the Jewish state proved far more robust than the perennially worried American Jewish establishment could have imagined. Between the beginning of the crisis and the war's end, the United Jewish Appeal alone collected $100 million, a fair portion of it coming from individuals whose Jewish identity seemed minimal at best. But if American Jews turned toward Jerusalem in unprecedented numbers, their mainline Protestant friends mostly preferred to remain on the sidelines. At a rabbinical meeting in Los Angeles, the head of Reform Judaism's interfaith activities, Rabbi Balfour Brickner, assailed the "Christian establishment" for not being willing to "take a strong stand on what it considered to be a political issue." At the other end of the denominational spectrum, Pesach Z. Levovitz, the president of the Rabbinical Council of America, expressed "deep disappointment" over the failure of "major segments of the world and American Christian community to raise their voices in defense of Israel when before the outbreak of hostilities President Nasser of Egypt was threatening the annihilation of its more than two million Jews." Levovitz called for an end to interfaith discussion until Christian leaders made clear their support for Israel's territorial and political integrity.[24]

In this regard, however, mainline Protestantism was less than forthcoming. Upon reading both rabbis' remarks in the *New York Times*, the former president of New York's prestigious Union Theological Seminary, Henry Pitney Van Dusen, dispatched a letter to the editor that read, in part:

All persons who seek to view the Middle East problem with honesty and objectivity stand aghast at Israel's onslaught, the most violent, ruthless (and successful) aggression since Hitler's blitzkrieg across Western Europe in the summer of 1940, aiming not at victory but at annihilation—the very objective proclaimed by Nasser and his allies which had drawn support to Israel.

As inflammatory as those words were to most Jews, the Protestant establishment, whose leaders had never been strong supporters of the Jewish state, did not hurry to dissociate itself from them. *Christian Century* magazine, the foremost organ of mainline Protestantism, declared that Christians would not "sign a blank check" for Israel.[25]

For its part, the National Council of Churches (NCC) struggled to maintain neutrality in the conflict. On the eve of the war, its general board adopted a resolution supporting the U.N.'s peacekeeping efforts. At a rally for Israel in Washington on June 8, news of the cease-fire interrupted the remarks being offered by the NCC's general secretary, R.H. Edwin Espy. Lest any of its readers construe his presence as pro-Israel partisanship, the *Century* published the disclaimer that he had been unable to deliver: "Our identification is not of course exclusively with any one community, one belligerent, or one set of national aspirations. ... Had we been invited to attend a corresponding meeting of the Arab community in the United States we would have been bound by our principles to bring the identical message—the plea for peace with justice and freedom which we derive from our Judeo-Christian heritage." On July 7, a new NCC resolution urged international "acceptance" of the state of Israel even as it criticized Israel's "territorial expansion by armed force" and "unilateral retention of occupied lands."[26]

The 1970s saw a slow pulling apart of the alliance between Jewish and mainline Protestant leadership. In their 1974 volume, *The New Anti-Semitism*, the ADL's Arnold Forster and Benjamin R. Epstein avoided rehearsing the story of the mainline Protestant lack of support for Israel at the time of the Six-Day War. Instead, in a chapter titled "The Clergy," they focused on a sermon critical of Israel that was delivered by Francis B. Sayre, dean of Washington's National Cathedral, on Palm Sunday of 1972.[27] Although it was still too early to openly contemplate the end of this durable alliance, in the course of the decade the two sides came to have less and less in common. Their shared civil rights agenda gave way to contention over affirmative action: in opposing policies giving preferential treatment to African Americans in employment and educational opportunities, the American Jewish community increasingly found itself at odds not only with the black community but also with the Protestant establishment.[28] Thus, in the prominent case of Allan Bakke, a white Vietnam veteran who claimed that he had been unjustly denied admission to the medical school at the University of California at Davis, the ADL and American Jewish Committee filed *amicus curiae* briefs on behalf of the plaintiff, whereas the National Council of Churches weighed in on the side of the state's affirmative action policy. Altogether, the Jewish policy agenda was marked by a pulling back from the broad societal issues of the civil rights era in favor of matters of communal self-interest, its two most prominent concerns being Israel and the plight of Soviet Jewry. Neither issue was, to put it mildly, high on the list of mainline Protestant concerns. However, there were other Protestants who felt differently.

Evangelicals on the March

Even as its romance with mainline Protestantism was fading, the American Jewish community was discovering a new object for its affections: evangelicals. The support of American evangelicalism for "Israel" was longstanding; it can be traced to an enthusiasm for the return of the Jews to the Holy Land that was expressed by the first exponents of the tradition in the 18th century. That enthusiasm, which never disappeared, led to great excitement among evangelicals when the state of Israel came into being in 1948. Indeed, the rise of premillennial dispensationalist theology (which postulated the ingathering and conversion of the Jews prior to the battle of Armageddon, followed by Christ's second coming and the final judgment) led many evangelicals to see the establishment of the Jewish state as a sign that the End Times was at hand.

For as long as its alliance with the Protestant mainline held sway, the American Jewish community paid little attention to the evangelicals. Notwithstanding the rise of Billy Graham and what was called "neo-evangelicalism" after the Second World War, revivalist Protestantism in the postwar period was considered to be a fading force in American religion, the last gasp of Scopes-era fundamentalism—and this, from the Jewish perspective, was a good thing. Evangelicals, after all, were proselytizers, "Christers" preoccupied with spreading the gospel and committed to the view that salvation could be obtained only through acceptance of Jesus as one's personal Lord and savior. It was the Six-Day War, which evangelicals viewed as "confirmation that Jews and Israel still had a role to play in God's ordering of history," that opened the door to a new relationship.[29]

In the wake of the war, Jewish leaders who engaged in interfaith dialogue began talking to evangelical leaders in a series of encounters, first between Jews and the Southern Baptist Convention and later, between Jews and the broader evangelical community.[30] Among the results was a 1978 volume, *Evangelicals and Jews in Conversation on Scripture, Theology, and History*, edited by Marc H. Tanenbaum and A. James Rudin (the director and assistant director of national interreligious affairs for the American Jewish Committee), and Marvin R. Wilson, the chair of the department of biblical and theological studies at Gordon College in Massachusetts. In his essay, Wilson made it clear that evangelicals had their own means of getting around classic supersessionist Christian claims, if they so chose. Focusing on Romans 9-11, where Paul seems to argue against the displacement of God's people, he wrote that "the great sensitivity on the part of evangelicals to the issue of biblical authority does not permit Paul's teaching concerning the Jews to go unheeded or to be passed over lightly."[31] Even as these efforts at dialogue went forward, however, the evangelical world was about to enter American public life in a way that no one anticipated, with political reverberations still being felt a generation later. In that context, the question of evangelical attitudes toward the Jews and Israel would quickly take center stage.

Indeed, it did so at the very moment the religious right emerged as a force on the national political scene. The occasion was the "national affairs briefing," a two-day event held in late August 1980 with the purpose of transforming white evangelicals into loyal and active Republicans. Shortly before the GOP nominee for president,

Ronald Reagan, addressed the assemblage, the newly elected president of the Southern Baptist Convention, Oklahoma pastor Bailey Smith, delivered a speech in which he declared: "It is interesting at great political rallies how you have a Protestant to pray, and then you have a Catholic to pray, and then you have a Jew to pray. With all due respect to those dear people ... God Almighty does not hear the prayer of a Jew. For how in the world can God hear the prayer of a man who says that Jesus Christ is not the true Messiah?" The resulting tempest led to a meeting in New York between Tanenbaum and Jerry Falwell, the Baptist minister who had emerged as the religious right's leading figure. The meeting produced a statement from Falwell acknowledging that God "hears the cry of any sincere person who calls on Him." Falwell, according to the *New York Times* story, declared that the "alignment of evangelical Christians and Jews" would "withstand the slurs and political exploitation of these days."[32]

Over the next three decades, the question of how to engage with evangelicalism would become the defining interfaith issue for American Jewry. On the one hand, evangelical support for Israel was staunch and unflagging, as the Israelis themselves would acknowledge by repeatedly embracing evangelical leaders. On the other, American Jews felt threatened by the rise of the religious right and its determination to inject its religious values and practices into public debate and public policy. Most Jews had long regarded a high wall of separation between church and state as the best guarantor of their equal status in American society, and they were horrified by the oft-expressed desire of the religious right to turn back the clock to the days when, for example, children recited Christian prayers in public schools.[33] In 1982, ADL national director Nathan Perlmutter and his wife Ruth Ann wrote *The Real Anti-Semitism in America* to calm Jewish nerves and smooth the way for an alliance with evangelicals against the enemies of Israel. With regard to the underlying issue of whether the supposed ally was prepared to recognize Judaism's religious claims, they wrote:

> Christian-professing attitudes, in this time, in this country, are for all practical purposes, no more than personally held religious conceits, barely impacting the way in which Jews live. Their political action, as it relates to the security of the state of Israel, impacts us far more meaningfully than whether a Christian neighbor believes that his is the exclusive hot line to "on high."[34]

The counter to this "Israel card," as deployed by liberal Jews, would invariably be an argument on the order of: yes, the evangelicals support Israel, but only for the sake of their own exclusivist ideas about salvation and the End Times, which envision that Jews will either convert or be damned.[35] To which the other side would respond: that's nothing for us to worry about now. Or as the Perlmutters put it: "If the Messiah comes, on that very day we'll consider our options. Meanwhile, let's praise the Lord and pass the ammunition."[36]

In fact, the extent to which evangelical support for Israel has rested on millennialist expectations is not easy to specify. Whereas such expectations have been part of the theological armory of conservative evangelicalism for more than a century, evangelicals need not, and often do not, refer to them as the basis of their support. They also cite the fact that the Bible says (for example, in Gen. 15) that God gave the land of Israel to the Jews. In a 2003 survey conducted by John C. Green, 84 percent of evangelicals said they sympathized with Israel because of this covenantal gift, while 75 percent cited biblical prophecy.[37] Evangelicals' support for Israel, in other words, is determined by biblical doctrine, which posits, among other things, that Jewish possession of the land is divinely warranted. In this, the evangelicals part theological company with many mainline Protestants, whose readiness to accept the continued validity of God's covenant with the Jews often stops short of a recognition of the centrality of the land of Israel to that covenant. In 1998, this lack of recognition came to public attention with particular clarity when Barbara Brown Zikmund, the president of Hartford Seminary and a church historian, contributed a short essay to the *Hartford Courant* on the occasion of the fiftieth anniversary of the state of Israel. "To survive into the next century," she wrote, "Jews will need to let go of the idea that a Jewish state located in a physical place is crucial to Jewish identity."[38] Not surprisingly, the Hartford Jewish community was shocked and dismayed, and in the ensuing uproar, Zikmund admitted that her words had been ill chosen. Yet even better chosen words would hardly have disguised her suggestion that Jews should embrace something like the heavenly Jerusalem of traditional Christian theology. The contrast with the evangelical perspective could not be starker. As the evangelical theologian Gerald McDermott noted: "[W]hile most [mainline] Protestant and Catholic scholars since the Holocaust fall over each other reaffirming God's eternal covenant with Israel, for the most part they ignore what for most Jews is absolutely integral to that covenant: the land." By contrast, McDermott writes, evangelicals "take seriously God's promises in Genesis to give a land to Abraham's descendants."[39]

The Divestment Problem and the Replacement Problem

In the first decade of the 21st century, Jewish-Protestant tensions over the status of the land of Israel centered on campaigns within particular denominations to engage in selective divestment of corporations doing business with Israel—in particular, those considered to be supportive of the continued Israeli occupation of Palestinian territories. The campaign focused on the Caterpillar corporation, which sells tractors and bulldozers used by the Israel Defense Forces, but other corporations were involved as well. Here is not the place to trace the details of these campaigns and how the organized Jewish community mobilized—with some success—to combat it.[40] In a paper written for the Jerusalem Center for Public Affairs, Eugene Korn, then serving as director of Jewish affairs at the American Jewish Congress, noted the differences between political activists (anxious to push the churches into advocating for Palestinian interests), denominational leaders (willing to go along with Palestinian advocacy, up to a point), and rank-and-file Protestants whose support for the state of Israel remained at a high level. Among the major players advocating divestment was the Sabeel Ecumenical Liberation Theology Center, a small Jerusalem think tank led by an Anglican clergyman named Naim Ateek. Visiting the center with a number of ecumenical officers from the mainline denominations on a fact-finding mission to Israel, Korn had the following exchange with Ateek:

He explained that he comes from Beit She'an in the Jordan Valley, and claims his family was evicted from there in the War of Independence. "Israel was born in sin. I can never recognize the right of Israel to exist," he shouted. When I challenged him about the Bible's view of the Land of Israel being essential to God's covenant, Ateek told me that any theology that takes land seriously is "immature." In one fell swoop he had delegitimized Judaism and the concept of the Jewish people.

This is nothing other than the old theology of supersessionism with its concomitant anti-Semitism, both of which are discredited by current Christian theologians and all major churches.[41]

It can be argued that Ateek's position is not at all supersessionist, but merely an anti-Zionist Christian interpretation of God's still-valid covenant with the Jewish people. Be that as it may, the theological basis of Korn's response is worthy of note. When it comes to Jewish-Christian relations, support for Israel is not merely a matter of politics, but rather goes to the theological nub of the matter.

Likewise, the theological dimension has been of central importance to Jewish criticism of evangelical Protestants. For example, in its 1994 report, *The Religious Right: The Assault on Tolerance & Pluralism in America*, the ADL takes pains to discuss dispensationalist theology and how it "emphasizes both the singularity of the Jews and the magnitude of their error in rejecting Jesus."[42] For this reason, it is telling that, in establishing Christians United for Israel in 2006, John Hagee abjured the supersessionist doctrine (also known as "replacement theology"), going so far as to claim that "a growing majority of evangelicals do not preach it."[43] The following year, in a book titled *In Defense of Israel*, Hagee wrote that the idea that "Israel has been rejected and replaced by the church to carry out the work once entrusted to Israel ... [that the] Jewish people have ceased to be God's people, and the church is now spiritual Israel" is a "misconception ... rooted in the theological anti-Semitism that began in the first century." It was "time for Christians everywhere to recognize that the nation of Israel will never convert to Christianity." Moreover:

> There are two Israels in Scripture. One is a physical Israel, with a physical people, a physical Jerusalem, and physical borders that are plainly defined in Scripture. There is also a spiritual Israel, with a spiritual people and a spiritual New Jerusalem. Spiritual Israel (the church) may have the blessings of physical Israel, but it does not replace physical Israel in the economy of God.[44]

Upon publication of his book, Hagee claimed that it would "shake Christian theology." And sure enough, his assertion that God's covenant with Israel was still intact drew considerable fire from fellow evangelicals who insisted that Christianity did indeed supersede Judaism and that Jews erred in failing to accept Jesus as their savior. In fact, Hagee did not say in so many words that Jews could be saved on the strength of their covenant alone. In an interview with the *San Antonio Express-News* on December 13, 2007, he insisted that his views were orthodox and promised further clarification—which, as of this writing, he had not provided.

It is this theological demarche, as much as his fundraising for Jewish causes, that accounts for the warm embrace given to Hagee by Jewish organizations such as AIPAC and individuals such as Senator Joe Lieberman. Speaking at the "Night to Honor Israel" sponsored by the Christians United for Israel in July 2007, Lieberman went so far as to compare Hagee to Moses:

> I begin by thanking your founder, Pastor John Hagee. I would describe Pastor Hagee with the words the Torah uses to describe Moses, he is an "Eesh Elo Kim," a man of God because those words fit him; and, like Moses he has become the leader of a mighty multitude in pursuit of and defense of Israel.[45]

Not all Jewish leaders were prepared to go along with this. In the spring of 2008, Rabbi Eric Yoffie, president of the Union for Reform Judaism, denounced the Jewish alliance with Christian Zionists in general and with Hagee in particular as bad for Israel, and he urged Jews to stay away from "Nights to Honor Israel."[46] Meanwhile, J Street, a new lobbying group intended to be a liberal alternative to AIPAC, collected more than 40,000 signatures to protest Lieberman's return engagement at the Night to Honor Israel held in July 2008.

Conclusion

In their interfaith Protestant journey, American Jewry will, for the foreseeable future, continue to navigate between the Scylla of mainline hostility to Israel and the Charybdis of evangelical supersessionism. Yet while this tricky passage is unlikely to be eased any time soon, it is important to keep it in perspective. As Korn points out, people in the mainline Protestant pews are very far removed from the anti-Zionist agitators who have the ear of the denominational leadership. Interfaith relations with mainline Protestants still come about far more naturally than with evangelicals, and on a host of domestic issues—abortion and gay rights, above all—the American Jewish community remains far closer to mainline Protestantism than it does to either the evangelical or the Catholic world. At the same time, evangelicals are a far cry from the theocrats their opponents sometimes make them out to be.[47] It is true that, in the aftermath of the attacks of September 11, their attachment to George W. Bush showed signs of generating an exclusivist political theology. But as the Bush presidency went into decline, their support for him also subsided. Neither antisemitism nor anti-Zionism enjoy much support in Washington, D.C. or on Main Street. Jews, for their part, no longer have need of the kinds of religious alliances they so eagerly sought in an earlier time.

It nonetheless remains a curiosity that the American Jewish community, more at home in the United States than Jews have ever been in the diaspora, should care so much what their Gentile neighbors think of their religion. Does this have more to do with America than with the Jews? The American religious order is predicated not only on the proposition that all must be free to worship according to the dictates of their conscience, but also on the polite conviction that the right to disrespect other Americans' religion, protected as it is by the First Amendment, should not be exercised in public. Yet the acceptance to which American Jewry feels entitled extends beyond civil equality and public civility. There is a conviction that American Christians should acknowledge that Jews enjoy the same access to Heaven that they do, and that Jews are entitled to the land of Israel on their own terms, and not for the sake of some Christian eschatological purpose. In a community whose members seem mostly indifferent to religious doctrine, the theological underpinnings still hold. The covenant, somehow, endures.

Notes

1. Zev Chafets, *A Match Made in Heaven* (New York: 2007), 54–55; *Tulsa World* (3 May 2000); Jewish Telegraphic Agency (12 March 2007), online at www.jta.org/cgi-bin/iowa/breaking/100522.html (accessed 26 April 2008); see Christians United for Israel (CUFI), online at www.cufi.org/site/PageServer?pagename=about_About CUFI.

2. Jim Forsyth, "Huckabee Angers Some Catholics," Reuters (23 Dec. 2007), www.reuters.com/article/topNews/idUSN2326769820071223?sp=true (accessed 2 March 2009).

3. See the blogger "Alexham," on the Redstate site, www.crosstabs.org/stories/elections/2008/huckabee_to_speak_at_church_headed_by_ant_catholic_bigot (accessed 31 March 2008).

4. Youtube.com/watch?v=uViQ0hVV57Q (accessed 31 March 2008). Left out of the discussion was the issue of Cornerstone Church's longstanding hostility to Catholicism in its local San Antonio context. Located on the Texas fault line between regions of Anglo evangelical and Latino Catholic dominance, much of Cornerstone's growth has been the result of Hispanic defections from the Catholic fold. Mary Navarro Farr, a Latino Catholic who regularly attended the church in the 1980s, described a pulpit filled with "hellfire and brimstone" and much talk about the role of "the City of the Seven Hills" in the coming Tribulation. "Someone would say I have a friend who is Catholic and we need to pray for their deliverance from that cult," she said. "I couldn't pray that prayer." One time, another Hispanic woman who had left Catholicism accosted her for wearing a holy medal with the image of the Virgin Mary. "I said, 'Why you're looking at me like I dropped my clothes.' She said, 'It's a graven image.' I said, 'You're frightening me into leaving this place.' Not long after that I decided to leave. It was time for me to go" (Mary Navarro Farr, telephone interview with author, 7 March 2008). See also Timothy Matovina, *Guadalupe and Her Faithful: Latino Catholics in San Antonio, from Colonial Origins to the Present* (Baltimore: 2005), 137.

5. "McCain Embraces Bigot—Links to Anti-Catholic Hagee Video," online at catholicleague.org/release.php?id=1393 (accessed 31 March 2008).

6. Samuel Rabinove, "How—And Why—American Jews Have Contended for Religious Freedom: The Requirements and Limits of Civility," *Journal of Law and Religion* 8, nos. 1–2 (1990), 140.

7. Leo Shapiro, "Religious Tensions in the U.S.—A Social Problem," *The American Catholic Sociological Review* 8, no. 1 (March 1947), 33.

8. Jennifer Siegel, "Evangelical's Endorsement Spurs Debate," *Forward* (5 March 2008).

9. For an overview of the Goodwill movement, see Benny Kraut, "Jews, Catholics, and the Goodwill Movement," in *Between the Times: The Travail of the Protestant Establishment in America, 1900-1960*, ed. William R. Hutchison (New York: 1989), 193–230.

10. Ibid., 201–202.

11. Mark Silk, "Notes on the Judeo-Christian Tradition in America," *American Quarterly* 36, no. 1 (Spring 1984), 65–85.

12. Beatrice Jenney (ed.), *Protestants Answer Anti-Semitism* (New York: 1941), inside front cover.

13. Julian Morgenstern, *Judaism's Contribution to Post-War Religion* (pamphlet of the Hebrew Union College [1942]), 5, 15.

14. Trude Weiss-Rosmarin, *Judaism and Christianity: The Differences* (New York: 1943), 11.

15. The Social Gospel was a theological movement that gained ascendancy in mainline Protestantism in the late 19th and early 20th century. Applying Christian ethics to poverty, war, and injustice, it tended toward an optimistic view of the ability of human communities to ameliorate social ills. The theology of crisis, which came into its own after the First World War through the writings of the influential Swiss theologians Karl Barth and Emil Brunner, took a dimmer view of man and his works.

16. Reinhold Niebuhr, introduction to Waldo Frank's *The Jew in Our Day* (New York: 1944), 4; idem, *The Nature and Destiny of Man* (New York: 1949), 2:36–37; idem, *The Self and the Dramas of History* (New York: 1955), 44.

17. Niebuhr, *The Self and the Dramas of History*, 117.

18. Ibid., 91.
19. A. Roy Eckardt, *Christianity and the Children of Israel* (New York: 1948), 146–147.
20. See Frank, *The Jew in Our Day*, 178-184; Alfred Kazin, in a symposium appearing in *Partisan Review* 17 (1950), 234; and Abraham Heschel, "A Hebrew Evaluation of Reinhold Niebuhr," in *Reinhold Niebuhr: His Religious, Social, and Political Thought*, ed. Charles W. Kegley and Robert W. Bretall (New York: 1956), 409.
21. Reinhold Niebuhr, "Christians and Jews in Western Civilization," in his *Pious and Secular America* (New York: 1958), 108.
22. Will Herberg, *Judaism and Modern Man* (Philadelphia: 1951), xi.
23. John Courtney Murray, *We Hold These Truths* (New York: 1960), 138, 125.
24. *New York Times* (23 and 27 June 1967). A more extended account of this controversy is found in Mark Silk, *Spiritual Politics: Religion and America since World War II* (New York: 1988), 144–146.
25. *New York Times* (7 July 1967); *Christian Century* 84 (1967), 883-884.
26. *Christian Century* 84 (1967), 884–885; *Interchurch News* (Aug.-Sept. 1967), 4.
27. Arnold Forster and Benjamin R. Epstein, *The New Anti-Semitism* (New York: 1974), 80–85.
28. On the role of affirmative action in splitting Jews and blacks, see Cheryl Lynn Greenberg, *Troubling the Waters: Black-Jewish Relations in the American Century* (Princeton: 2006), 236–244.
29. Gerald McDermott, "Evangelicals and Israel," in *Uneasy Allies? Evangelical and Jewish Relations*, ed. Alan Mittleman, Byron Johnson, and Nancy Isserman (Lanham: 2007), 136.
30. These encounters are summarized by Lawrence Grossman in "The Organized Jewish Community and Evangelical America: A Brief History," in ibid., 51–53.
31. Marvin R. Wilson, "An Evangelical Perspective on Judaism," in *Evangelicals and Jews in Conversation on Scripture, Theology, and History*, ed. Marc H. Tanenbaum, A. James Rudin, and Marvin R. Wilson (Grand Rapids: 1978), 23.
32. A more extended account of the Bailey Smith episode is found in Silk, *Spiritual Politics*, 159–167.
33. On the centrality of church-state separation to the American Jewish community, see Gregg Ivers, *To Build a Wall: American Jews and the Separation of Church and State* (Charlottesville: 1995).
34. Nathan Perlmutter and Ruth Ann Perlmutter, *The Real Anti-Semitism in America* (New York: 1982), 156.
35. This view was recently expressed by *Time* magazine columnist Joe Klein by way of a blog post criticizing Senator Joe Lieberman for his support of Pastor John Hagee:

> A few questions for Senator Lieberman: Hagee's flagrant support for Israel has its basis in Scripture, to be sure, but in weird Scripture—namely Revelation, the strangest book of the New Testament. Revelation is the source of the phantasmagoria known as the Rapture, in which the battle of Armageddon is fought (against the Arabs, one expects), Israel triumphs, Jesus returns in celebration, lifts all Believers to heaven ... and everyone who doesn't believe in Jesus is incinerated. So, Senator, what do you think of all this? I suspect you're following an, ummm, short-term strategy here: the enemy of my enemy etc. etc. (www.time-blog.com/swampland/2008/07/but_what_happens_to_jews_in_th.html, [accessed 8 Aug. 2008]).

36. Perlmutter and Perlmutter, *The Real Anti-Semitism in America*, 156.
37. John C. Green, "Evangelicals and Jews: A View from the Polls," in Mittleman, Johnson, and Isserman (eds.), *Uneasy Allies?*, 35-36. See also the essay by Timothy Weber in this volume, "American Evangelicals and Israel: A Complicated Alliance," esp. 146–147.
38. *Hartford Courant* (3 May 1998).
39. McDermott, "Evangelicals and Israel," 141–143.
40. For an account of the struggle over the 2004–2005 divestment campaign in the Presbyterian church, see Andrew Walsh, "Presbyterians Divest the Jews," *Religion in the News* 8, no. 2

(Fall 2005), 18-21. On the background of the divestment campaign, see the essay by Christopher Leighton in this volume, "The Presbyterian-Jewish Impasse," 116–119.

41. Eugene Korn, "Divestment from Israel, the Liberal Churches, and Jewish Responses: A Strategic Analysis," online at think-israel.org/korn.churches.html (accessed 6 May 2008).

42. David Cantor, *The Religious Right: The Assault on Tolerance & Pluralism in America* (New York: 1994), 71. For a discussion of this report, see Mark Silk, "The New Antisecularism, Right for the Jews?" in *Antisemitism in America Today: Outspoken Experts Explode the Myths*, ed. Jerome A. Chanes (New York: 1995), 295–310.

43. David Horovitz, "Most Evangelicals are Seeing the Error of 'Replacement Theology'," *Jerusalem Post* (21 March 2006).

44. John Hagee, *In Defense of Israel* (Lake Mary, Fla.: 2007), 145, 148, 146.

45. Lieberman's statement can be found online at http://lieberman.senate.gov/newsroom/release.cfm?id=279110 (accessed 2 March 2009).

46. Ron Kampeas, "Reform Leader Calls on Jews to Skip Hagee's Pro-Israel Events," Jewish Telegraphic Agency (3 March 2008).

47. Cf., for example, James Rubin, *The Baptizing of America: The Religious Right's Plans for the Rest of Us* (New York: 2006), 65:

> Christocrats are waging an all-out campaign to baptize America. It is a struggle that will decide whether the United States remains a spiritually vigorous country but without an officially established religion, or whether America will become "Christianized," a land in which the religious beliefs and practices of Christian conservatives become the dominant faith: a legally mandated American theocracy exercising control over all aspects of our country's public and private life.

American Evangelicals and Israel: A Complicated Alliance

Timothy P. Weber
(FULLER THEOLOGICAL SEMINARY)

Since the late 1970s, American evangelicals have established themselves as visible and unrelenting supporters of Israel. Usually identified with the so-called "new Christian right," they have founded numerous pro-Israel organizations, held large rallies in Washington, D.C. and elsewhere, aggressively lobbied Congress and the White House, and eagerly supported candidates who promise to oppose any efforts to pressure Israel to trade land for peace. Evangelicals have also raised money to help Jews immigrate to Israel or settle on the West Bank, promoted tours to Israel, and sold millions of biblical prophecy books showing Israel's role in the "End Times," the last days leading up to the second coming of Christ. In short, the evangelicals' support of Israel is hard to miss and a force to be reckoned with.

All this is well known; but it is hardly the whole story. American evangelicals comprise a large and diverse segment of American religious life; and though they overwhelmingly support Israel, they do so for vastly different reasons and envision different futures for the Jewish state.

Locating Evangelicals in America's Free-Market Religious Economy

Historians of American religion have long recognized that for the last century, American Protestantism has had three rather distinct foci. On the right are fundamentalists, who militantly oppose most forms of modernity, fiercely defend orthodoxy, and invariably separate from anyone they consider to be theologically or behaviorally deviant. On the left are liberals, who eagerly embrace modernity, prefer an ethical rather than doctrinal approach to the Christian faith, and view the Bible, theology, and social issues in progressive terms. In the middle are evangelicals, who build broad, trans-denominational coalitions, uphold a more or less traditional theology based on a strong belief in the inspiration and authority of the Bible, and take an activist approach to evangelism, missions, and certain kinds of social reform.[1]

Though all three groups can trace their roots to 19th-century mainstream Protestantism, the current divisions grew out of the fundamentalist-modernist controversy of the early 20th century, when rival understandings of science, the Bible, and Christian theology tore the Protestant fabric apart. During the 1920s and 1930s, liberals gained control of the historic Protestant denominations, nearly all of which were classified as evangelical in the 1800s. When fundamentalists failed to stem the liberal tide, they created an elaborate religious subculture of their own. While some evangelicals decided to remain in their now-liberal denominations as the vocal opposition, many others found a home in more theologically compatible but not always comfortable fundamentalist circles.[2]

Nothing remains the same for long in American religious life. By the end of the Second World War, many of the more moderate evangelicals within fundamentalism were clearly unhappy with the prevailing pessimism, separatism, and negativism of the Protestant right wing. They called for a more positive "new evangelicalism" to engage other Christians and American culture. By the mid-1970s, this "born-again movement" was being widely reported. When evangelicals helped elect Jimmy Carter, a Sunday school-teaching Southern Baptist, to the White House, even outsiders noted the "evangelical renaissance" that was underway.[3] Once again, evangelicals were rebuilding their old coalitions with other religious groups in hopes of playing a more constructive role in American life.[4]

The evangelical comeback had staying power, thanks in large part to mainstream Protestantism's huge losses in membership and cultural influence over the last forty years. In a recent article in *Foreign Affairs*, Walter Russell Mead noted the "monumental changes in the balance of religious power in the United States" and then elaborated:

> According to *Christianity Today*, between 1960 and 2003, membership in mainline [liberal] denominations fell by more than 24 percent, from 29 million to 22 million. The drop in market share was even more dramatic. In 1960, more than 25 percent of all members of religious groups in the United States belonged to the seven leading mainline Protestant denominations; by 2003 this figure had dropped to 15 percent. The Pew Research Center reports that 59 percent of American Protestants identified themselves as mainline Protestant in 1988; by 2002-3, that percentage had fallen to 46 percent. In the same period, the percentage of Protestants who identified themselves as evangelical rose from 41 percent to 54 percent.[5]

Pew's recent "U.S. Religious Landscape Survey" reported similar findings. Of the 35,000 American adults surveyed, 51.3 percent identified themselves as Protestants. To be more precise, 26.3 percent of those surveyed were evangelicals, 18.1 percent were mainline Protestants, and 6.9 percent belonged to historically black churches. At present, then, evangelicals comprise the largest religious group in America, with Catholics running a close second at 23.9 percent.[6]

As evangelicals' market-share increased, so did their influence in American education, arts and media, business, and politics. Sociologist D. Michael Lindsay documented this trajectory of success in his book *Faith in the Halls of Power: How Evangelicals Joined the American Elite*. While Lindsay found that many fundamentalists and evangelicals remain focused on fighting a "culture war" against progressives, he located and interviewed hundreds of other evangelical leaders in high places who actively interact with people unlike themselves in order to find the common ground necessary for the common good. Lindsay noted a significant difference between "movement leaders" who try to exert influence while remaining inside their religious subculture and "public leaders" who take their evangelical faith into government, business, and culture.[7]

Increasingly, then, evangelicals are full of surprises. Though they still rate abortion and family values as high priorities, their list of moral, ethical, and political concerns is expanding to include other issues as well. Recently the National Association of Evangelicals made headlines by affirming the crucial importance of climate change and the environment, by opposing torture, and by promoting programs to address global poverty and the AIDS crisis, especially in Africa. In May 2008, a group of eighty evangelical leaders issued an "Evangelical Manifesto" that took both fundamentalists and liberals to task for politicizing faith, "using faith to express essentially political points that have lost touch with biblical truth. That way faith loses its independence, the church becomes 'the regime at prayer,' Christians become 'useful idiots' for one political party or another, and the Christian faith becomes an ideology in its purest form. Christian beliefs are used as weapons for political interests."[8]

Drawing on their long history of political involvement, evangelicals have also become leaders in various causes related to U.S. policy, especially in the areas of humanitarian concerns, human rights, and religious freedom. According to Mead, who has tracked evangelicals' rising influence in U.S. foreign policy circles, evangelicals tend to be suspicious of state-to-state aid or large-scale development efforts and favor more hands-on, grass-roots, and faith-based efforts to solve problems. Although not everyone is sanguine about the evangelicals' efforts to shape U.S. foreign policy, Mead believes that their influence will continue to grow and that they have shown signs of working well with others in achieving common goals.[9] In this way, 21st-century American evangelicals are reclaiming their 19th-century activist and reforming heritage.

Evangelical Views on Israel

When it comes to U.S. foreign policy, evangelicals are still best known for their strong support of Israel. For the most part, this support is rooted in a variety of biblical and theological ideas about the relationship of Christians and Jews in God's ongoing redemptive program, as described below.

Replacement Theology

According to the doctrine of replacement theology, which is more formally called "supersessionism," the church is the New Israel. Most Christians since the second and third centuries of the Common Era have believed that when Jews rejected Jesus as their Messiah, God transferred all their rights and privileges as the chosen people to the church. Since then, becoming part of the New Israel has depended on one's faith in Jesus Christ, rather than one's genealogical descent from Abraham and Isaac. Karl Barth, a leading 20th-century Swiss Protestant theologian, summarized this doctrine:

> The first Israel, constituted on the basis of physical descent from Abraham, has fulfilled its mission now that the Saviour of the world has sprung from it and its Messiah has appeared. Its members can only accept this fact with gratitude, and in confirmation of their own deepest election and calling attach themselves to the people of this Saviour, their own King, whose members the Gentiles are now called to be as well. Its mission as a natural community has now run its course and cannot be continued or repeated.[10]

The most obvious implication of supersessionism is that Jews as a national or ethnic entity no longer figure in God's ongoing redemptive plans. Of course, Jews may still be saved, but only as they individually trust in Jesus as the Messiah and become part of the New Israel by faith. Thus there can be no biblical or theological significance to the continuation of the Jewish people after Christ—or the establishment of a Jewish state in the Holy Land.

Since the Second World War and the Holocaust, replacement theology has been criticized on the grounds that some Christians have used it to justify antisemitism or the targeting of Jews for evangelism. Simply put, in an age of growing interreligious sensibilities and dialogue, replacement theology can be a huge stumbling block. Consequently, some critics of supersessionism have argued for the concept of "dual covenants": that is, when God established a new covenant with the church, he did not abrogate the old covenant with the children of Abraham. By implication, Jesus Christ is the savior of the Gentiles, but not the Messiah of the Jews; Christians no longer need to evangelize Jews because the latter never lost their special covenant relationship with God. According to its advocates, by questioning the church's standing as the New Israel, the dual covenant approach fosters mutual appreciation and replaces proselytism with respectful dialogue.[11]

While American evangelicals repudiate antisemitic uses of replacement theology, they overwhelmingly reject the dual covenant view, insisting that if Jesus is not the Messiah of the Jews, he cannot be the savior of the Gentiles. They also continue to affirm the biblical mandate to take the gospel of Christ to *everybody*—Jews as well as Gentiles.[12] Old-style replacement theology is still held by a sizeable minority of evangelicals in the United States, especially among those in the Calvinist tradition. However, it seems unlikely that their numbers exceed 20 percent.[13]

Dispensationalism

In contrast to replacement theology, dispensationalism, with its emphasis on biblical prophecy, places the modern state of Israel in the center of events leading to the second coming of Christ. Biblical prophecy has a special resonance among American evangelicals, especially as it relates to a future millennium, a golden age of peace and justice that is closely connected to the return of Christ. Most 19th-century evangelicals were postmillennialists who believed that the second coming would occur *after* the millennial golden age was established through the "Christianization" of the world. Dispensationalism, a form of premillennialism, originated with John Nelson Darby, a 19th-century English Bible teacher who made a number of trips to the United States in the 1860s and 1870s and gathered a following of prominent evangelical pastors and Bible teachers. His teachings spread through the more conservative evangelical networks—Bible conferences, Bible institutes, and popular publications such as the

Scofield Reference Bible (1909). By 1920, dispensationalism was enormously popular among those who were already calling themselves fundamentalists.

Darby's teachings could get quite complicated. He divided all biblical and subsequent history into eras (dispensations) in order to keep track of God's changing plan of redemption, which he believed contained two distinct "peoples of God"—one "earthly" (Israel) and the other "heavenly" (the church). With Israel, God established a number of covenants that stretched from the call of Abraham to the coming of the Messiah and beyond. However, when the messiah Jesus came, Israel rejected him. In response, God *temporarily* suspended all dealings with Israel and created a new people, the church. Unlike replacement theology, Darby's teaching stressed that, instead of transferring all of Israel's covenantal privileges to the church, God simply stopped doing business with Israel by sending it into a kind of historical hiatus—what Darby called the "great parenthesis" of prophetic time—during which it rightly suffered the consequences of its sin and unbelief. In time, however, God intended to resume dealing with the people Israel by restarting the prophetic "clock" and fulfilling his ancient promises to them.

Taking a more or less literal approach to interpretation, Darby combined prophecies from the Hebrew Bible and the New Testament to fashion a remarkably detailed scenario of the End Times. He believed that God worked with only one chosen people at a time; this necessitated the notion of the "rapture," by which means Christ would bring the church (that is, the true believers) up to heaven. This act would allow Israel to reassume center stage in God's program.

From the outset, dispensationalists' prophetic expectations have depended on the restoration of the Jews in the Holy Land. In a nutshell, the dispensationalist scenario is as follows: soon after the restoration, the new Jewish state finds itself surrounded by hostile and threatening neighbors. "Kings of the north" and "kings of the south" (Russians and their Arab allies, according to dispensationalists since the 1830s) attack Israel in a pincers movement. But before the attackers can bring about Israel's destruction, God intervenes and destroys them. Thoroughly shaken by its close call, Israel forms an alliance with the charismatic leader of a ten-nation European confederacy (the revived Roman empire) who promises peace and security. For a while, all seems well—but this charismatic peacemaker is really the Antichrist in disguise. One day, he suddenly enters the rebuilt Temple in Jerusalem and demands to be worshipped as God; soon thereafter, he unleashes a reign of terror against all who refuse to recognize him as such. This is the Great Tribulation, a new holocaust that surpasses Hitler's. Jews in large numbers are slaughtered; those who remain beseech God to send the Messiah to save them. Finally, the Messiah does come: as the forces of Antichrist assemble at Armageddon to fight a huge army led by "kings of the east" (the Chinese), Jesus Christ returns with the previously "raptured" church and annihilates the combatants. The surviving Jewish remnant hails Jesus as its true Messiah and puts him on King David's throne in Jerusalem, where he reigns for a thousand years.[14]

By the 1920s, dispensationalism had become synonymous with fundamentalism, promoted by a network of fundamentalist schools, churches, and other organizations until it became an essential part of the fundamentalist subculture. Among more moderate evangelicals, its impact was less pronounced. Nonetheless, over time, dispensational teachings made their way into popular American culture, often by means of breakout best-sellers such as Hal Lindsey's *The Late Great Planet Earth* (1970) and Tim LaHaye's twelve-volume *Left Behind* (1995-2006) fictional series. These and other dispensationalist books can now be found in Borders, Dalton Books, Barnes and Noble, Wal-Mart, and other mainstream outlets.[15]

Although dispensationalists often claim to speak for all evangelicals, they actually make up only a small portion of the evangelical movement. In fact, as previously noted, most dispensationalists are best classified as fundamentalists. However, whereas fundamentalists and evangelicals differ substantially in terms of style and openness to the culture, they remain close theologically. As a result, poll-takers invariably place fundamentalists in the far right wing of the broadly defined evangelical movement. According to John C. Green of the Pew Forum on Religion and Public Life, no reliable survey has ever identified how many dispensationalists are in the United States. His estimate is that no more than 10 percent of evangelicals are committed and well-informed devotees, with possibly another 20 percent qualifying as "dispensationalists lite," that is, fundamentalists and more moderate evangelicals who have adopted parts of the dispensational system without really understanding it.[16] Nevertheless, though a distinct minority, dispensationalists often extend their reach far beyond their own boundaries. According to historian Paul Boyer, when times turn apocalyptic, even otherwise secular people are willing to listen to the Bible teachers who say they know where the world is headed and what is going to happen next.[17]

The Evangelical Middle

If approximately 20 percent of evangelicals accept replacement theology and 30 percent are dispensationalists, what about the other 50 percent? Despite the popular stereotype that they are obsessed with biblical prophecy, the chances are good that a majority of evangelicals rarely hear a sermon on prophetic themes. Consequently, most evangelicals do not have a well-developed eschatology: they do believe that Jesus is coming back and that God does have a plan for the future; but they do not know or care much about the details.[18] So where does the widespread evangelical support for Israel come from? The short answer: from a rather intuitive and instinctive reading of the Bible.

Before 1948, most evangelicals did not expect a restored Jewish state in the Holy Land. However, when this event came about, they quickly concluded that God must be behind it. As Bible-centered people, evangelicals grew up hearing stories of ancient Israel—the call of Abraham, slavery in Egypt, the Exodus, the conquest of Canaan, the great kings David and Solomon, the division of the tribes, their conquest and exile, and the eventual return to the land. They mastered the maps that were found in the back of their Bibles and that were hanging on their Sunday school walls. They knew that Jesus was a son of the covenant and that the land of Israel was where all the great works of redemption took place. In deeply personal ways, evangelicals viewed (and still view) the story of Israel as vitally related to their own story. Without giving the matter much thought, most evangelicals easily concluded that the new Israeli state was somehow connected to the Israel of the Bible; in a real sense, it could be seen as a continuation and confirmation of the biblical narrative. Could such an unlikely and seemingly miraculous event occur without God's blessing and intervention? Once evangelicals answered this question, it was clear that they should support the new Jewish state.

Evangelicals, then, do not need the dispensationalist scenario in order to be pro-Israel. Instead of relying on elaborate prophetic constructs, evangelicals who occupy this middle ground frequently refer to two biblical passages as crucial: God's promise to Abraham (Gen. 12:3) and Paul's assertion that Israel's current "blindness" is only temporary and that in the end "all Israel will be saved" (Romans 9–11). With regard to the former passage, God's promise to Abraham appears to be unconditional: "I will make you into a great nation and I will bless you; I will make your name great, and you will be a blessing. I will bless those who bless you, and whoever curses you I will curse; and all peoples on earth will be blessed through you." Evangelicals operate on the assumption that God's plan for Abraham and his descendants is still operational and that anyone who blesses the Jews will be blessed in return. They do not need to understand everything about God's future plan for the Jews (even the Apostle Paul called it a "great mystery"). It is enough to know that God has such a plan and that modern Israel might well be part of it; this is enough to ensure that Bible-reading evangelicals will be favorably disposed to the Jewish state.

Evangelical Support for Israel

How do such beliefs translate into politics? Despite the fact that dispensationalists are a distinct minority within the evangelical movement, they have long led the way in organized political support for the Jewish state. This was not always so. For the first hundred years of their history, dispensationalist activism consisted of preaching, teaching, and writing about the future restoration of the Jews. It was only after Israeli independence in 1948 and the expansion of its borders following the 1967 Six-Day War that their activism turned aggressively political.

Dispensationalists in the 19th century were content to predict the future; only William E. Blackstone, a successful Chicago businessman, tried to make it happen. He wrote one of dispensationalism's early best-sellers, *Jesus Is Coming* (1878), and in 1890, following an extensive tour of the Holy Land, he organized Chicago's first conference for Christians and Jews, at which he promoted the idea of a new Jewish homeland. In 1891, six years before Theodor Herzl organized the first Zionist conference in Basel, Blackstone sent a "memorial" to President Benjamin Harrison, signed by 413 prominent Americans, that advocated the establishment of a Jewish state. He sent similar petitions to Theodore Roosevelt in 1903 and Woodrow Wilson in 1916.[19] As a result of his efforts, Blackstone became friends with a number of Zionist leaders, who in 1918 acclaimed him a "Father of Zionism." In 1957, Israel dedicated a forest in his honor.[20] Blackstone also qualified as a father of Christian (or Gentile) Zionism, another name for those non-Jews, whether religious Christians or not, whose support for Israel is grounded in their prophetic views.[21]

In contrast to Blackstone, most early 20th-century dispensationalists were talkers, not doers. They noted the Balfour Declaration in 1917, the fall of the Ottoman empire, and the rise of the British mandate in Palestine. They watched as the British tried and failed to solve the mounting problems in Palestine. When Israel finally declared its independence, dispensationalists were ecstatic, but not entirely satisfied. To conform to their prophetic expectations, Israel needed to expand its borders—which it did, following the 1967 Six-Day War.

Organizing to Support Israel

During the 1970s, dispensationalists grew even more confident about their reading of biblical prophecy. Lindsey's *The Late Great Planet Earth* set sales records, and his follow-up, *The 1980s: Countdown to Armageddon*, offered ample evidence that the pieces in dispensationalism's prophetic puzzle were falling into place. During the 1980s, several prominent believers in biblical prophecy—among them, Jerry Falwell (Moral Majority), Ed McAteer (Religious Roundtable), and Pat Robertson (Christian Coalition)—founded grassroots organizations that became part of the new Christian right and placed support of the state of Israel high on their agendas.

Even before the rise of the new Christian right, American dispensationalists were building new relationships with Israeli leaders. In 1971, for instance, 1,400 Americans attended the Jerusalem Conference on Biblical Prophecy, which included a special address given by David Ben-Gurion. The conference organizer promoted it as "a ringside seat at the second coming," and most speakers agreed that Israel's existence and recent expansion were all part of God's plan.[22] This conference marked the beginning of a wave of evangelical tourism. The Israeli Ministry of Tourism recruited evangelical pastors for all-expenses-paid "familiarization" tours of Israel that were designed to turn them into tour guides accompanying their own flocks to the Holy Land. American dispensationalists launched a number of new travel agencies specializing in such "Bible Prophecy Tours," and leading dispensationalist pastors, including Jerry Falwell and Chuck Smith, headed numerous tour groups that, interestingly enough, refrained from contact with Palestinians, including Palestinian Christians.[23] Probably the most widely publicized gathering of evangelicals in Israel is the Feast of Tabernacles conference sponsored annually by the International Christian Embassy of Jerusalem (ICEJ), an organization of Christian Zionists that, despite its name, has no formal diplomatic standing. This worldwide gathering is customarily addressed by the Israeli prime minister, and its participants (generally numbering approximately 5,000) take part in the annual "Jerusalem Parade" conducted throughout the city and its environs. Sensitive to the charge of ulterior motives, the ICEJ claim is that "[w]e are not trying to fulfill an end time agenda, but are standing on biblical principles. We proclaim a message to Zion that her modern day restoration is not a historical accident, but the fulfillment of God's word."[24]

In the mid-1980s, the American Israel Public Affairs Committee (AIPAC), Israel's major lobbying group in Washington, decided to cultivate Christians on the political right. In response, conservative Christians established a number of organizations to foster strong U.S.-Israeli ties, among them, Christians Concerned for Israel, Christians for Israel, and the National Unity Coalition for Israel.[25] These groups dispensed information about the Middle East crisis, sent letters and faxes (and, at a later stage, emails) to the White House and members of Congress, and held rallies and meetings that sometimes numbered in the thousands. At one such event in 1998, Prime Minister Benjamin Netanyahu declared that "we have no greater friends and allies than the people sitting in this room."[26]

Other groups supported various humanitarian causes. Christian Friends of Israeli Communities linked Israeli settlements on the West Bank to American evangelical congregations, which provided money and materials for the Jewish settlers. Bridges for Peace sponsored various educational and lobbying activities for its supporters, in addition to running what it claimed to be Israel's largest food bank and assisting Jewish immigrants to the Holy Land. Undergirding these humanitarian activities were strong beliefs about Israel's place in biblical prophecy and the importance of taking an active role in bringing about the prophecies' fulfillment. As a Bridges for Peace promotional piece put it: "Don't just read about prophecy when you can be a part of it."[27]

One of the most successful of such groups was the International Fellowship of Christians and Jews, founded in 1983 by Yechiel Eckstein, an Orthodox rabbi from Chicago. Early on recognizing the importance of evangelical support for Israel, Eckstein cultivated friendships and mounted a one-man crusade to improve evangelical-Jewish relations. Soon he had people such as Jerry Falwell, Pat Robertson, Gary Bauer, and Pat Boone making infomercials for his organization. Eckstein has raised millions of dollars annually, mostly from evangelical sources. In 2003, for instance, he distributed $20 million to 250 social welfare projects in Israel. His own "On Wings of Eagles" program helped bring Jews from the former Soviet Union to Israel ("Just $350 can save one Jew"), and his "Guardians of Israel" and "Isaiah 58" projects sought to help the impoverished immigrants once they arrived. In 2006, Eckstein expected revenues to reach $80 million, thanks to advertising on the Fox News Channel and the addition of 30,000 new donors following the Israeli-Hezbollah war in Lebanon in 2006.[28] Eckstein knew how to appeal to Bible believers: "Your prayers and financial support will help us continue rescuing persecuted Jewish *émigrés* in the former Soviet Union ... in fulfillment of biblical prophecy."[29]

In 2003, Eckstein and Ralph Reed, former head of the Christian Coalition, launched the Stand for Israel initiative to mobilize one hundred thousand churches and one million Christians to support Israel through prayer and political action. At its first Washington, D.C. briefing, participants included Israeli experts on the Middle East crisis; U.S. Attorney General John Ashcroft; Congressional representatives Tom DeLay and Tom Lantos; and Janet Parshall, a prominent right-wing radio talk-show host. At about the same time, Pat Robertson teamed up with Ehud Olmert, at the time the mayor of Jerusalem, to initiate a Praying for Jerusalem campaign. In addition to prayer, this initiative raised money for the New Jerusalem Fund, which supported various cultural and urban improvement projects in Jerusalem. Robertson made it clear that he was praying for a particular kind of peace in the Middle East: "We should not ask [Israel] to withdraw from [occupied territories]—we should stand with them and fight." Rejecting all Palestinian claims, Robertson declared Jerusalem "the eternal, indivisible capital of the state of Israel" that "must not be divided."[30]

A Difficult Alliance

Pro-Israel evangelical groups invariably are the subject of mixed reviews on the part of American and Israeli Jews. Critics charge that evangelical support for Israel is nothing more than a cover for evangelizing Jews or an attempt to fulfill biblical prophecies. To be sure, dispensationalists have a long history of supporting missionary organizations that target Jews,[31] and even Yechiel Eckstein has urged his evangelical friends to "leave the conversion of the Jews to God."[32] But such complaints do not dissuade most evangelicals from their conviction that God wants them to share the gospel with *all* people. Believers in biblical prophecies see no contradiction between supporting Israel, on the one hand, and attempting to lead Jews to Christ, on the other. Nevertheless, some evangelicals active in the prophecy-driven pro-Israel organizations have decided to tone down their evangelistic activities for pragmatic reasons. For example, Christians for Israel, Christian Friends of Israeli Communities, and the International Christian Embassy have explicit policies against proselytism.[33]

The pro-Israel groups find it more difficult to deal with their critics' allegations concerning biblical prophecy. According to their literature and their websites, these groups are deeply motivated by their understanding of prophetic texts and what they believe God is doing in the world. Yet many outsiders see a dark side to these prophecies. The future that dispensationalists envision for Israel is full of suffering and slaughter: Jews must remain in the Holy Land in order to keep their rendezvous with the Antichrist, suffer the horrors of the Great Tribulation, and, in the end, welcome Jesus as the Messiah. Such a future, of course, is quite different from that envisioned by the Jews. According to Gershom Gorenberg, a Jerusalem-based journalist: "This is incredibly dangerous to Israel. [The dispensationalists are] not interested in the survival of the State of Israel. They are interested in the Rapture, in bringing to fruition a cosmic myth of the End Times, proving that they are right with one big bang. We are merely actors in their dreams."[34]

Eckstein and his compatriots have often had to defend their evangelical allies against such charges, claiming that the evangelicals' love for Israel is sincere. For instance, according to Eckstein's close associate, Gary Bauer:

> Among Christians, there's just a fundamental religious idea that the Jews are God's people and the land of Israel is covenant land that God granted them. Beyond that, what drives Christian support for Israel is that Christians tend to see U.S. foreign policy in very moral terms. We believe Israel and the U.S. are facing the same types of totalitarian forces, and we as two countries that share the same values should stand against that.[35]

Hoping to substantiate this point of view, Eckstein commissioned the Tarrance Group in 2003 to survey evangelicals' attitudes about Israel. The poll found that whereas 28 percent cited as influencing their point of view "reasons related to the End Times," 59 percent referred to their literal belief in Gen. 12:3, where God promised to bless those who bless Abraham's descendants. This finding came as a great relief to Eckstein: "The media portrays [evangelicals] as premillennialists who do this [support Israel] to get all the Jews to Israel . . . [so] those who don't accept Jesus will be killed. It's just hogwash. If anything, it's about Genesis 12:3." Yet despite his claims, Eckstein's message seems to depend on his audience. While he assures people who are suspicious of prophecy that it plays only a minor role among his supporters, his fundraising infomercials directly appeal to the belief in biblical prophecy: "The mosaic of events we see happening today is like a gigantic jigsaw puzzle with the pieces beginning to form the exact picture foretold by the prophets."[36]

No one maneuvers more successfully between these different positions than John Hagee, the pastor of the 18,000-member Cornerstone Church in San Antonio, Texas and the head of John Hagee Ministries, founded in 1979 to manage his television and revival work. In 2006, Hagee founded Christians United for Israel (CUFI), a well-financed and high-profile organization that provides weekly email updates on news about Israel in addition to sponsoring "Nights to Honor Israel" in churches and other venues throughout the country, organizing trips to Israel ("Summit in Jerusalem"), and conducting annual gatherings in the nation's capital at which participants receive high-level briefings and have an opportunity to meet with their elected officials. When asked about his motives and the theological ideas behind CUFI, Hagee denies that biblical prophecy has anything to do with his organization, citing God's promise to Abraham in Genesis 12 as the bedrock on which his organization is built.[37] In his telecasts, however, Hagee regularly preaches on the End Times; in his numerous books on biblical prophecy, he follows the standard dispensationalist line.[38] In fact, for more than 25 years, Hagee has made use of the Bible to make the case for supporting Israel. He has built strong personal relationships with Israeli leaders, starting with Menachem Begin, and has traveled to Israel more than 20 times. He has also turned Cornerstone Church into a center of prophetic teaching, preaching, and pro-Israel activity. John Hagee Ministries has collected millions of dollars for its Exodus II program, which helps Jews immigrate to Israel from the former Soviet Union. By contributing to this restoration project, Hagee claims, donors "become a part of biblical prophecy." The pledge card on which contributors indicate their level of financial support is equally explicit: "I want to be a part of the fulfillment of prophecy and the courageous effort to return Jewish families to their homeland."[39]

Why would Hagee separate Christians United for Israel from teachings he has been promoting for close to three decades? Clearly, it is because he seeks the broadest possible base of support for the organization. As has been seen, the dispensationalist doctrine held by Hagee is not embraced by a majority of evangelicals, whereas many of them do endorse God's blessing to Abraham.

Evangelical Divisions on Israel

For many fellow evangelicals, the biggest problem with Hagee is not prophecy, but rather politics. CUFI and virtually all the other aforementioned pro-Israel groups take a hard-line approach to the Middle East crisis, to the extent that they are often accused of supporting Israel "no matter what." Their view of the prophetic future includes the expansion of Israeli territory rather than territorial concessions. Thus they reject outright George W. Bush's "road map to peace," which advocates a two-state solution. Indeed, they fiercely oppose Israel's trading *any* land for peace, defending the continued presence of Israeli settlements on the West Bank and denouncing any concessions to the Palestinians. These views comprise what Hagee calls "God's foreign policy."[40]

In brief, dispensationalists believe that Israelis and their enemies are locked into an escalating conflict that no "road map to peace" or any other diplomatic initiative can resolve. The only solution to the problems of the Middle East is the return of Christ. Until then, the region will continue to fester and boil, with intensifying violence and one failed peace attempt after another. Biblical prophecy is the only "road map" that matters; and God's plans are unchangeable. Therefore, they believe, Christian options are few: support Israel, do nothing that impedes or opposes God's plan for the future, and be thankful that the rapture will occur before the horrors of the Last Days begin.

In accordance with these views, many American dispensationalist leaders have developed relationships with Israeli figures located on the far right of the religious and political spectrum, including Gershon Salomon and the late Stanley Goldfoot of the Temple Mount and the Greater Land of Israel Faithful Movement and Rabbi Yisrael Ariel, the head of the Temple Institute. High on the agenda of both groups is the rebuilding of the Jewish temple on the Temple Mount, where Muslims have their Dome of the Rock. As early as 1983, the *Jerusalem Post* noted the connection between dispensationalists and right-wing Jewish extremists: "There are growing numbers of Christians, many organized into small churches and larger groups, who see the construction of a Third Temple as the cornerstone of these beliefs. Though there is a clear divergence in religious belief between these Christians and Jews who work toward the rebuilding of the Temple, they willingly and enthusiastically cooperate."[41] Although most Israelis consider such people dangerous extremists, dispensationalists view their aspirations as dovetailing with their own prophetic expectations.[42]

In the view of dispensationalists, tampering with biblical prophecy carries dire consequences. In October 2004, at a time when Israeli prime minister Ariel Sharon had begun to explore the possibility of turning over the Gaza Strip to the Palestinian Authority, Pat Robertson and 4,000 supporters met in Jerusalem to protest. "I see the rise of Islam to destroy Israel and take the land from the Jews and give East Jerusalem to Yasser Arafat," Robertson declared. "I see that as Satan's plan to prevent the return of Jesus Christ the Lord." In fact, he continued, only God could decide if Israel should relinquish land that had been taken in the Six-Day War of June 1967: "God says, 'I'm going to judge those who carve up the West Bank and the Gaza Strip. It's my land and keep your hands off it.'"[43] Despite Robertson's warnings, Sharon persevered in his plan, which ultimately resulted in the withdrawal of Israeli armed forces and settlers from Gaza and parts of northern Samaria in the summer of 2005. When Sharon suffered a massive stroke in January 2006, Robertson assured his television audience that the prime minister had been punished by God. Sharon, he said, had been "dividing God's land, and I would say, 'Woe unto any prime minister of Israel who takes a similar course to appease the [European Union], the United Nations or the United States of America.'" Israelis, the White House, and fellow evangelicals were all outraged by his comments; within a week, Robertson had apologized profusely. But early on, while Robertson was still trying to ride out the storm, one of his spokespeople attempted to defend him: "What they're basically saying is, 'How dare

Pat Robertson quote the Bible?' This is what the word of God says. This is nothing new to the Christian community."[44]

Although such sentiments are common in certain evangelical circles, recent polls have indicated that most evangelical leaders now favor a two-state solution in the Middle East. In 2002, for instance, sociologist John C. Green conducted a foreign policy survey for the Ethics and Public Policy Center. He contacted 350 leaders of evangelical organizations and found that whereas nearly two out of three (60 percent) were in favor of backing Israel over the Palestinians, slightly more than half (52 percent) favored the establishment of a Palestinian state alongside Israel. According to Green: "Evangelical elites want to see peace in the Middle East. They believe the Palestinian people have legitimate aspirations to have their own country. These elites would not support a state if it threatened Israel."[45] According to Richard Land, president of the Southern Baptist Ethics and Religious Liberty Commission, Israel is covenantal land and God has a plan for the Jews—but the best way to support Israel is to seek a workable, two-state solution: "I would argue that nothing could be more secure for Israel than creating a viable, self-sustaining Palestinian state that agrees to live in peace and agrees to suppress terrorism."[46] Although some of the evangelicals point to obvious foreign policy implications in biblical prophecy, regarding the establishment of a Palestinian state as a serious repudiation of God's plan for Israel, others are inclined to be far more flexible. Richard Mouw, president of Fuller Theological Seminary, noted that there was no theological reason either to require or forbid the creation of a Palestinian state: "The question for me is one of prudence, and not of theological principle."[47]

If the polls are correct and a majority of evangelical leaders favor a two-state solution, why are their views not more widely known? Most likely, this is because they are more low-key in the dissemination of their message. Rather than organizing the masses, holding rallies in Washington, D.C., or sending out email messages to tens of thousands of supporters, they tend to write letters to selected, influential people. In July 2002, for instance, some 40 evangelical leaders sent a letter to President George W. Bush titled "Evangelical Christians and Israel/Palestine." The letter advocated "an even-handed U.S. policy towards Israelis and Palestinians," condemning suicide bombings and the failure of the Palestinian Authority to stop the violence against Israeli civilians, but denouncing as well the "unlawful and degrading Israeli settlement movement," the "theft of Palestinian land and the destruction of Palestinian homes and fields," and "the continued military occupation that daily humiliates ordinary Palestinians." The purpose of the letter was to let the president know that "the American evangelical community is not a monolithic bloc. ... Significant numbers of American evangelicals reject the way some have distorted biblical passages as their rationale for uncritical support for every policy and action of the Israeli government instead of judging all actions—of both Israelis and Palestinians—on the basis of biblical standards of justice." The signers included academics, CEOs of various evangelical denominations and "parachurch" organizations, and a few pastors.[48]

Five years later, in July 2007, 34 evangelical leaders (more than half of whom had signed the previous letter) sent another message to President Bush in which they endorsed his efforts to achieve a two-state solution. This second letter acknowledged that "both Israelis and Palestinians have legitimate rights stretching back for millennia to the lands of Israel/Palestine. Both Israelis and Palestinians have committed violence and injustice against each other. The only way to bring the tragic cycle of violence to an end is for Israelis and Palestinians to negotiate a just, lasting agreement that guarantees both sides viable, independent, secure states." As with the previous letter, this one sought to correct the "serious misperception" that all American evangelicals think alike about the Middle East. After embracing the biblical promise to Abraham ("I will bless those who bless you"), it declared that "perhaps the best way we can bless Israel is to encourage her to remember, as she deals with her neighbor Palestinians, the profound teaching on justice that the Hebrew prophets proclaimed so forcefully as an inestimably precious gift to the whole world."[49]

The idea for the second letter originated when four evangelical leaders attended the U.S.-Islamic World Forum in Qatar in early 2007. Muslims and U.S. diplomats in attendance were shocked to discover American evangelicals in favor of a Palestinian state. Ronald Sider, who was in Qatar and signed the subsequent letter, said that it would be translated into Arabic and distributed throughout the Middle East and Europe: "We think it's critical that the Muslim world realize that there are evangelical Christians in the U.S. in large numbers that want a fair solution." John Hagee, however, was not impressed. After reviewing the letter, he said that "Bible-believing evangelicals will scoff at that message."[50]

Yet what kind of influence do prophecy-minded evangelicals really have? They claim to have access in high places; elected officials often show up at their gatherings; and they utilize the same methods used by successful Washington lobbyists. As a result, many people are fearful that they are making a difference, forcing their views of biblical prophecy on American foreign policymakers. But this is hardly the case—while they certainly get the attention of those who are facing upcoming election, they have not been able to steer official Israeli or U.S. policy away from seeking a two-state solution. Richard Land's observation is correct: "I would point out that probably the most popular president ever among evangelicals is the first American president to officially make a two-state solution American foreign policy, and a majority of evangelicals support him in that."[51]

Not all evangelicals think alike.[52] While they overwhelmingly support Israel, they do so for different reasons and envision different futures in the Middle East.[53] Views of biblical prophecy seem to get all the press; but only a minority of evangelical believers share these views. Rather, for most evangelicals, support for Israel is founded on an intuitive reading of the Bible and some widely held political assumptions about the Middle East.

Notes

1. Needless to say, this division of American Protestants into a mere three groups may appear foolhardy in the extreme. At best such boundaries are only suggestive; at worst they are seriously misleading. Though evangelicals are distinct from fundamentalists in terms of style and the company they keep, they share much in common with them theologically. As will be seen, this has led some analysts to view fundamentalism as the extreme right wing of

evangelicalism, which is another way of saying that while all fundamentalists are evangelicals, not all evangelicals are fundamentalists. Furthermore, even the best polls obscure the fact that mainline Protestantism contains large numbers of evangelical members and congregations. Where do African Americans fit within the three categories? While they are closest to evangelicals theologically, they are more closely identified with the social views of mainline Protestantism. Finally, Pentecostals may appear to belong to both the fundamentalist and evangelical camps. All of this notwithstanding, the three labels do identify major differences and tendencies in American Protestant religious life.

2. William R. Hutchison, *The Modernist Impulse in American Protestantism* (Cambridge: 1976); George M. Marsden, *Fundamentalism and American Culture: The Shaping of Twentieth-Century Evangelicalism: 1870–1925* (New York: 1980); Martin E. Marty, *Modern American Religion,* vol. 2: *The Noise of Conflict, 1919–1941* (Chicago: 1991); and Joel A. Carpenter, *Revive Us Again: The Reawakening of American Fundamentalism* (New York: 1997).

3. George M. Marsden, *Reforming Fundamentalism: Fuller Seminary and the New Evangelicalism* (Grand Rapids: 1987); idem, *Understanding Fundamentalism and Evangelicalism* (Grand Rapids: 1991).

4. By the early 1980s—deeply disturbed by the legalization of abortion, the elimination of prayer from public schools, a culture-wide rejection of "family values," and what they believed to be a blatant strategy to push people of faith outside the public square—many conservative Protestants decided to fight back by identifying a few key issues and calling the faithful to action. They formed organizations such as the Moral Majority, the Religious Roundtable, and the Christian Coalition. Thanks to their militant, "take-no-prisoners" style, the leaders of the new Christian right often looked and sounded more fundamentalist than evangelical, yet they were able to rally people from both camps to their cause. In retrospect, the new Christian right was only partially successful in attaining its goals, although its members did play an important role in electing Republicans to Congress and the White House. After the 2004 election, the movement appeared to lose steam, and many evangelicals began moving on to other concerns such as poverty, racism, global warming, and the AIDS crisis.

5. Walter Russell Mead, "God's Country?," *Foreign Affairs* 85, no. 5 (Sept.-Oct. 2006), online at www.foreignaffairs.org/20060901faessay85504/walter-russell-mead/god-s-country.html (except as indicated, online citations for this essay were accessed on 15 July 2009).

6. Pew Forum on Religion & Public Life, "U.S. Religious Landscape Survey" (Philadelphia: 2008), online at http://religions.pewforum.org/reports.

7. D. Michael Lindsay, *Faith in the Halls of Power: How Evangelicals Joined the American Elite* (New York: 2007).

8. "An Evangelical Manifesto: A Declaration of Evangelical Identity and Public Commitment" (Washington, D.C.: 2008), 15, online at www.evangelicalmanifesto.com.

9. Mead, "God's Country?"

10. Karl Barth, *Church Dogmatics,* vol. 2, part 2 (Edinburgh: 1969), 584. A more recent explanation of supersessionism is found in the work of the evangelical Anglican bishop N.T. Wright. See his *The New Testament and the People of God* (Minneapolis: 1992), 457–458.

11. For an example of a rather moderate critique of supersessionism and advocacy of dual covenants, see General Assembly of the Presbyterian Church (U.S.A.), "A Theological Understanding of the Relationship between Christians and Jews" (New York: 1987), online at www.pcusa.org/theologyandworship/issues/christiansjews.pdf. For a stronger rejection of replacement theology, see Clark Williamson, *A Guest in the House of Israel: A Post-Holocaust Church Theology* (Louisville: 1993); and James Carroll, *Constantine's Sword: The Church and the Jews* (Boston: 2001). See also Luke Timothy Johnson, "Christians and Jews: Starting Over—Why the Real Dialogue Has Just Begun," *Commonweal* (31 Jan. 2003). Johnson's article may be accessed at www.bc.edu/research/cjl/meta-elements/texts/cjrelations/resources/articles/johnson.htm.

12. Craig Blaising, "The Future of Israel as a Theological Question," *The Journal of the Evangelical Theological Society* 44 (Sept. 2001), 435–450.

13. For a Calvinist defense of supersessionism, see O. Palmer Robertson, *The Israel of God: Yesterday, Today, and Tomorrow* (Phillipsburg, Penn.: 2000). For a variety of evangelical views

on supersessionism, see John S. Feinberg (ed.), *Continuity and Discontinuity: Perspectives on the Relationship between the Old and New Testaments* (Wheaton, Ill.: 1988).

14. Timothy P. Weber, *Living in the Shadow of the Second Coming: American Premillennialism, 1875 to 1982* (Chicago: 1987), 13–42.

15. Timothy P. Weber, *On the Road to Armageddon: How Evangelicals Became Israel's Best Friend* (Grand Rapids: 2004), 187–196.

16. John C. Green is senior fellow in religion and American politics, Pew Forum on Religion and Public Life. He provided these observations during a phone interview on June 20, 2006.

17. Paul Boyer, *When Time Shall Be No More: Prophecy Belief in Modern American Culture* (Cambridge: 1992), 1-18.

18. This point was forcefully made during a symposium ("God's Country? Evangelicals and U.S. Foreign Policy") at the Pew Research Center in Washington, D.C. on September 26, 2006 by Richard Land, president of the Ethics and Religious Liberty Commission of the Southern Baptist Convention; Alan Cooperman of the *Washington Post*; and Michael Cromartie, vice president of the Ethics and Public Policy Center. A transcript of their comments may be found online at http://pewforum.org/events/?EventID=127.

19. For a detailed account, see Yaakov Ariel, "William E. Blackstone and the Petition of 1916," in *Studies in Contemporary Jewry,* vol. 7, *Jews and Messianism in the Modern Era: Metaphor and Meaning*, ed. Jonathan Frankel (New York: 1991), 68–86.

20. Weber, *On the Road to Armageddon*, 102–106.

21. Stephen Sizer, *Christian Zionism: Road-map to Armageddon?* (Leicester: 2004), 70–74.

22. Carl F.H. Henry, *Confessions of a Theologian: An Autobiography* (Waco: 1986), 334-336.

23. Mark O'Keefe, "Israel's Evangelical Approach: U.S. Christian Zionists Nurtured as Political, Tourism Force," *Washington Post* (26 Jan. 2002), B11.

24. This statement originally appeared on the organization's website (www.icej.org), which has since been redesigned. For an extensive analysis of ICEJ, see Donald E. Wagner, *Anxious for Armageddon: A Call to Partnership for Middle Eastern and Western Christians* (Scottsdale, Penn.: 1995), 96–113.

25. Rod Dreher, "Evangelicals and Jews Together: An Unlikely Alliance," *National Review Online* (5 April 2002), accessed at www.nationalreview.com/dreher/dreher040502.asp.

26. Debra Cohen, "Premier Meets with Evangelicals," *Jewish News of Greater Phoenix* (11 April 1998).

27. See Bridges for Peace website: www.bridgesforpeace.com.

28. David D. Kirkpatrick, "For Evangelicals, Supporting Israel Is 'God's Foreign Policy,'" *New York Times* (14 Nov. 2006), online at www.nytimes.com/2006/11/14/washington/14israel.html?_r=1&sq=God's%20Foreign%20Policy&st=nyt&adxnnl=1&oref=slogin&scp=1&adxnnlx=1210431722-M7W7VNEkHSE9HI1w0Gm/FA.

29. See the International Fellowship of Christians and Jews' website: www.ifcj.org.

30. "Pat Robertson Forms Alliance with Mayor of Jerusalem," and "Christian Coalition Calls for Solidarity with Israel," *Religion News Service* (11 Nov. 2002).

31. Yaakov Ariel, *Evangelizing the Chosen People: Missions to the Jews in America, 1880-2000* (Chapel Hill: 2000).

32. Yechiel Eckstein, *What Christians Should Know about Jews and Judaism* (Waco: 1984), 299.

33. See Weber, *On the Road to Armageddon*, 230-232.

34. Gershom Gorenberg, quoted in Craig Unger, "American 'Rapture,'" *Vanity Fair* (Dec. 2005), online at www.vanityfair.com/politics/features/2005/12/rapture200512; see also Gershom Gorenberg, *The End of Days: Fundamentalism and the Struggle for the Temple Mount* (New York: 2000).

35. For the Eckstein and Bauer quotes, see Max Blumenthal, "Born-agains for Sharon," Academics for Justice (30 Oct. 2004), online at http://dir.salon.com/story/news/feature/2004/11/01/christian_zionism/index.html.

36. Ibid.

37. The Christians United for Israel website is found at www.cufi.org. See also David Brog, *Standing with Israel* (Lake Mary, Fla.: 2006).

38. A sampling of Hagee's books: *From Daniel to Doomsday: The Countdown Has Begun* (Nashville: 2000); *The Battle for Jerusalem* (Nashville: 2003); and *Jerusalem Countdown: A Warning to the World* (Lake Mary, Fla.: 2006).

39. See the church's website at www.sacornerstone.com; and John Hagee Ministries' website at www.jhm.org.

40. Kirkpatrick, "For Evangelicals, Supporting Israel is 'God's Foreign Policy.' "

41. *Jerusalem Post* (30 Sept. 1983), quoted in Randall Price, *The Coming Last Days Temple* (Eugene, Ore.: 1999), 159.

42. Weber, *On the Road to Armageddon*, 249-268. See also Gershom Gorenberg, *The End of Days*.

43. Associated Press (3 Oct. 2004), online at http://archive.newsmax.com/archives/articles/2004/10/3/214501.shtml.

44. "Robertson Suggests God Smote Sharon," CNN (6 Jan. 2006), online at www.cnn.com/2006/US/01/05/robertson.sharon/index.html (accessed 10 Nov. 2008); "Pat Robertson Apologizes for Sharon Slam," Associated Press (12 Jan. 2006), online at www.msnbc.msn.com/id/10825240.

45. Quoted in Todd Hertz, "Opinion Roundup: The Evangelical View of Israel?" *Christianity Today* (11 June 2003), online at www.christianitytoday.com/ct/2003/123/31.0.html (quote on p. 2).

46. Quoted in ibid., 3.

47. Ibid. See also Jeremy D. Mayer, "Christian Fundamentalists and Public Opinion Toward the Middle East: Israel's New Best Friends?" *Social Science Quarterly* 85, no. 3 (Sept. 2004), 695–712.

48. "Evangelical Christians and Israel/Palestine" (12 July 2002), online at www.cmep.org/letters/2002Jul12.htm.

49. "Letter to President Bush from Evangelical Leaders," *New York Times* (29 July 2007), online at www.nytimes.com/2007/07/29/us/evangelical_letter.html.

50. Laurie Goodstein, "Coalition of Evangelicals Voices Support for Palestinian State," ibid., online at www.nytimes.com/2007/07/29/us/29evangelical.html.

51. "God's Country: Evangelicals and U.S. Foreign Policy" (see n. 18).

52. A sampling of books that promote a different view of the Middle East than that of the dispensationalists include Gary M. Burge, *Whose Land? Whose Promise? What Christians Are Not Being Told about Israel and the Palestinians* (Cleveland: 2003); Colin Chapman, *Whose Promised Land?* (Grand Rapids: 2002); Elias Chacour, *Blood Brothers: The Unforgettable Story of a Palestinian Christian Working for Peace in Israel*, expanded ed. (Grand Rapids: 2003).

53. One evangelical organization that promotes this alternative future is Evangelicals for Middle East Understanding. See its website: www.emeu.net.

"Universal Temple"? Jewish-Christian Collaboration in Plans to Reestablish the Holy Temple in Jerusalem

Motti Inbari
(UNIVERSITY OF NORTH CAROLINA AT PEMBROKE)

Of all the diverse activities in the sphere of contemporary Jewish–Christian relations, the ties that have developed between Jewish and Protestant fundamentalist groups for the achievement of a common objective—the reestablishment of the Holy Temple on the Temple Mount in Jerusalem—are undoubtedly unique. This essay is devoted to an analysis of these ties.

The Temple Mount, where both the First and Second Holy Temples once stood, is Judaism's holiest site, whereas Muslims revere it as the location of Muhammed's ascent to heaven and regard it as the third holiest site of Islam, superseded only by Mecca and Medina in Saudi Arabia. The Temple Mount's sanctity has turned it into a focal point of the Israeli–Arab conflict. After the Israeli army captured it during the Six-Day War of June 1967, a status quo was established according to which day-to-day control of the Temple Mount compound was formally assigned to the Supreme Muslim Council (known as the Waqf), with Israeli authorities controlling the Western Wall plaza located directly underneath the Mount.[1] In addition, the Chief Rabbinate ruled that Jews were not allowed to enter the Temple Mount compound, as the site of the Holy Temple was out of bounds to anyone in a state of ritual impurity.[2]

Nevertheless, several individuals and groups challenged the status quo, in both the legal and religious areas. Among the most prominent of those opposed to the status quo agreement was Shlomo Goren, later to become the Ashkenazic chief rabbi of Israel, who at the time of the Six-Day War was serving as chief rabbi of the Israel Defense Forces. Goren, relying in part on his own measurements of the Temple Mount (which, he claimed, allowed him to determine more precisely which parts of the site were sanctified), demanded that Jews be permitted to pray in certain other sections of the compound.[3] Citing security concerns, this demand was refused by the police. At the end of the 1960s a group known as the Temple Mount Faithful (Neemanei har habayit) began its persistent efforts to enable Jews to pray on the Mount, and to this day holds a public demonstration every few months before its gates.

In addition to the overt public struggle for Jewish prayer on the Mount, a few clandestine plans were laid to destroy the mosques that were located there. In April 1984, a group that came to be known as the "Jewish underground" was apprehended. Comprising several leading members of the religious-nationalist Gush Emunim movement, this group carried out a number of terrorist actions that resulted in injuries and deaths among Palestinians. However, their most ambitious scheme was to blow up the mosques in order to pave the way for the establishment of the Third Temple. Later that same year, another clandestine group that became known as the "Lifta underground" (after the name of the abandoned Arab village on the outskirts of Jerusalem in which they lived) was apprehended. Members of this group were formerly secular Jews who had adopted a religious way of life that was strongly influenced by militant kabbalistic traditions; their plan, too, was to blow up the Temple Mount mosques.[4]

Ironically, the only person who actually caused any damage on the Mount was a Christian tourist, Michael Dennis Rohan, who, in August 1969, attempted to set fire to the al-Aqsa Mosque and succeeded in causing some damage to the mosque's furnishings, including an ancient wooden *minbar* (preacher's pulpit). Rohan was influenced by millenarian ideas that posited the necessity of restoring the Temple as part of a divine scenario for the Christian "End Times" that would lead to the second coming of Christ. This dramatic act on the part of a young man who was later declared to be deranged was one of the most extreme consequences of the importance assigned to the Temple Mount by some fundamentalist Protestants.

Historical Background of Protestant Fundamentalism

The interest that fundamentalist Protestants exhibit in Jews and in the concept of the return to Zion, as well as their support of modern-day Zionism, is deeply rooted in Christian millenarian beliefs regarding the second coming of Christ and the establishment of a thousand-year kingdom of God on earth. Belief in the second coming was characteristic of early Christianity, though it was abandoned in the 4th and 5th centuries when Christianity became the dominant faith in the territories of the Roman empire. The revival of Christian millenarianism came in the aftermath of the Protestant Reformation in the 16th century. Additional waves of messianism emerged in England during the revolutionary period in the mid-17th century and again in 19th-century Britain and elsewhere in Europe. During the latter wave, there were those who called for the return of the Jews to their ancestral homeland. Among them was Wilhelm Hechler, a German clergyman who developed friendly relations with Theodor Herzl and helped him both to contact leading Christian individuals and to mobilize German support for Zionist aspirations.[5] In addition to their pro-Zionist activity, such people were often active in missionary efforts among the Jews.

From the mid-19th century, messianic concepts began to penetrate Protestant denominations in the United States; by the end of the century, millenarianism had taken root among the more fundamentalist groupings of American Protestantism. For fundamentalist Christians, messianic beliefs lent an element of urgency to their call for a return to religiosity, spiritual rebirth, and acceptance of Jesus as a personal savior. The American fundamentalist movement became the largest and dominant group among conservative Protestant movements throughout the world, which adopted the concepts and ideas put forward by its American counterpart.[6]

Two eschatological schools of thought in Protestantism influenced fundamentalist Christian thinking. The first, less widespread today, is the "historical school" that predominated in the 19th century, which maintains that End Times events have already begun and that it is possible to identify certain occurrences and developments fitting in with biblical prophecies that relate to the millennium. The other school of thought, known as dispensationalism, maintains that events connected with the End Times have not yet begun. Beginning in the late 19th century, the dispensationalist school became more dominant among fundamentalists.

The central concept of dispensationalism is that the second coming of Christ will take place in two stages. In the first, Jesus will reappear in heaven but will not descend to earth. In heaven, he will meet the true believers—those who were "born again" by adopting Christ as their personal savior. In an act known as "the rapture," these believers will be miraculously drawn up to Jesus from the earth, while true believers who died prior to the appearance of the Messiah will be resurrected from the dead, also to be joined with Jesus. All of this is slated to happen in the near future, although no one knows exactly when.

The true believers will remain with Jesus for seven years (or three-and-a-half years, according to another interpretation), during which period the earth will undergo "the great tribulation." This will be manifested in natural disasters such as earthquakes, widespread floods, volcanic outbursts, hunger, and plagues, and also in wars, uprisings, revolutions, and a reign of terror in many parts of the globe. For the Jews this will be "a time of trouble for Jacob" (Jer. 30:7). Despite their return to their homeland, prior to or during this period, they will be considered "lacking in faith" because they will not have accepted Christ as their Messiah. Therefore, their state will not be the hoped for kingdom of God, only a stage in the developments that will precede the coming of the Messiah. During the period of "the great tribulation" there will arise a Jewish ruler—the Antichrist—who will pass himself off as the true Messiah and be accepted by the Jews as their redeemer. Taking over the rebuilt Temple, the Antichrist will institute a reign of terror. Jews who accept the kingdom of Christ during this period will be persecuted by the followers of the false messiah, and some of them will even be killed. There will be a series of attempted invasions of the Holy Land from all corners of the world, and about two-thirds of the resettled Jewish people will be destroyed. The period of the great tribulation will end with the return of Christ to earth, together with his true believers, to establish his kingdom. He will defeat the Antichrist, establish a regime of justice throughout the world, and make Jerusalem his capital.

With the start of the thousand-year kingdom of God on earth, the surviving Jews will accept Jesus as their Messiah. Humankind will still be divided into nations, each with its own territory, and the Jews will live in their ancestral homeland, whose borders will be those of the historic kingdom of David. Their status will stem from being the chosen people, and they will assist Jesus in ruling the world. The thousand-year messianic regime will be an intermediary period leading to a utopian era, a period in which humankind will learn to know the Lord and to serve him faithfully. As the intermediary period draws to an end, Satan will launch his final revolt and be everlastingly defeated. The earth will undergo cosmological, geological, and climatic changes; among other things, its physical area will be expanded. God the Father will join his son Jesus in ruling the earth, the day of the Last Judgment will be acted out, sin and death will be overcome, and the world will finally be at peace—"the wolf shall dwell with the lamb" (Isa. 11:6).[7]

From the outset, followers of dispensationalism naturally exhibited much interest in the fate of the Jews and their possible return to the Holy Land. To be sure, their attitude toward the Jews was (and remains) ambivalent. On the one hand, they consider them to be the Lord's chosen people, the nation that will once again play a leading role in the kingdom of God that will be established in the messianic period. This concept differs from the traditional Christian approach that considers Christianity to be the successor of Judaism. On the other hand, the dispensationalist cast of mind vis-à-vis the Jews is not always characterized by love and trust. Some fundamentalist authors claim that God continues to be angry at the Jews because they did not accept Jesus Christ as their savior, an act that would have brought about an earlier establishment of the kingdom of God on earth.

By the 1970s and 1980s, fundamentalist Christianity was on the rise in the United States. The Six-Day War of 1967, resulting in the Israeli conquest of Judea, Samaria, the Gaza Strip, the Sinai Peninsula, and the Golan Heights, was the catalyst that transformed many American fundamentalists into avid supporters of Israel, since the war's outcome was interpreted as a tangible omen of the End Times. Active involvement took the form of political lobbying of the U.S. administration on behalf of Israel, alongside philanthropic efforts within Israel. In addition, since Israel had captured the Temple Mount, some fundamentalists now broached the idea of rebuilding the Temple, a topic that became an increasingly central theme in fundamentalist discourse.[8] For example, Hal Lindsey's *The Late Great Planet Earth*, published only three years after the war (which eventually had sales of approximately 30 million copies), places Israel at the focus of the cosmic drama that will include the rebuilding of the Temple and the rise of the Antichrist as events leading up to the End Times.[9]

One of the most prominent Christian supporters of efforts to reestablish the Holy Temple is Jan Willem van der Hoeven, a Dutch pastor who received theological training in England and who, since 1963, has resided in Israel. Among other ventures, he founded the International Christian Embassy, a nongovernmental organization whose efforts are directed at enhancing the image of Israel among evangelical Christians throughout the world.[10] In 1997, van der Hoeven, a vociferous opponent of the Israeli-Palestinian peace process and its inevitable territorial compromises, withdrew from the International Christian Embassy in order to be free to promote his political views more vigorously. The new organization he created, the International Christian Zionist Center, has active ties with the Temple Mount Faithful.[11] Other Christian fundamentalists, as will be seen, have sought to collaborate with Jewish groups promoting the reestablishment of the Temple.

Jewish Movements for the Establishment of the Temple

In the wake of the Six-Day War, a new era began in the short history of the state of Israel. One of the indelible images of that war is a photograph of weeping paratroopers standing at the Western Wall in the just-captured Old City of Jerusalem. That photo, along with the declaration by Col. Mordechai (Motta) Gur that "the Temple Mount is in our hands," became two of the most outstanding symbols of the war.

As noted, not all Israelis agreed with the compromise status quo for the Temple Mount. About two years after the war, Gershon Salomon founded the Temple Mount Faithful group, which called for an end to Muslim control of the Mount and its transformation into the focal point of Israeli sovereignty. The movement's supporters came from the ranks of the Greater Land of Israel Movement (Hatenu'ah lema'an erez yisrael hashelemah), a broad-based movement founded in the immediate aftermath of the Six-Day War, which over the years became mainly (though not exclusively) religious and right-wing in orientation.

In the four decades of its existence, the Temple Mount Faithful has concentrated on public protest demonstrations held at the foot of the Temple Mount at regular intervals during the year, generally in conjunction with Jewish religious holidays and fast days. The demonstrations take the form of a convoy of pilgrims and usually include ritual elements connected with the Temple Mount, as described in the ancient Jewish sources. During Sukkot, for example, the procession route passes through the Siloam tunnel (which in ancient times provided water to Jerusalem from the Gihon spring), so as to symbolically recreate the water libation ceremony that was performed in the Temple during this festival; on Shavuot, the Temple Mount Faithful bring the first sheaves of harvested wheat. The group also conducts demonstrations on modern Israeli holidays and on days of commemoration—for instance, on Memorial Day (commemorating all of Israel's wars) and Jerusalem Day (which more specifically commemorates the reunification of Jerusalem).

All of these demonstrations take place at the Mughrabi gate (located near the Western Wall plaza), since Israeli authorities prevent the demonstrators from entering the compound. Members of the Temple Mount Faithful invariably demand that central state institutions such as the Knesset and the Supreme Court be moved to the compound and that military ceremonies regularly held in the Western Wall plaza be conducted on the Mount itself. As we shall later discuss, Temple Mount Faithful activities are publicized on an English-language website that is directed, in the main, to a Christian fundamentalist audience.

Over the years, the Temple Mount Faithful has lost some of its influence as many of its religious members have joined more narrowly based groups that emphasize the practical or spiritual (as opposed to political) aspects of reestablishing the Temple. One of these groups is the Temple Institute (Makhon hamikdash), founded in 1984 by Rabbi Yisrael Ariel and located in the Jewish quarter of the Old City. The institute's main objective is to enhance knowledge of the history and practices of the Temple. It operates a museum, a publishing house, *yeshivot*, and a workshop that reconstructs utensils used in the Temple; develops curricula for state religious schools; presents folkloristic recreations of ceremonies that were conducted in the Second Temple; and sponsors an annual colloquium on religious issues relating to the Temple. Thousands of pupils from state religious schools visit the Institute each year, along with dozens of groups of soldiers and thousands of evangelical Christian tourists. In 1999, journalist Gershom Gorenberg was informed that this last group accounted for 60 percent of the Institute's income from tickets and the sale of products in its store.[12]

A second group, the Movement for the Establishment of the Temple (Hetenu'ah lekhinun hamikdash) focuses on bringing Jews to the Temple Mount for purposes of prayer. This group, founded in 1987 by about 20 people who had left the Temple Mount Faithful, is headed by Yosef Elboim, a member of the Belz hasidic group, and, like the Temple Institute, appeals to a religiously observant population.[13] Some of its members are also identified with the extremist nationalist Kach movement founded by Meir Kahane (outlawed in 1994, following the massacre in Hebron that was instigated by one of its members, Baruch Goldstein). For Elboim, a haredi Jew whose life is devoted to the practice of religious ritual, establishment of the Third Temple is a religious issue par excellence. Contrary to Gershon Salomon, he believes that the demand for Jewish control of the Temple Mount is first and foremost a religious imperative—"And let them make Me a sanctuary that I may dwell among them" (Exod. 25:8)—that does not necessarily bear a nationalist Zionist stamp.

In view of Salomon's recurrent failure to receive permission from the authorities for public prayer on the Mount, the Movement for the Establishment of the Temple adopted a different tactic, avoiding publicity and receiving clearance from the police before organizing small groups of worshippers. In their view, "conquest" of the Temple Mount was contingent on a constant presence there, even if this presence consisted of relatively few individuals. Visits were conducted every Tuesday and Saturday until the Mount was closed to Jews after the outbreak of the second ("al-Aqsa") intifada in September 2000, and were renewed when it was opened once again to Jews in November 2003.[14] The movement's leadership deliberated about joining forces with Christians in their efforts, with the exchange of opinions on the matter being conducted in the pages of *Yibaneh hamikdash*, the movement's newsletter. While not all were of one mind on this issue, the group's attitude underwent change over time, as will be seen, and this enabled the establishment of cooperative ties with evangelical Protestants.

Fundamentalist Jewish Theological Justifications for Jewish-Christian Collaboration

Jewish temple activists were at first unable to fathom Christian interest in their cause. This was especially true of those who came from an Orthodox or haredi background, who found it difficult to find a common language with their fundamentalist Christian supporters. Notwithstanding, some of them began to consider theological arguments that might justify their forging ties with non-Jews.

In March 1990, for instance, Yisrael Schneider, a Bratslav hasid, published an article in *Yibaneh hamikdash* in which he justified accepting help from Christians by drawing on a talmudic tale involving an encounter between R. Shimon bar Yohai and a demon.[15] After first attacking those haredi *yeshivot* that did nothing to further the establishment of the Temple, Schneider recounted the talmudic story: R. Shimon bar Yohai once journeyed to Rome to request that the edicts forcing apostasy upon the Jews be rescinded. Upon reaching the gates of the city, he was met by the devil Ben Tamalion, whereupon he wept bitterly: why a devil, since even Hagar, the handmaid of Sarah, had encountered three angels when she fled her mistress?[16]

Schneider's explanation was that the times had changed: God Himself had regularly appeared to Abraham in the course of the latter's offering up of sacrifices, and because of this, even his wife's maidservant merited being visited by angels. However, by the time of Shimon bar Yohai, matters had taken a turn for the worse—the Temple had been destroyed, the revolt mounted by Bar Kokhba had failed, and the *parokhet* (the curtain of the Holy Ark in the Temple) was in Roman hands. Under such conditions, angels no longer appeared to men; assistance could be offered only by demons. As Schneider put it:

> And in our days, if only we could be privileged to have angels from Heaven build the Temple for us, but realistically—we can only hope for the help of devils. More simply put: if we cannot expect help from the *yeshivot*, who knows—perhaps our succor will come from the Gentiles? It is Jewish destiny that all the God-fearing do nothing and wait for the Temple to be revealed from Heaven, [and] only Christian fundamentalist sects believe that it is the Jews who must build the Third Temple. *May the miracle come from anywhere.*[17]

An even more innovative argument came from Yitzhak Hayutman, who, like Schneider, was an active member of the Movement for the Establishment of the Temple. Born in Haifa, Hayutman had become religiously observant while he was a university student in California during the height of the "flower children" movement of the late 1960s. In the late 1980s, he founded the Hayut Foundation for Renewing the Zionist Vision, whose basic objective was the establishment of a "universal temple" on the Temple Mount. This temple would be, in effect, a virtual museum in which visitors would be able to "reconstruct" the act of Creation by means of advanced technologies. It would also feature sacrifices, though not of live animals. Rather, visitors would symbolically "offer up" their negative traits and go through a process of self-correction while participating in the mystic experience of being partner to the Creation. Such a temple, wrote Hayutman, was meant for everyone—religious and secular Jews, and also Gentiles.[18] Indeed, nonreligious Jews and Gentiles were in particular need of such a temple:

> If we look at this from a sociological and religious standpoint, it would seem that the Jewish people have become accustomed to living without a temple, especially with regard to the religious experience sensed by the individual.... In contrast, those Gentiles who have begun seeking a close relationship with Israel [and who] are not obligated to observe the 613 commandments—and, truth be told, also those myriads of Jews who do not observe the commandments—both these groups may gain an understanding that ... participation in the holy ritual is the way to draw near to God.[19]

Hayutman pointed to fundamentalist Christians as the possible target audience for this project since they were a powerful body with tens of millions of believers. If people belonging to various nations appeared before international forums and demanded the reestablishment of the Temple in Jerusalem and the right to pray in it, he argued, this would undermine the claim that such efforts were being sought by Jewish zealots desiring to provoke the Muslim world.[20]

Hayutman's articles aroused lively debate within the ranks of the Movement for the Establishment of the Temple. His specific ideas regarding the "universal temple" were ultimately rejected.[21] However, his call for cooperation with fundamentalist

Christians was received more positively. Among those who wrote in favor of Hayutman's proposal was Elitzur Segal, one of the founders of the Jewish temple movement. In the mid-1990s, Segal (in the wake of another activist, Chaim Richman) developed close ties with a group known as B'nei Noah, or the children of Noah.

B'nei Noah, which currently numbers approximately 30,000 members, was initiated in the 1970s by two Protestant evangelical pastors, Vendyl Jones of Texas and J. David Davis of Tennessee.[22] In contrast to Christians who believe that after the period of the great tribulation they will be saved and thus remain untouched by the cataclysm, the Noahides, as they are often known, believe that they must perform specific acts in order to survive the apocalyptic inferno. Their central concept is based on fulfillment of the seven commandments of the Children of Noah as elaborated in the Babylonian Talmud (Sanhedrin 56a), which comprise prohibitions on idolatry, murder, theft, sexual immorality, blasphemy, and tearing a limb from a living animal, alongside the directive to establish and maintain just courts of law.

B'nei Noah's roots go back to ideas expounded by a 19th-century Italian rabbi, Elijah Benamozegh (1822–1900), who later became the mentor of a French Christian theologian named Aimé Pallière. The latter expressed interest in converting to Judaism, but Benamozegh dissuaded him, believing that Pallière's more important mission was to disseminate his teachings regarding the Noahide laws. Pallière thus engaged in a lengthy career as a spiritual guide for both Christians and Jews, and was also responsible for the posthumous publication of Benamozegh's book, *Israël et humanité* (1914). Years later, his writings were rediscovered by Jones and Davis and were used as the basis of the new Noahide movement.[23]

In his teachings, Benamozegh pointed to the affinity between the nations of the world as manifested in the similarity of many of their core beliefs. At the same time, there was an essential dissimilarity between Israel and the other nations. Israel, termed by Benamozegh "the firstborn," was "charged with teaching and administering the true religion of mankind."[24] Moreover, according to Benamozegh, the Hebrew Bible bears two messages. The first is directed at the Jews, who are obligated to fulfill all 613 commandments of the Torah and to maintain their national distinctiveness. The second, which is aimed at the rest of mankind, obligates them to observe a very limited number of commandments—the Noahide laws. Because these commandments were universally obligatory, they were given to the children of Israel generations before the revelation at Mt. Sinai.

The current B'nei Noah movement began in 1973–1974, when David Davis began to delve into the issue of the historical Jesus. This quest brought him to the Second Temple period and to the Mishnah. As he read the Mishnah, he realized that he needed to know more about Judaism; the more he studied, the more he (and later, a larger group of B'nei Noah) drifted from Christianity. At a certain point, their lack of knowledge, coupled with their feelings of isolation within the fundamentalist Christian community in which most of them lived, caused the Noahides to look for guidance and support among members of the Orthodox Jewish community.

Around the time of its first international conference, which convened in April 1990, B'nei Noah contacted the Chabad/Lubavitch movement—whose leader, R. Menahem Mendel Schneersohn, had long encouraged his disciples to spread the Noahide laws among the Gentiles—to ask for aid and instruction. Chabad declined to send formal representatives to the conference.²⁵ However, when the incumbent Sephardic chief rabbi, Mordechai Eliahu, was contacted sometime thereafter, he endorsed the movement's initiative. Subsequently, close relations developed between B'nei Noah and Rabbi Chaim Richman of the Temple Institute, to the extent that the B'nei Noah newsletter features a regular column about issues concerning the Temple, while a number of B'nei Noah leaders serve as the Institute's official representatives in contacts with non-Jewish organizations. The Temple Institute, for its part, disseminates information about B'nei Noah to groups of Christians visiting its premises in the Old City of Jerusalem.²⁶ In addition, Richman delivers regular lectures to B'nei Noah on the principles of Judaism, and the Institute assisted in drawing up the program for B'nei Noah's second international conference, held in 1992.²⁷

On January 9, 2006, B'nei Noah inaugurated a "high council" whose mandate included establishing contacts between B'nei Noah groups and certain groups among Orthodox Jewry. At this session, which I attended as an observer, the council was made subject to the authority and guidance of "the reestablished Sanhedrin," a body comprising a group of mostly extreme right-wing Israeli rabbis and individuals active in movements for the reestablishment of the Temple.²⁸ Representatives of B'nei Noah, foremost among them Vendyl Jones, were also formally charged with disseminating the message with regard to this new Jewish-Christian alliance.²⁹

Although the modern B'nei Noah movement was brought into existence by two individuals who, at the time, were Protestant evangelical ministers, its theology has evolved considerably since the 1970s, in large part as a consequence of the group's interactions with Jewish fundamentalists, notably Richman and Elitzur Segal. In 1995, Segal published an article in *Yibaneh hamikdash* that both elaborated and transformed the Noahide philosophy, with specific reference to the Temple. According to Isaiah's vision of the End of Days, the Temple would become a place of prayer for all peoples, who would be instructed there in God's ways (Isa. 2:2–3; 56:3–7; 66:18–23). Segal maintained that, with the establishment of the state of Israel, the groundwork had been laid for achieving Jewish hegemony over the nations. To this purpose, the ancient Noahide covenant had to be renewed. This covenant—which God had actually made with Adam, several generations prior to Noah—had been forgotten, but it had been renewed after the Flood, transmitted first to the children of Noah, then to Abraham, and so on down the line until the time of the giving of the Torah on Mt. Sinai. From that point onwards, the children of Israel were obligated by all the laws of the Torah, whereas those of other nations had a more limited obligation to observe the Noahide commandments. In the time of the First and Second Temples, sacrifices were brought both by Jews and by non-Jews who observed the Noahide commandments. This interrelationship between Jews and non-Jews, Segal claimed, was reflected in the fact that the Sanhedrin had seventy members—corresponding to the seventy nations of the ancient world—as well as in the bringing of seventy sacrifices during the holiday of Sukkot.

Segal went on to argue against the traditional view that Judaism does not seek proselytes. In fact, he claimed, it was permissible to renew efforts to disseminate the Abrahamic faith among the nations. The practice of placing obstacles in the path of those who wish to join the ranks of Judaism, he explained, was the outcome of constraints arising from Jewish existence in the diaspora: Judaism could not behave as a missionary faith for fear that this would increase tension between the Jews and Christians and Muslims. However, the true essence of Judaism is to attract all individuals to its faith. Hence, Segal's call for the establishment of an "Abrahamic commonwealth" of nations that would accept Judaism in its "light" form—that is, a form suitable for Gentiles—with Israel standing at its center, just as Great Britain stands at the heart of the British commonwealth.[30]

Tikun 'olam or repairing the world, he continued, is to be achieved by means of the Temple. Reestablishment of the Temple will mark the fulfillment of Isaiah's prophecy, which foresaw the nations of the world proclaiming: "Let us go up to the mount of the Lord, to the house of the God of Jacob, that He may instruct us in His ways and that we may walk in His paths. ... Thus He will judge among the nations and arbitrate for the many peoples" (Isa. 2:3–4).[31] Jerusalem will become the capital of the world and all nations will come there to learn and to be judged. Noahides, each of whom will have the status of *ger toshav*, or resident non-Jew,[32] will worship the Lord in the Temple through the mediation of the people of Israel, using the lingua franca of the Abrahamic commonwealth—Hebrew.[33]

What Segal essentially did was to take the vision of Elijah Benamozegh and transform it into a platform for the creation of Jewish hegemony centered on the Temple in Jerusalem. Benamozegh, who expounded his views before Zionism was a mass political movement, did not foresee a sovereign Jewish state or seek to convey a nationalist messianic message. Rather, his central concept was one of universalism, that of a world in which Jews interact with other nations and serve as a sort of moral compass for them. Segal recast this vision, replacing interreligious harmony with a far more particularistic scheme that emphasized Jewish superiority vis-à-vis the Gentiles. In this fashion, the "partnership" with B'nei Noah (which, as noted, was carried out mainly by Richman and others at the Temple Institute) was theologically justified, as the Jews were clearly understood to be the leaders and B'nei Noah the followers.

Searching for the Red Heifer

One of the more esoteric activities undertaken by the Temple Institute is the continuing search for a halakhically valid red heifer (*parah adumah*) whose ashes can be used in purification ceremonies. As has been noted, the site of the Holy Temple is considered out of bounds to those in a state of ritual impurity. Jewish law distinguishes between several levels of impurity, the most severe being that caused by contact with (or proximity to) a human corpse. In general, individuals today are considered to have the status of "corpse-defiled," and this status can be changed only by a ceremony utilizing red heifer ashes. Yet the conditions set down in the Bible (and later elaborated in the Mishnah) make it almost impossible to find a pure red heifer. It must be three years old and completely red—even two hairs of another color disqualify it. Its horns and nose, too, must be red; it must have no blemish and never have been yoked. According to rabbinic tradition, only nine red heifers were ever sacrificed and burnt, the first being prepared by Moses. Maimonides writes that the tenth will be sacrificed by the Messiah.[34]

To date, all efforts to locate a valid red heifer have failed.[35] In August 1996, a red heifer was born on a dairy farm in Kfar Hasidim, not far from Haifa. The owner, Shemarya Shor, called in the regional rabbi for a consultation, and he in turn invited Yisrael Ariel, president of the Temple Institute, to come and see it. Three leading figures from Temple Mount movements joined him: Gershon Salomon of the Temple Mount Faithful, Yosef Elboim of the Movement for the Establishment of the Temple, and Yehuda Etzion, who had led the "Jewish underground." Other rabbinical authorities soon followed, and the heifer, named Melody, became a local and even international celebrity. Among those who wrote about her were a number of Christian fundamentalist pastors. How great was the general disappointment about a year later, when a few white hairs appeared in Melody's tail and dashed the hopes of her becoming a halakhically valid *parah adumah*.[36]

In April 2002, the Temple Institute announced that, about a month earlier, another red heifer had been born in Israel. The announcement, prominently featured in the Institute's website, provided no details about the birth but was accompanied by a photo of the cow with Richman and Menahem Makover, the Institute's director, standing next to it. In November of that year, an announcement on the website reported that this cow, too, had been disqualified.[37] I have been unable to verify any of the details, as the Institute has been very discreet about facts that might reveal where this cow had been born.

A few years prior to these episodes, a Pentecostal clergyman named Clyde Lott contacted Chaim Richman of the Temple Institute to offer his assistance in the search. Lott, who had years of experience raising cattle, came to Jerusalem for the first time in 1990. Later, together with Richman and Ariel, he scouted places in Israel that would be suitable for raising a herd of red cattle that, it was hoped, would produce at least one valid red heifer. In 1994, he invited Richman to come to Mississippi to examine a number of red heifers that might meet all the halakhic requirements. It was estimated that the cost of bringing cattle over to Israel was about $2,000 per head. To finance the project, a non-profit company, Canaan Land Restoration of Israel, Inc., was established and a fundraising campaign, aimed at Christian fundamentalists, was launched throughout the United States.[38]

The project was never realized. In 1998, Richman and his Christian partners came to a parting of the ways, ostensibly because of economic difficulties. It was rumored, however, that the breakup was actually due to apprehension on the part of the Temple Institute that its Christian partners intended to engage in proselytizing among Jews in Israel.[39] This rumor was confirmed in an informal conversation I conducted with a leading Temple Mount activist who had been involved in the negotiations, who told me that the venture was called off after his colleagues viewed a video tape featuring Lott and another clergyman discussing their intention to engage in missionary activity as part of their preparations for the End Times.

Common Enemies, Different Visions

In October 2001, during the holiday of Sukkot, the Temple Mount Faithful held one of its demonstrations at the Mughrabi gate. One of those in attendance was Jan

Willem van der Hoeven, who declared that he and his followers loved the Jewish nation, and Gershon Salomon in particular. He asked rhetorically: Did God bring the remnants of the Jewish people from Auschwitz only for the sake of praying at this "Wailing Wall," or did He bring them to the Temple Mount? Van der Hoeven declared that he was ashamed of those rabbis who did not instruct their faithful to build the Temple, and he offered a blessing ("in the name of the Lord") to Salomon, with the hope that all other rabbis in Israel would follow in his path.[40]

The Temple Mount Faithful, the most veteran of the Jewish temple activist groups, has had ties with fundamentalist Christian groups since the early 1990s. Stanley Goldfoot, a South African-born journalist, was the initial intermediary between Salomon and a number of evangelical American Protestants.[41] In the course of time, these connections led to a shift in ideological rhetoric. Whereas the Temple Mount Faithful's message was once directly primarily at right-wing Israeli Jews who wanted to see the Temple Mount transformed into the epicenter of Israeli Zionist nationalism, it now places far greater emphasis on the reestablishment of the actual Temple, which will eventually serve as a site of prayer for all nations. This, at least, is the thrust of its English-only website (established in 1999, shortly before the onset of the new Christian millennium), which declares on its homepage: "Our goal is the building of the Third Temple on the Temple Mount in Jerusalem in our lifetime in accordance with the Word of G-d and all the Hebrew prophets and the liberation of the Temple Mount from Arab (Islamic) occupation so that it may be consecrated to the Name of G-d."[42]

Salomon's messianic ideas, based on Jewish biblical prophecies, are described in detail on the website and in Temple Mount Faithful publications. He foresees dramatic events in the near future that will be harbingers of the End of Days. The process will come to an end with the final salvation of humankind and the people's acceptance of God as king on the Temple Mount in Jerusalem. Before that, however, will be the war of Gog and Magog, which will pit the forces of good against absolute evil. In the cosmic drama envisioned by Salomon, the role of demon is assigned to the Palestinian national movement. As he notes in a message written in 2001 (when Yassir Arafat was still alive and serving as the head of the Palestinian Authority): "In G-d's end-time plans there is no place for the cruel enemies of G-d. The terrorist Arafat, and his "Palestinian Authority" will not succeed with their war. We do not fear them nor their violence. The great event of the redemption of Israel cannot be stopped. Who can stop the G-d of Israel?"[43] In another article, he combined a call to bring about redemption with a warning regarding those nations who are urging the state of Israel to agree to territorial concessions:

> G-d has given this great vision to our generation and we cannot run away from our responsibility to Him. The redemption of the people and land of Israel and the rebuilding of the Temple in this generation will open ways for the fulfillment of this vision all over the world. However, it must first be accomplished here in Israel. According to the Word of G-d the Temple must be rebuilt on Mt. Moriah in the midst of Jerusalem. Mashiach ben David will not come to Washington D.C, not to London, Paris or Rome, not to Cairo or Damascus, but to the place which G-d chose, Jerusalem. So my call to all the nations is to stop putting pressure on Israel to sign anti-godly so-called "peace" agreements which give the land, Jerusalem and the Temple Mount to the most cruel enemies of the G-d

and people of Israel. Do not join the enemies who want to destroy Israel. When you join with the enemies of Israel to destroy her you bring yourselves under the judgment of G-d which He promised to execute on the enemies of Israel.[44]

Similar rhetoric regularly appears in material put out by Christian fundamentalist groups such as the International Christian Embassy and the International Christian Zionist Center.[45] Like Salomon, they regard present-day Jerusalem as a holy city whose sanctity is not yet fully manifested: it is still subject to internal Israeli politics, which are hardly messianic, and it still contains a sizeable Muslim presence. Although these negative elements are due to disappear at the End of Days, the present state of affairs calls for positive action. Thus there is room for "Christian Zionists" to join in the efforts to bring about the messianic future. When the Messiah comes, Jerusalem will become the capital of the world, and all those who fought on his side during the battle of Gog and Magog will be worthy of heaven. The Temple Mount, according to both Jewish and Christian fundamentalists, plays a central role in the messianic future. Both groups are also in agreement that, so long as the Temple Mount is under Muslim control, final redemption is impossible. It naturally follows that all peace negotiations between Israel and the Arabs (the Palestinians, in particular—but not exclusively) are an obstacle to redemption. In the eyes of its Christian supporters, the Temple Mount Faithful (regarded by most Israelis as a marginal movement) symbolizes the true spirit of Zionism.

The inherent paradox of Jewish-Christian fundamentalist cooperation is that, while each group may be seeking the same short-term goal, the desired end is vastly different. Both groups envision a messianic future in which the kingdom of God is established for all time. But in the Christian version, Jesus occupies center-stage and Jews who do not acknowledge his kingship are destroyed. In the Jewish version, Jesus is, of course, entirely absent.

The question, then, is where this relationship is headed. Outward cooperation between Jewish and Christian groups masks a basic lack of respect that each side feels for the other. At times this basic distrust comes to the surface, as was the case in the abrogated cooperative venture between the Temple Institute and the Canaan Land Restoration company. Another instance involves Mel Gibson's film of 2004, *The Passion of the Christ*, which was vociferously attacked by Jewish groups across the political spectrum, both in Israel and abroad. Moshe Feiglin, who heads the extreme right-wing faction of the Likud party, and who is also identified with Temple Mount activists, criticized both the movie and the support that it received from conservative Christian audiences.[46] Jan Willem van der Hoeven sent a laudatory message to Gibson in which he expressed his hope that, in the wake of the movie, Jews would comprehend the evil they had wrought in the matter of the crucifixion; would repent; and would make the effort to rebuild the Temple.[47]

It may well be that Jewish temple activists view Christian support as useful but not absolutely crucial to their cause, and are thus willing to risk foregoing their assistance in the event that a given situation is felt to be untenable. Christian supporters, for their part, are unable to conceal their hope that the Jews will in time accept Jesus as their savior. In the meantime, given that messianism is central to their beliefs, it is reasonable to assume continuing fundamentalist Christian support for Israel and the

Jews, including efforts relating to the Temple Mount and the reestablishment of the Temple.

Notes

This essay was translated by Yohai Goell.

1. On the legal status of the Temple Mount, see Shmuel Berkovitz, *The Temple Mount and the Western Wall in Israeli Law* (Jerusalem: 2001).

2. The Temple grounds were divided into sections of varying levels of sanctity. Some areas were limited to the priests (*kohanim*), and entrance to the inner sanctum, or holy of holies (*kodesh hakodashim*), was permitted only to the high priest, and only on the holiest day of the year, Yom Kippur. The prohibition with regard to ritual impurity will later be discussed at greater length.

3. Yoel Cohen, "The Political Role of the Israeli Chief Rabbinate in the Temple Mount Question," *Jewish Political Studies Review* 11, nos. 1–2 (Spring 1999).

4. Nadav Shragai, *Har hamerivah: hamaavak 'al har habayit: yehudim umuslemim, dat upolitikah meaz 1967* (Jerusalem: 1995), 172–179.

5. On the relationship between Hechler and Herzl, see Amos Elon, *Herzl* (New York: 1975), 187–194.

6. Yaakov Ariel, "Doomsday in Jerusalem? Christian Messianic Groups and the Rebuilding of the Temple," *Terrorism and Political Violence* 13, no. 1 (2001), 1–14.

7. Yaakov Ariel, *On Behalf of Israel: American Fundamentalist Attitudes toward Jews, Judaism, and Zionism 1865–1945* (New York: 1991), 1–25; Stephen Spector, *Evangelicals and Israel: The Story of American Christian Zionism* (Oxford: 2009), 1–22.

8. Robert K. Whalen, "Israel," in *Encyclopedia of Millennialism and Millennial Movements*, ed. Richard A. Landes (New York: 2000), 192–196.

9. Hal Lindsey, *The Late Great Planet Earth* (Grand Rapids: 1970).

10. The International Christian Embassy was established in 1980. Earlier that year, the Knesset had passed a law declaring Jerusalem (including East Jerusalem) to be the eternal capital of Israel. In protest, most of the countries that maintained embassies in Jerusalem transferred them to Tel Aviv. The organization operates several philanthropic projects in Israel.

11. Gershom Gorenberg, *The End of Days: Fundamentalism and the Struggle for the Temple Mount* (New York: 2000), 161–162. The International Christian Embassy also supports the Temple Mount Faithful, but keeps a lower political profile. Although it publicizes events organized by Gershon Salomon, its officials do not participate in Temple Mount Faithful demonstrations.

12. Ibid., 174.

13. See a call for new members, dated 16 Dec. 1987, appended to the second issue of *Yibaneh hamikdash*.

14. Motti Inbari, "The Oslo Accords and the Temple Mount—A Case Study," *Hebrew Union College Annual* 74 (2003), 279–323.

15. Babylonian Talmud, Me'ilah 17b.

16. The talmudic text interprets Gen. 16:7–11 (in which the term "angel of God" appears three times) as referring to three *different* angels; cf. Rashi's commentary on Gen. 16:9.

17. Yisrael Schneider, "Beesh atah 'atid livnotah," *Yibaneh hamikdash* 29 (Mar. 1990), 6–7.

18. Yitzhak Hayutman, "Lesheelat miẓvat binyan hamikdash beyameinu," *Yibaneh hamikdash* 33 (July–Aug. 1990), 32–37.

19. Yitzhak Hayutman, "Beit tefilah lekhol ha'amim," *Yibaneh hamikdash* 31 (Apr. 1990), 28–31.

20. Ibid.

21. See letters to the editor, *Yibaneh hamikdash* 32 (May 1990), 27–28; ibid., 35 (Aug.–Sept. 1990), 24–25; ibid., 36 (Sept.–Oct. 1990), 11–13. After the Movement for the Establishment of the Temple declined to promote his "high tech" religious project, Hayutman attempted to interest visiting Christians in the idea, without great success (interview with Hayutman, 4 Aug. 2004). Eventually the universal Temple idea was developed into a book that was geared to a "New Age" audience; see Yitzhak Hayutman and Ohad Ezrahi, *Hayashan yithadesh vehehadash yitkadesh: he'arot lemashma'ut hamikdash* (Jerusalem: 1997).

22. Vendyl Jones is a former pastor and an archaeologist of some fame. Indiana Jones, the hero of some of Steven Spielberg's films, is partly based on his biography. On the growth of B'nei Noah, see Jeffrey Kaplan, *Radical Religion in America: Millenarian Movements from the Far Right to the Children of Noah* (Syracuse, NY: 1997), 42–47, 105–106.

23. Ibid., 110–115.

24. Elijah Benamozegh, *Israel and Humanity*, trans. and ed. Maxwell Luria (New York: 1995), 53-54; cited in Kaplan, *Radical Religion in America*, 111.

25. Ibid., 44–45. Certain elements within the Chabad movement do conduct instructional campaigns among Gentiles to introduce them to the laws of the Children of Noah. To this end, they make use of pamphlets, newspaper ads, and billboards. Channel 2 of the Israeli television network reported on March 29, 2004 that such a campaign took place in Arab villages in the Galilee on the eve of Passover.

26. See, for example, the brochure published by the Temple Mount Information Center, authored by Tsvi Rogin, and titled *The Seven Commandments of the Children of Noah: The Path for Gentiles to Enter into the World to Come and to Avoid the Flood of Immorality in this World* (Jerusalem: 2003).

27. As reported in the Institute's annual *Mah hadash bemakhon hamikdash* for the year 1992.

28. "The Reestablished Sanhedrin" was founded by active members of the Movement for the Establishment of the Temple, who also fill key positions within it. Yisrael Ariel, the head of the Temple Institute, also heads the "court for matters relating to the nation and the state"; Prof. Hillel Weiss, of the department of Hebrew literature in Bar-Ilan University, who has tried to unite all movements working for the reconstruction of the Temple, is its spokesman. The *nasi* (president) of the Sanhedrin is Rabbi Adin Steinsaltz. See its website: www.thesanhedrin.org/en/index.php/The_Re-established_Jewish_Sanhedrin (all online citations, except as indicated, were accessed on 19 July 2009).

29. This material based on my notes taken at the session conducted on 9 Jan. 2006.

30. Elitzur Segal, "Beit Avraham," *Yibaneh hamikdash* 90 (March–April 1995), 8.

31. The text follows the Jewish Publication Society's translation.

32. This status is conferred on Gentiles who take it upon themselves to observe the seven Noahide laws and accept Jewish rule in Eretz Israel (Babylonian Talmud, 'Avodah zarah 64b). A *ger toshav* is permitted to reside in the Holy Land.

33. Segal, "Beit Avraham"; see also Yair Sheleg, "Behazono, 'am yisrael 'omed bemerkazo shel 'hever 'amim Avrahami,' " *Haaretz* (1 Oct. 2002).

34. Mishneh Torah, Hilkhot parah adumah 3:12.

35. Nadav Shragai, *Har hamerivah* (Jerusalem: 1995), 137–140.

36. This episode is described in Gorenberg, *The End of Days*, 1–29.

37. The announcement originally appeared on the following link on the organization's website: www.templeinstitute.org/current-events/Red Heifer/index.html (accessed 3 Feb. 2009).

38. Gorenberg, *The End of Days*, 20–26.

39. Ibid., 28.

40. This paraphrase of van der Hoeven's comments is based on notes in Hebrew that I took at the demonstration (4 Oct. 2001).

41. Stanley Goldfoot was a particularly colorful figure. During the British Mandate period, he served as a correspondent for international English-language media while simultaneously working for the Lehi underground. Among other things, he supplied Lehi members with critical information that enabled them to assassinate U.N. mediator Count Folke Bernadotte in Jerusalem on September 17, 1948. In later years, he became active in the Temple Mount

Faithful movement. A biographical account of Goldfoot, who died in 2006, appeared in the Jerusalem weekly *Kol ha'ir* (13 Oct. 1995), 44–49.

42. See www.templemountfaithful.org.

43. "The Beginning of the End-Time Gog and Magog War against Israel and against Jerusalem," *The Voice of the Temple Mount,* 2001; online at www.templemountfaithful org/Newsletters/2001/5761-2.htm (par. 8).

44. "A Word from Gershon Salomon," *The Voice of the Temple Mount*, 2000, www.templemountfaithful.org/s5760.htm#HEADER1 (par. 19).

45. See, for example, the statement by David Parsons of the International Christian Embassy: "We can take encouragement [from the fact] that the Bible promises the destiny of this long journey is not Israel's annihilation, but rather her ultimate redemption in God" (www.icej org/article/the_struggle_within_the_dream); Jan Willem van der Hoeven: "We live in days of almost unprecedented coming to pass of biblical prophecy. For the past five plus decades, Israel has been the focal point of prophetic fulfillment as most of the events foretold in the bulk of Scripture have been set to take place here" (www.israelmybeloved.com/channel/history_prophecy/section/prophecy_in_our_day).

46. Moshe Feiglin, "Teshukat muḥamed," *Lekhathilah* 131 (2004). This is a 2-page leaflet.

47. Interview of Maria Leppäkari with Jan Willem van der Hoeven, 21 April 2004. I am grateful to Dr. Leppäkari for providing me with a copy of the text.

Essay

Between Socialism and Jewish Tradition: Bundist Holiday Culture in Interwar Poland

Daniel Mahla
(COLUMBIA UNIVERSITY)

The General Jewish Workers Union (Algemeyner yidisher arbeterbund), popularly known as the Bund, was one of the most influential Jewish political parties in interwar Poland.[1] Advocating a socialist society and international workers' solidarity, the Bund was successful in attracting thousands of Jewish workers to its ranks. At the same time, it had to deal with a tension inherent in the very concept of a Jewish socialist party that made universalist claims but also retained particularistic elements of Jewish tradition. Bundist leaders addressed this tension by characterizing their party as anti-Zionist and anti-religious, but still manifestly Jewish. In place of the Orthodox and Zionist concepts of *klal-yisroel*,[2] the Bund promoted the idea of an East European Jewish workers' community. Along these lines, it called for an autonomous status for the Jewish minority within the Polish state, particularly with regard to cultural affairs.[3]

Thus, in the interwar period the Bund not only played an important role in the political arena but also put much effort into establishing cultural and educational institutions with a distinctly anti-elitist character.[4] For example, the Kultur-lige (though not officially a Bundist institution, it had many Bundists among its leadership) supported Yiddish literature, theatre, and music; other institutions catered to women, young adults, and children.[5] A sports organization, Morgnshtern, promoted physical education among Jewish workers. In addition, together with two other groups, the Folkistn and Poale Zion, the Bund helped create a secular, Yiddish-language Jewish school system known as the Tsentrale yidishe shul organizatsiye (Tsisho).[6] The Bundist Yiddish press, and in particular its main organ, the *Naye folkstsaytung*, was a crucial element in the party's cultural enterprise. To be sure, the main task of Bundist newspapers was to spread socialist views and propaganda among the workers. However, the newspapers also aimed at educating and cultivating their readers by means of articles about Yiddish cultural events and literary contributions by writers such as Isaac Leib Peretz and Sholem Asch. In order to further enhance the establishment of a special community known as the "Bundishe mishpokhe," additional editions and supplements were published for women and children.[7]

The Bund also fomented a distinctly Jewish and socialist holiday culture. It sought to establish its own calendar of holidays and commemorative days as a radical alternative to the traditional Jewish calendar. To this end, it put out a "workers' calendar,"[8] and the Bundist press regularly reported on important dates and figures in the history of the movement. The central date of this socialist year was May Day, the *yontef fun arbet* (workers' holiday).[9] The workers' calendar stressed dates such as the outbreak of the French Revolution, which, though regarded as a bourgeois revolution, was nonetheless considered to be a progressive milestone.[10] In addition, it listed the Jewish high holidays as well as the birth and death dates of important Yiddish writers. In common with secular Zionists who offered their own version of the Jewish calendar, Bundists transformed religious holidays. However, in contrast with the Zionists, the Jewish socialists had a much more ambiguous attitude toward certain concepts, such as national liberation and the notion of the land of Israel as the Jewish homeland, that were central to holidays such as Passover.

Many scholars have pointed to the significance of rituals for the construction and affirmation of communities. Emile Durkheim was the first to highlight the way in which societies use rituals to develop self-consciousness; in his view, societies produced, refined, and advanced collective dogmas through what he termed "cult worship."[11] Similarly, through celebrations, social groups create separate, or "sacral," spaces in which they communicate and debate the basic assumptions of their communities.[12] This was the case with regard to the Bundist celebrations. As Jack Jacobs has pointed out, Bundist leaders considered the cultural and educational arenas to be crucial in fostering socialist values and convictions among the workers.[13] As opposed to promoting religious or bourgeois concepts, the Bund offered its own leisure activities and cultural events in an attempt to create an alternative socialist culture. Yet the implementation of a Bundist subculture was not a one-sided process in which the party's elite simply communicated its values to the workers. Operating in an environment in which Jewish religious traditions were pervasive, the socialists had to take them into account. Hence they found themselves striving to reconcile different and sometimes clashing concepts, namely, the universalist notion of an international working class (as dramatized in the May Day celebrations), as opposed to the particularistic notion, stressed in the traditional Passover hagadah, of the Jews as a unique and even chosen people.

These two very different holidays, May Day and Passover, are the focus of this essay. In analyzing the Bundist rituals connected with these days, I pay particular attention to the ways in which the party sought to create a vibrant new workers' culture combining socialist and Jewish traditions.

A Workers' *Yontef*—Jewish May Day Celebrations

First proclaimed by the founding congress of the Second International in Paris in 1889, the first of May, or International Labor Day, is marked by socialist parties around the world as a day for political action. In interwar Poland, Jewish labor leaders planned and organized May Day demonstrations well in advance. A special committee of leading Bundists discussed and arranged all of the processions. Every party member was asked to pay a special May Day tax, and workers were responsible for organizing themselves in their unions, arranging meeting points and procedures to be followed during the demonstrations, and preparing flags and banners. The actual proceedings commenced early in the morning on May Day. Following several introductory speeches and the singing of the Bundist hymn, "Di shvue" ("The oath"), the procession began.[14] The instructions were for workers to march in neat rows of five people each; in theory, anyone unwilling to comply with the strict rules laid down by the Bundist leaders would have no place in the demonstrations.[15] The emphasis placed on order and punctuality was an expression of the party leaders' concern that May Day demonstrations could easily turn chaotic.[16]

In preparation for the celebration, streets and houses in the workers' neighborhoods were festooned with red flags. Large banners were hung at the Bund headquarters, some of them featuring slogans and demands and others the portraits of former party leaders and martyrs. Many workers wore holiday clothes and red ties, or tucked red carnations in their buttonholes; members of the May militia,[17] the Morgnshtern sports club, and the Tsukunft youth club wore their distinctive uniforms. Despite the festive atmosphere, the underlying goals of May Day events were quite serious—both to bring public life to a halt and to impose a proletarian *yontef* throughout the country. This was particularly true in the case of Warsaw, where the strikes that commonly accompanied May Day demonstrations curtailed industrial production and paralyzed traffic, at least in the city center. Moreover, although Polish newspapers were published as usual, no Yiddish newspapers came out on May Day, since Bundists controlled the union of Jewish printers.[18]

The route of the march reflected the workers' struggle for public space. The marchers deliberately bypassed typical workers' districts such as Praga (a Warsaw suburb) in order to symbolically "take over" neighborhoods inhabited by the bourgeoisie. Downtown Warsaw was targeted for special attention. At the climactic point of the procession, workers headed toward Theater Square; during those years in which worker cooperation was at its peak, a mass rally was co-sponsored there by the Bundists, the Polish Socialist Party (Polska Partia Socjalistyczna [PPS]), and other, smaller socialist parties. They chose Theater Square because it symbolized the power of the Polish metropolis, whereas the march through the streets represented the irrepressible advance of socialism: "The proletarian world army marches toward victory."[19] In towns with a socialist majority, workers were able to advance this message by flying a red flag from town hall.[20] In Warsaw, though, there were many years in which the gathering at Theatre Square was banned. This was especially true in the late 1930s, when the right to demonstrate was almost exclusively granted to workers' organizations that identified with the regime, thus demonstrating the powerlessness of the socialist opposition.[21]

Socialist demonstrations were perceived to be a symbolic attempt to (re)write the script for Poland's future, a performative act that challenged the official culture's claims to authority and stability. The staging of demonstrations in the central squares of Polish cities and towns resulted in a "dialectical-theatrical split into protagonists and antagonists."[22] In 1938, a year after a child had been shot during the course of a May Day demonstration, Baruch Sheffner, a columnist at the *Naye folkstsaytung*, declared that the sidewalk had ceased to be neutral ground: bystanders were no longer like the audience at a play but had rather become part of the struggle.[23] Indeed, by this time, violence had become inextricably linked with Polish May Day demonstrations. Apart from Communist-inspired harassment and frequent police brutality, May Day demonstrators were often confronted by supporters of the extreme right-wing National-Democratic movement (Endecja) who sought to break up Bundist rallies by chanting anti-Jewish slogans, beating up Bundist demonstrators, snatching away flags and banners, and throwing smoke-bombs.[24] In Warsaw, student supporters of the Endecja regularly ambushed Jewish workers in front of the university. In most of these instances, the Bundist militia fought back.

As indicated, May Day events were marked by a certain amount of cooperation between the Bund and other socialist parties, most importantly the PPS. Bundist leaders went to great lengths to coordinate the day's events with their non-Jewish socialist counterparts because such cooperation reflected the ideal of Polish-Jewish brotherhood—an important theme in the Bundist worldview. Notwithstanding, May Day events were rarely the product of joint Polish-Jewish sponsorship. Political differences between the different groups, the fear of violent excesses on the part of the (other) group's members, and ever-increasing constraints by Poland's quasi-authoritarian government all worked to impede cooperation. Given these obstacles, the joint marches that took place in the years 1928, 1930, 1931, and 1934 took on even greater symbolic meaning. During those years, as the workers marched together through the center of Warsaw, their struggle appeared to be truly united. Ethnic antagonisms dissipated at least temporarily as Polish and Jewish workers jointly sang the "Internationale."[25]

Yet despite the mutual avowals of cooperation on the part of their leaders, it is doubtful whether the bulk of Jewish and Polish workers ever came into close contact. For one thing, Jewish and non-Jewish groups often followed different processional routes. And even when they marched in the same procession, Polish and Jewish socialists were grouped separately—a situation that reflected Bund leaders' determination to maintain their party's distinctive Jewish identity.[26] Otherwise, it was felt, Bundist demands such as equal rights for Jewish workers and state recognition of Jewish secular schools might drown in a sea of Polish flags. In a similar vein, the Bundists declined offers of assistance from the PPS militia, not wanting to rely on their "goyishe friends" to protect them as they were marching through "Polish" streets.[27] Then, too, there was the question of language: the Bundists' struggle for the recognition of their own language could hardly be waged by using Polish slogans. On several occasions, the Warsaw May Day coordinators addressed this last issue by setting up two separate stages in Theater Square. Although this measure somewhat undermined the notion of Jewish and Polish workers comprising a single, unified entity, it allowed the Bund to assert its separate demands for cultural autonomy while at the same time situating the Jewish collective of workers within the broader socialist movement.

Outside of Warsaw, the cooperation of different Jewish worker groups was easier to achieve. In smaller towns, activists were not subject to the same level of party scrutiny.[28] Moreover, Polish laws and restrictions were less carefully monitored in the provinces.[29] As in the larger cities, workers in outlying towns viewed the celebrations as vehicles for communicating and negotiating social values. This point appeared in many of the accounts of local demonstrations published in the *Naye folkstsaytung*.[30]

Bundist May Day propaganda generally adhered to the larger socialist narrative and conveyed Marxist tenets. In addition, however, the Bund leadership made use of Jewish concepts and rhetoric. Thus, for instance, the Bund was termed "a messiah" that would lead the workers "out of the czarist and capitalistic exile."[31] In a May Day article published in the *Naye folkstsaytung* in 1928, Baruch Sheffner drew a socialist lesson from a well-known talmudic story about a potential convert who wanted to study the Torah as quickly as possible. In the talmudic account, the Gentile first approaches the renowned scholar Shammai, who turns him away. He then seeks out Hillel, who grants the man's wish, explaining that the Torah in its entirety can be summarized in one phrase: "That which is hateful to you, do not do to your neighbor." According to Sheffner: "Thus there are two ways leading to every doctrine, to every religion. One leads through the intellect and the other through the heart. ... The same holds true with regard to socialism. There is one difficult way of socialist theory, that of hard studies. And there is a way in which 'the light of the sun is leading the workers,' the way through the heart."[32]

A statement by Bernard Goldstein, the leader of the Bundist militia, similarly demonstrates the extent to which some party members were still rooted in a traditional Jewish discourse. In order to denounce a political opponent, Goldstein labeled him a "geshmadter yid."[33] The word "geshmadter," translated as "baptized" or "renegade," has strongly negative connotations. By using this expression, as opposed to attacking the other leader on the grounds of his political identity, Goldstein relied on internal Jewish polemics. Moreover, by referring to his opponent as the embodiment of extreme assimilation, Goldstein was underscoring his own organization's folk-national basis. To be sure, leading Bundists had abandoned the religious observance typical of many East European Jews. Nonetheless, and in spite of their revolutionary and anti-traditional rhetoric, they continued to be deeply steeped in the symbolic system and language of Jewish religion and culture.

A Workers' Exodus—The Bund's Revisionist Passover Narrative

In creating their own holiday culture, the Bundists attempted to detach their adherents from religious concepts. Allegedly outdated values, ideas and behavior were to be discarded. At the same time, traditional holidays were deemed useful, both as targets of criticism and as a means of subversion. The Bundist strategy was to retain the outward trappings of traditional Jewish holidays while emptying them of religious content and imbuing them with socialist meaning.

Thus the Bundists (like the Zionists) took holidays such as Passover and filled them with new and ideologically relevant content.[34] They emphasized the festive element of Passover with activities such as sports events and communal dinners.[35] Yet even more significant was the way in which the Bundists attempted to read socialist meanings into the holiday by reinterpreting the biblical narrative. Such exegesis was carried out both in the party press and in Bundist revisions of the traditional Passover hagadah, one of which was published in Cracow in 1919.[36] Although it is extremely difficult to evaluate the extent to which workers accepted this revised hagadah, its frequent reprintings attest to the fact that Bundist leaders regarded it as an important vehicle for spreading their socialist message.

Written mainly in Yiddish, the Bundist hagadah marked a radical break with the traditional Jewish understanding of the Passover narrative and its significance. The first paragraph, for instance, describes a Jewish worker coming home and searching for leftover leavened food. This scene echoes the ritual search (*bedikat ḥamez*) that takes place on the eve of Passover, where the intention is to rid the home of leavened food. Here, however, the worker, tired and hungry, is searching for a piece of bread to eat. Taking this scenario as a starting point, the Bundist hagadah goes on to describe the hardships and bondage of the workers. Throughout the text, history advances in Marxist terms from slavery in Egypt to the current bourgeois exploitation of the proletarians. Beginning with its description of the workers' poverty, the story line proceeds to subjects such as self-liberation, freedom, and the belief in progress, and ends with the call for redemption in the form of socialism.

The Bundist narrative ignores or changes other key elements of the traditional Passover seder. For instance, the socialist hagadah hardly mentions the ritual foods that are an essential part of the traditional seder. There is only a brief allusion to *maror*, the bitter herbs symbolizing the bitterness of slavery in Egypt. In contrast, "matzo" (in Hebrew, *mazah*) undergoes an etymological and ideological transformation, becoming *masa* (burden). At the Bundist seder this matzo is not even meant to be eaten. Rather, it symbolizes the fact that oppressed workers are so poor that they have to "eat" one another in order to survive.[37]

In the Bundist hagadah, God is largely edited out of the narrative. One instance involves Psalm 146, appearing in its entirety in the traditional Hebrew hagadah, whose refrain repeatedly praises God, "for His kindness is everlasting" (*ki le'olam ḥasdo*). In the Bundist version, "progress" stands in the place of the deity and, as noted in the refrain, "its actions will last forever" (*zayn virkung doyert eybik*).[38] In another instance, the counting song "Eḥad mi yode'a?" (Who knows one?) is thoroughly reworked. Whereas the original text enumerates basic motifs of traditional Judaism ("two tablets of the Law, three patriarchs, four matriarchs…"), the Bundist version recounts the myriad evils of the time, among them capitalism, militarism, the religious establishment, and the oppression of the proletariat.[39] And whereas the final song in the traditional hagadah, "Ḥad gadya" (An only kid) allegorically describes a cycle of evil broken by God's slaying of the angel of death, the Bundist version features the struggle of socialism against capitalism. According to its upbeat conclusion: "In the end socialism will triumph and liberate everybody. Amen."[40]

Indeed, when mentioned at all, God is blamed for not following up on the divine promise of redemption. Since the workers still live in bondage, they have to free themselves. In lieu of appeals for redemption, the Bundist hagadah substitutes Georg Herwegh's famous declaration: "If your mighty arm wills it, all the wheels will come to a halt" (*Wenn dein starker Arm es will, stehen alle Räder still*).[41] The people—that is to say, the workers—take center stage in the process of salvation. Instead of God, "progress" is worshiped for its ability to accomplish miracles, bring light into the darkness, break the iron chains, defeat the despots, redeem the workers and, ultimately, usher in socialism.

Both the redemptive aspect of socialism and the Bund's rewriting of tradition are emphasized in a subtle play on words appearing near the end of the revisionist hagadah. One of the most controversial sections of the traditional Hebrew text is an appeal addressed to God: "Pour out Your wrath upon the nations that do not acknowledge You" (*shefokh ḥamatkhah el hagoyim asher lo yeda'ukhah*). In the Bundist version, the Hebrew term for "wrath," *ḥemah*, is replaced by *ḥamah*—deriving from the same root but translating as "heat" or "warmth" (it is also the biblical term for the sun)— and God is replaced by socialism. With this change in wording, a call for vengeance is transformed into a cry for unity. Instead of being destroyed by God's consuming anger, those nations that have not (yet) acknowledged the new social order will bask in the warmth of socialism.[42]

In line with its internationalist ideology, the Bundist hagadah also annuls the linkage between the Jewish people and the land of Israel. Thus, the Bundist version first cites the original Hebrew text when talking about "the land that was promised to our forefathers" (*haarez asher nishba' laavoteinu*) but then reinterprets "the land" as the emergence of a new world order:

> He will lead us to the land that was promised to our forefathers. ... Everybody has to understand that he has the same rights as anyone else. This holy idea (blessed be it) will grow stronger and stronger, and will teach us to build up the world that already has been promised to our parents. We will be redeemed and we will establish a society of true felicity for all working people.[43]

In observing the seder ritual, Jews symbolically reenact the historical scenario as well as renewing and replenishing their national memory. As Yosef Yerushalmi has noted, memory in this sense is not merely recollection, which preserves a certain distance, but re-actualization.[44] Such a performance of commemorative rituals opens the possibility not only of reviving and affirming older memories, but also of modifying them. In the Bundist retelling, the Exodus story that was transmitted throughout the generations—a tale of divine redemption of a specific people, the children of Israel—gives way to a narrative focusing on the self-liberation of the workers, the calling into question of the traditional Jewish laws, the axiom of all men being equal, and a Marxist understanding of history.[45] Thus, in the course of sabotaging traditional authority by launching an attack on the bourgeois elite, the rabbis, and even God, the Bundists abolished the conventional narrative and filled the void with its own "master fiction" (in the terminology of Clifford Geertz). At the same time, they did not strive for a complete breach with the past.[46] As Michael Walzer has argued, the biblical account lends itself to political interpretation as an alternative to messianic and millenarian thought, as a secular and historical account of redemption that does not require a miraculous transformation of the world.[47] In fact, other (non-Jewish) revolutionaries had previously alluded to the Exodus. For the Bundists, however, the biblical story had the additional significance of being a central component of Jewish tradition. Retaining the seder along with its narrative theme of liberation, the Bundists sought to infuse Jewish culture with elements of Marxist tradition and in this way create a "pre-history" for the latter that began much earlier than working-class struggles. Indeed, the Bundist hagadah goes so far as to claim that its narrative represents the "original" text as opposed to an "invented rabbinical tradition." The rabbis, it is claimed, were not satisfied with the *peshat*, the simple and direct reading of the text, and had therefore forged another version with the help of their sophisticated, but class-driven, exegesis.[48]

Another important disparity between the traditional hagadah and the Bundist version concerns their differing emphases on the past and future as opposed to the present. The traditional Passover ritual displays a certain tension in its turning both to a mythic past and a redemptive future while disregarding current circumstances as being unimportant. This stance complies with an aspect of Orthodox Jewish thinking that views current events as relevant only as indicators of the process of salvation. The socialist narrative takes the opposite approach. Although past and future also have significance, the focus is on the present; rather than relying on an inchoate future, workers are urged to change their present reality. This declaration is, of course, one of the basic tenets of Marxist ideology.

A Marxist understanding of history and historical processes is present throughout the revised hagadah, especially in its socioeconomic re-interpretation of the Passover myth. Traditionally, the Exodus does not merely bear the meaning of liberation from physical bondage but includes as well a strong spiritual dimension. It reminds the Jews that their forefathers had been idolaters—idolatry being understood as the worship of idols that are alien to Judaism (the Hebrew term *'avodah zarah* translates as "foreign worship"). In the Bundist text, the word *'avodah* (*avoyde*) is translated literally as "work," and the phrase becomes reinterpreted as "work for strangers," that is, the proletarian's selling of his labor to others. Accordingly, the socialist text continues with a short outline based on a socioeconomic understanding of history, and sacrality is transferred from God and His people to the new revolutionary community.[49] Whereas traditional Judaism teaches that the Jews help prepare the world for the coming of the Messiah and the ultimate revelation of God's glory, the proletarian Passover message transfers the eschatological mission to the workers, the new chosen people.

Particularism versus Universalism

Both Bundist May Day celebrations and Bundist leaders' attempts (as in the case of the Passover hagadah) to transform Jewish rituals and adapt them to their own ideological orientation reflect the tensions inherent in the concept of a Jewish socialist workers' culture. To what extent were the Bundists successful in their efforts? With regard to the Passover seder, it is difficult to provide a clear-cut answer, since this was a private ritual conducted among individual families.[50] May Day celebrations, in contrast, were public events that were the subject of numerous reports both in the Bundist and non-Bundist Polish Jewish press. Such reports provide evidence of broad and constantly growing support for the mass worker celebrations.[51]

Both cases, however, attest to a similar combination of socialist and Jewish elements. To be sure, the emphasis was on the socialist rather than the Jewish aspect. At the same time, as has been seen, the Bundists took socialist concepts and infused them with elements of the Jewish world and tradition. Such blending, in turn, created a tension that can be discerned in many accounts of the celebrations. At Bundist May

Day celebrations, particularism and universalism were yoked together but at times led to audible dissonance, as in the discussions concerning joint Polish-Jewish processions and the issue of Yiddish banners and speeches. On many occasions, Jewish socialists had to stand up for specifically Jewish interests in some areas while conceding to their Polish counterparts in others.

Perhaps the best example of the tension between universalism and particularism is provided by the phrase *yidisher arbeter-klal*. "Arbeter-klal," referring to the workers' community, stands in sharp contrast to *klal-yisroel* (the community of Israel), the ethno-religious notion advanced by both Zionist and Orthodox Jews. However, even though "arbeter-klal" stresses the priority of class affiliations over ethnicity, it also insists that a particular *Jewish* working class exists apart from the general labor movement.[52] Moreover, *yidisher arbeter-klal* was far from being a fixed concept. The question of how much emphasis should be given to its different and partly opposing components—ethnicity and class affiliation—was the subject of frequent debate.[53]

In a manner similar to that of the Zionists, the Bund contributed to a secularization of Jewish concepts. Such a process, however, was inevitably slow and subject to contradictory trends, as it proved to be impossible to build a modern Jewish national consciousness without referring to religious traditions.[54] For one thing, the origins of the Jewish people were inseparable from biblical events and therefore from the Jewish religion. In addition, the Yiddish language, containing numerous words and expressions deriving from Hebrew, was itself tightly linked to religious traditions and concepts. Thus, the Bundists had to adapt their new teachings and rites to Judaism's traditional symbolic system. And this process went in both directions. On the one hand, the teachings of socialism deeply influenced the Jewish workers. On the other hand, Jewish workers adjusted the socialist ideology to the religious traditions from which they could not entirely escape.

While similar strategies of Jewish labor leaders in the United States may be regarded as a manifestation of the gradual Americanization of the East European Jewish immigrants, the situation in Poland was quite different. There, the often hostile environment and the vulnerable civil and legal status of the Jewish minority fostered a strong feeling of social cohesion among Jewish workers and cast doubt upon the prospects of acculturation to the Polish majority.[55] Far from being a lopsided process, the interchange between socialist and religious tenets created a particular Jewish-socialist culture.[56] In interwar Poland, a "new song, a splendid song"[57] was clearly audible in the Jewish milieu, providing some of the workers with confidence and dignity.

Notes

I would like to thank Professors Ezra Mendelsohn, Kiran Patel, and Shaul Stampfer for their extensive comments on earlier drafts of this essay and their sustained support throughout the period of my research.

1. The Bund was founded in the Russian Pale of Settlement in 1897 and developed into one of the leading Jewish political movements in the empire. After the Russian Revolution and the liquidation of the Bund by the Bolsheviks, the party's center shifted to Poland. There, during the period of the Second Republic, the Bund was one of the main Jewish parties.

2. *Klal-yisroel* is an ethno-religious concept denoting the entire Jewish people, regardless of any religious or political divisions. The term acquired additional significance with the emergence of Zionism; see Ehud Luz, "The Limits of Toleration: The Challenge of Cooperation between the Observant and the Nonobservant during the Hibbat Zion Period, 1882–1895," in *Zionism and Religion*, ed. Shmuel Almog, Jehuda Reinharz, and Anita Shapira (Hanover: 1998), 45.

3. Bundist leaders only gradually came to appreciate the cultural aspect of their mission—it was only after 1905 that these issues were taken into account. See David E. Fishman, "The Bund and Modern Yiddish Culture," in *The Emergence of Modern Jewish Politics: Bundism and Zionism in Eastern Europe*, ed. Zvi Gitelman (Pittsburgh: 2003), 107–119.

4. Gertrud Pickhan, *"Gegen den Strom": der Allgemeine Jüdische Arbeiterbund "Bund" in Polen 1918–1939* (Stuttgart: 2001), 222–223.

5. The Kultur-lige was founded in 1918 in Kiev, but many of its socialist members left Ukraine in the early 1920s. In interwar Poland, the Kultur-lige was led by members of several Jewish parties; from 1924, it was dominated by the Bund. See ibid., 230–235.

6. Nathan Cohen, "The Bund's Contribution to Yiddish Culture in Poland between the Two World Wars," in *Jewish Politics in Eastern Europe: The Bund at 100*, ed. Jack Jacobs (Basingstoke: 2001), 112–130. For a detailed description of Tsisho, see Pickhan, *"Gegen den Strom,"* 236–248.

7. Pickhan disputes the allegedly unique character of the Bundist *mishpokhe* (*"Gegen den Strom,"* 110–177), arguing that the self-representation of the party as a family resembled self-depictions of the Polish socialists. On the Polish socialist community, see Stephanie Zloch, "Demokratie und Nationalismus in Polen (1918–1939)" (Ph.D. diss., Humboldt University of Berlin, 2007). I am grateful to Dr. Zloch for allowing me to read parts of her dissertation.

8. See, for instance, *Arbeter tashen-kalender 1930* (Sotsialistishe yugent-bibliotek, no. 7) (Warsaw: 1930).

9. *Yontef* (holiday) derives from the Hebrew *yom tov*, or good day. Originally, the term was used exclusively for Jewish holidays.

10. Whenever the Bundist press commemorated events of the bourgeois struggle, it made sure to point out the half-hearted aspect of that struggle as opposed to the dedication of the true revolutionaries—the proletariat. Thus, in an article appearing in the *Naye folkstsaytung*, the writer noted that the French Revolution should have taken place a few days before it did, but was deferred because of bad weather. See *Naye folkstsaytung* (4 May 1927), 4; see also ibid. (13 April 1933), 4; ibid. (30 April 1929), 3.

11. Emile Durkheim, *The Elementary Forms of the Religious Life* (London: 1976), 416–417.

12. For a very useful outline of the different theoretical approaches to rituals and their role in the process of fostering communities, see Malte Rolf, *Das Sowjetische Massenfest (1917–1941)* (Hamburg: 2005).

13. Jack Jacobs, "Creating a Bundist Counter-Culture: Morgnshtern and the Significance of Cultural Hegemony," in idem (ed.), *Jewish Politics in Eastern Europe*, 59–68.

14. See descriptions in the following issues of the *Naye folkstsaytung*: (2 May 1927), 1; (3 May 1929), 1; (2 May 1930), 1; (3 May 1931), 1; (2 May 1932), 2; (2 May 1933), 1–2; (2 May 1934), 1–2; (2 May 1935) 1–3; (2 May 1936), 1–3; (2 May 1937), 1–2; (2 May 1938), 1.

15. In their frequent appeals to workers, Bundist leaders urged them to be on time, warning that latecomers would not be allowed to take part in the proceedings. In this regard, it appears that the leaders were battling an allegedly ingrained element of Jewish behavior, "Jewish chaos." See, for instance, *Naye folkstsaytung* (30 April 1937), 12. Notwithstanding their frequent calls to order, Bundist leaders do not seem to have been notably successful in their attempts: neat rows of five workers each are not to be seen in photographs taken at the time.

16. The Bundists were well aware of the risk of chaos. Thus, they blamed the PPS for being against joint demonstrations merely because the Polish labor leaders feared losing control over the demonstrations; see *Nasza Walka*, nos. 5–6 (May-June 1926), 113.

17. The May militia was established by the Bund; one of its primary functions was to provide protection for Bundist events. For the May Day celebrations, the militia was reinforced

by additional Bundists. See Leonard Rowe, "Jewish Self-Defense: A Response to Violence," in *Studies on Polish Jewry 1919–1939*, ed. Joshua A. Fishman (New York: 1974), 105–149.

18. This was a point of considerable annoyance to the management of rival, non-socialist Yiddish newspapers, among them *Haynt* and the *Yidishe togblat*. The Bund, meanwhile, was vocal in its triumph. See, for instance, *Naye folkstsaytung* (2 May 1931), 3; cf. *Haynt* (30 April 1931), 4; *Yidishe togblat* (2 May 1933), 1.

19. *Naye folkstsaytung* (19 April 1929), 3. A similar point regarding socialist demonstrations in general is made by Winfried Gebhardt, *Fest, Feier und Alltag. Über die gesellschaftliche Wirklichkeit des Menschen und ihre Deutung* (Frankfurt: 1987), 135.

20. *Naye folkstsaytung* (29 April 1927), 7 (describing pre-May Day preparations in Zamość); ibid. (29 April 1928), 2 (describing preparations in Lublin and Lodz).

21. The workers supporting the Sanacja (the pro-government forces) had split from the PPS and became known as the PPS – Dawna Frakcja Rewolucyina' (PPS-F.R.). The Jewish parties referred to them as *frokes* (from "tailcoat," an allusion to their ambitious quest for power). See Bernard Goldstein, *20 yor in varshever bund 1919–1939* (New York: 1960), 116–117; Antony Polonsky, *Politics in Independent Poland, 1921–39: The Crisis of Constitutional Government* (Oxford: 1972), 264–265. On at least one occasion, the Bund itself acknowledged that the larger demonstrations of the PPS-F.R. in Theatre Square reflected the distribution of power. See *Naye folkstsaytung* (3 May 1931), 1.

22. Richard Schechner, *The Future of Ritual: Writings on Culture and Performance* (London: 1993), 88.

23. *Naye folkstsaytung* (6 May 1938), 4.

24. Reports on the most serious of these incidents for the period under question appear in the following issues of *Naye folkstsaytung*: (2 May 1928), 3–4; (2 May 1934), 1–2; (2 May 1937), 2.

25. See the following issues of *Naye folkstsaytung*: (2 May 1934), 1; (2 May 1931), 1; (3 May 1931), 1; (2 May 1934), 1f.

26. Goldstein, *20 yor in varshever bund*, 219.

27. Ibid., 219f.

28. On a number of occasions, the Bund's central committee explicitly came out against joint processions with the rightwing Poale Zion. Nonetheless, there are several accounts detailing such cooperation between the two groups. See *Naye folkstsaytung*: (2 May 1932), 7; (7 May 1935), 4; (12 April 1939), 9.

29. For instance, whereas joint Polish-Jewish processions were not allowed in Warsaw between 1936 and 1939, the workers in Grodno marched together. See *Naye folkstsaytung*: (3 May 1936), 2; (3 May 1937), 4; (2 May 1938), 3; (7 May 1939), 5.

30. In fact, editors of the *Naye folkstsaytung* often apologized for not being able to print all the reports that had been sent in; see, for instance, the following issues: (5 May 1936), 6; (3 May 1937), 4.

31. Emanuel Nowogrodski (ed.), *Beynish Mikhalewicz gedenk-bukh* (Buenos Aires: 1951), 199.

32. *Naye folkstsaytung* (30 April 1928), 2.

33. Goldstein, *20 yor in varshever bund*, 118.

34. The Zionist treatment of Jewish holidays has been examined widely. See, for instance, Anita Shapira, "The Religious Motifs of the Labor Movement," in Almog, Reinharz, and Shapira (eds.), *Zionism and Religion*, 251–272; Yaacov Shavit and Shoshana Sitton, *Staging and Stagers in Modern Jewish Palestine: The Creation of Festive Lore in a New Culture, 1882–1948* (Detroit: 2004); François Guesnet, "Chanukah and Its Function in the Invention of a Jewish-heroic Tradition in Early Zionism, 1880–1900," in *Nationalism, Zionism and Ethnic Mobilization of the Jews in 1900 and Beyond*, ed. Michael Berkowitz (Leiden: 2004), 227–246. Other socialist parties, among them the German SPD, also dealt with the relationship between socialism and religion, using sacral language and attempting to present socialism as the logical successor of Christianity: Christ himself was often depicted as the first socialist. See Lucian Hölscher, *Weltgericht oder Revolution. Protestantische und sozialistische Zukunftsvorstellungen im deutschen Kaiserreich* (Stuttgart: 1989); Heinrich Basilius Streithofen, *SPD und*

katholische Kirche. Eine Untersuchung über das Kirchenbild des Vorwärts (Stuttgart: 1974). On French revolutionaries and holidays, see Michel Vovelle, *Die französische Revolution. Soziale Bewegungen und Umbruch der Mentalitäten* (Munich: 1982), 127.

35. See, for instance, the following issues of *Naye folkstsaytung*: (8 April 1927), 8; (30 March 1931), 5; (10 April 1936), 1; see also Goldstein, *20 yor in varshever bund*, 129.

36. *Hagode shel peysekh, mit a sotsialistishn nusakh* (Cracow: 1919). For the purposes of this essay, this version of the hagadah is termed the "Bundist hagadah" though in fact it is a revision of a version originally written in 1887 by Jewish socialists in Vilna, which was reprinted several times and in different places, including London and New York. In 1900, three years after its founding, the Russian Bund published a considerably revised version of the text in Geneva. This revision was marked by a moderation in tone and content; former versions had called on the Jewish workers unambiguously to "take up their rifle" and "destroy the parasites," that is, the bourgeoisie. The version discussed here was used by Bundists during the interwar period in Poland.

For a history of the hagadah, see Yosef Hayim Yerushalmi, *Haggadah and History: A Panorama in Facsimile of Five Centuries of the Printed Haggadah from the Collections of Harvard University and the Jewish Theological Seminary of America* (Philadelphia: 1975). For additional background regarding both the socialist hagadah analyzed here and an earlier version written in Yiddish (with a Hebrew translation), see Haya Bar Itzhak, "He'arot lahagadah shel pesaḥ shel 'haBund,'" *Ḥulyot* 2 (1994), 255–271. See also David P. Shuldiner's *Of Moses and Marx: Folk Ideology and Folk History in the Jewish Labor Movement* (Westport: 1999), 119–140, which discusses an earlier socialist version of the hagadah produced in Yiddish for the American Jewish labor movement. On alternative versions of the hagadah that were used by members of the Jewish labor movement in Mandatory Palestine, see Derek J. Penslar, "The Continuity of Subversion: Hebrew Satire in Mandatory Palestine," *Jewish History* 20, no. 1 (March 2006), 19–40.

37. Matzo was the subject of an article appearing in *Naye folkstsaytung* ([4 April 1928], 3), where it was derided as a relic of ancient times. According to the article, whereas people in ancient times were unfamiliar with bread and thus prepared "a kind of cookie" with unleavened dough, it was now the case that this unleavened bread was being produced on modern, assembly-line machines. The Bundists regarded this as clearly absurd—yet another example of the inanity of religion. The article hints at the fact that there was an ongoing dispute among hasidim with regard to the halakhic status of mechanically produced matzo. On this issue, see also Mendel Piekarz, *Haḥasidut bepolin: megamot ra'yoniyot bein shetei hamilḥamot uvegezerot 5700–5705 ("hashoah")* (Jerusalem: 1990), 93–96.

38. *Hagode shel peysekh*, 17. The Germanized diction harkens back to the older version of the text published in New York, which included many *daytshmerish* (Germanizing) elements. Often coming out of a Russian-speaking background, many New York-based activists learned German before switching to Yiddish. Therefore their Yiddish absorbed many German expressions. See Tony Michels, *A Fire in Their Hearts: Yiddish Socialists in New York* (Cambridge, Mass.: 2005).

39. See *Hagode shel peysekh*, 20 ("Who knows two? I know two—mankind is divided into two parts: poor and rich. Who knows three? I know three—The Christian trinity embitters [*farfinstert*] the world. Who knows four? I know four—capitalism, militarism, religion, and the government enslave the working class"). Similarly, the Zionist movement (especially among certain kibbutzim in Palestine) inserted its own messages into the hagadah and used elements such as "Eḥad mi yode'a" to deal with current political and social problems, among them the unfulfilled promise of the Balfour Declaration and the Arab revolt of 1936–1939. See, for instance, David C. Jacobson, "Writing and Rewriting the Zionist National Narrative: Responses to the Arab Revolt of 1936–1939 in Kibbutz Passover Haggadot," *Journal of Modern Jewish Studies* 6, no. 1 (March 2007), 1–20; Penslar, "The Continuity of Subversion."

40. *Hagode shel peysekh*, 23.

41. This line appears as part of a song ("Bundeslied für den allegemeinen deutschen Arbeiterbund") composed in 1864 by Herwegh, a German revolutionary, for the General German

Workers Association. In the song, the lines are reversed: "Alle Räder stehen still, wenn dein starker Arm es will."

42. *Hagode shel peysekh*, 15. In the original Hebrew text, "nations that do not acknowledge You" refer to nations that oppress the people of Israel, as noted in the following verse: "For they have devoured Jacob and laid waste his habitation" (*ki akhal et ya'akov veet navehu hashemu*). The Bundist hagadah omits this reference.

43. *Hagode shel peysekh*, 13–14.

44. Yosef Hayim Yerushalmi, *Zakhor: Jewish History and Jewish Memory* (Seattle: 1982), 44.

45. *Hagode shel peysekh*, 3–4.

46. As has been argued for the French revolutionaries; see Lynn Hunt, *Politics, Culture, and Class in the French Revolution* (Berkeley: 1984).

47. Michael Walzer, *Exodus and Revolution* (New York: 1985), 17.

48. According to the "rabbis" quoted in the Bundist hagadah: "No, the simple *peshat* is not enough for us; we have to find another *derash* [a homilectical or interpretive meaning], we must not give [the workers] time to understand the simple *peshat*" (*Hagode shel peysekh*, 5). This, of course, is what the Bundists were doing as well.

49. *Hagode shel peysekh*, 8–9. Cf. Mona Ozouf's observations on the French revolutionary festivals in her *Festivals and the French Revolution* (London: 1988), 262ff.

50. What seems clear is that many Jewish workers, although not strictly observant, were nonetheless fairly traditional in their beliefs and practices, as evidenced by the fact that Bundist newspapers regularly carried advertisements for kosher food and beverages. See, for instance, *Naye folkstsaytung* (4 April 1928), 3, which contains both an article about the "anachronism" of eating matzo and advertisements for (kosher for Passover) matzos.

51. Although reporting lower numbers than the Bundist press, both *Haynt* and the Orthodox *Yidishe togblat* could not ignore the increasing numbers of workers participating in the demonstrations. Naturally, they tried both to downplay the significance of the demonstrations and to ridicule them. Concerned about the growing popularity of May Day observances, the Agudat Israel movement published a pamphlet in 1930 that explained why Jews should not celebrate the first of May. See L. Szetrzekacz, *Der ershter may – farvos m'darf im nisht fayern* (Warsaw: 1930).

52. On this distinction, see Yosef Gorny, "Bein ma'amadiyut le'amamiyut—ha'bund' hapolani 1917–1932," *Gal-Ed* 18 (2002), 194.

53. The constant renegotiation of these different components can be detected, for example, in the changing Bundist rhetoric with regard to Passover during the interwar period. In contrast to the Bundist hagadah, later Bundist propaganda reinserted the Jews (in place of the working class) as the protagonists of the Exodus story. While still refraining from characterizing the Jews as the "chosen people," this later material remained closer to the original Hebrew text. See, for example, *Naye folkstsaytung* (24 April 1929), 1; ibid. (1 April 1931), 1–2.

54. On the difficulties of abandoning old traditions, see Yehuda Eres, "Tanakh umasoret yehudit bitnu'at hapo'alim hayehudit," in *Sozializm yehudi uteun'at hapo'alim hayehudit bemeah ha-19*, ed. Moshe Mishkinsky (Jerusalem: 1975), 20.

55. On the connection between the workers' movement and Americanization, see, for example, Irving Howe, *World of Our Fathers* (New York: 1976). In contrast to Howe and others, Tony Michels makes a strong argument that the American Jewish labor movement should not be seen simply as an agent helping the East European immigrants to adapt to their new environment (Michels, *A Fire in Their Hearts*, 20–21).

56. Jack Jacobs recently published an excellent study about what he terms the "Bundist counterculture," in which he argues that Bundist institutions such as the Tsukunft and Morgnshtern were critically important to the party's political success during the 1930s. Roni Gechtman calls the same phenomenon "national-cultural autonomy in the making." See Jack Jacobs, *Bundist Counterculture in Interwar Poland* (New York: 2009); cf. Roni Gechtman, "'Yidisher Sotsializm': The Origin and Contexts of the Jewish Labor Bund's National Program" (Ph.D. diss., New York University, 2005), 17.

57. *Hagode shel peysekh*, 14 ("Un mir velen im zingen a nayes lid, eyn herlikhes lid").

Review Essays

The Second Edition of the *Encyclopaedia Judaica*: "Snapshot" or "Lasting Monument"?

Encyclopaedia Judaica, 2nd ed. Detroit: Macmillan Reference USA in association with Keter Publishing House (Jerusalem), 2007. Editor-in-chief: Fred Skolnik; executive editor: Michael Berenbaum. 22 Vols.

In his preface to the second edition of the *Encyclopaedia Judaica*, the executive editor, Michael Berenbaum, characterizes the first edition, published in 1971, as "authoritative, comprehensive, serious yet accessible" (vol. 1:5).[1] A new edition, he writes, is justified by the many changes that have taken place in Israel and in the world in general during the last three decades. In Israel, for instance, Golda Meir was Israel's prime minister when the first edition was published, but since then "Israeli culture has been transformed and its institutions have evolved" (ibid.). Elsewhere, the Soviet Union and the East European bloc no longer exist, and Jews living in these areas are free to emigrate as well as to search for their Jewish roots. American Jewry also has changed—getting older, on the whole, relocating to Sun Belt cities, creating new schools for the next generation, and forging new expressions of their religious identity, while at the same time experiencing profound changes as the result of the women's movement.

Berenbaum continues:

> The editors of this new edition of the *Encyclopaedia Judaica* are acutely conscious of these changes . . . and have endeavored to preserve much of the original writing [of the first edition], to add what must be added, to refine where refinement was in order and to change what must be changed with the passage of time. . . . Mindful that this work [the second edition] would be consulted for years and years, it is intended to be more than a snapshot of what is known at this time; its insights are meant to withstand the passage of time. . . . We have endeavored to be comprehensive and creative (vol. 1:7).

The purpose of this essay is to evaluate whether the intentions stated by Berenbaum have been fulfilled—that is, to determine whether the second edition is indeed "comprehensive and creative" as opposed to being a mere snapshot of Jewish knowledge at the beginning of the 21st century. In order to make this evaluation, we must first clarify the nature of the first edition, what it accomplished, and how it was received at the time. We will then compare the first and the second editions with regard to a number of key elements, including the scope and size of articles, the credentials of contributors, the accuracy and currency of information, and the quality of illustrations, bibliographies, and indexes. We will review some of the initial reactions to the second edition and, in conclusion, will attempt to place the second edition in the context of the changing publishing world of the 21st century.

Berenbaum traces the origins of the first edition to the unfinished German edition of the *Encyclopaedia Judaica* that was launched in Berlin in 1928 by Nahum Goldmann (1895–1982), of which only ten volumes, covering the letters A through L, were published before the Nazis took power. An additional volume was ready to go to press in 1933, and the remaining volumes were in the final stage of preparation. This material was saved when one of the editors escaped to Switzerland.

There are many comparable points between the German edition and the first edition of the *Encyclopaedia Judaica*, published in English in Israel: both engaged a large, international contingent of Jewish scholars, many of them senior and established, but also many young and then unknown scholars who would flourish in the following generation. The German edition featured a structure that was followed in the first edition of the *Encyclopaedia Judaica*: a number of "central" pieces—lengthy synthetic essays that summarized broad topics—alongside more "peripheral" articles on personalities, events, or places that were generally written in a brief and concise style.[2]

For Berenbaum, the first edition "was a product of German Jewry. ... It was produced in Israel and was perhaps the last and best manifestation of German Jewish scholarship that had migrated to Israel."[3] The field of history dominated; there was not as much in the way of social sciences, and less emphasis on personal as opposed to intellectual biography. The articles prepared for the first edition by Gershom Scholem (1897–1982) illustrate the kind of German Jewish scholarship to be found in Israel: Scholem contributed more than a hundred articles to the first edition, some of them short biographies of kabbalists, but also lengthier pieces such as the one on "Kabbalah," which, with 164 columns of text, was one of the ten longest articles in the first edition. Among Scholem's shorter contributions were "Yom Kippur Katan," "Dibbuk," "Lilith," "Metatron," "Chiromancy," "*Yezirah, Sefer*," and "Ein-Sof."

Cecil Roth (1899–1970), the first editor-in-chief of the first edition, is another example of a scholar trained in Europe. Roth settled in Israel in 1964 upon his retirement from Oxford. He contributed almost 300 articles, 165 of them brief biographies, though other, lengthier pieces dealt with such diverse topics as continents (Africa, America), the Inquisition, taxation, and Judaizers. Roth's successor as editor-in-chief was his deputy editor, Geoffrey Wigoder (1922–1999), a British scholar who had settled in Jerusalem in 1949. Wigoder contributed only a handful of articles to the first edition, but in an article published in *Conservative Judaism* in 1972, he provided a detailed account of the publishing process and some statistics on the contributors.[4] According to Wigoder, even though much of the material had survived the Holocaust, there was little to salvage from the German edition: it was easier to start from scratch rather than translate and update the articles. Certain subjects presented more of a challenge than others—it was less difficult to find contributors on biblical subjects than on rabbinical exegesis, or on the Second Temple period as opposed to the period following the Bar Kokhba revolt. Wigoder noted as well that most contributors failed to address the economic aspects of Jewish history, and some topics were either missing or almost entirely left out: for example, there were virtually no scholars to be found who could write about Balkan Jewry. Of the contributors, he wrote, 55 percent were from the United States and 35 percent from Israel (the remaining 10 percent were presumably mostly from Europe).

What was the emphasis of the first edition? Wigoder listed first the Holocaust, and then together, in a long and windy phrase, "the establishment and development of the State of Israel and the emergence of American Jewry to its role of leadership and predominance." In addition, he noted a modest emphasis on modern Latin American communities. On biblical studies, he believed that the first edition manifested a "more profound and balanced understanding" of these subjects than did the "higher criticism" propounded by Julius Wellhausen and other 19th-century Protestant Bible critics. Wigoder credited Yehezkel Kaufmann (1889–1963) for this. Similarly, the first edition had a more nuanced approach to Jewish historiography, as promoted by Salo Baron (1895–1989). Wigoder also listed kabbalah, Jewish law, history of Jewish law, contemporary Jewry, and Jewish art as areas in which the first edition had charted a new path.[5]

Publication of the first edition of the *Encyclopaedia Judaica* was a major financial undertaking that mobilized private foundations and even some government agencies in the United States and Israel.[6] This advance funding allowed for all of the volumes to be printed at the same time—an uncommon feat, as most encyclopedias until then were published one at a time, with the income from subscriptions used to finance the publication of subsequent volumes. Volumes 2–16 were all published in 1971, and Volume 1, consisting mainly of the index, appeared in January 1972. The first edition contained 11 million words, a total of about 12,000 pages, 25,000 entries, and 8,887 illustrations. There were approximately 2,000 contributors, and the project was coordinated by a staff of 150. Apart from lengthy and shorter topical and biographical essays, the first edition also featured "capsule entries," brief items providing lists of Jewish authors in various literatures, Jews in science and art, Jewish politicians, Jewish doctors, and Jewish inventors.

How was the first edition received? The reviews published at the time varied in length and focus: some were very short (less than a column), whereas others were much longer (at least one was almost 30 pages long); some were simply descriptive, others reviewed only parts or aspects of the first edition while a few addressed the entire project.[7] The negative reviews pointed to the numerous mistakes and misprints found in the first edition—in many cases, the consequence of a self-imposed tight schedule. Many reviewers compared the length of various articles, complaining that certain topics or subjects were not given the proper amount of space or else were missing altogether. One reviewer noted that the binding of Vol. 1 would not weather the wear and tear of regular public library use, while another reviewer had words of praise for the cover design. The illustrations, even though mostly in black and white, were considered a major plus, but some reviewers criticized the size of some pictures, or noted that small maps were not helpful. The index volume pleased most reviewers, but the bibliographies provided at the end of the articles were not as well received: some were considered irrelevant and lacking important bibliographic resources.

On a controversial topic, Bible, reviewers found "useful contributions in various areas, even masterful treatments of individual books of the Bible, valuable sections in archaeology and history, but they deplored the treatment of biblical religion, law, and ethics."[8] Reviewers did not feel that the encyclopedia was fully able "to bring to the reader all views, from the most traditional to the most critical," as had been promised in the introduction. Some claimed that the bias of certain contributors had been allowed to stand. A pronounced bias toward Israel was also commented on: the first edition covered life in the state of Israel in great detail while ignoring the views of diaspora-centered philosophers and historians (as is indicated, for instance, in Table 1, which shows that three of the five lengthiest articles are related to the state or land of Israel). The first edition was criticized for underrepresenting non-Orthodox trends within Judaism, especially Conservative and Reform Judaism in the United States.[9] Finally, reviewers complained that the quality of the entries varied from excellent to poor. According to Herbert Zafren, "too many less than qualified people did too much of the writing and editing ... the competence of at least 20% of the people listed among the contributors cannot be guessed from the data provided in the encyclopedia: they are almost anonymous 'researchers,' rabbis, journalists, 'historians.' "[10]

Within a year of the 1972 printing, the first *Encyclopaedia Judaica Year Book* was published. Additional volumes were issued in 1974, in 1975–1976, and in 1977–1978. These last three volumes, each heavily illustrated and running between 400–500 pages, contained a chronology of past events, a calendar, and some new entries. In 1982, the *Decennial Book* 1973–1982 was published, which, in 684 pages, presented material taken from the previous three year books along with some new entries and updates. The same pattern was used for the following decade, with subsequent year books covering the years 1983–1985 (three years instead of two), 1986–1987, 1988–1989, and 1990–1991. The *Decennial Book* 1983–1992 was published in 1994.[11]

Three years later, a CD-Rom edition, version 1.0, appeared, which extended coverage through the May 1996 elections in Israel. The CD-Rom version also contained multimedia features such as historic film clips, slide shows, music, and sound clips. Although most of the original maps, tables, and charts were transferred to the new medium, many of the photographs and portraits were missing. The search engine was limited to keywords or phrases (with no option for wildcard searching), and there were no hypertext links from the articles to the illustrations.[12] For the second edition, there is both a printed version and an e-book, the latter accessible only to institutions and their registered users.

It is against this background that we now examine the second edition of the *Encyclopaedia Judaica* and underline the major shifts between the two editions. One useful tool is the general introduction to the second edition (vol. 1:15–32), which follows the preface to the second edition written by Berenbaum. This general introduction, while largely based on the introduction that appeared in the first edition,[13] has a number of important emendations. I, for one, object to this rewriting of the history of the *Encyclopaedia Judaica*; it would have been wiser simply to reprint the original introduction.

However, the deletions and additions are revealing of the different emphases of the two editorial boards and of typographical improvements of the second edition.

For instance, three paragraphs of the original introduction, headlined "the new world of the Encyclopaedia," "the climacterics of the twentieth century," and "Bible," were removed from the introduction to the second edition, although Berenbaum worked some of this material into his preface. The first edition introduction emphasized the illustrations ("one of the outstanding advances of this Encyclopaedia") and the index ("one of the highlights of the Encyclopaedia"), whereas reference to both these features is relegated to the end of the second edition's introduction. The introduction to the second edition also omits a paragraph on "capsule entries." In the "principles of selection" section of the introduction to the first edition, reference is made to an "extreme proposal—which was not accepted—to exclude living people altogether" as subjects for biographical entries. This reference is deleted from the second edition introduction, probably because the policy with regard to biographies of living people had been further liberalized: there are many such biographies in the new edition.

One of the most irksome features of the first edition was its use of initials rather than full names of contributors at the end of each entry; readers had to refer to the index volume to find out that "C. L." referred to Curt Leviant or "G. Sch." to Gershom Scholem. In the second edition, the introduction informs us, full names are provided, and entries produced by the editorial staff, "the ubiquitous 'ED.'" of the first edition, are "unsigned, unless the second edition update or revision was significant enough to warrant its attribution to the second edition contributor alone" (vol. 1:31).[14] Moreover, in the bibliography following some of the entries, the second edition attempts to supply full names and full titles of articles that are quoted in the main body of the text, and updates are clearly marked "add. bibliography."

The introduction to the second edition also provides some statistics: work on the new edition, we are told, commenced in August 2003 and "concluded editorially in the first months of 2006" (vol. 1:19). The project employed 50 divisional editors (as against 150 for the first edition) and approximately 1,200 contributors (as against approximately 2,000). About half of the original entries of the first edition were revised, and 2,650 new entries were created. The bibliographies were updated with approximately 30,000 new references; in all, some 4.7 million "new words were written for the second edition" (ibid.).[15]

In his preface, Berenbaum notes various shifts in emphasis with regard to central topics of the two volumes. Table 1 illustrates the comparative length of selected articles in the two volumes. Among the most important shifts are those dealing with the Holocaust (which moved up, from eleventh place in the first edition to second place in the second edition); Jerusalem (which moved down, from second place to sixth); the United States (up, from twelfth to fifth place); and, most dramatically, "Woman," which was given only 7 columns in the first edition, as opposed to 53 pages in the second. Not indicated in the table is the extent to which each subject was rewritten or updated, as opposed to being left essentially unchanged. For instance, according to Berenbaum: "Gershom Scholem's major essay on the Kabbalah [was] left untouched. Moshe Idel filled in what had been learned since."[16] And in one instance relating to the Holocaust—Berenbaum's own field of specialization—he notes: "When we received the first entry on Hilberg [Raul Hilberg (1926–2007)] by his greatest disciple, Christopher Browning, I told him that he had to tell why Hilberg is controversial. I thus deliberately gave Hilberg a large entry of 1,800 words because of the central role he played in the emergence of Holocaust studies."[17]

Table 1. Ranking of the Lengthiest Articles in the Two Editions of the *Encyclopaedia Judaica*

First edition[a]	Second edition[b]
1. Israel, State of (744)	1. Israel, State of (561)
2. Jerusalem (215)	2. Holocaust (165)
3. History (210)	3. History (122)
4. Israel, Land of (194)	4. Kabbalah (107)
	Bible (107)
5. Kabbalah (164)	5. United States (102)
6. Bible (155)	6. Jerusalem (89)
7. Zionism (132)	7. Zionism (88)
8. Music (125)	8. Israel, Land of (80)
9. Hebrew language (102)	9. Hebrew grammar (66)
10. Hebrew grammar (98)	10. Music (65)
11. Holocaust (88)	11. Hebrew language (63)
12. United States (86)	12. Russia (56)
13. Education, Jewish (85)	13. Hebrew Lit., Modern (54)
14. Masora (81)	14. Masora (53)
	Resurrection (53)
	Woman (53)
15. Poland (80)	15. Education, Jewish (52)
16. Russia (73)	16. Hasidism (42)
17. Hasidism (49)	
18. Germany (47)	
Woman (7)	

[a] Numbers in parentheses refer to columns.
[b] Numbers in parentheses refer to pages.

Sources: For first edition, a manual count done by the author on 30 April and 21 July 2008; cf. Shimeon Brisman, *A History and Guide to Judaic Encyclopedias and Lexicons* (Cincinnati: 1987), 405 (n. 231). For second edition, data provided by John Magee (email message to author, 20 June 2008), which was checked against the printed volumes.

A similarly active role was taken by Judith Baskin with regard to the subject of "Woman." She was invited to join the editorial board in early 2004 as an associate editor, with a mandate both to "identify articles [in the first edition] that should be revised or supplemented to reflect recent developments in gender studies"[18] and to propose new articles. She wrote 41 entries herself, totaling some 30,000 words, and commissioned ten lengthy essays (up to 5,000 words) on feminism and its impact on contemporary Jewish life and culture, along with shorter contributions on subjects ranging from domestic violence to Jewish cookbooks. Baskin also solicited more than 200 biographies of "Jewish women of achievement."[19] In some instances, she writes, "I prepared entries in areas distant from my own academic expertise when it was clear that an important assigned article was not forthcoming"—an indication that not all the articles in the second edition were written by foremost experts in a given field.[20] Berenbaum, for his part, notes that the absence of a woman's perspective on the subject of the mikveh (the Jewish ritual bath) in the first edition was a "serious omission, one not repeated" in the second edition. The new edition, he explains, "represents a deliberate attempt to include women and the experience of women . . . because we cannot understand Jews or the Jewish experience without understanding the role of Jewish women" (vol. 1:7).

In the field of kabbalah and mysticism, the post-Scholem generation of scholars is not well represented. Only 18 entries are signed by Moshe Idel alone. There are no articles by Lawrence Fine, Arthur Green, Daniel Matt, or Elliot Wolfson. Jonathan Garb wrote one entry, the biography of Moshe Idel (a mere 500 words), whereas Shaul Magid deals with Zalman Schachter-Shalomi in less than 400 words. Rachel Elior contributed four pieces—one new article on the daughter of the founder of the Frankist movement, two revised short biographies, and one revision of the entry on "Chabad" in which her name is misspelled. In the entry "Zohar," only 1,800 words ("Later Research," written by Melila Hellner-Eshed) augment the 15,000 words originally written by Scholem. All in all, this cannot be considered a reevaluation of the field of kabbalah and Jewish mysticism that accurately reflects the last 30 years of research.

In vol. 1 of the second edition, a list of contributors and their contributions to both editions is provided (pp. 45–176). Getzel Kressel (1911–1986), described as a "writer and bibliographer," was the most prolific author of entries for the first edition—the list of his entries, including those on cultural life in the state of Israel, Hebrew newspapers, Zionism, and the Zionist congresses, runs to more than four columns of print (pp. 110–111). For the second edition, a free-lance writer, Ruth Beloff, who edited the U.S. general culture section, is the most prolific author, with nearly five columns of listed articles (pp. 55–57).[21] Although Kressel was not an academic, he did write several specialized books that appear in the catalogs of academic libraries. Overall, it appears that the academic credentials of contributors to the second edition are somewhat less impressive.

My analysis of Berenbaum's preface, along with the comparative ranking of various key articles and my evaluation of the academic background of the contributors to both editions, leaves me with the impression that a substantial portion of entries from the first edition have been left untouched in the second edition; that many of the entries that were modified simply had their bibliographies updated; and that prominent scholars did not participate in the rewriting of entries for this new edition. Furthermore, a significant number of new entries are factual biographies of Jewish women and men of achievement, rather than comprehensive reevaluations of various fields of Jewish studies at the start of the 21st century.

My general observations are largely corroborated by two early reviews of the second edition, one by Shnayer Leiman and the other by Marc Saperstein.[22] These reviews are worthy of examination, as they indicate the initial reception of the second edition among the Jewish scholarly community.

Leiman, in an online review of the second edition, notes the "almost complete lack of visual images . . . [which] is a fatal flaw that renders it the least attractive (and arguably, the least informative) . . . of all the Jewish encyclopedias." He also examines the textual content, concluding that "many key entries that needed to be revised and updated were neither revised nor updated." Leiman found serious errors of commission and omission in the new entries he examined, giving five examples—all biographies of rabbinical figures of the 19th and 20th centuries—and concluding in each instance that the second edition "does not reflect the present state of modern scholarship." Two separate entries for the same rabbi (identified in one place as "Bloch, Chaim Isaac [1867–1948]" and in another as "Bloch, Hayyim Isaac ben Hanokh Zundel Ha-Kohen [1864–1948]") indicate the "sloppiness of the editors." Among the sins of omission, Leiman lists several prominent Jewish women, rabbis, academic scholars, and a number of sizeable Jewish communities in the metropolitan New York area, that should have received entries. Concluding his "preliminary observations," Leiman recommends to "all public libraries and private collectors to retain their 1972 edition."

In his review for the *Jewish Chronicle*, Saperstein reaches similar conclusions. He notes the "surprising lack of consistency and some noticeable gaps in the British material." Although conceding that the "area of modern Jewish thought has been especially well served with new or significantly revised articles" on major contemporary Jewish thinkers, he criticizes the decision to retain all the articles written by Gershom Scholem (although, admittedly, some are supplemented with new entries) as "unjustified and excessive." In conclusion, Saperstein praises the simultaneous publication of the second edition as an e-book containing key words that can be accessed by clicking on the appropriate link; while noting some quirks in the system, he prefers the e-book version to the printed volumes.

Saperstein's preference for the searching capacity of the e-book version is explained in part by the lesser role played by the second edition index as opposed to that of the first edition. In the introduction to the first edition, the index is described as follows:

> Ordinarily, an encyclopedia can be consulted only through the alphabetical list of entries. In the case of the *Encyclopaedia Judaica*, this would give the reader some *25,000 subjects*. With the aid of the index the option is expanded *tenfold* to some 200,000 subjects, and the reader can at once see where he can find information on topics that have not received independent entries but have been treated under other headings.[23]

Although the language in the second edition is almost identical, there are some interesting changes in key details: there are said to be "22,000 subjects" (instead of 25,000), and, "with the aid of the index the option is expanded more than eightfold. . . ."[24] Be that as it may, the index to the second edition is easier to read, occupying three columns on each page instead of the four that appeared in the first edition. At the same time, it contains far less detailed information. For example, the first edition entry on Aaron ben Elijah, a Karaite, has seven subdivisions that list additional information (apart from the main entry) found in other volumes, whereas the entry in the second edition refers only to the main entry. Those with access to the e-book edition may be more successful in finding additional information: by doing a search of the "entire document," one can retrieve six results for Aaron ben Elijah, including the main entry (though I also received a result referring to a different Aaron ben Elijah, of Altona). The e-book search did not yield the mention of Aaron ben Elijah in the entry "Luzki (Lucki), Simhah Isaac ben Moses," since his name appears there as "Aaron b." (instead of "ben") Elijah. In similar fashion, Saperstein reports his disappointment that "a search for 'Haskalah' yielded 175 names associated with the movement of Jewish enlightenment, but not the main article."[25] To be sure, Saperstein and I may not have used the most efficient search strategy; there is no specific help menu designed by the publisher to help users refine their searches.[26]

One useful feature of the second edition is its "thematic outline," found both in the last volume, Vol. 22, and in the e-book. This provides a general view of the conceptual scheme of the encyclopedia—a regrouping of articles, and especially biographies, into sections and subsections. For example, the section on France is divided into "main surveys," "general entries," "communities," "organizations," "publications," and "biographies," whereas the section on biographies is divided into "academic life," "art," "literature," "music," "popular culture," "public and economic life," "religion," and "science."

Does the second edition of the *Encyclopaedia Judaica* live up to the claims put forward by Michael Berenbaum in his preface? Not entirely.

"*Authoritative*"—As a publication of the American Library Association notes, an encyclopedia derives its "authority from the credentials of [its] contributors and the general reputation of the publishers. While distinguished contributors may be listed as authors of articles, the editors determine what information to include as well as the format in which it will appear."[27] An examination of the second edition leads me to conclude—based in part on the fact that there is a smaller editorial staff and more limited participation of leading scholars—that the second edition is *less* authoritative than the first one.

"*Comprehensive*"—The American Library Association considers the question of comprehensiveness by asking: "Are 'hot' topics and contemporary issues covered or only those items that have been proven by the passage of time?"[28] In this regard, the second edition appears to pass the test. Although the biographies of some leading living scholars are missing, it retains most of the entries produced some three decades ago, and there are many new biographical entries. Yet with regard to the "core articles"—those defining concepts and major ideas of Judaism—there has been little substantive revision. For instance, both the drastic reevaluation of the field of Jewish mysticism and the transformation of research dealing with post-Second Temple rabbinic literature on the part of a new generation of scholars in Israel, the United States, and Europe are not reflected. Thus, the second edition is comprehensive only on the margins, not in the core.

"*Serious, yet accessible*"—Berenbaum seems to be attempting here to define the potential target audience of the second edition—namely, both serious scholars and a broader adult public. Judging by its writing style, which in general is clear, and its wide-ranging contents, the second edition appeals to both specialist and nonspecialist audiences—this, however, should be true of most encyclopedias. With regard to visual accessibility, the typography of the printed volume is clear and easy on the eyes, though the limited number of illustrations is, as already noted, a major drawback (in fairness, it should be noted that all of the second edition illustrations, in the form of one insert per volume, are in color).

Creative—Given today's world of interactive CD-ROMs complete with movie clips, musical excerpts, photographs, graphs, charts, and the like, "creative" was not the word that came to my mind the first time I approached the second edition, either in print or in electronic format. In fact, the e-book version is far less innovative than the 1997 CD-ROM, which included some clips, musical excerpts, and photographs. The e-book makes very limited use of hypertexts, whereas the print version, as we have noted, does not retain the rich iconography (even if only in black and white) of the first edition.

It would take a lengthy essay to properly evaluate the place of both editions of the *Encyclopaedia Judaica* in the larger framework of encyclopedias published during the 20th and 21st centuries. Overall, I would say, the second edition stands closer to the past than to the future. The standard for many specialized encyclopedias has long been the *Encyclopaedia Britannica*, regarded as a model of both scholarship and commercial success. The second edition of the *Encyclopaedia Judaica*, as with the current online version of the *Encyclopaedia Britannica*, tries to build on the reputation acquired by the first edition by recycling almost half of the articles published some 30 years ago. Institutions appear to be its main targeted audience—according to a listing posted on a discussion group of Judaica librarians, the e-book version was offered in 2007 at a discounted price to institutions purchasing the printed version as well.[29] This stands in marked contrast to the approach of online compendiums such as Wikipedia, the free, multilingual, open-content encyclopedia project, with 683 million visitors annually (as of April 2008). If Wikipedia represents the interactive model of the future, the second edition of the *Encyclopaedia Judaica* would appear to be more of a "snapshot of what is known at this time." Yet, given that the second edition of the *Encyclopaedia Judaica* has conceded at least some of its authority (as so many of its entries are not authored by prominent scholars), it would not be difficult to arrange for a community-wide effort to continually update its contents. Indeed, some encyclopedia publishers in Europe, among them Larousse, are already exploring hybrid models of publishing both in print and online, with some articles written by established professional editors and academics and others by registered users.[30]

In his review of the first edition of the *Encyclopaedia Judaica*, Geza Vermes noted: "All in all, though scarcely a masterpiece, the new Encyclopaedia displays enough general reliability and sporadic excellence to deserve to be ranked among the indispensable works of reference in the field of Judaica in the widest sense."[31] In the case of the second edition, I feel compelled to add the phrase, "but just barely." Unfortunately, the second edition is not the lasting monument promised by its publisher.

Roger Kohn
Library of Congress

Notes

I gratefully acknowledge the assistance of the following individuals: Zachary M. Baker, Joan C. Biella, David Gilner, Eric Chaim Kline, Cecile E. Kuznitz, John Magee, Peggy K. Pearlstein, Judith Pinnolis, Hélène Potter, Benjamin Richler, Fred Skolnik, and Laurel S. Wolfson. The views expressed in this essay are my own and are not official statements of my employer. I would, however, like to thank Lenore Bell, team leader of the Hebraica cataloging team, for her steadfast encouragement.

1. The preface also appears online, at www.galeuk.com/judaica/pdfs/Preface.pdf (accessed 28 Mar. 2008). The only difference I noted between the two versions is that the (later) print version thanks a collaborator, Jay Flynn, who brought the second edition to completion.

Although Berenbaum refers to the first edition as having been published in 1972, Shimeon Brisman writes that it was published in Jerusalem in 1971 and then clarifies his statement: the bulk was published in 1971, with Vol. 1 appearing a year later. See his *A History and Guide to Judaic Encyclopedias and Lexicons* (Cincinnati: 1987), 97, 99. Brisman also notes that a second, corrected printing of the entire encyclopedia was published in 1972 (ibid., 101).

2. The best English-language introduction to the German edition appears in Brisman, *A History and Guide to Judaic Encyclopedias and Lexicons*, 52–57. See also David B. Levy, "The Making of the *Encyclopaedia Judaica* and *The Jewish Encyclopedia*," Proceedings of the 37th Annual Convention of the Association of Jewish Libraries, Denver, 23–26 June 2002; online at www.jewishlibraries.org/ajlweb/publications/proceedings/proceedings2002/levy.pdf (accessed 28 Jan. 2008).

3. See Manfred Gerstenfeld's interview with Michael Berenbaum, "The Transformation of Jewish Knowledge over the Decades: The New Edition of the *Encyclopaedia Judaica*," *Changing Jewish Communities* 27 (16 Dec. 2007), online at www.jcpa.org/JCPA/Templates/ShowPage.asp?DBID=1&LNGID=1&TMID=111&FID=254&PID=0&IID=1950 (under subhead: "A Change of Mood," accessed 3 March 2008). Berenbaum notes in this interview that, despite its being the product of much German scholarship, the encyclopedia was nonetheless written in English, since this had become the predominant language in the post-Second World War Jewish world.

4. Geoffrey Wigoder, "On Producing an Encyclopedia," *Conservative Judaism* 26, no. 4 (Summer 1972), 40–45, esp. 41. According to Wigoder, Israeli scholars "have shown themselves outstanding and original. But they also display a tendency to be clique-ish and to denigrate the work of scholars in other countries" (ibid., 42). See also Brisman, *A History and Guide to Judaic Encyclopedias and Lexicons*, 405 (n. 235).

5. Wigoder, "On Producing an Encyclopedia," 44.

6. Brisman, *A History and Guide to Judaic Encyclopedias and Lexicons*, 98.

7. On reviews of the first edition, see Herbert C. Zafren, "Jewish Encyclopedias of the Last Fifteen Years," *Jewish Book Annual* 31 (1973–1974), 21–28; supplemented by Brisman, *A History and Guide to Judaic Encyclopedias and Lexicons*, 405 (ns. 236, 237).

8. Zafren, "Jewish Encyclopedias of the Last Fifteen Years," 25. The introduction to the first edition contains a section titled "Bible" that anticipates some of the criticism: "it was realized that the balance would be precarious, and that, in view of the strong feelings held on either side, it would be difficult and probably impossible to satisfy all the readers all the time" (*Encyclopaedia Judaica*, vol. 1 [Jerusalem: 1972], 9). The "Bible" section was deleted from the introduction to the second edition.

9. Zafren, "Jewish Encyclopedias of the Last Fifteen Years," 26.

10. Ibid. One of the most trenchant reviewers was Trude Weiss-Rosmarin, editor of the *Jewish Spectator*. See her article, "Another 'Non-Encyclopedia,'" *Jewish Spectator* 37, no. 8 (Oct. 1972), 3–6, 30. According to Weiss-Rosmarin,

> the index is riddled with so many mistakes and inconsistencies that it is of little use … the absence of even the most elementary criterion of editorial intelligence in [the] bibliographies may be judged from the fact that the bibliography of *Tailoring* is more than three times as extensive as the bibliography of *Talmud*. An identical deficiency of editorial judgment is evident in the disproportion of space allotments. … The editors also have a penchant for Jews prominent in the world of entertainment. For example the entries for *Max Reinhardt*, *Billy Rose*, and *Maurice Schwartz* are either longer or the same length as that for *Salo W. Baron* (pp. 4–5).

Altogether, she concluded, the first edition was "indescribably sloppy" (ibid., 30).

There was also an acerbic exchange between Solomon Zeitlin and Louis I. Rabinowitz (a deputy editor-in-chief of the first edition) in the pages of *The Jewish Quarterly Review*. According to Zeitlin ("Encyclopaedia Judaica: The Status of Jewish Scholarship," *Jewish Quarterly Review*, new series, 63 [July 1972], 1–28), "the publication of the *Encyclopaedia Judaica* is not a major accomplishment in the world of Jewish scholarship. ... Many articles are below the standards of a good encyclopedia, they are sophomoric" (ibid., 27). In the following issue, Rabinowitz attacked the "dogmatic assertions of Zeitlin" ("A Criticism of Criticism," ibid. 64 [July 1973], 71); Zeitlin was then given the last word ("The Encyclopaedia Judaica: A Specimen of Jewish Scholarship," ibid., 74–91). Zafren, for his part, calls for the "review of subject specialists, who stick to their specialties, that will yield both the detailed criticisms that are necessary and the consensus or lack of it that will validate or invalidate the generalizations of those bold enough to make them" ("Jewish Encyclopedias of the Last Fifteen Years," 24). The most balanced and informative review that I found is that of Geza Vermes, "Encyclopaedia Judaica," *Journal of Jewish Studies* 24, no. 1 (Spring 1973), 88–91, which I used as a checklist of the topics to address in this essay.

11. Brisman, *A History and Guide to Judaic Encyclopedias and Lexicons*, 101–102, supplemented by an online search of the holdings of the Library of Congress and Stanford University Libraries (16 July 2008). The only review of the yearbooks and decennials that I know of was written by S. Lehmann (on the first decennial book), which appeared in *Choice* (Sept. 1995), ref. 33–0018 (accessed 28 March 2008).

12. This description is based on the only review I found in the databases available at the Library of Congress: see W. Fontaine in *Choice* (Jan. 1998), ref. 35–2442 (accessed 28 March 2008).

13. Introduction, *Encyclopaedia Judaica*, 1st ed., 1:1–16.

14. In more than a year of using both the printed and e-book versions of the second edition, I have not encountered any unsigned articles. Members of the editorial staff are listed as contributors, and all the articles they contributed to, either as sole author or as editor, are listed at the beginning of Vol. 1.

15. Berenbaum gives a figure of 2,100 contributors, who wrote "six million new words"; quoted in Gerstenfeld, "The Transformation of Jewish Knowledge over the Decades" (under subhead: "Economics").

16. Ibid. (under subhead: "What to Preserve?").

17. Ibid. (under subhead: "Holocaust Studies"). My word processor gave me a count of 2,000 words for the Browning article.

18. Judith R. Baskin, "Adding Women and Gender to the Second Edition of the *Encyclopaedia Judaica*," *Journal of Modern Jewish Studies* 5, no. 3 (Nov. 2006), 344.

19. Ibid. I found 47 entries for "Baskin, Judith R." in the second edition (1:53). The word count for each of the articles related to women averages out to 730. "Feminism," for instance, contains 5,008 words (including the bibliography); "Cookbooks, Jewish," 2,373; "Birth," 2,232; "Domestic Violence," 1,454; "Lesbianism," 1,137; "Barrenness and Fertility," 930; "Salons," 428; and "Rebbetzin," 412—much less than 5,000 words on average per article.

The ratio of 10 lengthy essays versus 200 biographies means that for each new substantive article, there are 20 new biographies. Even if we assume that an average biography is much shorter than Christopher Browning's lengthy (2,000-word) piece on Raul Hilberg—say, 500 words on average—this amounts to approximately 100,000 words devoted to biographies of women, which is far more than the total word count of all of the more substantive essays in the "Woman" category.

20. Ibid., 347.

21. According to John Magee, who worked on the index of the second edition, Beloff wrote 194 articles and substantially revised an additional 367 pieces (email correspondence, 20 June 2008). All of the 194 articles written by Beloff are biographical sketches.

22. Shnayer Leiman, "The New Encyclopaedia Judaica: Some Preliminary Observations" (6 June 2007), http://seforim.blogspot.com/2007/06/shnayer-leiman-new-encyclopaedia.html (accessed 6 June 2007); Marc Saperstein, "Is the New Judaica Really Worth £1,000?" *Jewish Chronicle* (22 June 2007), 36. Leiman is a professor of Jewish history and literature in the

department of Judaic studies at Brooklyn College and visiting professor of Bible at the Bernard Revel Graduate School of Yeshiva University (according to the website of Brooklyn College, accessed 25 July 2008). As of July 2006, Marc Saperstein was the principal of Leo Baeck College, having previously held positions at George Washington University, Washington University, and the Harvard Divinity School (according to the website of the Leo Baeck College, accessed 25 July 2008).

23. Introduction to first edition, 1:6, emphasis added.

24. With regard to the contradictory figures, I corresponded with Hélène Potter, director of publishing, Macmillan Gale, who responded that the editors of the second edition had deleted a substantial number of entries of the first edition, mostly biographical entries. This would mean that some 5,600 entries were eliminated, and replaced with the 2,650 new entries mentioned above (email response to author, 28 July 2008). My own experience in using both editions concurrently does not support this explanation, as I have yet to encounter an entry in the first edition that is not in the second edition as well. A more plausible explanation is that the figure for the first edition was inflated—certainly there is an inherent contradiction to speak of a "tenfold expansion to some 200,000" subjects when the initial number of subjects is given as 25,000.

According to Fred Skolnik, the editor-in-chief of the second edition:

> when we made up our master list of entries from the 1996 CD-Rom we found fewer than 20,000, and this included over 1,000 entries added from the Year Books, so the true figure for independent EJ1 entries must have been around 18,500! Beyond human error I can't say what else went into producing the inflated EJ1 entry count. Conceivably, in family entries, each member whose name appeared in small caps in the text, was counted, and there may have been other cases of counting duplication as well (email response to author, 28 July 2008).

25. Saperstein, "Is the New Judaica Really Worth £1,000." It is also possible to search Hebrew terms, but these have to be entered exactly as they appear in the text.

26. In an attempt to be as thorough as possible, I generally use the "entire document" advanced search option. In cases that yield many results, the results are sorted in categories such as "overview" or "biography." In most instances, however, these categories are too general to allow for more precise sets of results.

27. Reference Books Bulletin Editorial Board of the American Library Association, *Purchasing an Encyclopedia: 12 Points to Consider*, 3rd ed. (Chicago: 1989), 8.

28. Ibid., 9.

29. "*Encyclopaedia Judaica* 2006 Purchasers," Hasafran (the electronic discussion forum of the Association of Jewish Libraries), 4 Dec. 2006; "Special Pricing for New *Encyclopaedia Judaica*" (posting by Susan Dubin on ibid., 27 Feb. 2008).

30. Olivier Dumons, "Larousse s'ouvre au Net," *Le Monde* (13 May 2008).

31. Vermes, "Encyclopaedia Judaica," 91. Vermes is the co-author of one article in the second edition, "Scherer, Emil° (1844–1910)."

Is There a "Jewish" Morality? Amalek as a Touchstone

Michael Walzer (ed.), *Law, Politics, and Morality in Judaism*. Princeton: Princeton University Press, 2006. 224 pp.

Is there any form of politics and morality that can authoritatively be identified as "Jewish"? Or alternatively, is there any way to establish ethics that could be widely accepted as Jewish, beyond the in-house manipulation of Jewish texts in insulated academic enclaves? Such questions bear particular weight for those like me who live in Israel, with its frequent political upheavals and daily, anguishing moral dilemmas. As I read this collection of essays, I found myself wondering: when will an ethical code of Jewish conduct catch up with the political realities of the state of Israel, whose Basic Law enshrines a hollow and potentially contradictory self-definition of Israel as both Jewish *and* democratic?[1]

As I mulled over these questions in February 2008, I idly turned on my television to the Knesset cable channel, which broadcasts both live reports from Israel's parliament and a variety of news and talk shows. The program being broadcast at that moment pitted a rabbi representing a group known as "The Committee to Rescue the People and the Land"[2] against an Israeli Arab/Palestinian lawyer. At issue was the latest round of violence between the Israeli army and Palestinian militants in Gaza, which had resulted in a large number of civilian casualties, among them women and young children. Armed with rabbinic rhetoric and justifications, the rabbi argued that such casualties were of no concern, since every Palestinian was a "descendant of Amalek," and consequently every dead Palestinian rid the world of an inherent enemy of the Jews. The Arab lawyer, though evidently outraged by this logic, seemed to be too stunned to mount an effective response: what could he say to someone who saw in him a latter-day Amalekite? As for the moderator, a mild-mannered religious Jew (judging by his *kipah*), he had no comment regarding the rabbi's racist diatribe, limiting his role to ensuring that each of the protagonists was granted a fair share of time and then thanking them politely before moving on to the next item.

Later that day, I happened to be present at a sermon focused on the upcoming holiday of Purim, given by a rabbi whose haredi, erstwhile anti-Zionist community has become increasingly nationalistic in recent decades. He enumerated the lineage of persecutors of Jews from Haman to Adolf Hitler and dwelt upon the fact that

Palestinians were continuing the tradition of persecution that was the lot of the children of Israel. All of these persecutors were descendants of Amalek, he said, and we should address contemporary Palestinian terror accordingly. The significance was clear: since the original commandment was to "blot out the remembrance of Amalek from under heaven" (Deut. 25:19), the present moment is a call to holy arms.

My sense is that these two rabbis represent a stance that is attaining widespread legitimacy among Israeli Jews. Stated crudely (but then, it is a crude form of reasoning to begin with), its logic is as follows: 1) by virtue of prior selection and consequent covenant, Jews are morally superior to Palestinians; 2) given that they are descendants of Amalek, Palestinians are inherently evil; 3) it is incumbent upon Jews to do away with descendants of Amalek; 4) consequently, if Jews do *not* get rid of Palestinians, they are being oblivious to a deterministic combination of natural selection, political reality, and the will of God.

Both the television program and the rabbi's sermon were very much on my mind as I pondered the issues raised in *Law, Politics, and Morality in Judaism*. For this reason, I will focus the following discussion on the question of whether one can accept or defend a specifically Jewish justification for labeling entire peoples as "our" preordained nemesis, or whether, conversely, one can refute racist perspectives by means of arguments drawn from classical Jewish sources.

There are two basic tensions underlying all of the essays in this volume. The first is that between the authority of the halakhah, on the one hand, and the authority of contemporary liberal-democratic states and values, on the other. In addition, there is a tension relating more specifically to the apparent disparities between Jewish morals that developed in non-Jewish, liberal-democratic states and political practices in the state of Israel.

Of the authors whose work is included in this collection, David Novak (who wrote two essays) adheres most strictly to an Orthodox point of view, and he appears to be more interested in redeeming the world than in setting up a political state based on a liberal constitution and a multiparty system of rule. Nonetheless, his attempts to reconcile Jewish particularism with human universalism while maintaining clear and nonapologetic distinctions between the two (in the essay titled "Land and People") are both creative and intellectually honest. Following an admirably intricate analysis of the route leading from the Jews' adherence to the covenant to their immanent preference to remain communally (and hence politically) separate from non-Jews, Novak suggests that the way to live in peace with non-Jews is to grant autonomy to non-Jewish communities presently subject to Jewish rule (p. 79). From his perspective, there is no halakhic reasoning that justifies a proactive endorsement of a political entity embracing diverse Jewish and non-Jewish communities (and, consequently, mingling in one polity competing sources of ethical conduct), since mundane political constitutions and processes inevitably lead to friction between divine and human sources of judicial authority. As noted by Noam Zohar, another contributor to this volume, Novak's view "accords priority to the definition of communal boundaries over the definition of territorial boundaries" (p. 83).

It seems to me that if Novak's way had been a viable political option for contemporary Israel, the Jewish state of Israel would have evolved into an autonomous communal entity within a larger multiethnic federative polity, and there would have been formally separate modes of communal and political life within that polity. I understand the appeal of this position, although for reasons other than those enumerated by Novak: it would be a tremendous relief if the Palestinian "problem" disappeared from my moral universe by means of its evaporation into a separate communal *and* territorial enclave. Yet history and politics did not take that turn, and one must address the material reality as it is. An additional drawback for anyone focusing on the issue of possible Jewish responses to racism is that Novak's basic distinction is not between Jews and non-Jews but rather between Orthodox Jews, on the one hand, and "secular Jews, liberal religious Jews, and non-Jews" (p. 71), on the other. Novak thus draws a clear boundary between those who adhere to halakhah and *all* of the rest, Jews and non-Jews alike. This results in an extremely particularistic political vision, an idealized variation on the Ottoman millet system in which no one community holds the trump in the constitutional deck of cards, and each community is relatively autonomous in determining its rules and laws.[3] Although theoretically interesting and personally enticing, such a system does not address the urgent issue of how best to arm oneself with a Jewish response to the kind of racism developing under the guise of halakhic rhetoric in sovereign, post-Ottoman Israel.

A different approach to the problem of the coexistence of Orthodoxy and modern state sovereignty is suggested by Menachem Fisch, a self-identified Orthodox Jew (p. 96). Although agreeing with Novak's assumption that most Orthodox Jews prefer "the culturally autonomous community, keeping politely to itself within a larger liberal state run by others" (p. 98), Fisch frames the issue in terms of existence in the political "liberal state" rather than in an apolitical, divinely ordained covenant. By doing so, he puts political reality on an equal footing with the textual reality of the halakhah and implicitly acknowledges the need for more creative interpretations of halakhah in its approach to issues regarding pluralism and state sovereignty.[4] However, to the extent that Fisch's analysis of halakhic attitudes toward tolerance and plurality deals with non-Jews, it is almost exclusively in the context of the diaspora. Little is said about the thorny relationship between halakhah and non-Jews in Israel, including the issue of how to apply the commandment regarding Amalek (or, conversely, how to disavow this commandment) in reference to Palestinian Arabs. This silence is striking against the backdrop of his clear and complex discussion of halakhic opinions guiding appropriate attitudes toward non-Jews in diasporic communities located in non-Jewish, liberal states. Thus, while going beyond Novak in seeking ways to justify and legitimize plurality from within the Jewish tradition, Fisch shies away from discussion of this issue with regard to Palestinian/Arab-Israeli non-Jews. Nonetheless, his inquiry does lay the foundations for such a discussion by drawing an analogy between Karl Popper's argument in favor of "otherness" and the talmudic disputes between the schools of Hillel and Shammai. He shows that both consider a dynamic meeting with opposing "others" in a favorable light, as this encourages the development of a "constructive skepticism" that gives rise to "a powerful method of critical reasoning" (p. 116).

Suzanne Last Stone, in common with several other contributors, explains why traditional Judaism is relatively amenable to liberal versions of civil society in non-Jewish states. The primary reason is that Judaism does not oblige a non-Jewish state "to conduct itself in accordance with Jewish precepts or to impose such precepts on non-Jewish society" (p. 26). What is at stake for Jewish citizens in non-Jewish states is to tolerate the state or its civil society "so long as [they] would not impinge on the halakhic practices and institutions of those desirous to observe the law" (p. 26). Judaism's initial neutrality with respect to a given state's political culture is another facet of its lack of a priori commitment to furthering a particular form of political regime.

But what about liberal values and practices in a *Jewish* state? Adam Seligman provides a succinct review of the sociological preconditions for a liberal polity that is absent from Orthodox (and therefore, "Jewish") commentaries. He concludes with the observation that Judaism lacks "the type of modern, post-Hobbesian vision of the individual upon which a politics of rights might rest" (p. 123). Reading Stone with Seligman's sober reading in mind, one is not surprised to note her disappointment with contemporary halakhah's insufficient attention to the fact that non-Jewish citizens of Israel are often not treated as equal members of the polity. In her incisive words, "the most glaring deficiency in the tradition that I have been reporting on is the lack of a model for the extension of equal citizenship rights in the Jewish polity" (p. 29). However, while exhorting us to exert intellectual energies to remedy this lacuna, Stone does not offer any new models of her own.[5]

What one does find in this volume are a number of recurring interpretive themes on the part of those seeking to glean halakhic precedents that would enable a Jewish state's political practices to be more commensurate with the standards of modern, liberal, and democratic law, politics, and morality. Two hermeneutic ploys, in particular, are worthy of attention: the discussion concerning the Noahide laws, and the responsa of Menahem Hameiri, the 13th-century French halakhic authority. With regard to the first, David Novak, in his essay "Judaism and Cosmopolitanism," offers the following explanation:

> The "Seven Commandments of the Noahides" is a term that appears regularly in rabbinic literature. It designates seven basic laws (actually, seven groupings of laws) that the rabbis assumed are binding on all human beings (who, after the Flood, are the descendants of Noah). These laws pertain to three areas of human relationships: those with other humans, those with God, and those with other sentient beings. They are: 1) the requirement to appoint judges, that is, establish a regular system of adjudication; 2) the prohibition of blasphemy; 3) the prohibition of idolatry; 4) the prohibition of incest, homosexuality, adultery, and bestiality; 5) the prohibition of murder (including abortion); 6) the prohibition of robbery; 7) the prohibition of tearing a limb from a living animal for food (apparently a common practice in the ancient Near East.)
>
> This body of law, however theoretical its origins might have been, has become the standard in the Jewish tradition for dealing with non-Jewish individuals and societies. By extension, it is the only cogent standard for dealing with the question of international society. This is important at a point in history when we Jews now have a state of our own, Israel, and when we are equal and active participants in states that have international interests and involvements (p. 134).[6]

One of the underlying assumptions shared by contributors to this volume is that those who adhere to the Noahide laws should be treated by Jews with respect and tolerance. Aviezer Ravitzky points to the use of this standard by R. Avraham Yeshayahu Karelitz (the Hazon Ish), the leading ultra-Orthodox halakhic authority in pre-state Palestine. Citing Maimonides, Karelitz forbade waging war against "those who had previously fulfilled the seven commandments" (p.170). Might this sort of reasoning serve as an intellectually powerful antidote to racist Amalekian rhetoric? In the words of Seligman: "This fascinating argument [concerning use of the Noahide laws] opens up the possibility of a legal pluralism based on common human morality, akin to natural law, as foundational of all social order, including presumably that of Jewish collectives" (p. 126). Unfortunately, there is no empirical basis to assume that reinterpretation of the Noahide laws would have any moderating impact on the hate speech directed at the "Palestinian descendants of Amalek." Largely unknown to the general Jewish public, this set of laws has had no discernable presence in Israel's political discourse.[7] Stone, for instance, notes that "this concept has been far less useful than one might suppose. Most Rabbinic authorities hold that Jews are not legally obliged to promote observance of Noahide law" (p. 28).

Similar to the interpretive strategy implicit in citing the Noahide laws within textual debates (which makes it appear as if these laws have actually had an impact on political practice) is the attempt to revive the works of Jewish scholars whose positions may have been unknown or relatively uninfluential in their own time, but who are now granted much more authoritative stature in the service of advancing a contemporary ethical position. In this collection, R. Menahem Hameiri—who himself made use of the Noahide laws in his writings—is granted the most attention as a newly (re)discovered authority.[8] I do not know the extent to which Hameiri is quoted in contemporary halakhic works, but he seems to be one of the main religious figures cited in scholarly works on Jewish and liberal political theory.[9] In this volume, he is widely cited as an authoritative figure in the essays of Novak, Zohar, Walzer, and Ravitzky; in fact, his name is often mentioned in the same breath as universally acknowledged giants of Jewish tradition such as Maimonides and Nahmanides. I found myself wondering whether this represented an attempt to recreate the textual—and, by extension, authoritative—Jewish halakhic universe. Again, a scholarly caution is voiced by Stone. Although citing him in support of her own reasoning, Stone is aware that Hameiri, "who equalizes the juridical rights of Jews and non-Jews" and whose writings "would provide an alternative basis for a theory that affirms the equality of all persons under the law," is in fact a thinker whose work "was lost for centuries [and] has only now begun to penetrate mainstream rabbinic thought" (p. 23).

Michael Walzer takes the theoretical discussion one step closer to political reality. His assumption—with which I agree—is that the traditional Jewish attitude toward war reflects a deeply ingrained assumption that the nations of the world seek to destroy Israel. For example, he points to the fact that wars of self-defense are allowed and at times even mandated:

> Since the nations of the world were assumed to be permanently hostile to Israel and forever plotting acts of aggression, any war against them, whatever its reasons in the king's mind, served in fact the purposes of prevention: "to diminish the heathen so that they do not come up against them [the Israelites]." This reductiveness is all-inclusive, justifying all imaginable wars (p.154).

When considering the ethics of such wars, Walzer cites a talmudic passage that discusses Saul's reluctance to kill women and children among the Amalekites. Saul is said to have asked God, "If the adults have sinned, what is the sin of the children?" The reply: "A heavenly voice came forth and said to him [Saul]: 'Do not be excessively righteous!' " Yet according to the same talmudic text, when Saul later ordered the killing of the priests of Nob, a heavenly voice came forth and said to him: "Do not be excessively wicked!" Walzer concludes: "Challenging God may be excessive (unwise? imprudent? presumptuous? self-righteous?); challenging kings is not" (p.157).

What do we learn from this tale? That previous generations have expressed concerns over biblical accounts of wanton aggression by Israelites, but that the discussion is closed by reference to God as both the source and the final word on the subject. In that case, what should a Jewish political theorist do? Accept the talmudic tale and use this as justification for remaining silent in the face of real—not textual—rabbis justifying and even calling for use of excessive force when dealing with the so-called contemporary embodiment of Amalek, namely, the Arabs/Palestinians? Walzer's talmudically inspired solution to this dilemma is to emphasize the extent to which the rabbis circumvented the commandment to exterminate Amalek:

> [T]he Rabbis labor, of course, under the burden of the biblical command to exterminate the Amalekites and the seven Canaanite nations. They cannot explicitly repudiate the command ... but they do succeed first in limiting it and then in permanently bracketing it, so that it has no present or future application (p. 161).[10]

Walzer chooses to highlight those rabbinical voices that labor under the "burden of the biblical command" rather than suggesting a fundamental reappraisal of the contemporary relevance of biblical commands. This is because he himself labors under the burden of changing the tradition from within, which in the context of a book about Jewish thought written by Jews is an understandable original position, although not entirely immune to criticism. He goes on to explain how Maimonides, for one, "bracketed" the commandment to annihilate Amalek by ruling that it was no longer possible to identify Amalekites (drawing on the mishnaic discussion of how "Sennacherib came and put all the nations in confusion" [Yadayim 4:4]). Walzer then adds: "I take this to mean that Maimonides and presumably many of his predecessors were not ready to countenance wars of extermination. But, again, he does not say that; nor do they" (p. 161). This silence on the part of the rabbis troubles Walzer. He ponders the absence of rabbinic decrees forbidding slaughter of women and children, and concludes that "the tradition is rather thin, for the usual reason: there were no Jewish soldiers who needed to know what they could and could not do in battle" (p. 163). An explanation is not a justification, of course. Hence his concluding comments, with which I concur: "The resources of the tradition have not yet been fully mobilized and brought to bear in this (highly politicized) debate" (p.165).

Following Walzer's essay, Aviezer Ravitzky provides an additional perspective that seems to cohere with my growing conviction that, sooner rather than later, we (Jews) have to develop our unique version of separation of church and state: to grant less weight to formal halakhic strictures and more to basic human sentiments; to delegitimize the *political* authority of rabbis and commensurably develop justifications (grounded in Jewish tradition) for greater political authority for the modern democratic and Jewish state. Contemplating the moral dilemma that arises with the decree to annihilate an entire people, Ravitzky cites R. Moses Sofer (the Hatam Sofer) as concluding that the king does not have the right to destroy "an entire human genus" (p. 173). He notes, however, an important qualification: the prohibition is inapplicable to Amalek or the ancient Canaanite nations (p.173; citing in an endnote a contemporary halakhic authority, R. Yehoshua Gershoni). Ravitzky glosses over this glaring lacuna without addressing its moral implications for Jewish politics in Israel. Although he makes no further reference to the specific issue of Amalek nowadays, he does tease out of the sources a reading regarding the "autonomous status [of human conscience] vis-à-vis the divine imperative" (p.175) and goes on to assert that "God invited, so to speak, the human initiative against warfare, and it is this initiative that underlies the primal notion of the 'prohibited war' in [halakhah]—that is, any war in which one does not initially call for peace" (pp. 175–176). Yet given the talmudic tale about Saul that was cited by Walzer, I wonder whether this moral stance, attractive as it is, can withstand halakhic rabbinic scrutiny.[11]

Ravitzky concludes his essay with the open-ended question of "whether the balance will now move from [the Christian notion of] 'just war' to 'holy war' or, conversely, toward a sharper distinction between a just war of defense and prohibited war" (p.179). A review of the essays in *Law, Politics, and Morality in Judaism* suggests that a universal directive prohibiting racial profiling or an unequivocal rejection of calls to annihilate entire peoples are not to be found in the mainstream of halakhic thought. While such positions do exist within Judaism, they are the opinions of individual thinkers, as exemplified in the works of the authors included in this volume. One may therefore conclude that if we (in Israel) wish to erect barriers against a "Jewish" form of racism, that is, the justification of "holy" rather than merely "just" wars, we need to turn to non-Jewish sources. In terms of the basic tensions addressed in these essays, it seems to me that the tradition of intragenerational halakhic give-and-take must give way to intense and immediate debate that will end Jewish moral meandering with respect to non-Jewish communities and individual non-Jewish citizens who are members of the Jewish sovereign state.

Paraphrasing Robert M. Cover's comment in his brilliant essay on obligation, in order to change the Israeli Jewish majority's ambivalence regarding the right of non-Jewish Israelis to enjoy the status of equality, we must move beyond mere rhetoric with regard to basic rights and examine what is actually happening (p. 9). There are worrying signs that, in both public and private forums, Jewish Israelis are drifting in the direction of legitimizing a policy of discrimination and perhaps even violence against those perceived to be the modern-day embodiment of Amalek. In this respect, David Biale offers a contrarian perspective in his review of Zohar's essay on civil society and government, which was written under the assumption that "the distance between traditional Judaism and democratic thought is smaller than is often suggested" (p. 34). In Biale's view:

> Biblical models appear utterly irrelevant to the present reality, for nowhere can we find either modern notions of democracy or of civil society. Neither are medieval models particularly useful, since they are drawn from quasiautonomous minority communities rather than from a state in which Jews held political power. It is therefore this confusion of categories and the lack of real historical precedent that suggest the great difficulties that Israel has experienced and will no doubt continue to experience… (pp. 53–54).

The essays in this volume provide stimulating groundwork for the gradual development and articulation of a morally sound Jewish response to the dilemmas that the state of Israel is facing. The logic and tradition of intra-Judaic dialogue necessitates a time span of generations before paradigmatic shifts in law, politics, and morality can occur. My concern is that insufficient attention to the political and moral exigencies of today's Jewish state is undermining the Jewish people's moral and political power to provide meaningful ethical guidance for the future. It seems to me that, in the meantime, we must abide by the "still, silent voice" (*kol demamah dakah*) informing us that basic respect of life—not only of human "others" but also of all creation and sentient beings—is in itself an authentic Jewish response to the demands of the political hour.

Law, Politics, and Morality in Judaism features a dozen uncommonly stimulating essays: it is rare to encounter a collection so reflective, serious, and intellectually passionate. Nonetheless, I would like to draw attention to a number of questionable editorial decisions made with regard to this particular volume, which is the twelfth to appear in the Ethikon Series in Comparative Ethics, published by Princeton University Press.

To begin with, ten of the twelve essays assembled in this collection were previously published in other volumes of the Ethikon series—in many cases, less than a decade ago. It is not clear why Princeton University Press chose to reprint a collection of essays so soon after they were originally published, and in the same basic forum. Moreover, considering the series' commitment to a diversity of ethical viewpoints, one wonders what was the rationale behind compiling a volume of essays written exclusively by Jews about Judaism. Do the editors of this series intend, similarly, to extract essays written exclusively by Muslims about Islam, or by Christians about Christianity? If so, it would be useful to apprise readers of this fact. If not, readers are still owed an explanation, and it is a pity that neither the editor of this volume nor the series' editor, Carole Pateman, saw fit to provide one.

Although the very process of compiling a collection of essays necessitates exclusion of various authors, topics, and themes, some of the exclusions here are troubling. In his preface, Michael Walzer notes that the essays were written exclusively by "Americans and Israelis" (p. x), and that they relate exclusively to the political practices of Jewish communities in North America and to the dilemmas confronting Jews with respect to minorities in Israel. His explanation is that "it is only in America where emancipation has, arguably, been most successful, and only in Israel is there full engagement with political sovereignty." Although Walzer feels that in this regard "the limitations of our contributors list is not necessarily a disadvantage" (p. 10), I do not agree. I am troubled, for example, when Walzer notes that "European Jewry is unrepresented here" (p. x) while overlooking mention of Jewish thinkers from other continents—most strikingly, those who draw upon Jewish traditions developed in North Africa and in South and West Asia. I was also puzzled by the near-total absence of women among the essayists (only one, Suzanne Last Stone) and by the fact that women's issues are barely mentioned. Surely one of the most fundamental challenges facing the Jewish tradition in an era of democratic and liberal values is the notion that men and women are politically equal? Political equality has enabled Jewish women to rise to positions of communal, theological, judicial, and scholarly authority—a development that is no less revolutionary than two others mentioned by Walzer, namely, the emergence in the 19th century of Jewish communities enjoying political liberties on the basis of civic equality, and the 20th-century establishment of a Jewish nation-state. It is not clear why this important topic was ignored.

Finally, the lack of a firm editorial hand does disservice to the excellent essays gathered in this volume. As noted, most of the pieces originally appeared in earlier volumes of the Ethikon series; in many instances, the editorial guidelines of the original volumes remain in place. Thus, for instance, Menachem Fisch, "reporting" from an Orthodox perspective, promises not to stray too far "from the guidelines we have been asked to follow"—presumably referring to guidelines given by the editors of the previous volume, *The Many and the One: Religious and Secular Perspectives on Ethical Pluralism in the Modern World*.[12] (Similarly, his essay makes no attempt to define the concept of "ethical pluralism" even though many readers of *Law, Politics, and Morality in Judaism* may be unfamiliar with the term.) Eight of the essays in this volume are paired—a long piece followed by a short commentary (a five-page piece by David Biale, for example, commenting on a 16-page essay by Noam Zohar), whereas four stand alone. (The pairings originate in other, previously published, volumes.) Only one essay (Stone's) includes recommendations for further reading, and only two of the endnotes in the entire collection refer readers to other essays in the volume. Significant themes, among them, "Amalek" and "solidarity," are absent from the index. And whereas Walzer the author contributes an essay that is characteristically thoughtful and original, as editor, he provides no introductory material apart from a brief preface, only part of which is devoted to an overview of the book's thematic content. This is a pity, because attention to such details would have sharpened the focus of this impressive and important work.

Dan Avnon
The Hebrew University

Notes

I would like to thank the following friends and colleagues who helped me think through the issues raised in this essay: Daphna Avnon-Amit, Jill Frank, Ruth Gavison, Daphna Saring, and the editors of this journal.

1. See Dan Avnon, "The Israeli Basic Laws' (Potentially) Fatal Flaw," *Israel Law Review* 32, no. 4 (Autumn 1998), 535–566.

2. To the best of my knowledge, this group (known in Hebrew as Hava'ad lehazalat ha'am vehaaretz) is a fringe organization. Nonetheless, by granting airtime to its representative, the Knesset channel essentially conferred legitimacy on the group and its racist ideology.

3. For an analysis of the millet system, see Bhikhu Parekh, "Balancing Unity and Diversity," in *Liberalism and Its Practice*, ed. Dan Avnon and Avner de-Shalit (London: 1999), 106–124.

4. Fisch notes: "As it stands, Jewish law contains nothing comparable with the sanctioning of an individual's right to cultural freedom or individual autonomy in modern liberal thought.

[Halakhic] Judaism tolerates the objectionable not in respect of someone else's rights but in order to avoid unnecessary trouble" (p. 100). In fact, the more strict the Orthodoxy, the greater the reluctance to intervene in other communities' ethics and lives.

5. On Judaism's deep-grained objection to unconditional civic equality, see Dan Avnon, "Haezraḥ bamikrah kemasad betoda'at haezraḥ hayehudi beyisrael," in *Sefat ezraḥ beyisrael*, ed. Dan Avnon (Jerusalem: 2006), 23–43.

6. Suzanne Last Stone provides a different listing of the laws on pp. 15–16. Novak, however, is the evident modern authority on the subject. See his comprehensive study, *The Image of the Non-Jew in Judaism: An Historical and Constructive Study of the Noahide Laws* (New York: 1983). It seems to me that this work, out of print for many years, merits republication with appropriate updating and revision.

7. I conducted an informal, nonscientific survey about the Noahide laws among my family, friends, students, and colleagues. Most had not heard of these seven laws, and no one could spell them out. Indeed, I have never heard Noahide laws cited in Israel's nonreligious public discourse.

8. According to David Novak, Hameiri turned to the Noahide laws in order to "avoid embarrassment"—that is, the embarrassment caused by "ethical flaws in the original law itself." See Novak, *Natural Law in Judaism* (Cambridge: 1998), 78. Modern commentators are simply following in Hameiri's interpretive footsteps, either consciously or by virtue of similar questioning and logic.

9. See, for instance, Jacob Katz, *Exclusiveness and Tolerance: Studies in Jewish-Gentile Relations in Medieval and Modern Times* (New York: 1962), 114–128.

10. Another essay in this volume, Geoffrey B. Levey's "Judaism and the Obligation to Die for the State," deals with the sages' position with regard to wars against Amalek and the seven idolatrous Canaanite nations. According to Levey:

> The sages agreed that that the wars expressly mandated by God are those waged against the Amalekites and the idolatrous Seven Nations in the pursuit and conquest of the land of Canaan. . . . Maimonides posited that both a communal obligation to wage war against these nations and a personal obligation to eliminate their members applied. . . . In the war against Amalek, where the individual's obligation to fight derives from the general obligation of the community to wage war, it is entirely fitting to speak of an obligation to die "for the state" (pp. 192–193).

Levey, it should be noted, repeatedly refers to the war against Amalek in a matter-of-fact manner, as it represents an explicit divine commandment. For example:

> The wars against Amalek and the Seven Nations represent in Jewish history, if not the founding, then the "grounding" of a nation. Ordained as they were by God Himself, their obligatory character is commanding. Only in the case of wars against Amalek, however, is the obligation to fight actually in behalf of the state... (p. 202).

11. For Ravitzky's view of this talmudic discussion, see pp. 174–175.

12. Richard Madsen and Tracy B. Strong (eds.), *The Many and the One: Religious and Secular Perspectives on Ethical Pluralism in the Modern World* (Princeton: 2003).

Book Reviews

Antisemitism, Holocaust, and Genocide

Steven Beller, *Antisemitism: A Very Short Introduction*. Oxford: Oxford University Press, 2007. 132 pp.

Steven Beller's introduction to the phenomenon of antisemitism is among the latest additions to a series of brief, stimulating, and accessible studies on a variety of topics in history, philosophy, religion, science, and the humanities that was introduced by Oxford University Press in 1995. His critique is learned, nuanced, and informed by a sophisticated knowledge of the Central European Jewish experience and Jewish/non-Jewish relations in modern times. He also provides a profound reflection on the relationship between antisemitism and anti-Zionism.

Beller focuses his study on "the components of the phenomenon of antisemitism, and the key, tragic interactions between these components that led to the Holocaust" (p. 8). In so doing, he downplays—though he does not entirely ignore—the historical evolution of anti-Jewish ideas and the ways in which these were transformed into secular tropes that resonated widely in the modern world. Intellectual currents, among them modernism, racism, social Darwinism, eugenics, irrationalism, and age-old Christian ideas about the Jew are discussed, but Beller is interested more in the national contexts within which these ideas were disseminated and within which they were manipulated and employed. More particularly, he is interested in the dialectic between the structural position of Jews in modern European society and non-Jewish perceptions of that position.

The chapter on the "Final Solution" is especially impressive. Here Beller is inclined to emphasize the importance of ideas. The Great War, the so-called "stab in the back," the fear of "Judaeo-Bolshevism," and the turn to genocide in the wake of the Nazi failure to expel Europe's Jews following its occupation of Eastern Europe are all considered, yet Beller's main argument is that "a particular German type of modernity" in "which *all* Jews were enemies" and "not just the 'foreign' ones" (p. 95) was what underpinned the Holocaust. Such ideas, according to Beller, were not regnant in other European nations.

In the case of Germany, then, ideas are important; for the rest, Beller challenges those scholars who emphasize the ideological roots of antisemitism. Indeed, he contends that, by stressing ideas of "the Jew" and ignoring the structural dialectic of Jewish/non-Jewish interaction, such scholars undermine Jewish agency and make Jews subjects rather than objects of history. This interactionist approach bears some fruit but inevitably fails to account sufficiently for why "the Jew" proves to be the ideal scapegoat.[1]

It is of some comfort that antisemitism, at least in the western world, has been marginalized since the Holocaust. Apart from a number of ugly, frightening, and distasteful phenomena—McCarthyism; the rantings of a Jean-Marie Le Pen, Jörg Haider, or Louis Farrakhan; and far-right Holocaust denial—respect for pluralism and multiculturalism, coupled with economic growth, has allowed Jews to be different. Such toleration is a far cry from the situation that prevailed in earlier times. In particular, Jewish-Christian relations became vastly improved in the wake of *Nostrae Aetate*, a Vatican declaration on the Jews that was enunciated by Pope Paul VI at the Second Vatican Council in 1965, and similar Protestant initiatives. Recent decades have witnessed further condemnations of antisemitism on the part of the Christian churches. In an act of major symbolic value, Pope John Paul II addressed congregants of the Central Synagogue in Rome in 1986.

The situation in the Muslim world is far different. Here we have classical antisemitic tropes expressed in Arab anti-Zionist discourse, including ideas directly informed by Nazism of the 1930s and 1940s.[2] Beller places this discourse firmly within the framework of the Israeli-Palestinian question, declaring it to be part of "Arab and Muslim resistance, revenge, and general hostility to the Zionist achievement of a Jewish state in Israel" (p. 113). In Beller's estimation, Arab antisemitism cannot be equated with the racial antisemitism of Europe. Yet while anti-Zionism and antisemitism cannot axiomatically be equated, the motifs and rhetoric of much anti-Zionist discourse—and not only that of the Arab world—is in fact reminiscent of the worst of European antisemitism, and it certainly goes beyond the bounds of normal political antagonism that is born of national conflict.

Beller devotes scant attention to the penetration of European ideas about the Jews into the Arab world long before Zionism evolved as a political ideology. These ideas built upon religious foundations and notions concerning "protected" non-Muslims (*dhimmi*) that were so central to medieval tensions between Jews (and Christians) and Muslims. As enshrined in the Pact of Umar—ascribed to caliph Umar (634–644) although consolidated only in the eighth century—Jews, albeit protected, were effectively second-class citizens. They were obliged to accept a range of discriminatory regulations, including special taxes, exclusion from government service, and rules concerning comportment, places of worship, proselytizing, and distinguishing clothing.

In addition, antisemitic calumnies such as the "blood libel" (originating mainly among the Greek Christian population in the 19th century) crept into Muslim discourse and were used to justify the looting, rape, and killing of Jews. In more recent decades, Arab anti-Zionist rhetoric has taken on the characteristics of delusional Christian antisemitism at its height. Jews are characterized as germs or as a malignant disease, and extensive commentary on the part of learned Islamic scholars depicts Jews as incurable pariahs, capable of the most evil and perverted deeds.

All of this is underplayed by Beller. More attention could also have been given to the ways in which "the Jew" has been constructed, starting back in antiquity. Although the language, idiom, and intensity of hostility have not always been the same, the notion of the Jew as a symbol of evil and as the classic "Other" has deep roots in the wellsprings of western civilization.[3]

Notwithstanding his rather narrow focus, Beller's introduction to a complex subject is carefully crafted, filled with insights, and replete with challenging observations. For the uninitiated, however, it is too complex. *Antisemitism: A Very Short Introduction* is not a historical survey of Jew-hatred, nor does it explain the myriad ways in which scholars from different disciplines have understood what the historian Robert Wistrich has termed "the longest hatred."[4]

Milton Shain
University of Cape Town

Notes

1. For examples of this approach, see Colin Holmes, *Anti-Semitism and British Society* (New York: 1979); and Albert S. Lindemann, *Esau's Tears: Modern Anti-Semitism and the Rise of the Jews* (Cambridge: 1997).
2. For a powerful exploration of these developments, see Matthias Küntzel, *Jihad and Jew-Hatred: Islamism, Nazism and the Roots of 9/11* (New York: 2007).
3. Gavin I. Langmuir, *Toward a Definition of Antisemitism* (Berkeley: 1990).
4. Robert Wistrich, *Antisemitism: The Longest Hatred* (New York: 1991).

Judith M. Gerson and Diane L. Wolf (Eds.), *Sociology Confronts the Holocaust: Memories and Identities in Jewish Diasporas*. Durham: Duke University Press, 2007. 389 pp.

In 1986, I spent a year in Israel at the Hebrew University working on a book about the postwar experiences of survivors in North America. One comment, made to me by Yehuda Bauer, was particularly memorable: "What is needed is a sociology of the Holocaust." That was true then, but in the decades since much progress has been made, as this fine collection of essays amply demonstrates.

The collection is a varied one, but this is due, in large part, to the field itself. Historians generally wait until decades have passed before commencing their research; sociologists do not, because their field focuses primarily (with the exception of collective memory and historical sociology) on the present. Consequently, the Holocaust, as a past event, was at first ignored by most sociologists. Even now, there is a certain imbalance—a sense of gaps in the material and a feeling that attempts are sometimes being made to fit a square peg into a round hole.

For instance, several contributors make the argument that research on postwar immigration to the United States should follow the models used for other groups of immigrants. One such model is that suggested by Ruben Rumbaut and Alejandro Portes, who divided postwar immigrants into two groups: those who came before 1965 (mostly from Europe) and those who came afterwards, mainly from Third World countries. Holocaust survivors, it is argued by Judith Gerson, Diane Wolf, and Rhonda Levine, fit into the latter model in numerous ways despite their pre-1965 entry. While it is true that Holocaust survivors, like later immigrants, came from a background of persecution, the organizational and communal support they received from American Jews was far greater than the support given to more recent arrivals from Africa and Latin America. Such issues and questions of transnationalism are well dealt with in the essays by Steven Gold, Rhonda Levine, Richard Alba, and Yen Le Espirita.

In order to integrate themselves into the current field of race, ethnicity, and immigration, researchers of the Holocaust explicitly state their wish to rely on the literature in the field. The problem is that the existing literature rarely even mentions the Holocaust. Between 1945 and 1980, the published material on the Holocaust was dominated by psychology and social work. Thus, whereas the work of Theodor Adorno and his colleagues that culminated in the classic study *The Authoritarian Personality* (1950) is grouped under "sociology" in this volume, it was actually a product of social psychology. In contrast are the studies of Nazis authored by Morris

Janowitz and Edward Shils, which fall squarely in the realm of sociology.[1] (I was also interested to learn that the renowned sociologist Talcott Parsons wrote nine essays on National Socialism.)

Moreover, as the editors of this volume, Judith Gerson and Diane Wolf, point out in an excellent joint essay, much of the initial focus was on the perpetrators rather than the victims—in part because sources were more readily available, but also because the field itself had not yet produced enough relevant work. This, I might add, was also the case with regard to the issue of American slavery: the oral narratives of slaves became the focus of research only after historians had exhausted the source material pertaining to the oppressors.

In their essay, Gerson and Wolf trace the history of sociological research in this area. Interest in the Holocaust, they note, increased significantly during the 1970s. This can be seen, for example, in the publication of Anna Pawelczynska's *Values and Violence in Auschwitz* (1979), a study of the camp's social organization. Another important work was Helen Fein's *Accounting for Genocide* (1979), which examined how different countries responded to genocide. Indeed, much of the material produced during the 1970s and 1980s focused on the Holocaust in the general context of genocide. Zygmunt Bauman's *Modernity and the Holocaust* (1989) centered on the Holocaust and the state, as did Irving Louis Horowitz's earlier book, *Taking Lives: Genocide and State Power* (1980), which is perhaps the strongest and most sophisticated of such works. Another very important volume, published in 1993, was Wolfgang Sofsky's *The Order of Terror*, which, like Pawelczynska's work, deals with the organization of camp life. In recent years, there has been increasing research on gender studies of the Holocaust.[2]

One of the dominant themes in *Sociology Confronts the Holocaust* is the impact of the Holocaust on contemporary Jewish identity. Debra Kaufman, David Schneer, and Caryn Aviv explore how young people with no direct experience with the Shoah integrate it into their Jewish identity. Chaim Waxman, who provides an excellent account of the contributions to American Jewish life made by the survivors, also calls our attention to the fact that the Orthodox were disproportionately represented among the survivors. To some extent this is because many of them (or their ancestors) had opted to remain in Europe during the great migratory movement of Jews to the United States in the late 19th and early 20th century, fearing that they would not otherwise be able to remain strictly observant. Arlene Stein argues that the disproportionate emphasis on traumatic stories of the Holocaust is in good measure attributable to a general interest in trauma on the part of U.S. researchers, as evidenced by the ample literature on trauma suffered by gays and lesbians, victims of rape and child abuse, war veterans, and others.

In a section dealing with memory and memoirs, we find an analysis of efforts to compare the Holocaust with other traumas (Gerson); accounts by those who hid survivors (Suzanne Vromen); and a critique of the Spielberg project's failure to pay greater attention, in its Holocaust survivor interviews, to the postwar experience (Diane Wolf). This section also features comparative essays by Irina Calota Silber and Ethel Brooks on memoirs written by survivors of traumatic events in Latin America, Bangladesh, and other Third World countries. In another section that is devoted to transnationalism, most of the contributions are not strictly within the purview of "sociology confronts the Holocaust," with the exception of Rhonda Levine's piece on German refugees from prewar Nazi Germany.

A final section is devoted to collective action, guilt, and memory. This section features an essay by Rachel Einwohner on resistance in European ghettos during the war; a piece by Jeffrey Olick on the collective responses of citizens in postwar Germany to the Shoah, and a contribution by Daniel Levy and Natan Sznaider on how the Holocaust is universalized into agendas focusing on general prejudice and human rights, and how it is invoked as a symbol of good and evil that everyone can relate to.

Clearly, there is a wealth of material in this book, and it is successfully held together by its relating, in one way or another, to the Holocaust. Still, we may ask why it has taken so long for social scientists to confront the Shoah.

This is a complex issue, but one of great relevance to the book under review. In the 1950s and the early 1960s, Jewish sociologists in general (two exceptions were Marshall Sklare and Nathan Glazer) tended not to focus on Jewish topics. For one thing, there was a fear—which had a basis in reality—that an interest in Jewish matters might brand them as parochial. It was even the case that a certain amount of prejudice existed against hiring Jewish sociologists at the time: Yale University, for example, did not hire sociologists of Jewish origin until after 1970. Second, most Jewish sociologists (both then and now) regard themselves as intellectuals who happen to be Jewish rather than the other way around. These social scientists form what the sociologist Milton Gordon, in his classic work *Assimilation in American Life*, has called "the fourth community"—liberal/left intellectuals who are uninvolved and even alienated from their religio-ethnic communities.

Finally, the comparative lack of interest in the Holocaust on the part of sociologists can be explained by the fact that sociologists tend to frame issues in terms of categories and general terminology (such as status, class, power, norms, and values). Thus, rather than viewing the Holocaust as a historical event, sociologists are more apt to focus on broader issues such as state power, genocide, or prejudice.

Happily, the situation is somewhat better today. Ethnicity is now regarded in a much more positive light, and the younger generation of scholars, less influenced by the above considerations, is unself-conscious about engaging in research on the Holocaust or Judaism. This volume is proof of the shift.

William Helmreich
CUNY Graduate Center

Notes

1. Edward A. Shils and Morris Janowitz, "Cohesion and Disintegration of the Wehrmacht in World War II," *Public Opinion Quarterly* 12 (1948), 280-315.
2. See, for example, Dalia Ofer and Lenore J. Weitzman (eds.), *Women and the Holocaust* (New Haven: 1998); Nechama Tec, *Women, Men and the Holocaust* (New Haven: 2003).

Diane L. Wolf, *Beyond Anne Frank: Hidden Children and Postwar Families in Holland.* Berkeley: University of California Press, 2007. 391 pp.

More than half a century after the Second World War, the wartime record of the Netherlands with regard to the Jews continues to be misrepresented—perhaps more so than is the case with any other country. The packaging and marketing of the Anne Frank story has played a major role in this distortion, which has resulted in the radically false image of widespread solidarity with the Jews on the part of the wartime Dutch population. In fact, the Dutch bureaucracy of the occupied Netherlands collaborated in many respects with Nazi Germany, and the country provided more volunteers to the Waffen SS than did any other West European state.

Only slowly has a true picture begun to emerge. The facts are these: of the 140,000 Dutch Jews at the beginning of the war, 75 percent were murdered in extermination camps throughout Eastern Europe, the largest percentage of any West European country. The Jews were arrested by Dutch policemen and transported mainly to the Dutch transit camp, Westerbork, and from there to the German border by means of the Dutch railway system. In the transit camps, the guards patrolling the periphery were Dutch. In summary: the Germans gave the orders while the Dutch carried them out, without any significant opposition.

Of the 24,000 Dutch Jews who went into hiding, approximately a third were arrested after having been betrayed by Dutch citizens. While there is still a debate concerning the overall impact of the Dutch resistance, it is clear that only a small percentage of the resisters provided assistance to Dutch Jews. The Dutch government in exile in London hardly cared about the fate of its Jewish citizens; among other things, it asked the Polish government-in-exile for information about deported Dutch Jews only a year and a half after the beginning of the deportations—this, despite the fact that the two governments were lodged in the same building (Stratton House). Moreover, in the postwar period, both the Dutch government and society in general often gave a cold reception to returning Dutch Jewish survivors.

Four Dutch resistance groups were involved in rescuing Jewish children and finding sanctuary for them with foster parents. One of the leaders of a group whose members were largely Calvinist Protestants was Gesina van der Molen, who later became the chairperson of the autonomous, government-appointed postwar commission whose purpose was to decide on the future deposition of surviving Jewish orphans. Van der Molen had been an influential figure before the war and was a friend of Queen Wilhelmina. In the legislation proposed by some resistance groups during the war, it was assumed that even surviving parents and family members should be made to forfeit their custody over children who had been placed with foster families. In part, this proposal stemmed from humanitarian concerns: several members of the commission who had a background in social work took the view that an additional separation would be traumatic for the children. In addition, however, there was a feeling—not always articulated explicitly—that it might be better if the children were raised as Christians. In the debate that ensued, members of the Gentile majority claimed that there was no such thing as a Jewish community and accused those who stood up for the rights of the surviving Jews as being "un-Dutch." Van der Molen belonged to this group, although with time her views evolved and she ultimately agreed to permit a large group of Jewish orphans to go to live in what was then Mandatory Palestine.

The Dutch Jewish community, for its part, was not silent in the matter. In a campaign led by the jurist Isaac Kisch and Abraham de Jong, a religious Zionist, Dutch Jews argued that it was a departure from established Dutch legal tradition to appoint an outside commission to rule on the future of children from the Jewish community, and that the community should be empowered to deal with issues of guardianship. Differences of opinion between the Jewish group and the commission, which were complicated by a clash of personalities between de Jong and van der Molen, resulted in an intense public debate. The commission was dissolved in 1949.

Joel Fishman, an American who was studying on a Fulbright scholarship in the Netherlands in the 1970s, was the first historian to publish several essays in English on the subject of the Jewish war orphans. He pointed out that, rather than calling them by their correct name, "Jewish war orphans," the majority invented a new term—"war foster children"—that minimized the Jewish identity of these children. A book (in German) on the trauma of these orphans was written by the psychiatrist Hans Keilson in 1979. In 1991, the journalist Elma Verhey published a book in Dutch on the institutional struggle concerning the hidden children. During a five-year period starting in 1994, the psychologist Bloeme Evers-Emden published four books in Dutch about hidden Jewish children and their relationships with their surviving parents and foster parents. These have been translated into Hebrew; regrettably, however, very little of Evers-Emden's writing is available in English.

This volume by Diane Wolf, who teaches sociology and who heads the Jewish studies program at the University of California, Davis, has a number of merits. It makes the war and postwar experiences of Dutch hidden children accessible to the English reader, and it also expands substantially the work of Evers-Emden. Wolf conducted extensive interviews for this book, and many insights can be gained from the cases she relates. Her main conclusion can be summarized simply: each case is unique. There were children who returned to their (often traumatized) parents, and were happy; others regret that they did not stay with their non-Jewish foster parents. Wolf found similar differences for those who remained in the family of their foster parents. Among these were a number who had been baptized, who later found their way back to the Judaism of their parents.

My own reaction to this book was ambivalent, in large part because of its omissions. Wolf acknowledges that she is not fluent in Dutch, and this fact is borne out by her bibliography, which contains far too few Dutch titles. Moreover, though a portion of her interviews were carried out in Israel, Wolf does not mention the work of Elah, an organization that deals with the socio-psychological problems of Dutch Holocaust survivors and their progeny. This is probably the one field in which organized Dutch Jewry in Israel has made a pioneering contribution to the country.

The book shows a lack of knowledge concerning contemporary and recent Dutch history, in particular with regard to the Jewish community. Several important studies concerning the postwar period as well as those detailing the shortcomings of the postwar restitution process were published in the late 1990s or shortly thereafter. These contain many insights into Jewish-Gentile relations in the immediate postwar period, which seem to be unknown to the author. One example of Wolf's lack of understanding of the Dutch context is her remark that the "number of antisemitic occurrences in the Netherlands remains relatively low" (p. 111). In fact, a major increase in antisemitism took place from 2000 onwards—calls for the murder of Jews have even been heard during anti-Israel demonstrations. (These became ever more frequent at the beginning of 2009 in various towns in the Netherlands, with the police only occasionally intervening.) Many antisemitic developments are documented in the annual reports of the Center for Information and Documentation on Israel (CIDI), which are not mentioned in the bibliography.

In light of all this, Wolf's remark that "it is crucial that we not conflate anti-Israel protest with anti-Semitism" (p. 111) does not withstand scrutiny. Scholarship, opinion polls, thousands of cartoons in the Arab world and in the media of various democracies, as well as outbursts of antisemitic violence under the guise of protest against Israel, have demonstrated that there is a major overlap between expressions of antisemitism and condemnations of Israel.

Toward the end of her book, Wolf makes a number of interesting remarks about the sociological conclusions to be drawn from her work. She states that hidden children grew up in "what we now call 'post-modern families,' shortly after 1945, many decades before the term was coined" (p. 336). She also raises questions about the notions of "family" as well as "bonding." However, she concludes with a short and unsubstantiated political discourse concerning, among other things, lessons of the Holocaust and genocide comparisons (p. 346). Her gratuitous instrumentalization of the Holocaust for political purposes may go over well in certain academic circles, but it detracts from the quality of her book.

Manfred Gerstenfeld
Jerusalem Center for Public Affairs

Cultural Studies and Religion

Simeon D. Baumel, *Sacred Speakers*: *Language and Culture among the Haredim in Israel*. New York: Berghahn Books, 2006. 232 pp.

Ultra-Orthodox Jews, or haredim, interest Simeon Baumel, a self-described Orthodox Jew raised in Brooklyn and long residing in Israel, as the only major Jewish group that "continued to adhere to a separatist tradition" (p. 1) into the modern era, eschewing what are perceived to be secular and non-Jewish cultural influences. In *Sacred Speakers: Language and Culture among the Haredim in Israel*, Baumel applies the tools of sociolinguistics, cultural linguistics, and cultural anthropology both to describe the diversity of attitudes toward language in four haredi communities in Israel (and beyond) and to explicate how a combination of religious ideology, political goals, economic and practical concerns, and habit all condition their actual use.

Baumel chose his subject populations—Habad and Gerer hasidim, mitnagdim, and Sephardic haredim—on the basis of their being among the largest of the haredi groups; in addition, there were those among them who were willing to participate in his study. He focuses on the Israeli branches of these global communities because of their demographic density, population variation, and political relevance. Despite a growing tendency toward religious-cultural radicalization and increased self-segregation, he notes, these sects remain linked to each other (and, it should be emphasized, to the general Israeli population) in "an almost Gordian knot formed by religious-political machinations of the Haredi world in the state of Israel during the last decade of the twentieth century" (p. 5).

To prepare readers for his subject, Baumel offers a useful but at times misleading account of language use among Jews since antiquity (to cite but one example, he attributes an important role to Reform Judaism in the acquisition and maintenance of German among Jews in Western Europe, while failing to mention the similar role played by Neo-Orthodoxy). The bulk of the book offers a comparative description and analysis of the history, values, and linguistic behavior of the three Ashkenazic sects as expressed in a multitude of forms in the private, public, and educational spheres—for instance, spoken language in the home; the language of rabbinic writings and spoken addresses; the language of instruction and of conversation in schools; and language in newspapers and magazines. An additional chapter discusses Sephardic haredim, a relatively new group that is treated separately because of its different cultural norms and distinct identity, both in Israel and in France (home to the largest population of Sephardim outside Israel). All of these chapters are based on fieldwork and observations made by the author among Israeli haredi families, in neighborhoods, and in educational frameworks. In contrast, a chapter comparing language ideology and practice in Great Britain, the United States, and Israel is based largely on secondary literature and includes information about additional groups such as the Satmar hasidim.

The haredi world defies easy characterization, and Baumel succeeds in depicting relevant aspects of it in a concise and nuanced manner. The low-status mother tongue of the East European Jewish masses, Yiddish, has become the international emblem of Ashkenazic haredi identity in the post-Holocaust world. It is venerated as a barrier against assimilation and as a quasi-sacred language both because of its association with a religiously idealized past and because it was the language of most of Hitler's victims. Despite this new prestige, Yiddish is known passively, at best, by most young haredim in Israel: boys may learn it orally in order to function in the yeshivas in which it is used, and girls may learn it formally in school if, for instance, they belong to the Habad movement and the aim is for them to understand the original text of the Lubavitcher rebbe's *sichos* (discussions). Mitnagdim and Sephardim, unless educated in certain Ashkenazic institutions, are less likely to know Yiddish, yet at the same time are more likely to be open to the notion of learning "foreign" languages and secular subjects.

In light of the massive linguistic assimilation of the post-Holocaust era (a phenomenon that existed as well among religious Jews in pre-Second World War Europe, which is worthy of more discussion than the author provides) and the desire, most notably in Habad, to integrate into their ranks both members of other sects and newly religious Jews, all of the groups surveyed in this work use the vernacular of the land as their dominant spoken language. In most cases, this language is also their mother tongue. Thus, Israeli haredim freely speak Israeli Hebrew (*'ivrit*), once considered taboo among Ashkenazic haredim, and the author suggests, perhaps correctly but without supporting evidence, that it enjoys "tacit, quasi-sacred status [owing to] its linguistic connection with Loshon Kodesh" (p. 176), the sacred register of Hebrew mixed with Aramaic. Haredi speech is virtually identical with that of other Israelis, apart from its avoidance of vulgarisms and slang terms (at least in the author's presence—haredi slang certainly exists, and I suspect there is also more deviance from community norms than Baumel observes or his interviewees have conceded). By and large, Baumel fails to emphasize significant linguistic markers (for instance, the "oriental" pronunciation of gutturals among Sephardim), though he does mention a number of characteristic terms in specific communities—for instance, the word "mamash," which regularly appears among Habad members; a somewhat greater use of Aramaic terms among Sephardim; and a preference for Yiddish-influenced pronunciation of a few words among Ashkenazic haredim.

As in generations past, language use is gendered. Males receive an overwhelmingly religious education and continue to study texts in *loshn-koydesh* and in Aramaic. Females, whose exposure to religious texts is deliberately limited, receive greater exposure to secular study and are more likely to acquire languages useful for earning a living outside their communities, since they increasingly serve as family breadwinners while their husbands ideally devote themselves to religious study.

In contrast to Israel, Yiddish is in more frequent use in the diaspora. Still, English is widely spoken as a mother tongue in the United States and in Great Britain, and French is the mother tongue of many haredim living in France. Interestingly, Baumel notes the emergence of "Yeshivish," a variety of English influenced by Yiddish, *loshn-koydesh* and *'ivrit*—among mitnagdic males, as evidence of a desire to create a distinctive manner of speaking among English-speakers who are decreasingly likely to be fluent in Yiddish.

Sacred Speakers would benefit greatly from a more thorough examination of a number of questions. For instance, what do haredim perceive as "foreign" languages—and do these include their own "foreign" mother tongues? What does the embrace of *'ivrit* suggest about haredi understandings of their relationship to other Israelis and to Israel as a Jewish state? It strikes me that here, as in many other areas of haredi conduct, the use of language suggests a higher degree of social and cultural integration into Israeli society than is often admitted by either haredim or outside observers.

Readers might also welcome more extensive—and at times more accurate—historical contextualization, as well as more explicit descriptions of the haredi linguistic corpus and broader, more systematic and consistent analysis of this material. On the more technical level, *Sacred Speakers* is marred by many typographical errors, idiosyncratic or incorrect transliterations of Yiddish (for example, the blatantly German "gepflantzt"), and undefined terms (what, for example, does "modern" mean in a haredi context?). Despite such flaws, however, this work performs an invaluable service by helping to shed light on a rapidly growing sector of Jewish society that has until recently received little attention from linguists.

Kalman Weiser
York University

Haim Chertok, *He Also Spoke as a Jew: The Life of the Reverend James Parkes*. London: Vallentine Mitchell, 2006. xii + 516 pp.

James Parkes, born on the picturesque English Channel island of Guernsey in 1896, was a sickly, lonely boy who loved to wander about and collect unusual objects. Orphaned of his mother at a young age, he was raised by his unsympathetic father, who favored Jimmy's vigorously masculine elder brother, David. Jimmy attended the Elizabeth College grammar school, excelling in Latin and Greek, and won a scholarship to Oxford. At about this time, his brother, serving as a combat officer, was killed in the First World War. The shy, diffident Jimmy followed him into army service, also as an officer.

Haim Chertok, who discourses freely and rather critically on Parkes' life in this long biography, finds a decisive moment in James Parkes' military career when he examines his subject's case of trench foot, an ailment common among soldiers confined at length to wet, muddy trenches. He concludes that Lieutenant Parkes induced his own trench foot, which hospitalized him as he desired and thus kept him out of the anticipated British offensive in the spring of 1918, where he might well have been killed. Chertok's analysis is keen, although not entirely conclusive. This less than flattering assessment regarding Parkes' trench foot is characteristic of Chertok's unsparing biography, although the evidence and conclusion seem stronger here than they do on some other topics, including Parkes' sexuality.

Chertok's account has at this point reached the end of the war and Parkes' enrollment at Oxford, but has in no way prepared the reader for the forceful, confident student activist who emerged. For a time, we learn, Parkes was that familiar type, the Big Man on Campus. Chertok follows his career into the 1930s as a functionary, based in Geneva, of the Student Christian Movement (SCM) and concurrently of kindred bodies such as the International Student Service. One of Parkes' duties in the SCM was to defend Jewish university students against antisemitic assaults on their academic rights, especially in Poland, Germany, and the Balkans. In order to do this, he was constantly on the move, visiting universities throughout Europe. His success, however, was very limited. Presumably it was during this period that Parkes' defense both of Jews and of Judaism became cornerstones of his Christian faith, though Chertok does not elaborate on this point.

Eventually the ceaseless round of meetings and conferences became wearisome. Moreover, the SCM and related bodies proved impotent against the rising tides of fascism and extreme nationalism in European student society. Parkes felt burnt out and returned to England in 1935. There he became a priest of the Church of England, though this came about only after difficulty over the required articles of faith was overcome thanks to the intervention of the Bishop of Manchester, William Temple (who later became the renowned Archbishop of Canterbury). The new Anglican priest was uninterested in serving a parish, although he did on occasion preside at some church functions, and he often had testy relations with his fellow clergy. Rather than serve in the church, Parkes was determined to devote himself to the sensitive field of Jewish-Christian relations, but not in the tiresome, cloying area of mutual goodwill: he meant to investigate in full the Christian basis of antisemitism. Before his fortieth birthday, he was in a writing mode that lasted for the rest of his life, during which time he produced the books and pamphlets that are his true legacy. Possessing neither a clerical nor an academic position and lacking a substantial personal income, Parkes was forced to cast about for a patron. There were no foundations at the time to which he could apply; instead, he was taken up by Israel Moses Sieff, one of the owners of the Marks and Spencer retail giant. Sieff provided a monthly stipend until the pressing needs of a huge number of German Jewish refugees compelled him to withdraw it. At this point, the commercial concern stepped in as Marks and Spencer bought up all the apples provided by trees belonging to Parkes (who owned a few acres of land) for its produce department.

Two major works show Parkes on his chosen path. *The Conflict of the Church and the Synagogue: Origins of Antisemitism* appeared in 1934, and a sequel, *The Jew in the Medieval Community: A Study of His Political and Economic Situation*, came out in 1938. Regrettably, Chertok deals quite summarily with these important books. Parkes' book of 1946, *The Emergence of the Jewish Problem*, synthesized many earlier essays and studies, but did not sell many copies. Parkes visited Israel several times as an invited guest, and he wrote and lectured with great warmth on the subject of the new state. By then he could tell audiences, "I speak as a Jew," a declaration that introduced his conclusions about the Jewish basis of Christianity.

From his Geneva days, Parkes collected books and printed material; over time, his library became a significant scholarly resource. In the years before his death in 1981, he was deeply concerned about the future deposition of his library. Almost by accident, it went to the recently founded University of Southampton, where it is now a separate collection that also provides a basis for that institution's noteworthy Jewish studies program. The Parkes library thus realizes in large measure James Parkes' hopes.

Lloyd P. Gartner
Tel Aviv University

Murray Friedman, *The Neoconservative Revolution: Jewish Intellectuals and the Shaping of Public Policy*. Cambridge: Cambridge University Press, 2005. 303 pp.

Published in 2005 at the start of George W. Bush's second term, *The Neoconservative Revolution: Jewish Intellectuals and the Shaping of Public Policy* offers a chronological narrative of American Jewish involvement in U.S. conservative politics of the 20th century and seeks to redress the liberal bias in the historiography of American Jewish politics. Its author, Murray Friedman (1926–2005), the founder and director of the Myer and Rosaline Feinstein Center for American Jewish History at Temple University, shared a biography similar to that of many of the subjects in his book. After a period of youthful left-wing affiliations, Friedman became disillusioned with Communism—crediting Whittaker Chambers and Arthur Koestler for his change of views—and later served in the Reagan administration as vice chair of the U.S. Civil Rights Commission. His views were adumbrated in an important volume of *American Jewish History* (1999) that he edited, and his essay there, "Opening the Discussion of Jewish Political Conservatism," is in many ways more analytic than this posthumous work.

The Neoconservative Revolution opens with a description of how Americanizing Jews in the pre-Second World War era sought to create a "neutral society" (to use Jacob Katz's term) by insisting on an impenetrable separation of church and state, as well as focusing on civil rights and laying the foundation for the Jewish liberal mystique. Yet as Friedman illustrates in his second chapter, "The Premature Jewish Neoconservatives," the participation of a group of young Jewish men (the "New York intellectuals") in the American military caused them to experience the justness of American power in the defeat of Nazism. Although individuals such as Daniel Bell, Nathan Glazer, Milton Himmelfarb, Elliot Cohen, and Irving Kristol remained in the liberal camp in the immediate postwar era, their earlier disillusionment with Stalinism laid the foundation for their ideological rapprochement with conservative trends in American politics.

Chapter 3 seeks to uncover the "forgotten Jewish godfathers" of neoconservatism, including Eugene Lyons, Ralph de Toledano, Morrie Ryskind, Frank Chodorov, Milton Friedman, Frank S. Meyer, and one godmother, Ayn Rand (née Alissa Rosenbaum), in an effort to prove that not all Jews were liberals in the 1950s and 1960s. But this chapter, as is true of most of the book, never analyzes why the Jewishness of these individuals mattered. Earlier, Friedman credited a vague "proclivity toward intellectualism" (p. 8) as the glue defining the group. In this chapter, he concedes that the "religious and Jewish identity views of these Jewish conservatives widely differed" (p. 56). The issue of what, apart from origins, makes neoconservatism a Jewish phenomenon is never addressed or resolved, which makes its use as a coherent analysis of the phenomenon very limited.

Friedman goes on to tell the story of the contentious 1950s, marked by a parting of the ways among a group of left-wing anti-Stalinists of Jewish origin, and the emergence of *Commentary* and *The Public Interest* as organs of the New York intellectuals' rightward shift. This story is well known. Chapter 5, "The Modernization of American Conservatism," the book's most original chapter, focuses on the very visibly Roman Catholic William F. Buckley, who moved American conservatism away from its bigoted (read: antisemitic) past, and popularized it through a magazine, *National Review*, and, most importantly, a television program, *Firing Line*, which first aired in 1966. This chapter illustrates how Buckley's explicit rejection of religion as a ticket for admission into conservative American public policy made room for Jews. The significance of Buckley for Friedman's story makes the "Jewish intellectuals" in his book's subtitle glaringly dissonant. So, too, the space spent on Barry Goldwater, whose Jewish roots could only be traced to his paternal grandfather, and on Daniel Patrick Moynihan. Why, exactly, did Friedman think neoconservatism is relevant to Jewish history?

An answer to that question lies in the year 1967, a watershed in postwar American Jewish politics. Chapter 6, "The Liberal Meltdown," describes the escalation of violence in Vietnam; the emergence of a militant black power movement; the standoff between the New York City teacher's union (representing mostly Jewish teachers in Brooklyn) and African-American activists who favored community control; and the support for adversarial politics among a new generation of American radicals, many of whom were of Jewish origin. Friedman, however, does not go beyond description to analyze why the New Left's politics became the focal point for a palpable shift among liberals.

In my view, when the New Left attacked the American university as a bastion of imperialism and privilege, Jewish intellectuals—who had once fought tooth-and-nail against social antisemitism and university quotas—went on a counterattack, defending the university as the safeguard of the liberal values that had allowed Jewish integration into American society. Similarly, when the New Left championed the cause of militant radicals, including the Palestinians, against colonial power, and equated Zionism with racism, liberal intellectuals of Jewish origin felt threatened *as Jews*. In the typological thinking of these former liberals turned neoconservatives, the militancy of the black power movement, of the Sandinistas in Nicaragua, and of the PLO all represented an unleashing of "the mob" with its accompanying violence. At the same time, the Soviet-backed agitation in South America and the oppression of Soviet Jews made the Soviet Union the embodiment of a state with a "mob" mentality, which affirmed the neoconservatives' earlier anti-Communism.

Whereas Friedman's book focuses on the American scene, a longer view of Jewish history might interpret the neoconservative preoccupation with antisemitism as consistent with a conservative Jewish political tradition that goes back to the earliest years of settlement in Europe—a tradition shaped by suspicion of political extremism and social unrest. Until the 1880s, Jewish elites in Eastern Europe often staked their community's security on the stability of Gentile authority and accommodated to its rule. These fears made a group of elite, postwar, and middle-class Jewish liberals ripe for a reassessment of the role of the American state in countering the international forces of "the mob"; in the 1980s, they embraced Reagan's international anti-Communist politics and trickle-down economic policies.

Adding to the neoconservative sense of instability and malaise was the assault on the middle-class family on the part of the New Left and the feminist movement. America, neoconservatives thought, was going to hell in a hand-basket, and the counterculture was to blame. What Friedman does not explore is the degree to which Jewish neoconservatives perceived the new social movements as threatening the Jewish family, the historical vessel for Jewish communal continuity. What links the neoconservatives' turn to Reaganite economics and international politics, alongside their rejection of multiculturalism and the "New History," is the quest for political stability and Jewish survival. Although some of Friedman's protagonists were not practicing Jews, they increasingly saw in religion a foundation for societal stability. Consequently, they sought to align themselves with public figures who articulated a need to return religion to the public sphere. This explains the neoconservative endorsement of school vouchers, a social program supported by members of the Christian Right—who, while not the usual political bedfellows of liberal Jews, were now comrades in the public defense of Israel and social morality.

Although Friedman intended his work as a revisionist attack on liberal Jewish historiography, *The Neoconservative Revolution* fails to do much more than outline the issues and name the many significant players involved with the movement. Given the resounding support American Jews gave to the Democratic party in the most recent presidential election, it appears that the neoconservative revolution has peaked and can now be assessed in terms of larger trends in modern Jewish history. The rise of the Jewish neoconservatives in postwar American politics should be seen as one expression of the process of acculturation of a group of mostly East European male Jewish children of the immigrant generation into mainstream American culture. They were an intellectual vanguard who brandished their pens at a time when the print media had vast public influence. But like all *intelligenti*, they were not necessarily in sync with the people they purported to lead.

Nancy Sinkoff
Rutgers University

Leonard Glick, *Marked in Your Flesh: Circumcision from Ancient Judea to Modern America*. New York: Oxford University Press, 2005. 370 pp.

In *Marked in Your Flesh*, Leonard Glick clearly explains the history of circumcision and how it has been viewed over time by Jews and Christians, and he also presents a social history of the medical research on circumcision. Trained both as a medical doctor and as a cultural anthropologist, Glick is well equipped to analyze ritual and, in this case, to decipher the science behind it. He is not, however, a disinterested party but rather a "scholar activist" with strong sentiments against circumcision. Although I learned a great deal from this book, it presents difficulties for a reviewer writing for a scholarly journal. For one thing, Glick does not engage in any primary research. As I am neither a scientist nor an expert on Hebrew texts, I cannot judge the quality of his secondary research. It seems to me, however, that his material on the history of circumcision in the West and medical research on circumcision is stronger than that pertaining to how circumcision has been viewed by Christians and Jews. Glick's description of circumcision in ancient, medieval and early modern Judaism is very interesting, but it is not as scholarly as the work of those such as Shaye Cohen who focus on the primary texts.[1] Finally, with regard to the activist part of the book, it is difficult if not impossible to make any kind of judgement.

Glick comes out clearly against circumcision on medical and humanistic grounds, though his opposition only surfaces toward the end of the book. He is courageous in critically analyzing and questioning the reasons underlying this deeply entrenched ritual in contemporary life. However, an unfortunate outcome of his strong opposition to circumcision is that many readers are likely to dismiss this book entirely. Glick may have been better served by a less polemical tone in his concluding section.

Because circumcision is linked to the very core of Jewish identity, any discussion about it hits a deep collective nerve. Significantly, although a majority of contemporary American Jews are not religious and thus do not necessarily regard it as symbolizing a covenant with God, the power of circumcision as an identity marker remains steadfast. The baby Jesus was circumcised (a topic of many artists' renditions) and his foreskin was supposedly on display in the Vatican until the relic was stolen at some point in the 16th century. Historically, however, circumcision separated and distinguished Jews from Christians. Paul realized that the requirement that Gentiles convert to Judaism in order to join Jesus' new form of Judaism was a serious obstacle, with circumcision being the greatest barrier. Dropping the requirement of conversion and, in consequence, circumcision, was thus highly significant in the growth of early Christianity. Indeed,

Glick also suggests that the way in which later Christians condemned and rejected circumcision may have contributed to the blood libel. Yet during the 19th century, some Christians began to view circumcision as a medically beneficial practice. At about the same time, a small group of Reform Jews in Germany argued that circumcision was not compatible with the cultural modernization and citizenship rights sought by German Jews. The Society of the Friends of Reform, a group of laymen established in Frankfurt in 1842, rejected most Orthodox practices in their platform. One member of that group put out a pamphlet in which he proposed what is now called a "Brit Shalom"—a ceremony welcoming any child, male or female, into the Jewish community—in lieu of circumcision. Rabbis were outraged by this idea; even the more progressive among them rejected the notion of abandoning the traditional practice of circumcision.

Glick shows how, before modern hygienic practices were introduced, babies were much more at risk for hemorrhaging and infections, in part because mohels (ritual circumcisers) used their thumbnails for part of the procedure. Another potentially hazardous practice was *mezizah bapeh* (oral suction), in which the initial blood on the infant's penis was sucked by mouth by the mohel. This was viewed as the first step in the healing process, but mohels who had any kind of mouth infection, herpes, syphilis, or tuberculosis were likely to transmit these diseases to the newborn child. Until the middle of the 19th century, this aspect of the ritual was seen as an essential and crucial component. Today, it is most common for the mohel to use a tube to suction the blood. However, some ultra-Orthodox groups still practice *mezizah bapeh* despite some publicized instances in which infants have been infected by herpes transmitted by the mohel.[2]

The early medical debates about circumcision are perhaps the most fascinating aspect of the book. In 19th-century Britain, some medical doctors were among the first Christians to advocate universal circumcision on the grounds that it prevented masturbation, promiscuity, and syphilis (probably in that order). A few doctors claimed that circumcision cured other serious diseases, including paralysis and insanity. American physicians subsequently took up the cause, such that by the late 19th century the U.S. medical literature called for widespread circumcision among the male population. This remained the default position for decades. In more recent years, various other medical reasons, such as preventing penile or cervical cancer, have been advanced on behalf of circumcision, although, according to Glick, each of these has been scientifically disproved. Glick also argues against the current assertion that circumcision prevents HIV-AIDs; after all, he points out, the United States has the largest number of circumcised adult males as well as one of the highest HIV infection rates in the developed world (p. 274). In the early 1970s, the American Academy of Pediatrics stated that there was no medical (as opposed to cultural or religious) reason to circumcise males. Thus, Glick argues, circumcision seems to be the only elective surgery on infants that is performed for nonmedical reasons, a fact that should give parents pause. Accordingly, the discourse used by those opposed to circumcision has become more militant, invoking such terms as "mutilation" and equating male circumcision with the mutilation of females in certain parts of the world. These debates have revealed a lack of nuance concerning circumcision.

As noted, most contemporary American Jews no longer connect their sons' circumcision with God's covenant or anything particularly religious, yet it remains one of the few rituals, if not the only one, observed by almost all Jews. To be sure, many opt to have a hospital-based procedure that omits the essential Judaic aspects of the ritual (unless the parents chose a doctor who is also a mohel). Glick points out that such a procedure—circumcising a son to signify his Jewishness in a ceremony devoid of traditional Judaic elements—misses the entire purpose.

Glick has provided an unusual perspective as an academic, a medical doctor, and a Jew. To his credit, he has given serious attention to some of the questions that are typically dismissed, such as the pain that circumcision can cause an infant. To this reader's disappointment, he completely ignores the question of circumcision among Muslims, which is performed, depending upon different customs and regions, anywhere between the age of seven and puberty. Overall, however, *Marked in Your Flesh* is a commendable book to which every reader will have his or her strong reaction.

Diane L. Wolf
University of California, Davis

Notes

1. Shaye Cohen, *Why Aren't Jewish Women Circumcised?* (Berkeley: 2005).
2. On the controversy and current practice with regard to *mezizah bapeh*, see www.ou.org/index.php/jewish_action/print/8976 (accessed 21 July 2009).

David Weiss Halivni, *Breaking the Tablets: Jewish Theology after the Shoah*, ed. Peter Ochs. New York: Rowman and Littlefield, 2007. 137 pp.

David Weiss Halivni is one of the last of the postwar generation's handful of talmudic scholars who received their early education in Europe, experienced and survived the Holocaust, and (in the case of Halivni) went on to do monumental work in the scientific study of the Mishnah and Talmud. Halivni, who today resides in Jerusalem, is of interest not only to students of the Talmud but to theologians as well, since despite his rigorously scientific approach to the Jewish tradition and his harrowing experience of the Shoah, "he has sought a life of piety" (p. xii). That is, he has remained a halakhically observant Jew who continues to believe in the revelatory nature of the Torah. There have been others, of course, who have retained their religious faith after Auschwitz. Halivni, however, has gone beyond mere faith by attempting to formulate a theology that would justify a relationship with God after the Shoah and at the same time show how the Torah may retain its claim to be Holy Writ. Thus, according to the book's editor, Peter Ochs: "This book is offered in answer to the question many of us have asked Halivni: What does it mean for you to be religious after the Shoah? How do you still pray?" (p. xiii).[1]

The theological background for his answer is given by Halivni in his prologue:

> There are two major theological events in Jewish history, Revelation at Sinai and Revelation at Auschwitz. The former was a revelation of God's Presence, the latter a Revelation of God's absence, the former indicated God's nearness to us, the latter God's distance. At Sinai God appeared before Israel, addressed us and gave us instructions. At Auschwitz God absented Himself from Israel, abandoned us and handed us over to the enemy. In between these two periods Israel's spiritual history took place, moving between God's embracing us at Sinai and God's withdrawing from us at Auschwitz, between Divine intervention and Divine abandonment, between our sense of connection and our sense of detachment.

Moreover, Halivni notes, "every aspect of our spiritual life is affected by whether we see ourselves in a period of God's Presence or absence: the way we pray, how we regard the Torah, particularly the Biblical text and its relation to the Oral tradition" (p. x). In the three brief chapters that follow, Halivni deals with two seemingly different issues: the ways in which a sense of God's absence in Auschwitz affected the prisoners' prayer; and how the history of the oral tradition (*torah shebe'al peh*) can best be understood as a response to the fluctuation between the mode of divine presence and that of its absence.

I have several general questions regarding Halivni's thesis. First, does he really mean to say that Auschwitz was a "revelation" of God's absence in the same sense that Sinai was a revelation of the presence and will of God? If the only evidence of God's absence is that Israel must confront its enemies on its own without divine intervention, in what sense was Auschwitz any more a revelation than were the Crusades or the expulsion from Spain or the Chmielnicki massacres? Surely it is not the number of victims that determines the degree of God's absence. Second, according to Halivni, from Sinai to Auschwitz "there was a gradual erosion of God's Presence so that Auschwitz was not a sudden eclipse of God but the ultimate outcome of a long process" (p. 108). If this statement implies that there was a steady erosion of spirituality over the course of the centuries, I would counter that post-biblical Jewish history has rather been marked by bursts of spiritual creativity, as manifested by such phenomena as the poetry and philosophy of rabbis and intellectuals in medieval Muslim Spain, kabbalistic mysticism, and Hasidism. Finally, while psychologically and theologically most agonizing, the problem of how one could pray in Auschwitz was in principle no different from that faced by Jews in any other time of troubles (*et zarah*).

If God's "absence" refers to a lack of divine intervention, Halivni is quite correct in saying that the prayer that "uniquely characterizes prayer in the camps is that which asks God to eliminate the free will of the perpetrators and take back the reins of government into His own hands"(p. 35). Such a plea, he notes, appears in a text traditionally recited in the course of the *musaf* service of Rosh Hashanah, which also forms part of the daily "'Aleinu" prayer.

Regarding the question why God did not intervene in the Holocaust to save His people, Halivni offers a speculative twist on the kabbalistic notion of *zimzum* (divine contraction), according to which God periodically withdraws, leaving the world completely to the vagaries of human freedom of will, for better or for worse. Unfortunately, Halivni explains, the last time this happened coincided with the coming to power of Nazi Germany. According to him, "the cause of [the Jews'] suffering was cosmic" (pp. 33–34). Perhaps he should have stayed with his first response: "I certainly have no answer to this question" (p. 32).

With regard to the evolution of the oral tradition, Halivni believes that, after the Revelation at Sinai, the Torah of revelation "passed through the conduit of humankind and has been affected by the journey. Both the written law and the Oral tradition did not escape unscathed. So that it cannot be said that the tradition we have received from the Rabbis is the perfect expression of God's will to Moses on Mt. Sinai" (p. 198). Nevertheless, "the text we possess today" (that is, one he believes was restored and reconstructed by Ezra, and then presented to the small remnant of the faithful returning from Babylon) was crowned with divine sanction and sanctity.[2] Halivni here is tackling a problem facing anyone who, like him, accepts the conventional historic view of what happens to documents or oral traditions over a period of 700 years of "neglect, forgetfulness and corruption" but who nonetheless wishes to continue the tradition of proclaiming, as the Torah is held aloft in the synagogue, "This is the Torah that Moses set before the children of Israel" (Deut. 4:44). His solution to this dilemma consists of three different theological claims. First, he argues, Ezra had the status of prophet, and because of this, his endorsement of the restored text may be considered divinely sanctioned. Second, the voluntary and enthusiastic acceptance of the Torah by a community that is largely free of the scourge of idolatry "renders the Torah authoritative." And finally (in contrast to the first two arguments, which make no reference to the presence or absence of God),[3] by the time of Ezra, "God's closeness was restored so that Ezra regained a considerable degree of the Sinatic power of interpreting God's 'literal word' " (p. 108).

Here, too, Halivni's claims raise questions. For one thing, if God's presence underwent "gradual erosion," how could it have suddenly reappeared in the time of Ezra? What is the evidence that it did, apart from the circular argument regarding the success of Ezra's "restoration"? Further, assuming the revelatory nature of Ezra's text, how do we get from that text to the halakhic codes of today? Halivni's "theological solution" (pp. 98–100) is first to justify the oral law in general by saying it is "necessary and indispensable"—that is, to live as a Jew is to "have a law to live by" and "we must be governed by fidelity to what we have inherited." And next, he argues, we must critically examine the entire talmudic tradition and distinguish the essential oral tradition from what he calls "extra-scriptural teachings" that are "pontifical" or simply "opinions" (p. 99). It is, of course, in devoted pursuit of this end that Halivni has developed a methodology often referred to as "source-critical analysis," which has yielded to date seven volumes of impressive talmudic scholarship.

Halivni's attempt to place his theory concerning the transmission and interpretation of the revealed Torah within the wider context of the theological concept of God's presence/absence adds nothing to its cogency or elucidation. As we have seen, the reasons given by Halivni for accepting the Torah text presented by Ezra as Holy Writ are quite coherent as far as they go. Similarly, his methodology for distinguishing the different layers of interpretation in the oral tradition has to be judged on its merits, independent of theology.

Finally, I would draw the attention of the reader to two sections not central to the larger theme in which we see Halivni at his scholarly best. In one section, basing himself on rabbinic sources, he shows how it cannot be said that the destruction of the six million came about because of their sins (pp. 17–27); elsewhere, he critiques the claim that the oral law was a separate corpus revealed at one time in a single encounter by God to Moses (pp. 77–88). These important views are well-researched and convincingly argued.

Shubert Spero
Bar-Ilan University

Notes

1. Of the 116 pages that remain after deducting the bibliography, indexes, and biographical information about the author and editor, more than 40 consist of introductions and commentary by Peter Ochs, a professor of modern Judaic studies at the University of Virginia and a longtime student of David Weiss Halivni. My review focuses on Halivni's portion of the book.

2. See David Weiss Halivni, "Revelation, Textual Criticism and Divine Writ," *Judaism* 47 (Spring 1998), 209.

3. These two arguments can be found in ibid., 201–202; this article was adapted from Halivni's book *Revelation Restored: Divine Writ and Critical Responses* (Boulder: 1997).

Anita Norich, *Discovering Exile: Yiddish and Jewish American Culture during the Holocaust*. Stanford: Stanford University Press, 2008. 232 pp.

When and how did the Holocaust come to exert such a massive influence on American Jewish cultural life, defining its moral imagination and setting its expressive limits? Anita Norich's *Discovering Exile* is presented simultaneously as a literary-historical investigation of the roots (or perhaps *pre*-history) of that redefinition of Jewish cultural life from the late 1930s through 1945; as an intensely personal but also ambivalent protest against that redefinition; and as a methodological essay on the centrality of Yiddish-language writing in any adequate investigation of 20th-century American Jewish culture. Relevant to both historians and literary scholars, *Discovering Exile* joins Eli Lederhendler's *New York Jews and the Decline of Urban Ethnicity* (2001) as a compelling effort to reestablish the postwar cultural history of American Jewry on a properly critical (and bilingual) foundation.

This last dimension of the work intersects fruitfully with Norich's literary history to yield the book's most compelling findings: that, whereas the destruction of European Jewry had surprisingly little effect, in the short term, on Anglo-Jewish definitions of the Jewish cultural condition in terms of "alienation" and the danger of exclusion, American *Yiddish* writers responded to it almost before it began with a fundamental redefinition of their cultural horizons in terms of "exile" and "erasure." For Anglo-Jewish literati such as Alfred Kazin or Phillip Rahv, the Holocaust simply strengthened the emerging notion that the Jewish writer was called upon to represent the universal alienation endemic to the modern condition, and that the defining cultural danger to American Jews was exclusion from full American/western cultural citizenship. By contrast, for Yiddish writers, the destruction converted their previous ambivalence toward the East European Jewish home they had left behind into an awareness of their being exiles in the truest sense. Unlike Thomas Wolfe or, for that matter, American Jewish writers born in the Bronx, they quite literally could not go home again. Spurred on by this fact, and by the looming erasure of Yiddish-language culture in favor of English, it was the Yiddish writers of America who anticipated American Jewry's eventual consensus that the Holocaust must in many ways define the parameters of Jewish culture.

Discovering Exile makes use of several heated Jewish literary controversies of the period to investigate how American Yiddishists and, to a lesser extent, English-language American Jewish critics began to rethink American Jewish culture in the face of the unfolding calamity in Europe. Norich focuses on four clusters of text and controversy. Chapter 1 sketches the institutional contours of American Yiddish(ist) writing, and explicitly Jewish English-language writing, and then homes in on the debate inspired by two symposia on the subject of the task of the Jewish writer that appeared in 1943 and 1944, one in Yiddish in Kadya Molodovsky's journal *Svive* and the other in the English-language *Contemporary Jewish Record*. Norich's sociological analysis yields two especially interesting observations. First, in the 1940s, lines of communication between the Yiddish and Anglo-Jewish press were more substantial and mutual than generally assumed. Second, at the start of this period, at any rate, the Yiddish press was arguably *more* expansive in its cultural aspirations and in its sense of what belonged in a "Jewish" journal than was its English-language counterpart, which defined its concerns more narrowly around explicitly "Jewish-interest" matters. Strangely, Norich seems almost reluctant to make this point, which stands in a peculiar tension with her defense of contemporary Anglo-Jewish culture (see below). Perhaps this is because it was precisely this greater breadth—the avoidance of a narrow concern with Jewishness—that Yiddish writers were in the process of questioning as they confronted news of the Holocaust.

Chapter 2 takes up this transition by revisiting its most compact expression: Yankev Glatshteyn's famous 1938 poem, "A gute nakht, velt" (Good night, world), which seemingly renounced European civilization in favor of a demonstrative "return" to "the ghetto." At the time and since, this poem has been read as the signpost of a larger "end of modernism" in Yiddish literature: it is taken to represent a general Holocaust-era renunciation by Yiddish writers of their youthful claims to expressive freedom from collective Jewish concerns and traditions, and of their high modernist vision of literature as a realm of individual self-formation through literary experimentation. Although one can hardly deny the general accuracy of this observation, at least for the Yiddish literary mainstream outside Israel (the story of Yiddish literature in Israel is considerably different, as Norich briefly acknowledges toward the end of her book), this work offers a moderate revision with regard to Glatshteyn himself. In a careful argument, Norich contends that Glatshteyn remained "very much a modernist" in certain ways. Most interesting is her argument that Glatshteyn's shift to prose writing in the late 1930s, epitomized by his two autobiographical novels, *Ven Yash iz geforn* (1938) and *Ven Yash iz gekumen* (1940), should be seen as the search for a genre that could allow him the formal resources to confront the great questions of the Jewish present without the spurious clarity he had assayed in "A gute nakht"—a quintessentially modernist search. Narrating the experiences of a Glatshteyn-like American Yiddish writer returning to 1930s Poland to see his dying mother, the *Yash* novels mark one of the most extraordinary achievements of modernist writing in Yiddish prose. Yet as though to spite their formal achievement, they furthered the harsh accounting to which Glatshteyn was subjecting the larger hopes of prewar Yiddish culture. Depicting a Jewish culture and society disintegrating from within, these bleak narratives gave further expression to the renunciation of Yiddishism's cosmopolitan dreams that "A gute nakht, velt" had already encapsulated.

Chapter 3 reconstructs the response to novelist Sholem Asch's wartime Christological trilogy—*The Nazarene, The Apostle*, and *Mary*—fleshing out the dimensions of the furious reaction in the Yiddish literary world in contrast to the intensely positive responses by Jewish critics in English. Norich's key claim is that the rage with which many American Yiddish critics greeted Asch's *Nazarene* was not due simply to its Christological content, but at least as much to the *linguistic* politics of its publication and reception: the novel appeared first in English translation and only four years later in the Yiddish original. This chapter further develops Norich's argument concerning the different dimensions of Yiddish and English-language Jewish cultural imagination in the 1940s. Whereas most Yiddish critics were infuriated by *The Nazarene* because it signaled the erasure of Yiddish in America at the very moment most of its native speakers were being murdered in Europe, American Jewish writers liked it because it accorded with their fundamental desire to claim full cultural membership for Jews in western civilization while also preserving some sort of vague Jewish distinctiveness.

Chapter 4 takes up the pained discussion in the Yiddish press of the future tasks and fate of Yiddish culture, as occasioned by Y. L. Peretz's thirtieth *yortsayt* in 1945. The few voices insisting on the importance of reading Peretz first and foremost as a writer and creator whose work could inspire further creation were drowned out by a chorus that now read Peretz "synecdochically, to represent the world whose destruction he could not have imagined" (p. 102).

Norich's findings make a convincing case for her core empirical claim that students of American Jewish culture are obliged to take Yiddish letters seriously. They also resonate with another important recent work on the postwar history of American Jewry, the aforementioned work by Eli Lederhendler. Strangely, Norich does not engage Lederhendler's study. Perhaps this is because Lederhendler's book is at odds with the dominant tone in American Jewish historical writing: one of relentless celebration of American Jewish creativity and a marked resistance to any suggestion that the history of 20th-century American Jewish culture involved compromise, loss, and diminution. At times, especially in her introduction and conclusion, Norich seems to sound this same note, polemically warning the readers against taking her findings on the transformation of culture into "identity" and "commemoration" as evidence of such a diminution. Arguably, though, that is exactly what *Discovering Exile* so compellingly shows. And indeed, even as she warns against this interpretation, Norich lets us hear some of her most interesting historical actors bear witness to its truth, in fascinating asides on A. Leyeles, Yankev Leshtshinsky, Avrom Golomb, Rokhl Oyerbakh, and of course in her analysis of Glatshteyn himself. But to dissent from some of Norich's views on the present is not to slight the importance of *Discovering Exile* as a work that yields new insights into the histories of Yiddish literature, American Jewish culture, and the study of Holocaust representation, reminding us that the latter two cannot be written seriously without attention to the first.

Kenneth B. Moss
The Johns Hopkins University

Eugene R. Sheppard, *Leo Strauss and the Politics of Exile: The Making of a Political Philosopher*. Waltham: Brandeis University Press, 2006. xi + 191 pp.

In the early 1980s, I suggested to a Columbia University professor that Leo Strauss' *Natural Right and History* be included on the reading list for a graduate colloquium in 20th-century U.S. intellectual history. He raised an eyebrow, summarily dismissing the suggestion. I did not imagine at the time that Strauss (1899–1973) would eventually become a subject of major historiographical interest. But he has. Throughout the George W. Bush years, the U.S. intelligentsia engaged in a spirited debate on Strauss' putative influence on the intellectual formation of high-ranking administration officials. At the same time, a young academic generation rediscovered the Weimar era's German-Jewish thinkers and explored their critiques of liberalism. The result was a wave of new publications on Strauss.[1]

Focusing on Strauss' intellectual and political development in Weimar Germany, the new works quickly superseded the barren polemics of the 1970s and 1980s regarding the Straussian reading of Machiavelli and the Greeks, as well as the more recent (and disturbing) exchanges regarding the alleged Straussian conspiracy to reshape U.S. national security policy. They have shifted the emphasis from Straussianism to Strauss, from postwar United States to interwar Europe, from the elusive and elliptical old exegete, the Chicago mandarin, to the agitated, struggling, youthful Jewish intellectual. Analyzing the making of Strauss as a philosopher, they have begun drawing a rich and complex portrait of Strauss as a young intellectual. He emerges as no less original or eccentric, no more liberal or likable, than the Strauss we had known, but he is now quintessentially historical, a mastermind shaped by and responding to the exigencies of the time.

Eugene R. Sheppard has gone further than anyone to date in historicizing the young Strauss. If earlier works recovered Strauss' engagement in Weimar debates on philosophy and political theology, Sheppard now relates them to the changing historical contexts. He charts Strauss' intellectual development from Weimar Germany (1921–1932) to his exile in Paris and London (1932–1937) to his New York years at the New School (1938–1948). His focus is on Strauss before Straussianism, before the 1948 appointment at Chicago transformed the beleaguered émigré into a formidable academic authority, and later, even a cult figure. The transitions between the three milieux signaled intellectual shifts from heterodox Zionism and young conservative anti-liberalism to an affirmation of the "medieval Enlightenment," the contemplative life, and the limits of politics; and from there to the championing of "esoteric" writing as both quintessential philosophy and as a strategy of avoiding the subversion of liberal democracy. The unifying theme running through Strauss' youthful intellectual life is the critique of modernity—of liberalism, historicism, and relativism. He sought to understand the roots of the modern western predicament by analyzing the formation of the "liberal" project in Hobbes and Spinoza and by exploring medieval and classical alternatives: Maimonides, Plato, Xenophon.

Sheppard goes systematically through Strauss' early writings, highlighting his work on Jacobi, Spinoza, and Maimonides and his discourse on Zionism. He draws attention to Strauss' intellectual associations, including Franz Rosenzweig, Martin Heidegger, and Carl Schmitt, and also traces Nietzsche's formative influence. Strauss took part in the rebellion of Weimar's young intelligentsia against liberal philosophy, theology, and politics. For young Jews, this entailed rejection of the Enlightenment, emancipation ideology, and Reform Judaism. Following Rosenzweig, Strauss emphasized the centrality of revelation in Judaism, yet at the same time, following Nietzsche, proclaimed his atheism. He pursued relentlessly the antinomies of liberal Jewish philosophy (among others, of his *Doktorvater*, Ernst Cassirer), striving to show the liberal failure to negotiate philosophy and religion. Yet this only deepened Strauss' quandary as a Jewish philosopher. For more than a decade he was a Zionist, but he felt that secular and modern nationalism sat badly with Jewish religion and history, which were predicated on exile and on the Jews being outsiders.

Strauss' intellectual guides outside the Jewish camp were the leading lights of the German rebellion against modernity and liberalism. He was enraptured both by Heidegger (although the latter's intellectual import for Strauss remains unclear) and by Schmitt, whose parsing of liberal democracy he admired. But, as a Jew, he could not follow the anti-liberal orgy to its German nationalist end. Thus, while choosing the worst possible intellectual guides, Strauss' rejection of historicism and relativism put brakes on their excesses. The shining examples of classical political philosophy and the Jewish spirit induced loftier reflections than Schmitt's *Realpolitik* or Heidegger's death anxieties. In a now famous 1932 review, Strauss insisted that, so long as Schmitt refused a discussion of values, his politics remained beholden to the modern liberal worldview.[2]

The Nazis' rise to power and Heidegger's and Schmitt's betrayal, Sheppard intimates, were transformative experiences. Strauss, on a Rockefeller fellowship in Paris, became an overnight exile: he would not return to his *Heimat* (homeland), where he would be considered an *Untermensch*. He defiantly refused *teshuvah* (religious repentance and return): he would not "crawl to the cross of liberalism" and, for a while, continued to identify imperial magnanimity—"to spare the vanquished and crush the arrogant"—with fascism. But this was bravado in the midst of despair. In truth, his position changed. Throughout the 1920s, Strauss had excelled at showing the impossibility of the present, using his razor-sharp intellect to deconstruct any bridge to the past, to unmask as fraudulent any appropriation of tradition. Now he accepted the limits of politics and turned them into the very precondition of philosophy.

Philosophers (that is, atheists) could not speak openly. If they did, they would undermine the political order—not to mention putting themselves at risk. The youth would be bound to misunderstand them, turn to nihilism and revolutionary politics and, in the end, put philosophy itself in danger. The medieval Jewish and Islamic philosophers, Maimonides and Alfarabi, showed the way out of this predicament. Accepting revelation as the origin of the perfect law, they freely reinterpreted "revealed" law philosophically, turning the prophet into a philosopher-king. They envisioned perfection and practiced philosophy for the discerning few without ever putting the political order in danger. Modern philosophy's fault was dual, and Heidegger and Schmitt were merely its recent embodiment: it relinquished the search for the Good (lowering standards to make realization possible), and it did so openly. It ended in a disaster.

Sheppard is especially acute in showing the convergence of Strauss' dilemmas as a Jew and as a philosopher. Given the Jews' predicament of the 1930s, political Zionism seemed more than ever an imperative, yet it provided no solution for the philosopher. Exiled from his *Heimat*, Strauss, like liberal émigrés, began talking about "we, 'men of science,'" whose intellectual search transcended national affiliation. Unlike the liberals, he identified the seekers and wanderers with the medieval philosophers and not with the Enlightenment's "republic of letters." Philosophers lived in a permanent exile, their search for truth putting them at odds with the city or nation. Just as, to Rosenzweig, Jewish homelessness induced a spiritual search, to Strauss, alienation, or exile, became a precondition for philosophy. Strauss discovered how an atheist may remain a loyal Jew: namely, by becoming a philosopher.

But was the philosopher's exile "Jewish"? In the name of authentic religion, Rosenzweig, Strauss, and their generation rebelled against liberal Judaism and historical theology as disingenuous modern hybrids that ignored both the centrality of revelation and belief and the implications of atheism and heresy. Yet belief and heresy were central to Christian theology in ways they never were to Jewish orthopraxis. There was no obvious Jewish parallel, *pace* Rosenzweig and Strauss, to Barth's revaluation of the 19th-century theology that informed their generation. The rebellion of the Weimar Jewish youth was vested in Christian discourse. Historicity exacted vengeance on Strauss. Rejecting historicization in search of universal norms, refusing to admit modern philosophy into Jewish tradition, Strauss was condemned to live the antinomies of revelation and atheism—neither of them obviously Jewish—rather than the comfort of attenuated revelation and historical tradition, the coexistence of religion and philosophy. Would Strauss have taken refuge in the philosopher's exile had he recognized its predominantly Christian origin?[3]

Strauss' decade in the predominantly leftist New School, the émigrés' "university in exile," witnessed the consolidation of his mature philosophy. He developed a distinctive writing style, corresponding to philosophy's need to reveal and conceal at the same time, along with a pedagogic program for training youth to enter into conversation with the great philosophers. He also worked on classical, medieval, and early modern philosophy, some of this work being published only in later years. Sheppard's discussion of Strauss' works subsequent to "Persecution and the Art of Writing" (1941) is less extensive, as his major concern is to elucidate the political import of esoteric writing. Using Strauss' correspondence (especially with Karl Löwith), his 1941 lecture on German nihilism, and his 1962 address, "Why We Remain Jews," Sheppard correctly discerns Strauss' irritation at his colleagues' liberal complacency and his continued ambivalence about democracy. But Sheppard may not appreciate sufficiently Strauss' new commitment to liberal democracy. Strauss' 1941 analysis of National Socialism as a revolt of the closed against the open society and as the vengeance that nihilist youth (bespeaking heroism and a discredited *Kultur*) visited upon civilization is remarkable both for its autobiographical dimension and for its similarities with the theory of a despised liberal protagonist and fellow Central European émigré, the philosopher Karl Popper. Whereas Popper yearned for the open society's triumph, Strauss' affective attachment was to the closed: so-called "open societies" were closed societies in disintegration, he thought. But both believed that the British empire, a bridge between the old and new, represented humanity's best hope.

This was a far cry from Strauss' fascist sympathies during the Weimar years. Although he never expressed regret, Strauss did do *teshuvah* for the rest of his life by educating youth about the imperfectability of politics and the philosopher's responsibility to resist subversion. To be sure, his was not a complete *teshuvah*, and Sheppard rightly suggests that Strauss' esoteric writing, his refusal of open communication, reflected deep mistrust of the liberal public sphere. But it is equally true that, whereas Strauss considered liberal society to be morally inferior to a well-governed aristocratic polis, he also regarded it as the best existing society for philosophers and Jews. Anyone doubting the positive influence of life in the United States on the politics of reactionary émigrés would do well to read the works of the postwar German mandarins—Strauss' teachers—who stayed behind.

Sheppard appropriately ends by quoting from Strauss' introduction to *Natural Right and History* (1950; the Walgreen lectures at Chicago, 1949). Posing as a defender of the Declaration of Independence against historical relativism, of the "self-evident" truth "that all men are created equal" against German philosophy, Strauss proceeds to show how the early modern Natural Right project, which underlay the Declaration, collapses under its own contradictions. This is the embodiment of Strauss' project: philosophy supporting liberal democracy (publicly) while interrogating modernity (surreptitiously). His endorsement of the Declaration is not disingenuous. He may think that Plato's questioning of self-evident democratic truths is on target, yet these have become the foundation of the existing order, political principles that must be avowed just as revelation was by medieval philosophers.

To Strauss, relativism threatens both philosophy and democracy—German nihilism showed as much. In response, he first affirms liberal Natural Right and rejects relativism, then turns the table and interrogates liberal Natural Right. *Natural Right and History* is a multivalent text seeking to persuade on different levels, the introduction written for the beguiled many and the rest of the book for the discerning few. Unsurprisingly, many readers have tired in attempting to negotiate Strauss' subterfuges. There is no need to accept any of his political presuppositions or conclusions in order to recognize that his close readings can be revelatory. Liberals dismissing them off-hand, as my Columbia teacher did, squander a learning opportunity. Sheppard's fascinating trajectory of the philosophical development of the young Strauss should make them rethink their position.

Malachi Hacohen
Duke University

Notes

1. Leora Batnitzky, *Leo Strauss and Emmanuel Levinas: Philosophy and the Politics of Revelation* (New York: 2006); David Janssens, *Between Athens and Jerusalem: Philosophy, Prophecy, and Politics in Leo Strauss's Early Thought* (Albany: 2008); Heinrich Meier, *Carl Schmitt & Leo Strauss: The Hidden Dialogue*, trans. J. Harvey Lomax (Chicago: 1995); Leo Strauss, *The Early Writings (1921–1932)*, ed. and trans. Michael Zank (Albany: 2002); Daniel Tanguay, *Leo Strauss: An Intellectual Biography*, trans. Christopher Nadon (New Haven: 2007).

2. Leo Strauss, "Anmerkungen zu Carl Schmitt, Der Begriff des Politischen," *Archiv für Sozialwissenschaft und Sozialpolitik* 67, no. 6 (1932), 732–749; trans. by Harvey Lomax as "Notes on Carl Schmitt, The Concept of the Political," in Carl Schmitt, *The Concept of the Political*, trans. and annotated George Schwab (Chicago: 2007), 99–126.

3. Nathan Tarcov (University of Chicago) (email correspondence, 7 July 2008) takes exception: "The medieval philosophers through whom Strauss came to understand the philosopher's exile were Jewish and Muslim, not Christian."

Alan M. Wald, *Trinity of Passion: The Literary Left & the Antifascist Crusade*. Chapel Hill: North Carolina University Press, 2007. xviii + 317 pp.

In this, the second volume of a proposed trilogy on the literary left in the United States, Alan Wald produces a vibrant and insightful reading of American sociopolitical literary culture. The book is of interest both as literary criticism and as social history.

In his first volume, *Exiles from a Future Time: The Forging of the Mid-Twentieth-Century Literary Left* (2002), reviewed in this journal in 2004, Wald dealt with writers (most of them poets), who began writing in the early years of the 20th century. This was the period in which Communist politics and party affiliations were first taking hold in the United States. There, as in this later volume, Wald was concerned with what he calls the "elective affinities" among writers—the ways in which individual writers, often with different personal styles and varying sociopolitical, economic, racial, gendered, and religious profiles, nonetheless fit together as "components of a 'humanscape'" (*Trinity*, p. xiv). This humanscape is produced by "force fields" and "networks" of publication, cultural activism, and literary theory (*Exiles*, p. xiv). That is, it is constructed through the many interactive yet decidedly divergent strands that produce anything but a homogeneous group of writers.

"In *Exiles from a Future Time*," Wald explains, "the writers discussed were principally shaped by the interplay of modernist impulses homologous to the 1920s and the feeling of civic emergency induced by the domestic crisis of the early 1930s. In *Trinity of Passion*, most of the authors initiate careers in the middle and later 1930s; they are drawn to what is by this time a dynamic and bustling movement whose predominate theme was opposition to fascism at home and abroad" (p. xiii). This notion of *opposition to* rather than *affiliation with* is one key to the book's own resistance to broad and reductive generalizations. Throughout his study, Wald is concerned with tensions between and among concerns (including literary versus political objectives) rather than with the happy harmonies of purpose such issues might produce. As he notes:

> The argument of *Trinity of Passion* is not that Communism has been the secret glue of U. S. literature in the 1930s, 1940s, and 1950s. To the contrary, Communism, or even political commitment in general, is by itself a deficient and distorting prism through which to view the narrative imagination. Too often a preoccupation with Communist affiliations leads to the deductive fallacy of making presumptions about the artistic process according to the supposed political loyalties of authors. *Trinity of Passion* is

intended to offer a judicious assessment of the intricacy of the lives of those writers in which a shared yet individualized political commitment played an indispensable part. It also aims to consider the implications of the transit through the antifascist crusade that are dispersed across the horizon of mid-twentieth-century literary history (pp. 14–15).

Accordingly, Wald's strategy is to provide detailed biographies of the major figures of the literary left, some of them by now largely forgotten novelists such as Alvah Bessie, William Herrick, John Oliver Killens, Albert Maltz, Irwin Shaw, Ann Petry, and Ruth Seid (Jo Sinclair); others more canonical figures, such as Henry Roth and Arthur Miller; and even a poet or two (Aaron Kramer and Norman Rosten). Wald also includes probing synopses of their writings. Since many of the works of fiction deal with real historical figures, Wald's discussions of the writings introduce still other biographical narratives into the ever-expanding and deepening humanscape.

Each of these stories is told by Wald in loving and exquisitely fine detail. This indepth portraiture gives the work a painterly quality, a feature that is augmented by Wald's inclusion of a fine selection of amazing photographs. His narrative skills as a teller of fascinating stories are prodigious, and the book deserves to be read not least because it is such a fine model of exciting storytelling.

Indeed, the quality and sheer quantity of biographies offered in this book make it impossible to summarize fairly in a review; I would only destroy its fabric by rendering it in paraphrase. Suffice it to say that Wald's humanscape emerges very powerfully as writers and characters are layered onto each other and viewed from perspectives both of juxtaposition and difference and of similarity. Wald treats lesser-known writers within the context of canonical figures; and he treats different groupings of writers in relation to one another. "Tough Jews in the Spanish Civil War," for example—Milton Wolff, Alvah Bessie, and William Herrick—are viewed with Hemingway in mind. Then this entire grouping is placed in relation to African American leftists such as Jon Oliver Killens and Chester Himes (who are discussed in relation to Ralph Ellison); and so on and so forth. Most of Wald's chapters tend to alternate between Jewish American and African American writers, taking into account the interactions between these two groups as well as the various external social and political events (such as the Holocaust) that bring pressure to bear on the writers. Wald also treats such separable issues as gender and sexual preference. (An exception to this structure is the chapter on Arthur Miller, in which Wald deals exclusively with this canonical figure.)

The conclusion to the book is a tour de force and a model of the book as a whole in one condensed reading. Wald brings together the "three lives" of Chester Himes, Dan Levin, and Jo Sinclair as those lives converged in the inaugural issue of a literary quarterly called *Crossroad*. None of these authors, Wald points out, is "cited in literary histories or reference works as principally a writer who had been associated with the Communist movement." Nonetheless, all of their "origins" are "intimately coupled with their early experiences with Communism" (p. 236). Therefore, reading them within the context of the anti-fascist crusade of the 1930s provides insights into their texts that might otherwise be lost to the contemporary reader.

As Wald puts it toward the end of this concluding chapter, looking forward to volume three of the trilogy: "[T]he literature of the antifascist crusade, intermittent in its quality, recounts many stories pivotal to apprehending the lives of idealistic yet diversely flawed men and women committed to the revolutionary fashioning of a better world in the mid-twentieth century" (p. 259). Aspiration is the key to Wald's admiring portraits of his writers, as well as to the writers' own portraits of African and Jewish American men and women, as Wald interprets them. Such a chain of aspirations makes this reader aspire as well to a better, more engaged relationship with America's writers on the left and the world that they created and inhabited.

Emily Budick
The Hebrew University

History and the Social Sciences

Steven E. Aschheim, *Beyond the Border: The German-Jewish Legacy Abroad.* Princeton: Princeton University Press, 2007. xi + 194 pp.

Steven Aschheim has long been interested in borders. His first book dealt with how German Jews viewed their brothers and sisters across the border in Eastern Europe. Eschewing institutional and economic history, he has more recently focused on the inner lives and contributions of uprooted emigré Jewish intellectuals from Germany. In particular, he has lectured and written on Gershom Scholem and on Hannah Arendt. In this volume, consisting of expanded versions of three lectures originally delivered at the University of California, Berkeley, in October 2004, he brings together previous work in a broad, though not lengthy, new study of three categories of displaced German Jewish intellectuals: Zionists who left for Palestine, historians who ended up in the United States, and a third group whose members have gained what Aschheim calls "iconic status." Not only did all three groups migrate beyond the physical borders of Germany, not less significantly, all of them in some sense transgressed the invisible borders of conventional thought.

    The first chapter focuses on German Jews who ended up in Palestine, some by choice and before the Nazi period (Scholem, Shmuel Hugo Bergman, Arthur Ruppin, Ernst Simon, Hans Kohn), others, though Zionists, mostly in response to Nazi oppression (Robert Weltsch, Martin Buber). What interests Aschheim about these men is that they all gravitated to the binational solution for the Arab-Jewish problem that was advocated first by Brit Shalom and then by the Ichud. Yoram Hazony has portrayed these individuals and their organizations as traitorous to Zionism; Aschheim, in contrast, is sympathetic, if not admiring, especially of those who, unlike Kohn and Arendt, stuck it out in Palestine despite efforts by the East European establishment to exclude them from positions of power and influence. He weighs various explanations for these Central European immigrants' attraction to a humanitarian, if probably naïve, dream of Arab-Jewish harmony, finally concluding broadly that, however much they may have rejected the bourgeois liberalism of German Jewry, it was that Jewry's ideal of spiritual and moral cultivation (the *Bildung* so much stressed in the writings of Aschheim's teacher, George Mosse) that best accounts for their rejection of chauvinism and their willingness to adopt an unpopular and unreciprocated ideology.

Of the large number of German Jews who reached the United States, Aschheim has chosen to focus on four historians: Mosse, Peter Gay, Walter Laqueur, and Fritz Stern (the last formally a Christian, though judged a Jew by Nazi racial standards). Not only did they spend most of their lives beyond the borders of their native Germany, their historiography, though certainly varied, crossed the border from a dominant social history, developed by non-Jewish historians in Germany in the 1960s, into the realm of a new cultural history that, while aware of social context, focused on the influence of ideas and the historical agency of persons rather than forces. Beyond method, the two groups of historians were divided on purpose. The social historians were determined to explain conditions that led to 1933; the cultural historians were more concerned to understand the ideological trends that produced, or at least contributed to, the collapse of Weimar democracy. Clearly, if social structures and processes were at fault, guilt was, at best, diffuse; if ideology mattered, then one could point to persons who invented or espoused it. Was it the German, the Jewish, or the American experience that resulted in their particular insights? In various measures it was undoubtedly all three, even if the affirmation of Jewishness in most of them possessed little positive content. Although eventually the German social historians began to reassess the work of their emigrated Jewish colleagues, Aschheim rightly deplores their very limited reception in Germany, especially that of Mosse.

The third chapter is devoted to a more diverse group of intellectuals: Theodor Adorno, Hannah Arendt, Walter Benjamin, Franz Rosenzweig, Leo Strauss, and (again) Gershom Scholem. They are not united by discipline or by country of emigration (Rozenzweig died in Germany; Benjamin committed suicide during a failed flight from the Nazis). Aschheim's reason for bringing them together is because they all became icons for western intellectuals and continue to possess that status down to the present. In the case of Arendt, Aschheim rightly notes, adulation has taken on the trappings of a cult; Benjamin is a favorite of name-droppers. Aschheim explains this extraordinary prominence within the framework of an idealized image of Weimar culture as well as, in the case of Arendt, feminism, and in that of Strauss, the rise of a conservative intellectualism in the United States. But that is not to deny their individual virtues: they were all thinkers "beyond the border," each, in a particular way, original—or, to use Aschheim's term: heretical. One might add that they also had a penchant for obscure writing that lent itself to multiple interpretation, a virtue for postmodernists. Toward the end, Aschheim asks an interesting question: why does a liberal society make icons of intellectuals who were so critical of its failings? And how could the unreconstructed liberal, Isaiah Berlin, attain similar status? Aschheim's answer is that we iconicize both types because intellectuals (and surely Aschheim himself) tend to be simultaneously pursuers of complex, troubling truths and seekers of safety within the bounded freedoms of liberalism.

To the icons Aschheim discusses one could add others. Einstein, Freud, and Kafka come immediately to mind, though one could argue over whether they fit into the category of intellectuals. Aschheim might have qualified the originality of the emigrant Jewish historians by considering that Peter Viereck had written of the ideological roots of the Nazi mind well before Stern and Mosse. A more careful proofreading would have removed the excessive typographical errors, especially in the extensive and helpful notes. But the final conclusion must be that Aschheim has successfully presented and analyzed a complex subject, one that carries immense dangers of false generalization, and has carried it off with the requisite nuance and care. *Beyond the Borders* is itself an outstanding example of cultural history.

Michael A. Meyer
Hebrew Union College-Jewish Institute of Religion, Cincinnati

Jocelyn Cohen and Daniel Soyer (eds.), *My Future Is in America: Autobiographies of Eastern European Jews*. New York: New York University Press, 2005. 368 pp.

In 1942, the Yiddish Scientific Institute, or YIVO (then based in New York City), organized an autobiography contest for immigrant Jews. Contestants were to write their life stories, explaining specifically why they left Europe and what they had accomplished in America. A total of 223 people (176 men and 47 women) submitted manuscripts ranging in length from a few sheets to hundreds of pages. About 90 percent of them were written in Yiddish, with the rest in English, Hebrew, and German. Garment workers, shopkeepers, housewives, professionals, and communal activists were among the participants. Their manuscripts—treasures of information about Jewish life in Eastern Europe and the United States—would sit in YIVO's archives for more than six decades, read mainly by scholars. *My Future Is in America* brings nine of these autobiographies, carefully translated and edited by Jocelyn Cohen and Daniel Soyer, to the English-reading public for the first time. It is a highly important volume that should prove valuable to researchers, students, and lay readers alike.

In an introductory essay, Cohen and Soyer explain that, consciously or not, YIVO's contestants wrote in one of three autobiographical genres. The first (although the least influential, it seems to me) was that of the East European Haskalah, in which the author struggles to obtain "worldly knowledge beyond or in opposition to traditional Judaism" (p. 10).[1] That core theme is indeed evident in the YIVO autobiographies, but considering that few of the contestants appear to have read maskilic autobiographies, it probably derived from other, more immediate, sources—one of them being "Socialist autobiography" (p. 10). According to the conventions of this second genre, the narrator begins as an unenlightened worker, blind to the forces of capitalism, and becomes a devoted socialist through a sudden conversion. The themes of socialist autobiography are evident in the YIVO collection because, as Cohen and Soyer explain, many of the authors were members of the Workmen's Circle, the largest left-wing fraternal order, which encouraged its members to participate in the contest. Members of the Workmen's Circle would have absorbed a socialist conceptual structure for understanding their own lives from years of constant exposure to socialist speeches, articles, and, at least for some, autobiographies. A third, and final, tradition influencing YIVO's contestants was the American "bootstraps" narrative, in which a poor immigrant of any given ethnic background rises economically through individual initiative and hard work (p. 12). Whereas the socialist genre defines success in terms of self-development and commitment to social justice, the bootstraps narrative stresses the accumulation of wealth.

Although diametrically opposed as genres, the bootstraps and socialist narratives were actually intermingled in immigrant Jewish autobiographies, as Cohen and Soyer observe. It is perhaps a peculiarity of immigrant Jewry that many of its members gravitated toward socialism while striving at the same time for success in business, a phenomenon that Soyer has analyzed at length in an important article published in the journal *Labor History*.[2] A determination to leave the ranks of wage labor, in other words, did not necessarily preclude a commitment to social justice. Thus, Minnie Goldstein, who settled in Providence, Rhode Island, writes of teaching herself how to read the socialist daily *Forverts* (which she took to as "a fish takes to water" [p. 31]), learning English, becoming a landlady, and sending her two sons to college. Goldstein was a lifelong member of the Workmen's Circle. Although her husband did not fare as well in business, having failed four times at becoming self-employed, the family "always had enough to live on" and Minnie felt proud of her role in supporting the family (p. 31). Similarly, Ben Reisman, who won first place in YIVO's contest, was an active Socialist party member his entire life, even as he prospered in real estate and the sheet metal business in Pittsburgh. In his concluding paragraph, Reisman affirmed his belief that "more than in earlier times ... the social democratic principle is best for humanity" (p. 102). Both Reisman and Goldstein also expressed hope that a Jewish homeland would be created in Palestine.

Although the authors represented in *My Future Is in America* followed certain autobiographical traditions, their narratives reflect a diversity of individual experiences. For instance, while many of the authors emigrated from Eastern Europe for economic reasons, contingencies played a role in shaping their choices. Thus Rose Schoenfeld and her family did not simply leave Galicia because they were poor. In their case, the family actually prospered after the discovery of oil in their town, only to lose its wealth as a consequence of poor judgment, intrafamilial conflicts, and bad luck. Other Jews in the town, however, successfully exploited the opportunities supplied by industrialization. Had the Schoenfelds been able to do the same, Rose probably would not have immigrated to the United States. Accounts like hers provide rich details of family relations, the immigration process, work, religion, intellectual awakening, and political activism.

My Future Is in America does not represent a cross-section of immigrants: secular and left-wing Jews were more apt to respond to YIVO's call, as were those who considered themselves successful (however defined) versus those who did not make it in America. (Cohen and Soyer, however, did ensure that women were well represented: of the nine authors included in this volume, five are women.) Yet Cohen and Soyer correctly note that, "taken collectively, these autobiographies present a dynamic portrait of an immigrant generation in its encounter with an epic historical moment, and they testify to the power of storytelling as a historical practice" (p. 2).

Tony Michels
University of Wisconsin-Madison

Notes

1. Page numbers refer to the hardcover edition. A paperback edition was published by New York University Press in 2008.
2. Daniel Soyer, "Class Conscious Workers as Immigrant Entrepreneurs: The Ambiguity of Class among Eastern European Jewish Immigrants to the United States at the Turn of the Twentieth Century," *Labor History* 42, no. 1 (2001), 45–59.

Henry L. Feingold, *"Silent No More": Saving the Jews of Russia, the American Jewish Effort, 1967–1989*. Syracuse: Syracuse University Press, 2007. 400 pp.

The international attempt to extricate Jews from the Soviet Union during the last third of the 20th century will surely be recorded as one of the major movements in modern Jewish history. Not only did a remarkable number of Soviet Jews take part in the emigration, but the coordinated effort on the part of many people in the United States, Canada, Israel, Great Britain, France and other European as well as South American countries was almost unprecedented. While Henry Feingold's *Silent No More* deals specifically with the American Jewish effort, he would have been well advised to give some attention to the impressively international nature of the campaign.

To his credit, Feingold makes it very clear that, in the United States, a pivotal role was played not only by various cooperating (and sometimes competing) Jewish organizations, but also by individuals who were not at all Jewish. As he points out, many of the key players in Congressional attempts to convince or pressure the Soviets to liberalize their emigration policy, most famously Henry Jackson, were non-Jews representing an overwhelmingly non-Jewish constituency. Without these people, there would have been far less leverage exerted on the Soviet leadership.

Indeed, one of the best aspects of this highly informative book is the historic approach that Feingold, a well-known expert on American Jewish history, brings to his study. In his first chapter, Feingold reviews earlier American Jewish campaigns in comparison with the efforts on behalf of Soviet Jewish emigration that took place in the 1970s and 1980s. In the 19th and early 20th centuries, he points out, congressmen and Christian leaders spoke out against the tsarist government in defense of positions espoused by American Jewish activists. "The strategy," he writes, "was to project the campaigns for abrogation [of the Russian Extradition Treaty of 1887] as not a Jewish fight but an American one" (p. 12). Similarly, during Richard Nixon's presidency, the congressional fight for the addition of the Jackson-Vanik amendment to the trade bill was couched in terms of human rights and was supported by non-Jewish public figures as well as by Jews. In general, this chapter provides considerable historical insight as it harkens back to the early days of the formation of American Jewish community interests. Then, as in the 1970s, various Jewish groups (and individuals) struggled for power and fought over turf even when pursuing a common goal.

In the postwar years, many American Jews looked back on the period of the late 1930s and the war with strong feelings of regret—the Jews at that time, they believed, had not done enough to save their coreligionists from the Holocaust. Thus, the campaign to "save" Soviet Jews can be seen as an attempt to correct a previous failing and rehabilitate the Jewish community. Furthermore, participation in the campaign came, in a way, to fulfill the need for a strong communal tie, a connection that, for many Jews, had been fading in the postwar era.

Feingold discusses all the intricacies connected with the campaign for the Jackson-Vanik amendment, a piece of legislation that was noteworthy for its linkage of human rights issues with U.S. economic policy. The amendment to what would become the Trade Reform Act of 1974 was first introduced in 1972 as a reaction to the hefty education tax that the Soviet government had begun to impose on would-be Jewish émigrés who possessed a post-secondary school education. According to the terms of the amendment, "most favored nation status" (which enabled trading partners to enjoy particular trade and credit benefits) would be denied any country practicing a restrictive emigration policy. Both Nixon and Secretary of State Henry Kissinger opposed the amendment, but it was eventually passed, though the trade act was only signed into law in January 1975, under the administration of President Gerald Ford. Long before that happened, the Soviets had already backed down on the education tax, which was in force for less than a year. Feingold refers to Marshall Goldman as saying, with reference to linkage, that the best results were achieved when the bargaining was still going on. In a positive assessment of the Jackson-Vanik amendment, Feingold notes (in several places) that it catapulted the Soviet Jewish issue onto the world stage. This may be true, but if Jackson-Vanik is judged on the basis of results, it must be deemed a failure: in the years following its passage, the number of Soviet emigrants declined markedly.

Notwithstanding, other attempts grew out of the Jackson-Vanik amendment, most prominently the inclusion of the right to emigrate as part of Basket III of the Helsinki Agreement, which dealt with humanitarian issues including free emigration and the unification of families. Feingold treats this subject thoroughly, as he does the whole issue of "drop-outs," that is, the question of whether Jews leaving the Soviet Union on Israeli travel documents had the moral right to change their route upon reaching Vienna. On this issue, Feingold traces the conflicting positions of numerous American Jewish groups as well as that of the Israeli government. Israel, as he points out, was intent on amassing as many Soviet Jewish immigrants as possible in order to bolster the Jewish population of the country, even if it meant taking away their right to choose their destination. Ironically, after so much effort on the part of American Jews to open up the gates to Jewish immigration, the Israelis, under prime ministers Menachem Begin and Yitzhak Shamir, did their utmost to convince the United States to close them.

Whereas *Silent No More* is in many ways a well thought-out and useful book, it is far from perfect. Feingold is relatively reliable when he writes about the United States but much less so when he discusses matters connected with the Soviet Union. It is instructive that, in his acknowledgments, he does not thank anyone for going over his manuscript. It is to be assumed that he did not show his work to a competent colleague; had he done so, myriad errors might have been caught and corrected. It also seems to be the case that, at Syracuse University Press (where Feingold serves as editor of the Modern Jewish History Series), the decision was made to leave the editing in his hands. Various typographical and syntactical errors might have been avoided had the publisher done an adequate job of editing and proofreading.

In the interests of scholarship, here is a very small sample of the errors to be found in this book. Although he uses the term correctly in some contexts, there are many instances in which Feingold uses "refusenik" (referring to someone actually denied an exit visa) when he really means "activist." The Jewish Anti-Fascist Committee was set up in the Soviet Union in 1942, not in 1943. Although Feingold refers to the trial of the so-called "killer doctors" in the 1953 Doctors Plot, no trial ever took place; those who had survived imprisonment were simply released after Stalin's death in March of that year. Although twice referred to as "President," Levi Eshkol was in fact the prime minister of Israel. The well-known dissident Vladimir Bukovskii was not involved in the Leningrad hijacking. Mikhail Zand emigrated to Israel in 1971, not in 1970. Potential emigrants in the 1970s did not need to receive an invitation from a first-degree relative in Israel, but rather from someone who merely appeared to be a relative. The well-known refusenik and Israeli politician is Yulii (not Yuri) Edelstein.

Although this book covers many of the issues connected with the struggle for Jewish emigration from the Soviet Union, there remains a need for a serious global study of the movement. Such a work would synthesize not only the accounts of all the efforts made by various organized groups in the United States, Israel, and elsewhere on behalf of Soviet Jews, but also those of the activists, who carried out their campaign—at great personal cost to themselves and their families—from within the Soviet Union.

Edith Rogovin Frankel
The Hebrew University

Marcie Cohen Ferris and Mark I. Greenberg (eds.), *Jewish Roots in Southern Soil: A New History.* Waltham: Brandeis University Press, 2006. xiii + 384 pp.

For more than a generation, scholars of Southern Jewish history have cogently argued that there is much more to the American Jewish saga than the big city (and especially, New York) experience. Indeed, the case has been made that there is an intriguing and complex story to be told about this region's stable, limited Jewish population, where the small numbers of Jews was a major factor accounting for how they constructed their social lives and maintained or reformulated their religious practices. Southern Jewish historians also have averred that their community's saga of communal survival, cultural adaptation, and accommodation to their host society is unparalleled in America. Here, however, their contention of special status is less than fully convincing. The essays that appear in *Jewish Roots in Southern Soil: A New History*, most of which are well-conceived and executed, both assert and question the concept of Southern exceptionalism.

Hasia Diner's important essay, which revisits the oft-told saga of immigrant Jewish peddler-community builders, implicitly argues against the notion of exceptionalism. As she reminds us, these intrepid fellows (in America, it seems, all of these adventurous entrepreneurs were men) took household goods from established urban areas to the countryside, where they serviced frontier customers. In many instances those who were successful at their enterprise opted to sink their roots in developing towns that later became cities, and the more observant among them became forces in the incipient local Jewish religious life. Yet these Southern merchants' experiences were quite similar to those of their archetypal Midwestern counterparts. Diner is quick to point out that this form of Jewish economic activity was also international in nature, being a particularly robust enterprise in early 19th-century German locales.

Gary Phillip Zola's exploration of the ascendancy of Reform Judaism in the postbellum South raises its own questions concerning what is unique to that region. In explaining how and why three early American synagogues south of the Mason-Dixon line transformed their ritual approach to Judaism while three comparable congregations up north retained their fidelity to traditional practices, Zola argues that a distinctive set of circumstances prevailed in the South. The Jews in Charleston, Richmond, and Savannah feared being viewed and judged as "aliens," were "in relative isolation" from one another, and "lived constantly within a Christian context," unlike their counterparts in Philadelphia, New York, and Newport, Rhode Island. Yet Zola's essay succeeds only in documenting the ways in which these smaller cities differed from the northeastern

Jewish metropolises of New York and Philadelphia. (Newport and its historic synagogue had a totally idiosyncratic history of rise and decline.) If anything, the process that Zola describes—that of three Southern congregations oscillating over time in their feelings toward traditional Jewish religious practices and moving fitfully down the road toward Reform—is highly reminiscent of synagogue experiences all over the United States at that time. Coping with their minority status among the Christian majority and often isolated, Jews nearly everywhere "Americanized" their houses of worship, often to a radical degree.

Similarly, while Stuart Rockoff's evocative examination of the economic and ecological changes that caused Southern Jews, in the post-Second World War era, to abandon the towns and areas of their birth is surely a Southern story, it is concomitantly the saga of the decline of Jewish life in Northeastern and Midwestern rust-belt environments and of group relocation in Sunbelt locales, including that very different southern city—Miami.

In the end, what makes the Southern Jewish experience special is its constant and compelling intersection with the dominant theme in that region's history: race relations. To be sure, this enduring American dilemma is a part of Jewish history elsewhere in this country—including New York, where Jews and blacks have been both allies and foes. However, it was in the South that the issue of race most dramatically and directly influenced the ways in which Jews, whether newly arrived immigrants or longstanding residents, ordered their lives, found their places within the host society, and understood their own status as a minority group. In this realm of scholarship, two essays—that of Eric Goldstein, which focuses on Southern Jews during the era of Jim Crow, and that of Clive Webb, which carries this tangled story well into the 20th-century desegregation era—are the most comprehensive and instructive contributions to this volume. It is this central theme of race, appearing repeatedly in the essays as a whole, that accords a unique dimension to *Jewish Roots in Southern Soil*, which thus offers an important contribution to American Jewish historiography.

Jeffrey S. Gurock
Yeshiva University

Robin Judd, *Contested Rituals: Circumcision, Kosher Butchering, and Jewish Political Life in Germany, 1843–1933.* Ithaca: Cornell University Press, 2007. 296 pp.

It began in 1843 with a few fathers who refused to circumcise their sons. Following a number of widely reported injuries and infections in the German lands, these fathers—unsurprisingly, some of them were physicians—were afraid to harm their children by submitting them to the ritual of Jewish circumcision (*brit milah*). Their rebellion and subsequent battle to have their uncircumcised sons acknowledged as members of the local Jewish communities opened a public debate involving rabbis, community officials, and physicians, Jews and non-Jews alike, throughout the German lands. At the time, circumcision served not only as a symbol of the covenant but as a condition for a Jewish male's being written into the communal birth registries. When rabbis refused to register the children, the concerned families turned to the city municipalities, and the debate shifted from being an internal communal issue to one involving Jewish versus state law.

Opening her work with a discussion of the various circumcision disputes of 1843 and the years that immediately followed, Robin Judd goes on to develop a whole new narrative of German Jewish life within the context of the longstanding debates regarding both circumcision and another central Jewish rite, kosher slaughtering (*shehitah*). Apart from sharing several important characteristics—both involve sharp knifes and a certain amount of bloodshed—circumcision and kosher slaughtering are essential markers of Jewish difference; as such, they became a natural subject of controversy in the age of emancipation and integration. Against the background of German nation-building, the debates on religious and administrative autonomy versus governmental involvement gained growing significance for Germans and German Jews alike.

Spanning more than four generations (from 1843 to 1933) of drastic social and economic changes, the debates on circumcision and kosher slaughtering reflect an entire spectrum of political agitation on the part of Jewish communal institutions and the wider German society. Relying on extensive documentation including communal records, court documents, medical records, memoirs, newspaper reports, and even cartoons, Judd successfully links administrative and religious questions with the growing importance of medicalization and racial antisemitism. To be sure, similar debates occurred throughout Europe during the 19th century, but the issue aroused the greatest and most enduring controversy in Germany. In contrast to the common approach that regards Jewish religious practice as a marginal phenomenon among post-emancipatory Judaism, Judd demonstrates "why rituals matter" in the process of examining German Jewish life as a whole. Moving her scholarly gaze away from a "traditional dependence on texts written by members of the German-Jewish intelligentsia" (p.14), she has produced a book that is cultural history at its best.

As Judd shows, the German-Jewish debates on circumcision were greatly influenced by contemporary trends such as the Jewish Reform movement and the "medicalization" of society. Whereas the impact of the anti-traditionalist Reform movement was mainly part of an internal Jewish discourse, the involvement of physicians opened the question of circumcision to a general public. Jewish and non-Jewish medical authorities became involved in disputes on the benefits versus the hazards of circumcision, as part of a general affirmation of Jewish physical difference. Not coincidentally, this all occurred during a period of integration and growing legal equality, when Jews as a group became far less visible in German society.

Although the situation in the periods before and after unification differed in various German lands, Judd identifies a general tendency toward increased government intervention: from overseeing birth registers to training and licensing the *mohelim* and, subsequently, influencing various hygienic aspects of the circumcision rite. Under the influence of animal protectionist groups, a parallel debate emerged in the 1860s with regard to kosher butchering, which resulted in state licensing and regulation of the *shohatim*. At the same time, the general discussion regarding both rites shifted to the broader issue of the alleged cruelty of Jewish rites versus the ideal of religious tolerance. Time and again the question was raised as to how far Jewish religious practices were compatible with the culture of a unified Germany.

From the 1880s until the First World War, the public discourse on Jewish ritual focused mainly on *shehitah*. Over time, both the rhetoric and the official response to it became increasingly radicalized. In 1892, for instance, the kingdom of Saxony made illegal the slaughtering of an animal without first stunning it; since stunning animals is forbidden according to Jewish law, kosher slaughtering was effectively banned. The widespread debate that followed—involving newspapers, the Reichstag, and the state parliaments—was avidly followed by the German middle class, and it largely internalized the rhetoric of race science, radical antisemitism, and German nationalism. As Judd demonstrates, there was a gap between ideology and practice: kosher slaughtering was not banned outside of Saxony. Yet Jewish communities understood the legislation in Saxony as a troubling precedent and responded with newly assertive forms of political behavior. In the counter-campaign launched on behalf of *shehitah*, Jews were supported by a number of scientists and inventors of animal-friendly methods of slaughtering such as "Niederlegen" (shackling) apparatuses, and (surprisingly) the Catholic center party. Such lobbying was ultimately successful in preventing a nationwide ban as well as in repealing the Saxonian ban and other local anti-*shehitah* initiatives.

Ongoing Jewish efforts to safeguard the ritual of kosher butchering in the years following the First World War reflected the internal contradictions of the Weimar republic. Overall, however, religious freedom was respected by Weimar Germany; despite continual attacks on Jewish ritual slaughtering, no laws were passed against it. Only in 1930 was another public campaign launched against *shehitah*, which eventually resulted in the April 1933 ban on kosher slaughtering by the Nazi government. Even then, the debate regarding Jewish rituals continued. While Nazi officials expounded on the theme of Jewish cruelty, Jewish rabbis and communal leaders engaged in an internal debate regarding the extent to which the halakhah might be adjusted to the circumstances, as well as the best means to distribute whatever kosher meat was still available.

Following her discussion of ninety years of German debates on Jewish ritual questions, Judd draws an important conclusion: post-emancipatory German Judaism was never restricted to the private sphere, as evidenced by the ongoing involvement of government officials, politicians, and the press. Her ambitious project to examine ritual questions in order to "complicate and de-exceptionalize the Jewish experience in Germany" (p. 11) is both impressive and successful.

Mirjam Zadoff
University of Munich

Victor Karady, *The Jews of Europe in the Modern Era: A Socio-Historical Outline*. Budapest: CEU Press, 2004. xix + 474 pp.

The Jews of Europe in the Modern Era has had many lives. First written in French, Karady's text initially appeared in German translation (1999), then in Spanish and Hungarian (2000), and now, in a revised and expanded edition, in English (2004). The publication history of Karady's book reflects its far-reaching content, which cogently analyzes the structural transformations of European Jewry from the 18th century to the present, with data drawn from cases as disparate as liberal England and Bolshevik Russia. The book's four long chapters examine demography and social stratification, Jewish emancipation, identity strategies after the Haskalah, and antisemitism and the Shoah; a long epilogue ties together these themes for the era after 1945. Lucidly written and well translated, Karady's book offers many important insights into the main historical processes and structures of the modern era.

The first chapter is a tour de force that draws upon Karady's earlier research into educational and professional stratification. After first describing the demographic foundations of European Jewry, Karady outlines the main economic and sociological transformations of the 19th century. As part of this analysis, he provides compelling answers to fundamental questions: Why did Jews choose to live in cities more readily than non-Jews? What accounts for the particular Jewish occupational structure in the modern era? Why were Jews statistically overrepresented in gymnasia, universities, and a wide range of cultural initiatives? In Karady's telling, the marginal and threatened position of Jews in all European societies defined nearly everything that followed. Yet the book also draws attention to the long-term importance of religious practices (keeping kosher, for example), Jewish traditions of literacy and learning, and the skills honed in the narrow occupational niches that were available to them before emancipation—all of which combined to make Jews the agents of modernization across much of 19th-century Europe. One of the pleasures of Karady's book is its analysis of less obvious phenomena, and this chapter offers interesting asides on Jews' traditional aversion to alcohol, conspicuous consumption, and physical violence.

The book's middle section covers Jewish emancipation (ch. 2) and Jews' individual and collective responses to it (ch. 3). Although Karady stresses that Jewish integration into wider societies faced obstacles across the continent, the discussion of emancipation maintains a familiar distinction between Western and Eastern Europe. In the West, relatively stable, centralized states with homogenous cultures offered a clear path to linguistic and cultural assimilation, whereas in the East, states such as Russia and Romania resisted Jewish emancipation and sanctioned anti-Jewish violence. Karady's most illuminating analysis focuses on Central Europe, where enlightened absolutism opened an era of social integration and gradual emancipation, but where the multiethnic environment held both rewards and risks for assimilating Jews, who often had to "choose sides" in the increasingly fierce competition among national groups. But as the following chapter on identity construction shows plainly, Jews everywhere in Europe grappled daily with the many challenges associated with assimilation, which Karady characterizes as a "life strategy that often demanded the daily mobilization of energies" (p. 113) and as one that was ultimately "an impossible undertaking" (p. 205). Karady offers a subtle exploration of the Jews' many responses to the growing crisis of assimilation, including psychic disturbances and pathologies (Jewish "self-hatred"), as well as the founding of new political movements at the turn of the 20th century (Agudath Israel, the Bund, and Zionism). This section also features brief biographical sketches of Theodor Herzl and Max Nordau (pp. 262–263), which stand out in a volume that otherwise pays little attention to individual agency.

The final chapter traces the emergence of a virulent antisemitism in the last decades of the 19th century and follows its path to the Holocaust. Here Karady's focus shifts from long-term processes and structural transformations to the realm of ideology and images. Karady defines antisemitism "as nothing but a basic ideological disposition in certain sections of modern societies, an attitudinal factor, an in-built need, the 'reasons' for which are merely the products of contingent rationalizations" (p. 303). For him, modern antisemitism in all its forms can be traced back to Christian doctrines that defined Jews as radically "other" and provided a justification for abuses and violence against them. The bulk of the chapter surveys the various functionalist models of antisemitism (scapegoating, antisemitism as a "cultural code," and so on), the topoi of antisemitic discourse, and the genealogy of racial theory from Gobineau to Hitler. Here, too, Karady includes many insights, as with his brief explanation of why soccer matches have so often provoked crude displays of antisemitism (pp. 315–316).

The Jews of Modern Europe closes with a long epilogue of nearly 70 pages. In it, Karady surveys the radically altered demographic landscape after the Shoah, the changing definitions of Jewishness that have emerged in the past sixty years, and the "philo-Semitic turn of sorts" (p. 441) that has defined postwar Jewish social life, particularly in Western Europe. In the book's final pages, however, Karady strikes a more pessimistic tone, warning against the belief that "all danger of a destructive reaction to Jewish 'otherness' has passed" (p. 454). The conclusion is in fact a mere two pages, and if there is a fault with this book, it is the lack of a sustained introduction and conclusion, both to the book as a whole and to the individual chapters. Karady does supply a country-by-country bibliography and, less helpfully, biographical notes (a good index would have been much more useful). One suspects that the length of his book may have kept Karady from using footnotes: their absence, however, means that readers may not always appreciate the many areas in which he is breaking new ground and the points on which he disagrees with the existing historiography (the text does not mention any contemporary scholars by name). But these distractions do not take away from his original and thought-provoking analysis of important questions at the heart of modern Jewish history.

Robert Nemes
Colgate University

Richard Mendelsohn and Milton Shain, *The Jews in South Africa: An Illustrated History.* Johannesburg: Jonathan Ball Publishers, 2008. 215 pp.

On the face of it, a book belonging to the genre of "illustrated histories" might not merit review in as judiciously selective an academic journal as *Studies in Contemporary Jewry*. However, this work should not be mistaken for just another beautifully illustrated coffee-table book. Indeed, therein lies its extraordinary merit; for its authors, Richard Mendelsohn and Milton Shain, both accomplished historians at the University of Cape Town, have produced a veritable model of the illustrated history genre of historiography at its best. As well as having broad public appeal, the book provides a coherent and well-nigh exhaustive synthesis of all the professional historical research ever done on South African Jewry, alongside the authors' own original and insightful contributions. Written with elegance and admirable economy and illustrated most discerningly with photographs and concisely composed sidebars (including cameo biographies, source extracts, and vignettes relating to well-known controversies and events), this book exposes to a wide audience an up-to-date, authoritative historical narrative of the Jews in South Africa. Although not following standard academic footnoting methods, the detailed subject-by-subject bibliographical listing at the book's end is perfectly adequate.

The Jews in South Africa opens with a brief chapter tracing the arrival and early activities of Jews who came mostly from, or via, Britain in the course of the 19th century. Following this is a well-informed narrative of the origins and characteristics of South African Jewry's formative wave of "Litvak" (Lithuanian) immigration, which is richly supplemented by sidebars on a variety of engaging subjects. An example is the important role of the Poor Jews' Temporary Shelter in London in the migration passage from Lithuania. Another example is the self-interested role of Sir Donald Currie's Castle Line shipping company in the promotion of Jewish migration to South Africa. True to the authors' declared intention of telling the story "warts and all," one also finds an intriguing description of the Jewish underworld in the early immigration years, which draws upon the innovative research of South Africa's foremost social historian, Charles van Onselen. This history features the infamous Joe Silver, whose notorious career in the criminal underworld was of international scope.

Two richly documented chapters are devoted to the period 1930 to the present. The first, covering the period 1930 to 1970, focuses on rising antisemitic agitation that created a grave "Jewish Question" in South Africa and on the peak years of apartheid; the second deals with the period from about 1970 until the 1990s. The authors' conceptualization of South African Jewry's historical experience is encapsulated in their choice of titles for these chapters. The first is titled "South African Jews," implying the predominant drive to conform quiescently to the dominant white minority's norms, including apartheid. By contrast, the inverse title, "Jewish South Africans," is given to the period after 1970 (sometimes described as the era of "reformed apartheid"), implying a new Jewish self-confidence and rising expressions of discomfort with apartheid. These manifestations have led to an outward embrace of the new non-racial South Africa, as well as an internal reassertion of Jewish identity, mainly expressed in greater religiosity and community coherence.

Throughout, the authors admirably live up to their declared intention of attempting "to encompass a broad swathe of Jewish life, from the *bimah* and the board-room to the bowling green" (p. ix). Indeed, every significant aspect of Jewish life is given discerning attention. The innovative and prodigiously productive entrepreneurial, commercial, industrial, literary, and professional achievements of individual South African Jews is examined; all of which amount manifestly to a record at least as impressive, in proportionate terms, as that of Jews in the United States. So, too, are the manifold social, charitable, cultural, and sports activities of Jews; the dominating stance of the Orthodox religious majority in relation to minority Reform Judaism; the energetic activities of the Zionist movement; the special role of women in the community and in politics; the effects on South African Jewry of the sharp vacillations in their country's relations with Israel, and much more.

Of course, a book limited in length to about 200 pages, much of which is taken up by photographic illustrations, is bound to disappoint those who expect it to encompass every personality of note, as if it were an encyclopedia. At the same time, it may well fall short of the demands of scholars who seek both analytical profundity and a comparative analysis of common issues facing South African Jewry and Jewish communities in other parts of the world. The foremost of such issues is how Jews behave when they share in the privileges of a societal and political system based on legalized racial discrimination. This marks the very unusual, although not absolutely unique, historical experience of South African Jewry, especially under the infamous apartheid regime from 1948 until 1994. This is one of several subjects on which the authors fall short of analytical depth. In a section devoted to what they describe as "roads to radicalism" they limit themselves to a superficial reference to various explanations that have been offered to account for the paradoxical fact that Jews were significantly overrepresented in the ranks of the radical opposition to apartheid, yet such Jews were generally alienated from the organized Jewish community.

A noteworthy feature of this work is the special attention Mendelsohn and Shain pay to the relationship between historical writing and collective memory. In this respect, two interrelated features of their narrative conceptualization are discernible. One is the relative de-emphasis of the near hegemonic status of Zionism and profound identification with Israel in the history of this community. The other is a contrasting narrative emphasis that conveys the impression of pervasive Jewish rejection of the apartheid regime and self-confident "at-homeness" and well-being in post-apartheid South Africa. The authors point out that Jewish collective memory during the apartheid era was nourished by contemporary historical writings, most notably the book *The Jews in South Africa: A History*, edited by Gustav Saron and Louis Hotz and published in 1955. Noting that such writing promoted a "usable past" that encouraged conformism to the racial social order and political quietism, they go on to say that since the demise of apartheid, "South African Jewry has begun to grapple with its past. ... What was formerly disquieting or even taboo has been recovered, valorized and often proudly publicized. In particular, Jewish radicalism, once embarrassing to the community and requiring explaining away, has been given pride of place in the search for a new 'usable past' " (p.198). Indeed, the book under review provides proof of the perceptiveness of the authors' observation.

Gideon Shimoni
The Hebrew University

Emanuel Trevisan Semi, *Jacques Faitlovitch and the Jews of Ethiopia*. London: Vallentine Mitchell, 2007. 204 pp.

Emanuela Trevisan Semi has written what is, to date, the definitive work on Jacques Faitlovitch (1881–1955). Also known as Yaacov Faitlovitch or simply Dr. Faitlovitch (it is interesting that Semi has chosen to use his French name, without his academic title), Faitlovitch is best known as "the father of the Falashas"—the Ethiopian Jews (or Beta Israel).[1]

Faitlovitch was born in the Polish city of Lodz, and moved to Paris to study Semitic languages under Joseph Halévy, a professor of Ge'ez at the Sorbonne. Like his doctoral supervisor, Faitlovitch traveled to Ethiopia, where he, too, came into contact with the Beta Israel. His first journey, which Semi calls "Faitlovitch's First Mission among the Falashas," was undertaken in 1904 with the support of the French banker Baron Edmond de Rothschild. Faitlovitch returned to Ethiopia in 1908, following which he wrote a detailed book on the plight of the "Abyssinian Jews."[2] All in all, he made eleven journeys to Ethiopia —most of them documented by Semi in exquisite detail—and he brought a total of 25 students back with him to study in the capital cities of Europe and the Middle East. In addition, he put together a collection of dozens of Ethiopian manuscripts, objects, and books (now located in the Sourasky library at Tel Aviv University). Faitlovitch also established committees on behalf of the Falashas in Europe and the United States and mobilized the international community, Jewish and non-Jewish alike, to support the cause of these "forgotten Jews."

As Semi demonstrates, Ethiopian Jewry was not the only cause that Faitlovitch championed. He became involved with the San Nicandro converts (residents of a small village in the Apulia region of southern Italy in the 1930s, who were embraced by the Jewish Brigade and who subsequently emigrated to Israel in a flurry of messianic fervor). He also took a special interest in the "Black Hebrews" of Harlem, who were researched by his favorite student, Taamrat Emmanuel. Indeed, in many ways, Semi's book on Faitlovitch is also about his students, many of whom became scholars in their own right.[3]

Faitlovitch's personality was as complex as the peoples and issues he supported. Semi shows how he was not merely an adventurer or a man in search of a cause. At times, he acted as a "Jewish missionary" who sought to bring about the redemption through rapprochement with far-flung tribes; at other points, Semi describes him as a "schnorrer" (pp. 71–83) who devoted much of his energies to fund-raising—not least, for himself. In addition, he was a scholar familiar with a wide range of Semitic languages, including Hebrew, Ge'ez, Amharic, and Tigrinya, who published books and other writings in several European languages, mainly German and French. His religious outlook was close to today's Modern Orthodox Judaism, and he was friendly with such personalities as Rabbi Avraham Yitzhak Kook in Palestine and Rabbi Zvi Margulies in Italy. He gained the support of a wide range of leading European Orthodox rabbis for the Ethiopian Jewish cause, and he undertook almost single-handedly the conversion of the Beta Israel to talmudic, normative Judaism at a time when they were still strictly observing the rules of purity and making animal sacrifices as prescribed in the Torah. In addition, Faitlovitch kept in touch with various Jewish organizations, among them the Joint Distribution Committee, the Alliance Israélite Universelle, and Hilfsverein des Deutschen Juden (later known as Ezra); he also associated with world leaders and government officials, including Emperor Haile Selassie and Yitzhak Ben-Zvi.

Officially, Faitlovitch made his home in Tel Aviv, marrying only in 1937 at the age of 56; the couple never had any children. Restless by nature, Faitlovitch made numerous yearly trips between Palestine, Ethiopia, and the United States, as documented in his extensive correspondence. After the state of Israel was declared, he advocated the emigration of the Beta Israel to Israel, but he never lived to see their communal exodus. Faitlovitch died in 1955; the Beta Israel heard of his death in the village of Ambober in Gondar province, Ethiopia, some time thereafter.[4]

Faitlovitch's impact is only beginning to be felt. Clearly, the immigration of Ethiopian Jews to Israel was long in the making, but their adaptation to normative Judaism began with Faitlovitch. The recent immigration of the so-called "Felesmura" (Beta Israel who, from the middle of the 19th century, converted to Christianity) had its roots in Faitlovitch's quest to bring even converted Ethiopian Jews in line with the Jewish world. Similarly, Faitlovitch's interest in "lost tribes" and their eventual ingathering in the state of Israel is only recently finding a wider audience. According to Semi, the causes promoted by Faitlovitch and those groups that supported him, including Modern Orthodox Zionists, had an impact on policies that were later implemented by the Israeli government.

Semi's work is based on years of scholarship, not only in the aforementioned Faitlovitch collection, where his diaries are to be found, but also in other archives in Israel, France, England, Italy, and the United States. It is a pity that the book does not contain a methodology section in which the author explicates her own private quest for material about Faitlovitch. Although her volume brings to light some amazing details, there will undoubtedly be future works dealing with this multifaceted and intriguing figure.

Shalva Weil
The Hebrew University

Notes

1. Shalva Weil, "Kinuyim kolektiviyim vezehut kolektivit shel yehudei etiopiyah," in *Yehudei etiopiyah beor hazarkorim*, ed. Shalva Weil (Jerusalem: 1997), 35–48.

2. Jacques Faitlovitch, *Quer durch Abessinien: Meine zweite Reise zu den Falaschas* (Berlin: 1910).

3. See, for example, Carlo Guandalina, "Gete Yirmiahu and Beta Israel's Regeneration: A Difficult Path," in *Jews of Ethiopia: the Birth of an Elite*, ed. Tudor Parfitt and Emanuela Trevisan Semi (London: 2005), 112–121; Shalva Weil, "Abraham Adgeh: The Perfect English Gentleman," in ibid., 101–111; Emanuela Trevisan Semi, "From Wolleqa to Florence: The Tragic Story of Faitlovitch's Pupil Hizkiahu Finkas," in *The Beta Israel in Ethiopia and Israel*, ed. Tudor Parfitt and Emanuela Trevisan Semi (London: 1999), 15–39; Shalva Weil, "Tadesse Yacob of Cairo and Addis Abeba," *International Journal of Ethiopian Studies* 2, nos. 1–2 (2006), 233–243.

The most famous of Faitlovitch's students was Taamrat Emmanuel. For a collection of his letters, see Emanuela Trevisan Semi, *La correspondence de Taamrat Emmanuel: intellectuel juif d'Ethiopie dans la premiére moitié du XXième siécle* (Turin: 2000).

4. Shalva Weil, "Kinah 'al mot doktor Ya'akov Faitlovitch," *Pe'amim* 33 (1987), 125–127.

Oren Soffer, *Ein lefalpel! 'Iton "Hazefirah" vehamodernizaziyah shel hasiah hahevrati hapoliti* (There is no place for pilpul! "Hazefirah" and the modernization of sociopolitical discourse). Jerusalem: Mosad Bialik, 2007. 240 pp.

The Jewish press was an important factor in the modernization process among East European Jewry. During the second half of the 19th century, Yiddish and Hebrew newspapers, though having relatively few paying subscribers, were reasonably accessible to a large number of readers. Distributed far beyond the areas in which they were printed, these newspapers functioned as a source of information and general knowledge. On the one hand, they served to shorten the distance between various communities; on the other, they contributed to the transformation in Jewish communal discourse, which shifted from a traditionally religious set of concerns to a more secular and modern political, social, and cultural discourse founded on scientific rhetoric and facts.

Oren Soffer's book focuses on a single publication, *Hazefirah*—the first "Polish" Hebrew newspaper. It traces the gradual development of the paper from its inception as a weekly in Warsaw in 1862 to its becoming a daily in 1886, following its path until the outbreak of the First World War in 1914. During the first stage of its existence, *Hazefirah* was published and edited by Haym Zelig Slonimsky (1810–1904), a maskil who was born and brought up in Bialystok, became a Hebrew cultural activist in various Jewish communities inside and outside of Lithuania, and finally settled in Warsaw. Slonimsky's worldview, which naturally found expression in the newspaper, combined religious conservatism and scientific skepticism. Under his tutelage, *Hazefirah* at first devoted very little space to political issues or literature, instead emphasizing developments in the natural world and in the realm of science, often by means of charts and illustrations. This emphasis gradually changed, largely through the influence of Nakhum Sokolov (1860–1936), who eventually took over as editor. In its second phase of existence, *Hazefirah* gave increased attention to current affairs and political issues. At the same time, Soffer maintains, it strove to maintain its political neutrality so that it could function as a "marketplace" (p. 88) for the exchange of ideas and positions. The third stage, which began with the transformation of *Hazefirah* into a daily, was marked by the paper's growing importance in the realm of political, social, and cultural debate. (This did not mean that the paper abandoned its emphasis on the "scientific" point of view—Sokolov frequently made use of statistical data in countering Jewish opponents or antisemitic accusations.) With the passage of time and parallel to the ideological changes in Sokolov's worldview, the newspaper, which had initially expressed reservations regarding the Hibat Zion movement, became clearly Zionist in its orientation. In addition, it devoted more space to belles-lettres.

Slonimsky's enterprise, continued by Sokolov, can easily be identified with the principles of the school of Warsaw Positivism (1860s to 1880s). In contrast to the contemporary, activist Romanticism that sought to renew Polish sovereignty, the Positivists championed "organic work" and "work at the foundations," regarding society as a harmonious organism that should be strengthened not through obscurant nationalist or religious ideas, but rather through equal rights for all (including Jews and women) and through the dissemination of knowledge (literacy, sciences, arts). Relevant information about this school and its various journals, which probably influenced *Hazefirah,* can be found in two works written by Zenon Kmiecik, *Prasa warszawska w latach 1886–1904* (1989) and *Prasa polska w latach 1864–1918* (1976); unfortunately, neither is mentioned by Soffer.

Who were Slonimsky's intended readers, and who in fact read *Hazefirah*? In this regard, Soffer provides a short summary (pp. 47–50) of various cultural influences on 19th-century Polish Jewry (mainly German, Polish, and Russian). One might expect to find in this context some mention of the "Litvaks" (Jews from the Pale of Settlement) living in Warsaw in those days. Most of these mainly young people had emigrated from the northern (mostly mitnagdic) provinces to Warsaw, where the Jewish population was largely hasidic in orientation. The Litvaks in Warsaw were regarded as agents of russification and as maskilim. They read contemporary Hebrew literature and newspapers, and some of them also took part in the creation of modern Hebrew culture. Both Slonimsky and Sokolov were typical "Litvaks," but for some reason there is no reference to this in the book.

In any event, *Hazefirah*'s circulation was never very large. By 1886 the newspaper had reached a circulation of 2,000 copies, with most of the subscribers living outside of Warsaw and possibly even outside Congress Poland.[1] According to official data from 1906, *Hazefirah* was distributed in 3,000 copies (less than the other two daily Hebrew newspapers, and far less than contemporary Yiddish newspapers in Warsaw).[2] Apart from interesting details regarding Slonimsky's relations with Alexander Zederbaum, the editor of the competing Hebrew newspaper, *Hameliz*, Soffer provides very little information about *Hazefirah* and other Hebrew newspapers. There is also nothing about *Hazefirah* with respect to contemporary Yiddish newspapers such as *Kol mevaser* (1862–1872), *Yidishes folks-blat* (1881–1890) and *Der yid* (1899–1901). As it happened, Sokolov himself turned in later years to Yiddish and even tried—with very little success—to publish a daily newspaper of his own in Warsaw (while he was serving as editor both of *Hazefirah* and of the Polish-Jewish *Izraelita*). This, too, goes unmentioned.

There is no doubt that Soffer is very well acquainted with *Hazefirah*'s content and with the biographies of its two prolific editors. What is disappointing is his failure to approach the topic of his research from a wider perspective and to set it in its proper context. In particular, the book's conspicuous lack of references to sources in Yiddish or Polish caused me to feel a sense of missed opportunity. Although Soffer's work discusses an important theme in the area of East European Jewish modernization and cultural change, significant aspects of this theme remain to be addressed.

Nathan Cohen
Bar-Ilan University

Notes

1. Yankev Shatzki, *Di geshikhte fun yidn in varshe,* vol. 3 (New York: 1953), 308–309. In Warsaw that year there were 146,246 Jewish inhabitants (Gabriela Zalewska, *Ludność żydowska w Warszawie w okresie międzywojennym* [Warsaw: 1996], 343).

2. Marian Fuks, *Prasa żydowska w Warszawie 1823–1939* (Warsaw: 1979), 298.

Zionism, Israel, and the Middle East

Eliezer Ben-Rafael and Yochanan Peres,
Is Israel One? Religion, Nationalism, and Multiculturalism Confounded. Leiden: Brill, 2005. xvi + 332 pp.

"Is Israel One?" is the most detailed analysis yet of the growing complexity of Israeli society. A number of recent works by sociologists such as Moshe Lissak and Don Horowitz, Calvin Goldscheider, and Baruch Kimmerling have pointed out that Israeli society is far from monolithic.[1] Building on this previous research, Eliezer Ben-Rafael and Yochanan Peres dissect the social divisions within Israel, adding details derived from four opinion surveys that they commissioned in 1999–2000 and bringing their analysis up to date as of the book's publication.

According to Ben-Rafael and Peres, there are 13 distinct albeit often overlapping social elements within Israeli society: Ashkenazim; Mizrahim; third-generation Israelis (the authors' questionable assumption is that, by the third generation, Israelis lose their association with diaspora cultural heritage); four levels of Jewish religiosity (nonreligious, traditional, religious, and ultra-Orthodox); the national religious (settler movement); Russians; Ethiopians; Arabs; Druze; and foreign workers (represented in this study by Filipinos). In the four opinion surveys, data was collected from representative samples of each of the societal elements except settlers. (Information on this last population was obtained from publications and informal interviews.) Respondents were asked about their allegiances to, and attitudes toward other social groups and the society as a whole, their perceptions and feelings of social distance (that is, their similarity to or dissimilarity from people in other social groups), and their political attitudes and behavior. From this information, the authors build a two-stage analysis of Israel's social complexity.

The first major section of the book covers nine of the social elements, each of which is described individually and in considerable detail. The chapters in this section serve both as perceptive descriptions of the place of the various groups within Israeli society and as a means of characterizing each group in terms of the data categories in the surveys (religiosity, nationalism, group identity, social distance, and feelings toward other groups). The book begins with chapters on two groups whose identity is driven by religion, the ultra-Orthodox and settlers (national religious). It then focuses on the two largest groupings within Israeli society, the Ashkenazim and Mizrahim, taking note of the fact that most nonreligious (secular) Israelis are Ashkenazic, whereas most "traditional" Israelis are Mizrahi. Following this is a discussion of two newer and less extensively analyzed segments of Jewish society, Russians and Ethiopians. Finally, the book turns to non-Jewish sectors of society—Arabs, Druze, and foreign workers. Ben-Rafael and Peres' treatment of the Arab and Druze segments of society is noteworthy for its accuracy and sensitivity; although many official institutions (including the census bureau) and analysts treat the Druze as socially distinct from Israeli Arabs, most Druze are in fact part of the Arab sector in terms of culture, language, and individual identity.

The second major section of *Is Israel One?* addresses the nature of Israeli multiculturalism with a lengthy series of analyses in which eleven of the social groupings are compared with one another. Topics such as social distance, group solidarity, common culture represented by language, and aspects of national identity (authority, allegiance to society, the religious nature of the state, "Middle Easternness," westernization, and the debate regarding a Jewish state versus a democratic state) are considered both in terms of individual attitudes and behaviors, and in terms of how respondents view other groups in the broader society. Finally, trends in political affiliation of each of the groups, and comparisons of political attitudes, are presented.

The book's concluding section takes up the question of whether there is a dominant "national identity" or "Israeliness," or whether Israel has lost its central identity in the current age of multiculturalism and post-modernity. Ben-Rafael and Peres conclude that in Israel, as in most complex societies, whereas there is an underlying allegiance to the nation state and a "family resemblance" among social groups, the notion of a hegemonic national identity has been replaced by the recognition that the society is diverse and that the groups within it have varying degrees of commitment to the overall social corpus. The authors corroborate the social structural conceptualization that drove the study and that is reflected in the book's title. That is to say, social groupings within Israel are tied to the state through links of religion, religiosity, culture and/or nationalism—but definitions of each concept vary from group to group.

The book is not an easy read. The style is ponderous. Many strange usages appear—social identities, for instance, are called "tokens," and a monotonic pattern in a data table becomes a "glissando." Some tables are not well explained or labeled and thus can be difficult to interpret, an example being the key table outlining the samples in the surveys (p. 58), which lacks horizontal lines making clear the "double counting" between religiosity (nonreligious, traditional) and ethnicity (Ashkenazic, Mizrahi). Moroever, although Ben-Rafael and Peres are experienced scholars, their book has the format, structure, and style of a doctoral dissertation. There is an extensive introductory theoretical discussion and a review of literature from many sources and places, although the study itself focuses exclusively on Israel. There is also a numbered list of "research questions' and no fewer than 98 tables of data.

Clearly such a wealth of information takes its place as an important reference source for scholars studying Israeli society. The book would have excellent potential as a classroom text were its price not so prohibitive ($206 list price; $175 on Amazon.com). The publisher, Brill, has a longstanding reputation for exorbitant prices, and this book is no exception. In its present form it will likely become a source to which students are referred for library consultation.

Russell A. Stone
American University

Note

1. Moshe Lissak and Dan Horowitz, *Trouble in Utopia: The Overburdened Polity of Israel* (Albany: 1989); Calvin Goldscheider, *Israel's Changing Society: Population, Ethnicity and Development* (Boulder: 1996; 2nd. ed. 2002); Baruch Kimmerling, *The Invention and Decline of Israeliness:* State, Society and the Military (Berkeley: 2001).

Meron Benvenisti, *Son of the Cypresses: Memories, Reflections and Regrets from a Political Life,* trans. Maxine Kaufman–Lacusta in consultation with Michael Kaufman–Lacusta. Berkeley: University of California Press, 2007. 253 pp.

In *Son of the Cypresses,* Meron Benvenisti—a historian, journalist, political activist (he served as deputy mayor of Jerusalem under Teddy Kollek between 1965 and 1971), and thoroughgoing nonconformist—presents his personal reminiscences and insights regarding the Israeli-Palestinian conflict. Autobiography is an intrinsically egocentric project, the consequence of its author's belief that his or her life holds important lessons for others. When the author has a big ego and a clear message but no real expectation that others will pay attention, the product is a book marked by bitterness. Benvenisti notes that his thinking is "totally irrelevant to the Israeli public discourse" (p. 52), and this fact makes him "a sad and pessimistic person" with regard to his grandchildren's future in Israel (p. 232). Reflecting on the fact that, three generations after the War of Independence in 1948, the Israeli army is still engaged in expropriating Palestinian land and in expelling Palestinians from their homes, his conclusion is stark: "Something is fundamentally wrong here" (p. 109).

Benvenisti sees himself as an authentic Israeli, the very embodiment of Israeliness. When he portrays Yitzhak Rabin as the archetype of the second generation of the Zionist revolution (pp. 100–101), the reader understands that Benvenisti puts himself in the same place. "I am exactly what my father wanted me to be ... I am from here. I am as much a part of this land as its stones," he declares (p. 230). However, unlike many of his compatriots today, Benvenisti makes no claim for exclusivity: "To me Eretz Israel without Arabs is a barren land" (p. 230). His self-identity is based on the heritage of the Labor movement's founding fathers, about whom he writes nostalgically. He is proud of the achievements of his father's generation (David Benvenisti, Meron's father, was a well-known geographer and educator), and he rejects the charges leveled against them by the "new historians" and critical sociologists. For Benvenisti, today's Israeli "identity" is a kitsch version of that of the previous generation.

A dominant theme of this book is the author's personality—as Benvenisti acknowledges, "I am a walking mass of internal contradictions and have become marginalized" (p. 231). Contradiction is indeed amply in evidence. Teddy Kollek, for instance, is referred to as "Mr. Annexation" and is credited for successfully managing the incorporation of East Jerusalem into the Israeli portion of the city in the wake of the Six-Day War. Elsewhere, however, Benvenisti describes Jerusalem as being deeply divided along ethnic lines. Writing as a historian, Benvenisti acknowledges the fact that, during the War of Independence, Israel expelled Palestinians and made them refugees. At the same time, he cannot tolerate Edward Said's claim that Israel should feel guilty about this transfer. More fundamentally, Benvenisti is known for his "irreversibility theory": first propounded during the 1980s, it posits the impossibility of ever attaining a real Israeli-Palestinian peace agreement, particularly with regard to Jerusalem. Moreover, he writes disparagingly about the "peace plans industry" (p. 87) that creates illusions by attempting to impose international relations solutions on what is essentially a tribal, intercommunal conflict (pp. 122–123). At the same time, Benvenisti takes part in this type of "alchemy experiment" when he indulges in his own vision of building relations of tolerance across Jerusalem's fault lines. The Old City, he argues, should be transformed into "a museum-like heritage site, a center for pilgrims and tourists, administered jointly by representatives of the communities involved" (p. 93). Moreover, between 1999 and 2001, Benvenisti initiated and led a "peace team" composed of young scholars. This "morning after" project, as described in Chapter 5, was devoted to analyzing the various transformations required in order to bring about peace.

In Chapter 7, titled "Description and Prescription," Benvenisti argues that there is no way back to partition. Convinced of the impossibility of a two-state solution, Benvenisti maintains that the bi-nationalism paradigm, that is, a bi-national state with political and cultural "soft borders," is not so much a political alternative as it is a de facto reality. Although Benvenisti discusses the models of Cyprus and Bosnia, he glosses over the legal issues involved in setting up a bi-national state—the constitutional framework is a "secondary issue" (p. 227)—and he also appears to have no practical advice as to how to bring such a model about.

Despite an overall lack of coherence, *Son of the Cypresses* does offer interesting and creative insights into the Israeli–Palestinian conflict. For instance, the author regards the separation barrier in the West Bank, the unilateral disengagement from the Gaza Strip, and the popularity of Mediterranean identity as all being manifestations of an Israeli wish to transfer the Palestinians from the Israeli collective mind and to deny the existence of the 1948 refugee problem. His style can be pithy and provocative: "In 1967 Zionism won one victory too many" (p. 232), he writes, and in other places he sums up the conflict by noting, memorably, that "Israelis walk and with them walks their shadow – the Palestinian people; they beat the shadow with a big stick but it does not leave them alone" (p. 127).

Menachem Klein
Bar-Ilan University

Yael Chaver, *What Must be Forgotten: The Survival of Yiddish in Zionist Palestine*. Syracuse: Syracuse University Press, 2004. 238 pp.

In the enumeration of the achievements and missteps of the Zionist movement, the "creation" and dissemination of modern Hebrew has nearly universally been regarded, by both historians and the Israeli public, as a stunning and praiseworthy success. In the common narrative of the Zionist movement, Yiddish, the language of the East European Jewish diaspora—like numerous other Jewish mother tongues—was the necessary jetsam of a powerful Hebrew current destined to propel the Jewish nation forward.

"The essence of a nation," Ernest Renan wrote memorably in 1882, "is that all individuals have many things in common and also that they have forgotten many things."[1] Yiddish, Yael Chaver suggests in this important study, was seen as one such "must-be-forgotten" thing. And yet, as Renan himself knew, the process of forgetting is never absolute. The language that had to be "instantaneously and totally repudiated" (p. xiii), was in fact highly regarded by many and actively developed by a few. In shining a critical light on the politics of Yiddish in Palestine, Chaver points to a lacuna in the historiography and literature of the Hebrew revival and presents a passionate project to recover the work of three neglected or misunderstood Yiddish writers, using the techniques of a close literary-critical study.

There are two major, interwoven points in *What Must be Forgotten*. First, Yiddish was deeply ingrained in the consciousness of even those Zionist leaders who propelled the pro-Hebrew cultural project; although the language was largely suppressed publicly, it was not cast aside willy-nilly by its speakers. A survey of writings by Hebrew cultural figures reveals the anguish of abandoning the mother tongue—the labor activist and writer Rachel Katznelson went as far as to use the phrase "*milḥemet safot*" (language war) to describe the situation in her divided Hebrew-Yiddish psyche (p. 40). Second, despite its repression, Yiddish indeed survived in Palestine in the writings of a cadre of Yiddish writers. Yiddish expression did not take place in isolation from Zionist society. On the contrary, using the forms of European modernism and the characteristic flexibility of Yiddish (a dynamic fusion language that could encompass disparate languages and linguistic features), Yiddish writers used their art to offer a deeply invested critique of the Zionist project and its assumptions about both Eastern Europe and its "other other," the Arab population of Palestine.

Chaver claims that her study lies "in the indeterminate ground between historical and literary study" because, "as the cultural process unfolds, literature and history necessarily inform each other" (p. xxiii). In fact, the space between history and literature is quite determinate in the organization of the book, which neatly divides the two disciplines by assigning different chapters to each. Chapters 1 and 3, the historical chapters, look primarily at writings about language by pro-Hebrew figures and at a selected set of historical controversies surrounding the presence of Yiddish in public life. In Chapter 3, Chaver attempts to read Yiddish back into episodes that are generally seen as victories for Hebrew: the decision made in 1910 by the Marxist Zionist organization Po'ale Zion to publish its newspaper in Hebrew rather than Yiddish; the outrage over the visit to Palestine of Yiddish writers in 1927; and a proposal to create a Yiddish language chair at the Hebrew University. Those on the "pro-Hebrew side" of these conflicts were not necessarily univocal in their opposition to Yiddish. For instance, Eliezer Shteynman, the editor of the Hebrew journal *Ketuvim* and one of Hebrew's advocates in the Yiddish writers' controversy, was also a regular contributor to Yiddish periodicals; as Chaver notes, he was "waging a war on a culture in whose production he was still actively participating" (p. 110). The insistence on Hebrew and the rejection of Yiddish, as clear as it was in many instances, was tempered by feelings of loss and ambivalence.

Chapters 2, 4, and 5, which stand largely independent of the historical chapters, offer close readings of selected works by three writers. Chaver's chosen figures, though disparate, are linked by a common language and related themes. Zalman Brokhes was a Zionist and his work was ultimately co-opted into the Hebrew canon in translations that elided both its original nuances and its more subversive strains. Avrom Rivess was one of the founders of the Yiddish Writers and Journalists club and a regular contributor to the Yiddish periodical literature in Palestine. His work is notable for its portrayals of fracture and alienation in the Yishuv setting. Rikuda Potash, the chronological outlier in a survey nominally about pre-state Palestine, offers a critique of "monocultural and monolingual nationalism" (p. 166) in a series of Yiddish stories written in the 1950s and 1960s, which were inspired by the disjointed, defamiliarizing tropes of German Expressionism.

These three authors deftly plied both the Yiddish language and the field of European modernist thematics. Over time, they became significant contributors to the rich literary communities of Zionist Palestine (and, in Potash's case, the early state of Israel). They did so, moreover, in a language that was more subtle, supple, and variegated than the still unwieldy Hebrew of the time. Yet Chaver goes further than simply crediting their writings with an aesthetic advantage over contemporary Hebrew literature, hinting as well at a possible moral advantage when she suggests that Yiddish texts offered a "counterversion" to the norms of Hebrew literature (p. xxiv). Potash, she notes, "did not automatically subscribe to all components of the mainstream Zionist cultural ethos, with its negation of Yiddish and its collective imperative to settle the land" (p. 172). While the statement is no doubt true for this writer, and indeed for Rivess and Brokhes as well, the implication that Yiddish writers set themselves against a mass of pro-Hebrew conformism underestimates the diversity of Yiddish- (and Arab-) related thought within the pro-Hebrew community (which, indeed, Chaver herself effectively demonstrates in her historical chapters). Moreover, such assessments fail to consider the fact that, although Yiddish writers employed a marginalized language and voiced cogent critiques, they were nonetheless participants in the larger (Ashkenazic) Zionist cultural project in Palestine and a party to its outcomes, for both good and ill.

The recovery of Yiddish literature and politics in Zionist Palestine becomes a study in a series of psychological contradictions. Yiddish speakers and readers were at one and the same time "others" who were pushed out and insiders who were very influential in the Zionist movement. Yiddish texts, rich, complex, and probing, stood in complex but active relationship to the ideologically tinged but still unsettled Hebrew literature of the time. Chaver's project to return the Yiddish linguistic margins to the story of Hebrew and Zionist culture is a welcome and important contribution within a growing set of studies that question the linearity of the Zionist move to Hebrew, the movement's detachment from both diaspora Jewish and foreign cultures, and, ultimately, Zionists' collective claim to have forgotten the past.

Liora R. Halperin
University of California, Los Angeles

Note

1. Ernest Renan, "Qu'est-ce que une nation?" (1882), rpt. in *Nation and Narration*, ed. Homi K. Bhabha (London: 1990), 8-22; cited in Chaver, 16.

Raymond Cohen, *Saving the Holy Sepulchre: How Rival Christians Came Together to Rescue Their Holiest Shrine*. New York: Oxford University Press, 2008. 320 pp.

Scholars of interfaith relations in Israel will welcome Raymond Cohen's new book, which explores the history of attempts throughout the 20th century to renovate the Holy Sepulchre in Jerusalem. Since the 4th century, when the Roman emperor Constantine constructed a shrine on the site where Christians believed that Jesus had been buried, the Holy Sepulchre has been one of Christianity's most esteemed objects of pilgrimage and piety. Following the Muslim conquest of Palestine in the 7th century, Christian leaders were concerned with protecting the integrity of the Holy Sepulchre and ensuring the safety of pilgrims who continued to make their way to Jerusalem. In 1095, Christian resentment over the Muslim dominance of Christian holy sites culminated in the first crusade, which was launched by Pope Urban II in order to liberate the Holy Land. The first orders of knights, the Templars and Hospitalars, were established in early 12th-century Jerusalem; their members combined monastic vows with the ethos of knighthood and confronted the initial challenges of protecting the road to Jerusalem and providing medical services to the exhausted pilgrims who arrived at the holy site. The Crusaders built a new Romanesque building on the remains of the Holy Sepulchre that has served, with some modification, until the present time.

Not surprisingly, almost all pre-Reformation Christian groups wished to take possession of the church or parts thereof. During the Byzantine and Crusader periods, governance of the Holy Sepulchre was in the hands of either Greek or Latin Christians, while Muslim rulers had to arbitrate between conflicting demands of different Christian groups. The final division of territory and privileges in the Holy Sepulchre took place only in 1757. The Ottoman rulers of Jerusalem supported the Greek Orthodox, who at the time were the most influential ethno-religious minority in the empire (in part because they were backed by the Russian state). Other groups, namely the Roman Catholics and the Orthodox Armenians, received lesser shares. In addition, the Copts, Ethiopians, and Orthodox Syrians were represented at the Holy Sepulchre, albeit as minor partners. Over time, Roman Catholic attempts to change the status quo proved futile, although they did inspire Catholic plans for the destruction of the existing compound and the construction of a totally new building. These plans, however, were contingent on the Axis Powers' taking over Palestine, and thus never materialized.

By the beginning of the 20th century, as Cohen describes in detail, the building had sustained major physical and structural damage, including the damage inflicted by a series of fires and earthquakes. British officials worried that the building might collapse altogether, with disastrous human, cultural, and political consequences. Hence they attempted to repair the church, utilizing British expertise in the restoration of ancient monuments. Their initiatives, however, were only partially successful, as the various Christian churches represented at the site refused to cooperate for fear of losing long-held privileges. According to Cohen, a breakthrough in the negotiations occurred in the 1950s. He credits Jordanian officials as being more successful than their British predecessors in persuading local church leaders to overcome differences and agree on a plan of work, division of labor, and shared expenditures. It is likely, however, that cooperation came about because of the rise of the ecumenical movement in the late 1950s and early 1960s, which led to a rapprochement between Greek Orthodoxy and Roman Catholicism and allowed restoration efforts to begin in earnest. These continued until 1967, when Israel conquered East Jerusalem. The Israeli government wished to demonstrate its benevolence toward Christian groups, but Israeli officials had neither the will nor the skills to intervene constructively in intra-Christian intrigues.

Cohen does an excellent job of narrating the history of attempts to bring the different church bodies to cooperate and save this unique historical and architectural monument. Some chapters read at times like a suspense novel, with the reader wondering what new twists and turns will be revealed in the next paragraph. The author has done an admirable job of uncovering the various exchanges that took place between Christian leaders, civic officials and architects, archaeologists, and restorationists in Palestine and beyond. Some of his discoveries are real gems. For instance, in Chapter 5, he recounts how, following the Lateran Agreement between Fascist Italy and the Vatican in the 1920s, a number of Italian church leaders in Palestine advocated a mixture of Italian patriotism and Catholic hegemony. Anticipating the takeover of Palestine by Axis forces in 1942, they prepared plans for the destruction of the older building and its annexes, the banishing of "schismatics" (non-Catholics) from the site, and the building of a completely new basilica. Cohen also shows how the delicate balance of power in the Holy Sepulchre brought the British to enforce the status quo in other places, such as the site of the Temple Mount and the Western Wall, that were sacred to Muslims and Jews.

Cohen writes in a particularly readable and witty style—a literary achievement that should not be taken for granted. He presents all the "dramatis personae," bringing them to life and placing them within the cultural and political settings in which they labored. Likewise, he is to be commended for his mastery of the topography, archaeology, and architecture of the site, as well as for his coherent analysis of architectural plans and debates, which he presents (for what is presumably a nonspecialist audience) in a very clear manner.

Saving the Holy Sepulchre is not without minor limitations. The author relies heavily on interviews, sometimes accepting at face value the claims made by individuals (or their associates) who were highly invested in the struggles surrounding the various stages of restoring the Holy Sepulchre. The testimony of Rafi Levy, who served as the district officer of Jerusalem following the Six-Day War and who characterizes his efforts at building inroads into the local communities as highly successful, is but one example (p. 187). Moreover, whereas Cohen has examined documents in Israeli, British, French, and Catholic archives, he did not delve into the records of Eastern churches or documents in Greece or Russia. It seems that the Catholic sources were more readily available—perhaps for that reason, the descriptions tend to exhibit a slightly pro-Catholic bias, with Catholics appearing to be more committed than the Greeks to high-quality restorations of the holy site. Such drawbacks aside, *Saving the Holy Sepulchre* is a remarkable achievement and a very welcome addition to the not very extensive literature on the relationships between religious communities in the Holy Land.

Yaakov Ariel
University of North Carolina

Zvi Ganin, *An Uneasy Relationship: American Jewish Leadership and Israel, 1948–1957.* Syracuse: Syracuse University Press, 2005. xix + 255 pp.

Although the nexus between the United States and Israel in the period of Israel's founding has prompted an outpouring of studies, the connection between the two countries in the years following the establishment of the Jewish state has hardly been researched and written about. The present work, therefore, is a very welcome contribution to our appreciation and understanding of the problems that marked the relationship between the Israeli and American governments, as viewed through the prism of America's Jewish leadership during the years after 1948. Zvi Ganin is a recognized authority on Israel's founding period. His major study, *Truman, American Jewry and Israel, 1945–1948* (1979), is a classic, and the current book is, in a real sense, a sequel to the previous volume. In both works, the focus is not only on the role of the U.S. government, but also on that of American Jewry—namely, its influence, or the lack thereof, on Israel and on U.S. policy in the Middle East. Appropriately enough, *An Uneasy Relationship* is divided into two parts: the first half deals with the adjustment in relations between American Jewry and Israel as necessitated by the establishment of the Jewish state, while the second half is devoted to analyzing U.S.-Israeli relations in the period leading up to the 1956 Suez Campaign.

The fundamental question engaging American Jews after the Jewish state was proclaimed in 1948 was—what is our relationship with Israel? In the view of David Ben-Gurion, Israel's fiery prime minister, every Jew, wherever he or she might be, was a potential *'oleh* (immigrant) to Israel and was obliged to fulfill the obligation of aliyah as soon as possible. The Jewish state, he maintained, was created not simply to cater for refugees fleeing from persecution or having nowhere else to go; it was meant for every Jew intent on living a more meaningful and intensive Jewish life. Thus, American Jews, no less than the refugees from the DP camps in Europe, should be moving en masse to Israel. For Jacob Blaustein and his colleagues in the American Jewish Committee, this notion was absurd. American Jews were Americans in the fullest sense of the word. Their citizenship committed them to total loyalty to the United States, their social and economic status assured them of full equality in the American milieu, and they had no intention or desire to leave. Ben-Gurion's repeated calls for aliyah from the United States only threatened to compromise American Jews' status as patriotic Americans. Their attachment to Israel was not one of citizenship but of sentiment. They cared for the Jewish state and wished it well, and they were willing to support it and contribute to its prosperity and success. But there was no obligation to go beyond that.

Ganin describes the numerous encounters that ensued between American Jews and Ben-Gurion in the process of straightening things out between the two camps. In leading the struggle to exact a clear retraction from Ben-Gurion, Blaustein was confronted by domestic voices in the American Jewish community that contended that Israel's very existence threatened to undermine the political emancipation and integration of Jews in the United States. After all, the Reform movement, with which most of these Jews were associated, had declared in 1898: "We are unalterably opposed to political Zionism. The Jews are not a nation, but a religious community [and] America is our Zion" (p. 3). Certain groups, most particularly the American Council for Judaism, expressed deep fears that the emergence of Israel would raise serious questions about the possible dual loyalty of American Jews.

In one respect, Jews were no different from other ethnic groups that maintained an attachment to their native homes, such as Italians with Italy, Germans with Germany, or Poles with Poland. Israel's situation, however, was unique in that sentimental ties would not suffice: the ties had to be more substantive. Under siege from Arab states that vowed to wipe it off the map, Israel was dependent on financial and political support from both American Jews and the U.S. government. Such aid was essential for Israel's very survival, yet this raised questions about the proper role of American Jews. In line with its ideology, the American Council for Judaism opposed American support (whether by the government or by American Jewry) for the Jewish state. Blaustein rejected this policy of alienation from the Jewish state, but felt that he had to ensure that Ben-Gurion would take into account the unique status of American Jews, and that Israel would refrain from seeking to serve as the representative of Jews worldwide.

After several abortive attempts to obtain a clear-cut commitment from Ben-Gurion that he would not campaign for American Jewish aliyah, Blaustein finally succeeded in securing the necessary statement. Meeting at the King David Hotel in Jerusalem on August 23, 1950, Ben-Gurion finally acknowledged that American Jews were not exiles and that the program of ingathering did not apply to the American scene. He also recognized that Israel could not interfere in the domestic affairs of the American Jewish community. Furthermore, the Zionist Organization of America would not be designated as Israel's sole representative body in the United States, and Zionists and non-Zionists would be equally entitled to work on behalf of Israel by presenting its case before the American people and its government.

Settlement of the Zionist/non-Zionist controversy enabled Blaustein to take a more effective role in strengthening the U.S.-Israeli relationship. In the second part of his book, Ganin shows how Blaustein succeeded in promoting warm relations between the two countries during the Truman administration, despite State Department obstruction. Under the following Eisenhower administration, however, American policy careered off in a vain search for a northern tier security pact, known as the Baghdad Pact, which led Washington into a series of diplomatic dead-ends.

Although Truman was sympathetic to the Jewish state, the State Department, which had failed to forestall Israel's emergence, was now intent on improving its relations with the Arab world. The logic was that the Arabs must be won over so as to reconcile them to Israel's existence. Three major issues, Ganin explains, engaged Washington in its search for a peaceful resolution to the Arab-Israeli dispute: Arab refugees, the status of Jerusalem, and Israel's final borders. In rejecting a proposal for Israel to accept a quarter of a million Arab refugees, Israeli diplomats explained that the admission of "vengeful and hostile refugees" would threaten the stability of the state. Moreover, Israel had accepted twice that number of Jewish refugees from Arab states, from where they had been expelled, so it was only fair that the Arab states would resettle Arab refugees in their own territories. On the question of Jerusalem, it was not the Arab states alone that sought to dislodge Israel from its sovereignty over the western part of the city and to deny it the right to proclaim Jerusalem as its capital. The Vatican, too, apparently fearful that its influence in the area would wane were the Holy City to remain under Israeli (and Jordanian) control, was vehement in its demand that Jerusalem be proclaimed an international city under U.N. auspices. As a result of Catholic pressure, Washington never recognized Israel's sovereign control of its sector in Jerusalem, which, in practical terms, meant that the status of Jerusalem remained indeterminate. And with regard to the final borders of the Jewish state, State Department policy repeatedly sought to sever off part of Israel, such as the Negev, and award it to Egypt.

Blaustein's personal friendship with Truman aided him in his role as Israel's advocate. In contrast to leading personalities in the Zionist movement who were personae non gratae at the White House because of their support for the Republicans, Blaustein was a long-standing and loyal Democrat who had helped finance Truman's successful reelection campaign. His strategy was to present Israel as a strategic asset to the United States, pointing out the benefits Washington stood to gain from a close association with the Jewish state.

When Dwight Eisenhower came into power in 1953, American policy vis-à-vis Israel took a decided turn for the worse. Secretary of State John Foster Dulles joined the British government in seeking to detach the Negev from Israel, and only desisted when Egyptian president Gamal abd al-Nasser refused to cooperate in settling for this gesture. This did not stop Eisenhower and Dulles from agreeing to join a Middle East security pact against the Soviet Union on condition that Egypt become fully sovereign (a reference to its demand for the evacuation of British forces from the Suez Canal). Washington accordingly pressured Britain to remove its armed presence. However, once the last British soldier departed, Nasser signed an arms agreement with the Kremlin. Refusing to acknowledge that they had been tricked and that the balance of power in the Middle East had been radically altered, Dulles and Eisenhower rejected every Israeli appeal to rectify the military balance. Dulles' pursuit of a northern tier defense pact only aggravated the situation. It infuriated Nasser, jeopardized Israeli security, and paved the way for a revolt in Iraq that toppled the pro-western monarchy. Blaustein's efforts to moderate Dulles' views were completely ineffective. Instead, U.S. policy under Dulles ultimately led to the Aswan crisis and Nasser's nationalization of the Suez Canal, followed by the British-French expedition in conjunction with Israel, which Eisenhower did so much to frustrate. The Suez crisis resulted in the exact opposite of what Dulles had sought to forestall—the dramatic entry of the Soviet Union, as a major actor, into the heart of the Middle East. Ganin concludes his review of American policy by noting that, in the wake of the

Suez conflict, Dulles failed to induce Jewish leaders to pressure Israel to evacuate the Sinai even before its security situation had been taken into account. Their rejection of Dulles' request revealed that American Jewish leadership "had come of age psychologically and politically. They had acquired sufficient self-confidence as American citizens to have their own concept of America's national interest" (p. 217).

Ganin's analysis of American policy in the era of Eisenhower-Dulles is an eye-opener. Among its merits is its repudiation of the thesis promoted by Stephen Walt and John Mearsheimer with regard to extraordinary Jewish influence in Washington.[1] Like any pressure group in the American capital, Jewish organizations can score on some occasions and fail on others. Theirs is a voice that should be listened to, no less than the voice of vested interests, such as oil, that promote a different policy for the United States.

Shlomo Slonim
The Hebrew University

Note

1. John J. Mearsheimer and Stephen M. Walt, *The Israel Lobby and U.S. Foreign Policy* (New York: 2007).

Benjamin Pinkus, *Meambivalentiyut levrit bilti ketuvah: yisrael, zarfat veyehudei zarfat 1947–1957* (From ambivalence to tacit alliance: Israel, France and French Jewry, 1947–1957). Sdeh Boker: Ben-Gurion University of the Negev Press, 2005. 755 pp.

Research on the origin of the state of Israel and its first years has generally been focused—and understandably so—on the role of the United States and Great Britain. It is only recently that other countries, including France, have begun to come under consideration, first by Tsilla Hershko in her *Between Paris and Jerusalem: France and the Creation of the State of Israel 1949–1945* (2000) and now by Benjamin Pinkus, whose work brings us to the period immediately following the Suez Campaign of 1956. Until now, Pinkus has been better known for his major contributions to the history of the Jews in modern Russia and to the history of Zionism. This volume marks both a change in direction and an important addition to the available literature.

Pinkus' study is divided into three chronological sections: 1947–1949, marked in part by Israel's struggle for recognition on the part of France; 1949–1954, when relations between the two countries moved from normalization to rapprochement; and 1955–1957, a period of strategic alliance between Israel and France. Each section deals with various problems connected with the two countries' diplomatic and political relations and with the growing involvement of French Jews in efforts to influence their country's foreign policy vis-à-vis the Jewish state.

In the first section, Pinkus describes French hesitation and unease in the wake of Israel's establishment. On the one hand, France had an axe to grind against English policies at that time, as it had not yet forgotten its ejection from neighboring Syria and Lebanon a few years before. On the other, it could neither neglect its interests as a colonial power in Muslim North Africa nor abandon its traditional role as a defender of western and Christian interests in the Middle East. Before May 1948, France assisted the Zionist movement by allowing it to organize illegal immigration to Palestine from French ports and camps, on condition that these actions remain undercover. The situation changed, however, when the matter involved public recognition of the new state. At this point, French policy became far more ambivalent. Pinkus describes in detail the difficulties and prejudices that French leaders and higher civil servants had to overcome in order to decide (in May 1949) to grant the state of Israel formal recognition.

All these events, the proclamation of the new state as well as its victorious war for survival, did not leave the Jews of France indifferent. France was the only western country dominated by the Nazis and their allies in which no less than two thirds of the Jewish population had managed to survive. Following the war, the French Jewish community set about reviving (or creating new) communal institutions, among them the Conseil représentatif des israélites (later: juifs) de France (CRIF), which evolved into an umbrella group of French Jewish organizations; the Fonds social juif unifé (FSJU), which was intended to centralize and expand Jewish social work in France; and, of course, a fund-raising organization, l'Aide à la Haganah, for the new Jewish state. All of these groups, along with French Jewish politicians of various political stripes, supported the establishment of the state of Israel.

A new period of normalization began in 1949, as Israel increasingly oriented itself toward the West, though it refrained from identifying too closely with either the United States or the Soviet Union, the two superpowers of the day. This orientation expressed itself in a more cordial relationship with France, which was to bear fruit in later years. According to Pinkus, this period also witnessed a weakening of Jewish identity among French Jews. His contention that the memory of the Holocaust was already fading is hard to accept, but it is true that most French Jews at this point were becoming more interested in their social and economic advancement. It is also the case that French Jewry's former enthusiasm for Zionism was now manifested mainly in financial support for the new state. Aliyah continued, but at a trickle: the total number of French Jews who emigrated to Israel during this period was 1,716, compared with 2,305 in the period covering 1948–1949. Although support for Israel did not diminish, it became less vocal as the local community busied itself with reconstruction and the establishment of new institutions.

The third part of Pinkus' book deals with the de facto alliance between France and Israel, which found its full expression in the Suez Campaign. The nationalization of the Suez Canal by Egyptian president Gamal abd al-Nasser—who had also, either tacitly or actively, encouraged terrorist attacks to be launched against Israel—brought about a convergence of French and Israeli interests. In this new situation, French Jews had no problem in publicly supporting Israel, as it was now an ally of their country. Moreover, the successful campaign carried out by Israeli military forces convinced the skeptics, both Jewish and non-Jewish, that the new state had a future.

In this 755-page volume, Pinkus has made an attempt at writing a "total history" of the period in question. He has been successful in many respects, and there is no doubt that this richly detailed study has opened new scholarly horizons. Nevertheless, and as could be expected, he leaves us with a few questions. The most important one relates to his understanding of the psychology of western, "assimilated" Jewry. Although he is quite aware of the inherent danger of describing western Jews in nationalist terms, Pinkus frequently resorts to such terminology. In fact, French Jews consistently rejected being defined as a separate nationality. Léon Meiss, then president of the Consistoire Central, warned against the use of the word "Jew" in the name of the new state-in-the-making; integrated French Jews—*les israélites français*—greeted the choice of the name "Israel" with relief. Pinkus does not pinpoint the rather remarkable fact that it was precisely these Jews who were very active in French political and public circles when the issue of the French vote at the United Nations and later, the formal recognition of Israel, were debated. In their view, Jewish solidarity was not predicated upon the existence of a Jewish nation. The recognized Jewish national minorities in Eastern Europe between the two world wars had disappeared during the Holocaust. Moreover, the state-imposed national minority status of the Jews in France by the Vichy regime no longer existed: French Jews had no intention of bringing it back to life.

It is unfortunate that Pinkus did not gain access to the archives of the major Jewish organizations of the time, which are unmentioned among the numerous sources listed for this volume. Instead, in gauging French Jewish reactions to the events and issues of the time under study, he relies mainly on contemporaneous press reports and later publications. There was obviously no independent Jewish press in France in the late 1940s and 1950s, and one must also keep in mind the fact that publications during this era had clearly defined political points of view, which, among other things, found expression in a widespread tendency to overestimate the power and influence of whatever political party a publication was affiliated with.

A work of this importance cannot avoid a few minor mistakes such as a confusion between the Paris Consistory and the Central Consistory—although both are located in Paris, they carry out different activities (p. 210). The Paris consistorial schools have nothing in common with the Alliance schools; they also teach general courses (p. 212). Porto Riche, not Bergson, was the first Jew to sit in the French Academy (p. 233). *La Terre Retrouvée* was never a daily (p. 259). Michel A. Mayer was not a rabbi in Paris (p. 261). Although Orthodox, the Conseil représentatif du judaïsme traditionaliste de France (CRJTEF) was hardly a "Haredi" organization (p. 410). The chief rabbis are elected by a body of electors (mostly Consistoire members), not by their dues-paying members (p. 407). There were never 100 students at the Rabbinical Seminary, not even in the early 1950s (p. 434). *Les Cahiers sioniens* is hardly a Jewish or Zionist publication (p. 436). The comparison between the number of bar mitzvah ceremonies in 1926 and 1948 does not take into account non-consistorial synagogues (p. 446). The Jews of Metz do not come from Alsace (p. 451). It is not known whether Edouard Depreux was Jewish (p. 712).

Despite such minor flaws, Pinkus' book fulfills the two most important aims of scientific historical research: he has uncovered a great mass of new information, and he has proposed original methods of investigation in his examination of the variety of French Jewish communal organizations and the ongoing responses of French Jewish leaders to government policies. All students of modern Jewish history are in his debt.

Simon Schwarzfuchs
Bar-Ilan University

Studies in Contemporary Jewry
XXV

Edited by Eli Lederhendler

Symposium—Ethnicity and Beyond: Theories and Dilemmas of Jewish Group Demarcation

Sarah Bunin Benor and Steven M. Cohen, *Talking Jewish: The "Ethnic English" of American Jews*

Bethamie Horowitz, *Old Casks in New Times: The Reshaping of American Jewish Identity in the 21st Century*

Tony Michels, *Communism and the Problem of Ethnicity in the 1920s: The Case of Moissaye Olgin*

Ewa Morawska, *Ethnicity as a Primordial-Situational-Constructed Experience: Different Times, Different Places, Different Constellations*

Joel Perlmann, *Ethnic Group Strength, Intermarriage, and Group Blending*

Riv-Ellen Prell, *The Utility of the Concept of "Ethnicity" for the Study of Jews*

Uzi Rebhun, *Jews and the Ethnic Scene: A Multidimensional Theory*

... plus essays, review essays, and book reviews

Note on Editorial Policy

Studies in Contemporary Jewry is pleased to accept manuscripts to be considered for possible publication. Authors of essays on subjects generally within the contemporary Jewish sphere (from the turn of the 20th century to the present) should send two copies to:

> The Editor, *Studies in Contemporary Jewry*
> The Avraham Harman Institute of Contemporary Jewry
> The Hebrew University
> Mt. Scopus, Jerusalem, Israel 91905

Essays should not exceed 35 pages in length and must be double-spaced throughout (including intended quotations and endnotes).

E-mail inquiries may be sent to the following address: studiescj@savion.huji.ac.il.

Abstracts of articles from previous issues may be found via our website: http://icj.huji.ac.il/StudiesCJ/studiescj.html.